THE WORK OF SOVEREIGNTY

Publication of this book and the fellowship from which it resulted were made possible with the generous support of the Ethel-Jane Westfeldt Bunting Foundation and The Brown Foundation, Inc., of Houston, Texas.

School for Advanced Research
Resident Scholar Series

James F. Brooks
General Editor

THE WORK OF SOVEREIGNTY

Tribal Labor Relations and Self-Determination at the Navajo Nation

David Kamper

School for Advanced Research Press
Santa Fe

School for Advanced Research Press
Post Office Box 2188
Santa Fe, New Mexico 87504-2188
www.sarpress.sarweb.org

Managing Editor: Lisa Pacheco
Editorial Assistant: Ellen Goldberg
Designer and Production Manager: Cynthia Dyer
Manuscript Editor: Margaret J. Goldstein
Proofreader: Kate Whelan
Indexer: Catherine Fox
Printer: Sheridan Books

Library of Congress Cataloging-in-Publication Data

Kamper, David.
  The work of sovereignty : tribal labor relations and self-determination at the Navajo Nation / David Kamper.
       p. cm. — (Resident scholar series)
  Includes bibliographical references and index.
  ISBN 978-1-934691-25-0 (alk. paper)
  1. Navajo Indians—Economic conditions. 2. Industrial relations—Southwest, New. 3. Self-determination, National—Southwest, New. 4. Navajo Indians—Politics and government. 5. Navajo Indians—Government relations. 6. Gambling on Indian reservations—Southwest, New. I. Title.
  E99.N3K27 2010
  323.1197'26—dc22
                             2010010904

© 2010 by the School for Advanced Research. All rights reserved.
Manufactured in the United States of America.
Library of Congress Catalog Card Number: 2010010904
International Standard Book Number: 978-1-934691-25-0
First edition 2010.

 This book was printed on 30% PCW paper.

Cover illustration: Shonto Begay, *Since Nights' Victory*, 2003. Photograph by Tom Alexander.

Contents

	Acknowledgments	vii
	Abbreviations and Acronyms	x
1.	Introduction	1

Part I. Labor Relations in Indian Country

2.	The Legal, Political, and Social Contexts	23
3.	Tribal Structuring of Labor Relations	69

Part II. Organizing in Indian Country: Navajo Labor Relations

4.	Navajo Nation Politics and Pragmatic Unionism	101
5.	The Campaign for Union Recognition	135
6.	Grassroots Expressions of Tribal Labor Relations	163

Epilogue: The Uncertain Future of Tribal Labor Relations		201
	Notes	213
	References	231
	Index	251

Acknowledgments

First and foremost, I must thank and acknowledge the people of the Navajo Nation, particularly Navajo Area Indian Health Service and Tuba City Regional Health Care Corporation employees for their patience with my inquisitiveness and their tolerance of yet another anthropologist. I particularly want to thank the grassroots activists at these locales for taking interest in my research. I have agreed not to mention your real names in this book, but you know who you are. I have unending admiration for your courage, tireless work for social justice, and commitment to your communities. I also want to thank former chairman Deron Marquez for his time and his patience with my inquiries about the inner politics of tribal gaming labor relations. Additionally, thank you to Ron Maldonado and Judy Arviso from the Navajo Nation Historic Preservation Department for all your help in the cultural resources permit process.

I would be nowhere as an academic if it were not for those at UCLA who taught me how to closely attend to and care about the world and people around me. First, I thank my dissertation committee. Karen Brodkin and Paul Kroskrity: You were excellent co-chairs, whose advice and friendship I value to this day. Duane Champagne and Mariko Tamanoi: You both added invaluable insights to my work and productively challenged my assumptions in ways that have made me a far better scholar. I also want to thank other UCLA faculty who helped educate me and contributed to my overall project: Carole Goldberg, Ruth Milkman, and Cecelia Klein. My American Indian studies graduate school colleagues always helped keep me in line and tolerated my pestering them to participate in union activities; special thanks to Stephanie Fitzgerald, Joe Nelson, and Kazushi Yabe. Several UCLA anthropology graduate student colleagues also helped shape me as a thinker, and in particular I want to thank those who continued to push me long past grad school: Rod Labrador, Justin Richland, Cynthia Strathmann, Jennifer Reynolds, Keith Murphy, and Andrew Schwalm. Justin and Rod: I hope our collective love for basketball and "intellectual trash talk" about it never dies. I'm forever indebted to both of you for your friendship and advice through the early challenges of becoming a professional academic. I must also thank my brothers and sisters of SAGE/UAW, particularly Mark Quigley, Mike Miller, Susan Markens, Dan Rounds, Connie Raza, and Daisy Rooks, who taught me more about sweat and love of workplace activism than any book I could ever read. Miller: I could never thank you enough (or forgive you) for the way you sucked me into the labor movement and taught me how to be and think like an organizer.

Although relatively brief, my stop at the University of Texas–Austin established lifelong friendships that greatly benefited my formative years as an academic. Lisa Moore, Asale Ajani, Steve Marshall, Ann Cvetkovich, Shirley Thompson, Jim Cox, Julia Mickenberg, and Dan Birkholz: Thank you all for helping me refine my research questions and the kind of academic I wanted to be. Steve: May we always have the Lakers!

I could not have had a better summer than the one I spent as a research fellow at the School of American Research (now the School for Advanced Research). I want to acknowledge the whole SAR staff and particularly James Brooks, Nancy Owen Lewis, and Catherine Cocks, for creating such a fabulous environment for research. I thank all the SAR summer fellows in my program. I learned a ton from you all and certainly had fun doing it. Nancy Parezo: Thank you for all your excellent advice on how to be a functioning academic and most of all for your sweetness toward me. Kim Christen and Rachel Heiman: I thank you both for your insightful comments on many pages of this project, but more importantly for being such fast, fabulous friends. May we periodically discuss culture over Trader Joe's prepared dinners for the rest of our careers.

I also want to thank those at SAR Press who patiently shepherded this project: Catherine Cocks, Lisa Pacheco, and Lynn Baca. Thank you to my peer reviewers, whose superb comments and suggestions improved this work enormously. I appreciate your careful attention to detail and the larger picture.

Faculty and staff of the San Diego State University Department of American Indian Studies have been tremendously supportive and have given me a great environment in which to grow as an academic and a colleague. Thank you, Margaret Field, Linda Parker, Alan Kilpatrick, Kate Reagan, and Kristen Bubb. I also thank my two research assistants at SDSU, Sarah McGinnis and Shelbe Wilkins. Shelbe: Your kid-sitting was obviously no less helpful than your research assistance. And to my other SDSU colleagues, Bill Nericcio, Brad Cook, Brian Finch, and Kerri Hame: I appreciate all the support you have given me in this process. Kate Spilde: It is always a pleasure to share knowledge and advice with you. You labor tirelessly to make sure that good and meaningful work happens, and I sincerely appreciate you for that.

Ed Blum and Jim Lee: I know few who understand and can explain the publishing business better than you two. Thank you for guiding and sheltering me through the process in such a loving way. (Jim: A special thanks for your help with these acknowledgments.) And Edsie: Thank you as well for all your free, wise editorial advice and all the quality time you willingly spent at our kitchen table.

Sarah Hardin: Thank you for your excellent friendship and meticulous copyediting. Jessica Cattelino and Colleen O'Neill: Thank you for always being able to maintain such deep, interesting thoughts and fun, casual conversation at the same time. I have truly appreciated every opportunity I have had to talk with both of you about Native and labor studies and the genuine support you have shown for my work. I also want to thank Darien Shanske, Walter Heiser, and Noah Zatz, who helped me better understand the inner workings of labor and Indian law—in particular Darien, who acted as my "in-house counsel" and ad hoc legal research assistant on this project. Who knew we'd make it from 408 Carmen Hall to here? Huge thanks are in order to Bob Purcel and Mary Ann Massenburg; without your generosity of time and trust, this project would not have been. I also want to thank LIUNA organizers Ellis Miller, Bill Keaton, Ron Meyers, and Julie Claymore for letting me tag along with them all across the Navajo Nation. Christian Sweeney: Thank you for the insightful exchanges and conversations about organizing in Indian Country.

Research for this project was generously funded by a UCLA Institute of American Cultures Predoctoral Fellowship, a UCLA Dissertation Year Fellowship, a UC Institute for Labor and Employment Doctoral Fellowship, the School of American Research Ethel-Jane Westfeldt Bunting Summer Fellowship, a Sycuan Institute on Tribal Gaming Research Grant, and SDSU faculty research grants.

To Clyde Van Arsdale and 3 Squares Gourmet: Thank you for the free wireless and excellent food and tea consumed during the writing of the overwhelming majority of this book. Huge thanks to the Davises, Boyers, Rangarajans, Rentchler/Hawleys, Hohenstein/Masons, and Newells for helping us find a nurturing community in San Diego and for all your love and support of our family in this process—particularly all the crucial, free kid-sitting hours that gave me time to write. Joey and Caroline: Your love and friendship span this continent, and I'm always a better person for it.

Aunt Michelle and Randy: You always made the Phoenix pit stops/detours well worth the trip. All my LA relatives: Thank you for your support and loving teasing about my quirky career and lifestyle choices. I could never have made it through graduate school sanely without cousins' night, and huge thanks are in order to all my aunts and uncles.

Thanks to Michele and Jim and the whole Brooks clan for your loving encouragement during the (many, many) years of this project.

Mosi the rez dog: You're a tireless bundle of energy and smiley stares and a daily reminder of how beautiful Navajoland is.

To Mom and Dad: All that I have that is good in my life can be traced back to you. Never could anyone imagine more supportive parents. I thank you for the solid foundation you have given me, and I love you dearly.

To Ella American and Rosa Lucille: No distractions from work are smarter, sweeter, or more fun than you two. I love every minute of cuddling, laughing, singing, and dancing with you, and I cannot wait to see what wonderful things you grow up to do.

Joanna: Being able to share my life with someone like you is the reason I got into this business. If it wasn't for the prospect of getting to see you at that union meeting thirteen years ago, this project would have likely never happened. You are a tireless supporter, mentor, and role model to me—all the while tolerating my LMJness. I adore your mind, creativity, and compassion. You make every day beautiful for me.

Abbreviations and Acronyms

BIA	Bureau of Indian Affairs
CTER	Council for Tribal Employee Rights
CWA	Communications Workers of America
HECMC	Hospital Employees and Community Members Committee
HERE	Hotel Employees and Restaurant Employees International Union
HPAIED	Harvard Project on American Indian Economic Development
IGRA	Indian Gaming Regulatory Act
IHS	Indian Health Service
IRA	Indian Reorganization Act
IUOE	International Union of Operating Engineers
LIUNA	Laborers' International Union of North America
MPLRL	Mashantucket Pequot Labor Relations Law
NCAI	National Congress of American Indians
NHCSC	Navajo Health Care System Corporation
NIGA	National Indian Gaming Association
NLRA	National Labor Relations Act
NLRB	National Labor Relations Board
NNC	Navajo Nation Council
NNCBC	Navajo Nation Collective Bargaining Code
ONLR	Office of Navajo Labor Relations
SEIU	Service Employees International Union
TCRHCC	Tuba City Regional Health Care Corporation
TERO	Tribal Employee Rights Ordinance
TLRO	Tribal Labor Relations Ordinance
UAW	United Auto Workers
ULP	unfair labor practice
UMWA	United Mine Workers of America
UNITE	Union of Needletrades, Industrial, and Textile Employees
UNITE-HERE!	Union of Needletrades, Industrial, and Textile Employees–Hotel Employees and Restaurant Employees Union

one
Introduction

It was by coincidence that I originally began to consider the relationship between labor unions and American Indian communities. Like many living in California in the 1990s, I gave little thought to how labor relations might play out in a contemporary indigenous context until they became a significant public issue in the debate surrounding the federally mandated regulation of tribal governmental gaming casinos. This public debate stemmed from two referendum campaigns (Proposition 5 in 1998 and Proposition 1A in 2000) meant to establish a legal regulatory relationship between the State of California and indigenous nations operating casinos within the state's boundaries. During these campaigns, most of the state's population supported tribal nations' efforts to improve their socioeconomic conditions by engaging in the enterprise of high-stakes gaming. Apart from the relatively minor voices of moral objection to gambling, the only significant opposition to Indian gaming in California swirled around concerns of corporate oversight of casino operations (see Bruyneel 2007; Goldberg and Champagne 2002; Rosenthal 2004). By questioning enforcement of environmental, labor, safety, and criminal codes, political campaigns and television ads (mostly funded by Las Vegas casinos) provoked fears of reservation lawlessness and of "unregulated" Indian gaming corporations. Some of the most active proponents of this position, and thereby the most vocal opponents of Indian gaming, were labor unions. They called attention to the labor relations of casino operations and sought to secure collective bargaining rights for casino employees.

At the time of this debate, I was in graduate school at UCLA, studying for a master's in American Indian studies and working as a union organizer. The union for which I worked—the United Auto Workers (UAW)—took no official stance on Prop 5, but many of my friends in the Los Angeles labor movement were progressive and proactive organizers for the Service Employees International Union (SEIU) and the Hotel Employees and Restaurant Employees International Union (HERE). As the two major representatives of casino employees in the United States, these unions were the most vocal opponents of Prop 5. Representatives from SEIU and HERE claimed that, as constructed by the proposition, the tribal–state gaming compacts did not allow enough protection for worker rights. In contrast, the sentiment in the Department of American Indian Studies, in which I was enrolled, was decidedly in favor of Prop 5. The department became an unofficial campus headquarters for the pro–Prop 5 campaign. Flyers and posters were hung in many offices, and the department lounge became a central distribution center for buttons and stickers. The department even co-hosted a debate on Prop 5, broadcast live in advance of the election. In this forum, the most significant opposition to the proposed tribal gaming structure, as described by the Prop 5 compact, came from prominent Los Angeles–area union leaders. These leaders claimed to speak on behalf of the majority nontribal members who would work at the casinos, and they criticized the proposition's lack of comprehensive protections for workers' rights to collectively organize and bargain. In the debate, both sides of the campaign framed unionism and tribal governmental gaming as being nearly irreconcilable.

I found my own political and social allegiances torn. Indeed, in the month leading up to the election, I wore a pro–Prop 5 button while walking around campus doing my duties organizing graduate teaching assistants. Although I respected the new labor movement's commitment to social justice, spearheaded locally by many of my friends and colleagues from SEIU and HERE, I could not help but feel that they were on the wrong side of the battle. Despite my involvement in and commitment to the labor movement, I got into many spirited debates with these friends and colleagues, usually provoked by my support of Prop 5. But I did not maintain my stance without internal conflict. I often cringed inside when some of the Native folks who avidly supported Prop 5 marshaled outdated and oversimplified tropes to attack labor's opposition to the proposition. On more than one occasion, in discussion with friends and classmates from the American Indian studies department, I felt the need to defend the historical necessity and overall objectives of the labor movement. Yet, in the next breath, I took pains to explain that despite my intimate connection to unions and union organizing, I was completely in favor of tribal gaming and tribal sovereignty and the proposition sustaining them in California. The thought-provoking discussions with friends, classmates, and union colleagues, on and around all sides of the gaming issue, led me to consider questions for which Indian gaming is only part of the answer: What is the nature of tribal labor relations? How do workers in Indian Country relate to corporate management in Indian Country?[1]

These questions strike at the heart of contemporary indigenous economic development and at broader issues of the process of indigenous self-determination. At stake are how much control indigenous communities have over shaping their economies and governing structures and how to do this in a way that is responsible to the people who participate in and are meant to benefit from economic development and political self-determination. This means considering the ways people enact economic and political self-determination from the top down and the ground up. Workers, who are the engine of indigenous economic development, have as much at stake in the process as policy makers, in large part because the jobs in these developing economies are often the only opportunities for miles around and years to come. Attending to tribal labor relations gives us a chance to look at what happens when indigenous leaders take on the power and responsibility of corporate management. As elected or appointed tribal economic administrators, they manage some employees who are tribal members and some who are not. With the former, they manage people they are meant to work in behalf of, in a broad political and economic sense, and at the same time to supervise in a more technocratic workplace setting. With the latter, they manage people who are not their political constituents and are not equally invested in the larger political, cultural, and social agendas of tribal economic development. Examining tribal labor relations, then, adds depth to our understanding of how globalization leads to unique and intricate economic, political, and civic relations at multiple levels.

Examining tribal labor relations is also important for what it can teach us about tribal sovereignty. In simple terms, tribal sovereignty is the right of tribes as political, cultural, and economic communities to decide how to govern themselves for themselves: it is the right of self-governance and self-determination. The goal of labor unionism is to secure for workers a collective say in terms of their work conditions. At first blush, these two agendas might seem at odds with each other in the context of tribal labor relations. Indeed, in the case of tribal gaming in California, labor unions sought to put legal limits on tribes' sovereign rights to make unilateral decisions about tribal economies and workplaces. But focusing on tribal labor relations shows us more than just the limits of tribal sovereignty; it gives us a new view of the characteristics of sovereignty as well. Tribal labor relations can be seen as a way for tribal governments to expand their governing jurisdiction and further enhance their day-to-day sovereignty. Moreover, asserting control in the affairs of tribal workplaces gives rank-and-file tribal members a say in how economic and political self-determination is enacted—not just for themselves as individuals but also for their communities as a whole. Hence, studying tribal labor relations reveals how the process of tribal sovereignty and self-determination is an interactive one between multiple on- and off-reservation forces.

Indian gaming is at both the center and the periphery of these questions of economic development, tribal sovereignty, and labor relations. The economic success of tribally operated casinos has put them at the heart of debates about tribal labor relations. As some of the most economically successful enterprises in Indian Country, with relatively large, stable, and generally non-Native workforces, tribal casinos present a prime opportunity for labor unions seeking to expand membership. Moreover, local and global political and economic forces have created the context wherein the strongest and most aggressive unions in the United States are the ones that represent service employees such as casino workers.[2] Thus, certain prominent unions have directed concerted energy toward proactively participating in tribal labor relations. For these reasons—and because of a general fascination with anything Indian gaming related—tribally operated casinos have increased the public profile of the issue of tribal labor relations. Most recently, tribal casinos have become a venue for legal and political battles between indigenous nations and U.S. labor unions. In these courtroom and legislative battles, the terms of the debate have been defined as a zero-sum game between labor unionism and tribal sovereignty. And current legal decisions on tribal casino labor relations threaten to have drastic impacts not just on tribal labor relations in general but also on the exercise of tribal sovereignty, even outside the realm of tribal labor relations. The story of tribal labor relations, however, does not begin and end with tribal gaming.

As publicly prominent as gaming is, successful tribal gaming operations are only a small percentage of tribal economic enterprises. Moreover, only a small percentage of tribally operated casinos are tremendously financially successful (HPAIED 2008). In terms of overwhelming financial success, tribal casinos are the exception rather than the rule.[3] Tribal casinos can also be considered peripheral to the rest of economic development in Indian Country in that they are among the few tribally run economic enterprises wherein the majority of employees are not tribal members. Tribal labor relations and their connection to tribal self-determination are influenced differently when tribal citizens are the employees of the tribal enterprise. In this context, unions are not as readily coded as foreign intrusions seeking to infringe upon tribal sovereignty. Indeed, unions can become a tool with which indigenous workers can expand their voices in the economic *and* political processes of tribal self-determination.

It is the exceptionalism of tribal gaming that allows it to be simultaneously at the center and on the periphery of tribal labor relations and, for that matter, economic development in Indian Country as a whole. That is, the few outlying Native nations whose financial success is so threatening to nonindigenous commerce and polities are made examples of by non-Indian critics who call for regulation of Indian casinos and the tribal sovereignty that allows for them. Although the criticisms are leveled at and the limitations designed for a specific enterprise, they go beyond just the "offending" Native nations and threaten to restructure the whole order of indigenous sovereignty (Corntassel and Witmer 2008). When attention gets so focused on tribal gaming, it can drive trends throughout the political economy, federal Indian policy and law, and even indigenous discourse in Indian Country. At the same time, this intense focus obscures a whole host of things in Indian Country that have little or nothing to do with tribal gaming. Tribal labor relations span the tension between gaming and nongaming concerning issues and questions that are central to any tribally run economic enterprise.

The Work of Sovereignty explores political, economic, and cultural forces that structure and influence economic development in Indian Country from the perspective of workers. A fundamental goal of this book is to view indigenous self-determination from the vantage point of work and workers. My considerations coalesce around what I call tribal labor relations, the unique ways in which relationships between workers and management play out in Indian Country. I hone in on this relationship because it allows me to stitch together structural forces such as law, politics, governments, and markets with the people who are affected by and influence these institutions. I am particularly concerned with the people most affected by tribal labor relations: workers. My analytical privileging of workers comes from the fact that most research on tribal sovereignty and economic development focuses on the legal, governmental, and economic structures that delimit sovereignty, not on the people who experience and enact it through their everyday labor. Most American Indians experience tribal economic development not as theorists, policy architects, or legislators but as workers. *The Work of Sovereignty* is interested in how individuals as workers contribute to the larger collective goals of tribal sovereignty.[4]

Labor relations in Indian Country can be delineated by the interrelation between four variables: (1) tribal employees; (2) nontribal employees; (3) tribal enterprises; and (4) nontribal enterprises. I use the term *tribal labor relations* specifically to describe the interrelationship between variables 3 and 1, 3 and 2, or 3, 1, and 2. This definition of tribal labor relations is not just a geographic designation—that is, labor relations happening in Indian Country—but rather is based on the participation of tribal enterprises in labor relations. Arguably, this definition emphasizes the composition of management over the composition of labor, but it is the participation of a tribal enterprise that makes the labor relations inherent to the enterprise distinctly "tribal labor relations."

In talking about a tribal enterprise, I mean an economic venture that is owned, sponsored, or run by a Native national government. This definition is critically important for understanding tribal labor relations; although some enterprises may appear to be commercial in nature, a tribal enterprise is a governmental entity, and therefore its employees are governmental employees. Not all the employees are tribal members with a distinct political/electoral relationship to the tribal government, but most U.S. labor laws construct the definition of governmental employees differently than that of private-sector employees. The difference is in large part a recognition that governmental enterprises are established for the benefit of citizens as a collective, not for individual investors or private shareholders. This is the case in almost all instances, whether a governmental enterprise is for profit or nonprofit. In the former, profits go into governmental coffers to support governmental activities and administration. In the latter, the enterprise is dedicated to serving the public, and any additional revenue created in this process goes back into the governmental enterprise or toward supporting other governmental services. Because of the importance of governmental enterprises to the act of governance, the relationship between these enterprises and their employees is often conceived of and regulated differently than it would be in private industry.

Tribal governmental enterprises are particularly important because in most cases they are the primary source of employment and generate much of the governmental revenue in Indian Country.[5]

Lastly, when talking about the labor side of tribal labor relations, I am not necessarily talking about unions' relationship to employees of tribal enterprises collectively, but about management's. In general U.S. labor relations, labor unions are the most common expression of workers' collective relationship with management.[6] Still, in this book, I also focus on tribal employees working concertedly for their workplace rights without being under the auspices of a union—unionization was one of the goals they were working toward.

Tribal labor relations is a phenomenon relatively unexamined, particularly from the perspective of indigenous workers. Much of this has to do with a general (nonindigenous) neglect of Indians as workers and of the work they do. As a corrective to this neglect, a growing number of historians and social scientists have begun to focus on how indigenous people experience work and the workplace. Also, public policy research on tribal economic development may focus on job creation and industrial development; however, little is mentioned of what effect this has on labor relations. The one academic discipline that has specifically attended to tribal labor relations is legal scholarship. The juridical approach has focused on how common law debates have structured formal jurisdiction over tribal labor relations. This approach is highly abstracted from people's everyday work experiences in Indian Country, though.

Disregard for indigenous work and workers has its roots in the larger and long-held settler colonial project of rationalizing the appropriation of Indian land by denying the work Indians did. Patrick Wolfe (2001:868) argues that "settler colonialism" is distinguished from other kinds of colonialism because its agenda is "to replace the natives on their land rather than extract surplus value by mixing their labor with a colony's natural resources.... [Settler] colonizers come to stay, expropriating the native owners of the soil...[and] introduc[ing] a zero-sum contest over land on which conflicting modes of production could not ultimately coexist." Settler colonialism overwrites Native occupancy with the argument that the land was not improved—not *worked* by indigenous peoples. Being unimproved meant that the land was not being used in a way (or through a mode of production) that implied possession. Therefore, it was surplus available for white expropriation. A counterpart to this logic of expropriation, or what Wolfe (2001) calls "the logic of elimination," was an attempt to assimilate Indians by compelling them to do certain kinds of work. Nineteenth- and twentieth-century assimilationist policies tried to make Indians into yeoman farmers through the Dawes Act of 1887 or into industrial laborers through boarding school vocational training (Littlefield 1991; Pfister 2004). The implication of these policies was that before they were enacted, Indians existed in a state of nature that did not qualify as "work." And, even if turn-of-the-past-century job training did assimilate some Indians into market economies, nonindigenous scholarship from the early twentieth century on ignored the class aspects of assimilationist tactics and focused instead on issues of cultural assimilation. For example, salvage ethnography privileged a "vanishing," "traditional" culture over the multiple ways in which indigenous peoples were actively engaged in contemporary economic systems. It assumed that cultural or "traditional" beliefs and practices kept Natives from entering market economies. This logic took either the extreme racist, social Darwinist perspective, that Indians were not prepared for or capable of participating in market economies, or a more seemingly neutral perspective, that Indians were too isolated to join market economies, either because of the historic economic and geographic limitations of reservations or because Natives actively chose to opt out of modernity and capitalism.[7]

Confronting these biases, many historians and historical anthropologists have recovered accounts of the working lives of American Indians. This research has emphasized three issues: (1) Native participation from the beginning in the growth of capitalism and modernism in America (e.g., Littlefield 1991; Pfister 2004; White 1991; Wolf 1982); (2) Native participation in wage labor on and off reservations (e.g., Hodge 1971; Hosmer and O'Neill 2004; Littlefield and Knack 1996; Meeks 2007; Norrgard 2009; O'Neill 2005; Weppner 1971); and (3) the extent to which we should read cultural activities such as arts, crafts, and tourism as labor—in addition to reading these activities for their meanings in terms of cultural representations (Dilworth 1996; Knack and Littlefield 1996; Raibmon 2005). This scholarship teaches us that blindness to indigenous work reinforces a version of the primitivist trope that constructs Native life as a cultural artifact not participating in but only affected by modernity. Attention to tribal labor relations further distinguishes our understanding of indigenous participation in the work spaces produced in modernity in that it illustrates how the meaning and terms of work are negotiated in Indian Country as part and parcel of the growth of tribal economies.[8] Above and beyond the historical and anthropological scholarship on the work indigenous people do (and have done), a focus on tribal labor relations looks at indigenous management of labor.

Much of the literature on tribal economic development treats indigenous peoples as fully modern subjects engaged in the process of nation building. This scholarship comes out of policy studies and social science research, and it analyzes and proscribes how to develop tribal economies and governments hand in hand. This indigenous nation building, though, seeks to be different from the model set up by modern, twentieth-century European nation-states. The policy analysts and social scientists propose a Native nation building that combines the form and structure of Euro-American economic and governmental institutions with traditional indigenous values and modes of relations.[9] The goal is tribal constitutionalism and tribal capitalism. However, the focus on the cultural aspects of economic development overlooks the notion of Indians as workers. Indeed, the only real discussion of employment comes in terms of job creation, and even this rarely deals with who is doing the actual work of tribal economic development and how they relate to tribal management and governments.

One thing lacking when work and workers are left out of discussions of tribal economic and political development is a discussion of the connection between markets and citizenship. As tribes further develop their economies and governments, the relationship between tribal citizenship and labor in Indian Country will become increasingly significant because of two factors: (1) many tribes need to hire nonmembers to fully staff their economic ventures; and (2) the workplace can be used as a venue for both tribal members and nonmembers to assert their economic *and* political rights. In terms of the first factor, the demographics of most tribes demand that to a varying extent they staff their tribal enterprises with labor from outside Indian Country.[10] However, this is not to suggest that there is not a huge need for jobs for tribal members in many Native communities. This is where the second factor comes in; a major goal of tribal economic development is to reduce reservation unemployment. The availability of work, the kinds, and how work will be distributed have always been political questions in Indian Country, and this is particularly the case for employment in tribal governmental enterprises. Because tribal governmental enterprises are operated in behalf of tribal members, there is often public discussion of whether these enterprises are being run in the interest of the people. The workplace is a key forum for this discussion because employees of tribal enterprises have insight into day-to-day operations and are directly affected by them. In this regard, active participation in tribal labor relations can be about more than just localized work conditions; also it can be about holding tribal leaders accountable for how they enact economic development in behalf of the community. This partaking in the political life of the community fits conventional notions of citizenship as participation (see Bosniak 2000). Moreover, citizenship has long been thought to be articulated in, around, and through work (e.g., Bosniak 2000; Goldberg 2007; Gordon 2007; Kessler-Harris 2003; Marshall 1964; Ong 2006; Shklar 1991). Examining tribal labor relations illustrates how this happens in Indian Country because it reveals how tribal members and nonmembers relate to the public-sponsored venture of tribal nation building and tribal capitalism.

Tribal capitalism is an ideal model of Indian Country economic development because it envisions tribal government–sponsored economic enterprises that value a tribe's natural and cultural resources and that redistribute the revenues these generate (Champagne 2004; Smith 2000). The emphasis on the way Native cultural values are infused into tribal capitalism is generally approached from the perspective of tribal corporate management and the tribal political leaders who structure and oversee these enterprises. Although certainly a very important and significant perspective, it has left out the standpoint of Native employees and employees in general. How do indigenous and nonindigenous employees interact with tribal economic development, whether it is operated by their own tribal government or by an outside firm working in conjunction with the tribal government? And to what extent are indigenous people, as individuals, relevant to these models of development as tribal employees, not just as tribal members? Furthermore, this literature does little to reflect on responsible labor relations as part of responsible economic development. Instead, workers' significance to the project of tribal economic development and its success is understood by the way in which cultural identity and values of tribal members and nontribal members harmonize or clash with a given strategy for economic development. The question of compatibility is primarily contemplated from a cultural perspective, not from the perspective of tribal members *as workers*. In decisions about tribal economic development, the collective labor resources of an indigenous community ought to be given the same weight as the cultural and natural resources. This is not to say that paying attention to tribal labor relations should be done at the expense of issues of cultural and ecological values, but rather in addition to them.[11]

Moreover, considering tribal economic development and nation building from the perspective of labor relations may shed a different light on our understanding of American Indian communities' relationships to globalization and labor relations in general in the current age of globalization. Tribal economic development that is responsible to the concerns of workers ensures that Indian Country does not become what Aihwa Ong (2006) describes as a zone of neoliberal exceptionalism, in which the drive to attract foreign capital investment and to compete on a global economic scale becomes so extreme that governments distribute rights in terms of what is expedient for profit margins rather than democratic notions of citizenship. If tribal capitalism is distinguished as being based on the ideals of redistribution over those of accumulation (Champagne 2004), then indigenous governments and tribal enterprises ought to be wary of implementing political, economic, and legal strategies that are used as neoliberal policies around the world. Attending to tribal labor relations means, then, considering how union-busting tactics and right-to-work laws affect indigenous communities and whether anti-unionism, or even unionism for that matter, is compatible with localized indigenous values. Equally relevant, examples of unionism that work in Indian Country because they are highly attuned to local needs might be instructive in the way unions ought to act in indigenous (and, potentially, nonindigenous) communities throughout the world.

Similarly, considering citizenship in the context of work in Indian Country and labor relations could contribute to broader ongoing discussions of postnational citizenship. Many scholars of globalization debate whether citizenship is still primarily a nation-state phenomenon and the extent to which it is becoming "denationalized," in the words of Linda Bosniak (2000), through transnational forces. As part of this debate, questions of citizenship are coalescing around globalization of labor, in the way labor migrates to find employment and in the way global capital travels the world to capture the cheapest labor market (see Barry 2006; Bosniak 2000; Chander 2006; Gordon 2007; Kessler-Harris 2003; Ong 2006). Ong claims that this process has led to

> components formerly tied to citizenship—rights, entitlements, as well as nation and territoriality...becoming disarticulated from one another and rearticulated with government strategies that promote an economic logic in defining, evaluating, and protecting certain categories of subjects and not others.... We are beginning to see a detachment of entitlements from political membership and national territory, as certain rights and benefits

> are distributed to bearers of marketable talents and denied to those judged to lack such capacity or potential. (Ong 2006:16)

She and others have noted how globalization and neoliberalism allow certain economic elites to cross different national territories in ways that grant them the same rights and benefits as local citizens or exceptional rights and benefits above and beyond those of local citizens.

Indian Country is also feeling the effects of the global movement of labor and capital as nontribal members come to reservations to work for, help manage, or even help capitalize tribal enterprises. In some cases, these people live on reservations or live near them and commute. What seems to be different about the movement in and out of Indian Country is the expectation that citizenship rights will travel with nonmembers to reservations. This is not just neoliberal exceptionalism for economic elites, but also for undifferentiated labor. The expectation of traveling citizenship likely has its roots in the assumption of continuity of citizenship and territory in the United States—Indian Country is not thought of as a distinguishable locale, because it is within U.S. national and territorial borders. U.S. courts have supported the expectation of traveling citizenship by limiting the authority of tribal governments mainly to members, not nonmembers (Aleinikoff 2002; Frickey 1999).

What this system creates is overlapping and crosscutting citizenship within one territory, where nontribal citizens have some important legal rights, such as criminal and civil rights protections, but not the same political rights and entitlements that tribal members have, such as voting rights, indigenous social services, and a share of tribal income. At its highest potential, this overlapping citizenship can be expressed in ways that allow for alliances against forces of neoliberalism. Tribal and U.S. citizenship rights can be conjoined to forestall neoliberal efforts to distribute rights based on profit margin, not on democratic ideals. At the same time, this overlapping can lead to contentious debates about which government's model of citizenship is the most valuable, just, or sacrosanct. My research on tribal labor relations bears out both collaborative and contentious overlapping as nontribal members and tribal members at the Navajo Nation work together to increase the accountability of tribal leaders or as tribes and unions fight in courtrooms about whose laws will most adequately protect tribal employees. Both examples of overlapping citizenship ought to further fine-tune our understanding of postnational citizenship.

Within Indian Country, the issue of citizenship is also paramount, because the legal right that tribes have over nontribal citizens demarcates and defines the limits of tribal sovereignty. Tribal labor relations play an important role in this debate as the courts adjudicate what legal jurisdiction tribal governments have in regulating nonmember employees. It should come as no surprise, then, that the academic field that has given the most detailed consideration to tribal labor relations is legal scholarship. Its main focus is how tribal labor relations relate to tribal sovereignty. Analysis of opinions made by the National Labor Relations Board (NLRB) and state and federal judiciaries has charted the complicated and often contradictory development of the common law that structures tribal labor relations (Buffalo and Wadzinski 1994–95; Grez 2005; Kemp 1995; Limas 1993; Rice 1996; Singel 2004; Thompson 2001). The main question of this legal analysis is, Under whose jurisdiction do tribal labor relations properly lie? From this perspective, tribal sovereignty is considered a question of jurisdiction: What governments and whose body of law should adjudicate what kind of tribal labor relations and under what circumstances? The debate in these court cases is whether federal labor law, specifically the National Labor Relations Act (NLRA), applies in Indian Country. This debate has structured jurisdiction as a zero-sum game and thus has played out as an adversarial relationship between labor unionism and tribal sovereignty. Argued and decided in this way, these cases have the potential impact of drawing tighter boundaries around tribal sovereignty in general, not just for the issue of labor relations. In this regard, it is important to pay attention to the jurisprudence of tribal labor relations for the way in which it may affect other aspects of federal Indian law and fit into larger patterns and judicial trends. Indeed, the contemporary jurisprudence of tribal labor relations provides an interesting barometer with which to measure juridical attitudes about both organized labor and tribal sovereignty. In recent years, the federal courts have not been friendly to either cause (see Aleinikoff 2002; Frickey 1999; Wilkins and Lomawaima 2001; Williams 2005 on tribal sovereignty; see Gross 1995; Lichtenstein 2002; Logan 2002; Tomlins 1985 on labor unions). As two causes that are under significant judicial attack are pitted against each other, judicial opinions on tribal labor relations might give us some sense of just how hostile the courts are to labor rights and tribal sovereignty rights.[12]

At the time of this writing, the most recent outcome of these adversarial legal deliberations has been rulings that favor union rights over tribal sovereign rights. Whether this will be the final word remains to be seen. But there is no denying the growing importance of tribal labor relations, particularly in regard to how tribal governments and enterprises need to make this issue a policy priority. Indeed, many have; they are increasingly developing their own legal structures for handling tribal labor relations, in the form of tribal ordinances and regulatory codes. This is in large part why tribal labor relations are so significant, because they represent the nexus of economic development and self-determination. Tribally run workplaces are among the key sites where tribal citizens (and noncitizens) directly experience—and have the potential to shape—the day-to-day enactment of tribal sovereignty. The economic articulation of tribal citizenship is at least as important as more purely political or cultural forms that might take shape through participation in electoral processes and governmental institutions or in ceremonial practices and kin networks. In fact, much of *The Work of Sovereignty* deals with how the tribal workplace and the labor relations therein become a forum for the expression of the political agendas of tribal self-determination. We should view the nexus of workers' rights and tribal sovereignty rights not in terms of conflict but in terms of the tremendous potential for expansion of tribal sovereignty—both in increasing the domain of tribal governance and law and in broadening democratic and grassroots participation in the exercise of tribal self-determination.[13] This is how attention to tribal labor relations can make a significant contribution to the crucial ongoing conversations about tribal sovereignty and self-determination.

Tribal self-governance and communal identity have always been critical aspects of indigenous communities, but in the past thirty-some years, as the field of American Indian studies has developed, tribal sovereignty has been among the central concerns of both the academic discipline and the indigenous communities with which the discipline seeks to work collaboratively. In many ways, academic considerations of tribal sovereignty have their genesis in the U.S. and international indigenous political and legal activism that has pushed for recognition of the sovereign status of indigenous communities within settler colonialist boundaries (Alfred 1995; Anaya 2004; Barker 2005; Barsh and Henderson 1980; Biolsi 2005; Bruyneel 2007; Cobb 2005/2006; Ivison, Patton, and Sanders 2000; Warrior 1994; Wilkinson 2005). What these indigenous activists sought and continue to seek is the collective right of self-governance without interference from settler colonial nation-states and their political subgroups.[14] Activists and Native community leaders in the United States and Canada have increasingly described self-governance in terms of nationhood and peoplehood and have called for government-to-government relations between indigenous nations and settler colonial nation-states. In the United States, the executive branch has proclaimed this government-to-government relationship as the baseline framework for federal Indian policy decisions, but Congress still maintains a stance of plenary power over Native communities.

What is often debated and misunderstood—particularly from the outside—in the drive for indigenous collective rights of sovereignty and self-determination is the extent to which indigenous sovereignty means independence or separatism. Indigenous rights within settler colonialism are certainly based on notions of distinction and difference (Povinelli 2002; Simpson 2000), but this does not necessarily mean autonomy. Indeed, it is likely that the (mis)emphasis on sovereignty as autonomy has driven the hostility toward indigenous sovereignty. This certainly seems to be the case on the international stage. The world's major settler colonial nation-states were unwilling to be party to the United Nations Declaration on the Rights of Indigenous Peoples because they feared a disruption caused by autonomous polities within what they perceived to be their territorial boundaries (Scott 1996). Sovereignty as autonomy does not accurately describe the political, economic, and cultural nature of our globalized world today (if it ever did) (Deloria 1979; Stacey 2003; Wilkins and Lomawaima 2001; Young 2000, 2001). Sovereignty is more appropriately thought of in terms of relatedness or, as Jessica Cattelino (2008) calls it, "interdependent sovereignty." This notion of sovereignty acknowledges the extent to which political communities depend upon one another but ought to be free from domination by one another. The sovereignty and self-determination of nondomination require that polities work out relationships based on compromises that allow for the mutual expression of political voice and need (Young 2001).

Following Iris Marion Young (2000, 2001) and Jessica Cattelino (2008), I read tribal labor relations through the notion of interdependent sovereignty. "Interdependent sovereignty" is the best way to describe the collaborative relationships within much of the noncasino-industry-based labor relations in Indian Country. Moreover, viewing sovereignty from an interdependent perspective seems to be the only way to break the legal and political stalemate that is growing around casino-industry-based tribal labor relations. The assumption that sovereignty means autonomy has created an argument, in which labor unions claim that tribal labor relations should be adjudicated solely on their terms—the NLRA—and tribes claim the converse—that their sovereignty trumps intervention of foreign regulation of labor. So far, the courts that have ruled in favor of labor unions have employed the logic of sovereignty as autonomy by setting untenable expectations of what tribal activities ought to look like to be exempt from NLRA jurisdiction. At the same time, tribal enterprises should not be too quick to label labor union organizers as foreign agitators who inherently contradict efforts toward tribal self-reliance. Although the extremes of this debate are almost exclusively engaged with tribal labor relations in the Indian gaming industry, the way in which the debates are settled legally and politically will likely affect the way labor relations are handled throughout Indian Country.

This book argues that what is needed is a greater balancing of workers' rights and sovereignty rights, and viewing sovereignty as interdependent allows for this. I am not calling for indigenous communities to sacrifice their sovereignty to achieve this balance. On the contrary, I am suggesting that indigenous nations expand their exercise of sovereignty by more thoroughly taking labor relations into account and developing more detailed labor codes that include indigenous-based, independent judiciaries to adjudicate tribal labor relations. Undoubtedly, this change would require greater concessions from certain labor leaders and changes in federal court interpretation of federal labor law. Nevertheless, in settler colonial situations, the cards are inherently stacked against indigenous groups, so in almost all cases, balance can be achieved only by the settler colonial nation-state making the greater concessions. At the same time, indigenous political and economic leaders must recognize the interdependent nature of their sovereignty, engage unions in negotiation, and respect certain fundamental collective rights of tribal employees (whether or not they are tribal citizens). These employee rights and protections can be achieved just as thoroughly through indigenous forms of governance as through nonindigenous forms, if not more. Young's (2001) notion of interdependent self-determination relies on a theory of freedom equal not to autonomy but rather to nondomination. Applied to tribal labor relations, this theory would put the onus on both labor *and* management to negotiate relationships that value and institutionalize workers' voices through a democratic system of governance that simultaneously respects indigenous sovereignty. Labor relations are, after all, processes of negotiation, and tribal labor relations are ideally processes of equality, nondomination, and open negotiation.

Of course, the process can get tricky where the rubber hits the road. So *The Work of Sovereignty* is not just about the legal jurisdictional debates over tribal gaming labor relations. Much of this book is about how labor relations play out on the ground in Indian Country, how tribal employees view their relationships with their bosses and tribal enterprises, and how this view connects to their enactment of indigenous self-determination. It is worth noting here that for the most part, I use the terms *sovereignty* and *self-determination* interchangeably. However, I do think there is a subtle but significant distinction, in that *self-determination* is a more process-oriented term. The word *sovereignty* in the political arena clearly originates in European monarchs' descriptions of their own power as heads of state (see Bartelson 1995). But with the advent of the nation-state, the term acquired meaning beyond just individual heads of state, and indigenous communities have adopted the term, if not the complete philosophy, to describe the collective rights of nationhood.[15] Indigenous peoples often use the term *self-determination* to talk about the same issues. But I feel that the active sense of self-determination—the "determining," if you will—implies the enactment of or process of carrying out sovereignty.[16] Indeed, Robert Warrior (1994), interpreting the philosophies of Vine Deloria Jr., talks about sovereignty as a process rather than a thing or a static state of being. It is the exercise of sovereignty, the act of self-determining, that I am trying to get at by looking closely at how Navajo Nation health-care workers experience, impact, and reflect on indigenous sovereignty through tribal labor relations.

The Navajo Nation health-care workers' everyday experience of tribal labor relations provides a valuable contrast to the legal and political wrangling common to tribal casino–based labor relations. First and foremost, their experiences illustrate that unionism is not inherently contradictory to the goal of tribal self-determination. Their union—the Laborers' International Union of North America (LIUNA)—has made noninterference with tribal sovereignty an official policy. This position is easier to sustain, given that the Navajo Nation has its own collective bargaining code. Therefore, following the regulations of the code, LIUNA and its members are not just maintaining noninterference but also are participating in tribal self-determination. Moreover, as part of participating in the procedures of the tribal labor code, tribal citizens exercise self-determination through processes that parallel and supplement tribal electoral and governmental politics. Navajo Nation health-care workers use their positions as tribal employees to articulate their political voice in the enactment of tribal self-determination. These workers have used workplace activism, such as petition campaigns and public protests, to politicize tribal labor relations in ways that express their views on how tribal economic development and self-determination should be conducted. In this case, tribal labor relations offered a space in which to hold indigenous leaders accountable to what workers believed was a legitimate and responsible enactment of self-determination.

This Navajo Nation example provides an excellent case in which to examine tribal labor relations, particularly the relationship between indigenous self-determination and tribal sovereignty. The Navajo Nation has a well-developed export economy, much of which is based on mineral extraction and energy production. Additionally, civil service—both federal and tribal governmental jobs—provides many jobs for the Diné (the Navajo people, literally translated, "The People"). More importantly, the Navajo Nation has one of the most comprehensive systems of tribal governance (Wilkins 1999). The tribal government consists of a well-developed tricameral structure, in which the executive, legislative, and judicial branches all enjoy a significant amount of independence. In addition to this centralized government, significant power is distributed to local and regional forms of governance and administration. Although the Navajo Nation operates without a constitution, it has a highly sophisticated set of codes that is very comprehensive in its coverage of issues and that generally attempts to blend traditional philosophies of governance with Western forms (Nielsen and Zion 2005; Wilkins 1999).[17]

The Navajo Nation's sophisticated form of governance has a lot to do with its tremendous geographic, human, and natural resources—both those that can be tapped into and those in need of protection. The Navajo Nation is the largest Native nation in the United States in terms of geographic area and the second largest in terms of population. This prodigiousness, almost in and of itself, necessitates a comprehensive and detailed form of governance. The vastness of Navajo resources has also made the Navajo Nation a coveted space for external investment in extraction and energy production and has led to a long history of economic exploitation of Diné land. The origins of the modern Navajo centralized governments come out of this history; the Bureau of Indian Affairs (BIA) helped the Navajos form a centralized council in the 1930s with nearly the sole purpose of signing agreements with outside investors. The longevity of the interconnectedness between the growth of the Diné economy and the development of the modern Navajo Nation government has also created longevity of experience dealing with labor relations on the Navajo Reservation. Some of the earliest attempts at unionization in Indian Country happened at Navajoland (O'Neill 2005). The first key NLRB court case dealing with labor relations in Indian Country (*Navajo Tribe v. NLRB*, 1961) involved the Navajo Nation. And the Navajo Nation was one of the first tribal governments to pass its own collective bargaining code.

Given all these factors, the Navajo Nation might seem an exceptional place to study tribal labor relations. However, although other Native nations might not share legal, economic, political, and demographic facets to the same degree as the Navajo Nation, many reservations have similar enough experiences with tribal economic development to make aspects of Navajo labor relations analogous and generalizable to them. For example, a significant reason to study labor relations at the Navajo Nation is the fact that tribal policy and communal expression of labor relations are being worked out almost exclusively in the absence of tribal gaming. Tribal gaming—with its conventionally high instance of imported labor—has been driving many of the current trends in tribal labor relations, although gaming is unrepresentative of most tribal economies.[18] Therefore, studying tribal labor relations in a primarily nongaming context can be more instructive about what is going on in the rest of Indian Country, particularly in regard to civil service work.

It is also worth noting that by looking at health-care workers, I consider a form of employment similar to service-sector employment in tribal casinos. Of course, health-care workers and casino workers do not do the same kinds of work, but they are arguably more similar to each other than casino employees are to the industrial or construction workers common to other parts of Indian Country.

More importantly, though, a key reason to study health care as a location of tribal labor relations is that a growing number of Native nations are taking over the administration of health care for their communities. In the United States, this is happening through the Indian Self-Determination Act, and indigenous governments are enacting these takeovers to expand both tribal self-governance and tribal control of economies. Under this federal law, reservation health-care facilities become tribally run enterprises, and the employees become tribal employees. Even more significant, the most recent NLRB ruling (*Yukon II*) asserts that labor relations in the context of tribally run health-care facilities (unlike tribal casinos) can be negotiated under the jurisdiction of tribal governments, not the NLRA. In fact, this ruling was designed to be read in conjunction with a recent NLRB ruling on tribal gaming to jointly set the legal precedent for adjudicating tribal labor relations. Tribally run health-care facilities, like casinos, are key locales at the intersection of tribal labor relations and indigenous sovereignty.

In addition to the policy- and law-oriented significance of labor relations at Navajo Nation health-care facilities, this example allows me to follow the experiences of tribal employees through dramatic changes to their workplace and to evaluate how the changes affected perspectives on tribal labor relations. The health-care workers who agreed to share their stories with me went through a pivotal change in management of health-care facilities, initiated by the Navajo Nation Council. Many employees' responses to this change were strong collective actions that publicly asserted the importance of worker voices in tribal labor relations and even in how to manage a tribal enterprise undertaken in behalf of indigenous communities. Much of *The Work of Sovereignty* studies organizing campaigns and grassroots, ad hoc collective political actions carried out by employees trying to increase control over their workplaces and their say in the political life of their communities. By studying them, I take an on-the-ground approach to tribal labor relations that puts tribal workers at the center of the action. I focus on how indigenous community members square their economic, political, and social selves in ways that overlap, contradict, and run parallel to one another. Attending to indigenous peoples as both economic and political members of their community also sheds light on processes of indigenous self-determination that are not always as readily visible as those in courtrooms and tribal council chambers. As much as centralized tribal governments are key to sustaining indigenous self-determination, it must also come from the people, from the grassroots upward (e.g., Alfred 1995, 1999; Simpson 2000).

Methodologies

In *The Work of Sovereignty*, I take my methodological cues from the interdisciplinary nature of American Indian studies—drawing on history, anthropology, sociology, political science, and policy studies, among others. The field of American Indian studies has traditionally critiqued, retooled, and marshaled these key disciplinary approaches to illuminate Native experience and Native concerns from a Native perspective (Deloria 1988). More recently, scholars and activists working in and around indigenous studies have been committed to decolonizing the traditional methods of studying indigenous peoples, in order to make the academy more responsible to and useful for Native people's needs and agendas (e.g.,, Smith 1999). I heed these concerns by centering a significant portion of my research on tribal labor relations involving the experiences of indigenous workers.

The Work of Sovereignty is quite different from what I first envisioned. While working toward my PhD in anthropology, I originally conceived of a more traditional ethnographic study that would combine cultural and linguistic anthropology to answer questions about how union organizing happened in Indian Country. Following a union organizing campaign among Navajo Nation health-care workers, I sought to explore differences in the way non-Native professional organizers and Native workers and volunteer organizers approached and thought about language use in organizing conversations. So I followed union organizers as they talked to Navajo Area Indian Health Service (IHS) employees about a potential tribal government takeover of the management of their health-care facilities and convinced them to sign a petition affirming their collective bargaining rights. I then interviewed several Navajo employees and non-Navajo and Navajo organizers about these conversations. The more I interacted with Navajo health-care workers, the more I realized that this question of language use was not particularly interesting to them (and it soon became less interesting to me as well). What mattered more to them was how their work conditions might change and that they have a say in how the changes would take place. This concern persisted through the transition to tribal administration as workers at one hospital began various kinds of public protest to improve their working conditions. After the protests, I began interviewing workers at this facility and attending some of their community meetings. I learned from these employees that it was critically important for them to have a say in their labor relations. The interactions I had with these workers motivated me to change my focus to how labor relations play out in Indian Country, particularly how employees experience tribal labor relations.

This project on tribal labor relations is the product of relationships with labor organizers and Native workers and activists at the Navajo Nation over the course of seven years. I also work in an American Indian studies department in a state university and in a region of the state where questions of labor and indigenous political economy are acute. These experiences have certainly shaped my understanding of tribal labor relations as a whole. In my ongoing relationship with union organizers and health-care employee activists, I have shared this manuscript with them and invited and incorporated their feedback to make this story of tribal labor relations as much as possible their story.

I have used various ethnographic methods—interviewing, spending time with workers and organizers, attending organizing and planning meetings, and observing and participating in a union recognition campaign—to get at how these people experience tribal labor relations. My research was conducted with approval from the Cultural Resources Office of the Navajo Nation Historic Preservation Department, along with notification to the chapter houses in areas where I conducted ethnographic research. All research with Navajo consultants was conducted with signed consent.

As Vicki Smith (2001) notes, ethnographic research in the workplace can be challenging, particularly when it involves issues of labor relations. Access to employees at their workplaces during working hours is understandably limited, given the potential for interference with normal workplace activities, and this concern is even greater in health-care settings such as hospitals. Moreover, specific precautions must be taken when talking to employees about their superiors. Most employees feel comfortable having conversations about their work conditions and labor relations out of earshot of their superiors and while remaining anonymous. Given the need to be circumspect, I do not use the real name of any person who consulted with me on this research, and many interviews with workers were conducted off the job site.[19] At the same time, through personal and professional connections, I was granted significant access to a union organizing campaign conducted at Navajo Area IHS facilities.[20] In this context, much of my ethnographic participant-observation time was spent in health-care facilities, where I joined LIUNA organizers during their many hours of the campaign and observed several hundred of their conversations with Navajo Area IHS workers. The organizers also let me sit in on many strategy sessions and planning meetings. However, I did not audiorecord any of the organizing conversations or strategy conversations, unlike my interviews. Nor did I record ad hoc meetings to discuss protest plans or meetings between workers and public officials. I decided that audio recording would disrupt the security and sanctity of these conversations and meetings. I did, however, take many field notes, on which I have based much of my analysis.

Another issue with ethnography in the workplace, as Smith (2001) notes, is the extent to which limited access to the workplace can hamper a researcher's ability to observe events that happen without much warning. For this study, I was unable to attend some important meetings and protests. For some events, my consultants shared their personal recordings with me.[21] But for all events discussed in this book—those I participated in and those I did not—an important part of my analysis is based on people's interpretations and recollections. These personal reflections are just as valuable, if not more, than my own participant observation. I think that getting at people's interpretations of their own experiences is one of the most important parts of studying human activities. This is most often where their values, beliefs, and opinions emerge.

My research for this project began in 2001, when I observed LIUNA's eight-month organizing campaign for Navajo Area IHS employees. The campaign sought to secure union recognition for the employees in the event that the Navajo Nation took over administration of IHS facilities. Following the campaign took me all over the Navajo Nation and its surrounding border-town communities. I visited health-care facilities and communities of various sizes in different regions of the approximately 26,000-square-mile reservation, in the Four Corners region of the United States. Visits included larger hospitals in sizable reservation population centers such as Tuba City, Arizona; Shiprock, New Mexico; and Fort Defiance, Arizona; and large hospitals in large reservation border towns such as Gallup, New Mexico. Additionally, I went to smaller clinics in the medium-sized towns of Crownpoint, New Mexico; Kayenta, Arizona; and Chinlee, Arizona; and to remote clinics such as Inscription House in Arizona and Dzilth-Na-O-Dith-Hle in New Mexico. In addition to the multiple trips made in the course of observing organizing in these facilities, I returned to many of them to interview employees there. These travels gave me a comprehensive cross section of the different communities and regions of the Navajo Nation and a sense of the various sizes and kinds of workplaces. Moreover, at all the facilities, I interacted and consulted with a broad range of workers, from medical staff such as doctors, nurses, and physician's assistants, to janitorial and maintenance staff, to clerical and administrative employees.

The second phase of my field research took place in the summer of 2005, when I did a more intensive study of one health-care facility, the hospital at Tuba City. This research was done during a time when hospital employees were actively protesting the state of labor relations at the hospital and attempting to improve their work conditions. This research included many intensive interviews with employees and workplace activists and attendance at public meetings held to address problems with tribal labor relations at the Tuba City hospital. My research at Tuba City provided a valuable complement to my work following the union organizing campaign, because it allowed me to look in further depth at labor relations in one facility. Moreover, it provided an important longevity component to my project in that it allowed me to follow the process of the tribal takeover of health care and to look at the effect this had on labor relations. Between and after these two concentrated periods of fieldwork, I went back to the Navajo Nation communities multiple times each year to maintain open conversations with my consultants.

The Book's Structure

This book is divided into two parts: Part 1, "Labor Relations in Indian Country," and Part 2, "Organizing in Indian Country: Navajo Labor Relations." The first part contains two chapters that trace the historical, legal, economic, political, and sociocultural development of workers' rights in Indian Country. Some scholars have argued that capitalism is uniquely practiced in Indian Country because of indigenous values placed on community responsibility and group benefit over individual benefit (Champagne 2004). In chapter 2, "The Legal, Political, and Social Contexts," I make the case that tribal labor relations are also unique because of the legal and political specifics of tribal sovereignty and tribal sociocultural values. This chapter reviews federal legislation and NLRB and federal case law, as well as policy decisions made by tribal leaders, tribal corporations, labor unions, and nontribal corporations that have shaped contemporary tribal labor relations. Chapter 3, "Tribal Structuring of Labor Relations," looks at how tribal governments have attempted to regulate labor relations through tribal labor laws and governing structures. Here I consider local political decisions and sociocultural values as they are expressed in tribal labor codes that have the potential to offer local models of tribal labor relations and innovative realizations of workers' rights, such as using tribal judiciaries and peacemaker courts to adjudicate labor relations.

The second part of this book, "Organizing in Indian Country: Navajo Labor Relations," is a case study of tribal labor relations at the Navajo Nation, divided into three chapters. Chapter 4, "Navajo Nation Politics and Pragmatic Unionism," historicizes recent expressions of labor relations at the Navajo Nation within the context of Navajo tribal politics and previous Navajo worker participation in unionism. Here I look at how Navajo politics often is expressed as tension around actions and decisions made by the centralized tribal government, the Navajo Nation Council. From its inception, the Navajo Nation Council has played an active role in economic development decisions, and the Navajo people have engaged in public debate about how its decisions affect their lives. At different times, the Navajo government and Navajo workers have engaged unionism as part of public political debates—on both tribal-wide and local levels. This engagement has been more frequently characterized by a pragmatism that uses labor unions to meet the expediencies of particular political and economic needs than by a long-term commitment to labor movement unionism. In chapter 5, "The Campaign for Union Recognition," I examine tribal labor relations and employee activism during a 2001 campaign to maintain union recognition for Navajo Nation health-care employees. This chapter looks at how Navajo health-care workers utilized workplace politics and union organizing tactics to assert their voice in the larger processes of tribal self-determination. Moreover, their support for unionization staked a claim for what they considered responsive tribal labor relations; Navajo health-care workers were no more willing to go without the mediating force of union representation when dealing with tribal management as when working under federal management. And lastly, chapter 6, "Grassroots Expressions of Tribal Labor Relations," is the story of a bold ad hoc group of workers and community members who protested what they perceived to be mismanagement and abusive treatment of Tuba City hospital employees. The group utilized grassroots tactics such as picket-line protests, pamphleteering, and newspaper editorials to make their voices heard. Through the sheer will of their workplace and community activism, they were able to force the resignation of two CEOs, restore the jobs of terminated employees, and gain institutionalized accountability over members of the hospital's board of directors. To this day, they continue to demand union representation. Their example illustrates the extent to which community members see their work conditions and tribal labor relations as vital components of responsible tribal economic development and self-determination. Risking their jobs, grassroots activists asserted their voices in the political life of the tribe and influenced the implementation of tribal labor relations, economic policy, and self-determination. Finally, in the epilogue, I conclude the book with my thoughts about the direction in which tribal labor relations might be headed.

PART I
Labor Relations in Indian Country

two
The Legal, Political, and Social Contexts

In *Playing Indian* (1998) and *Indians in Unexpected Places* (2006), Philip Deloria masterfully explains American Indians' relationship to notions of modernity by examining non-Native performative enactments and expectations of Indianness. These performances and expectations of how Indians should look and act are generated by the deep-seated, dominant Euro-American tropes of savagery and civilization that code Indians as both antithetical and antecedent to America modernity. Generally, Indians have been characterized alternately as barbaric savages—in their violent opposition to progress and civilization—or as noble savages, with a primitive wisdom that preceded modernity and could act as an antidote to the ills of modernity. For much of the twentieth century, the concept of the noble savage was the prevailing lens through which white America understood Indianness: either through the earlier vanishing race, salvage anthropology, and assimilationist mentalities that presumed a tacit acceptance of the march of progress and an honorable forfeiture of an obsolete culture or through the more recent countercultural appropriation of Indian "wisdom" to advance antimodernist agendas of pacifism, New Age spiritualism, and environmentalism.[1] Deloria's research illustrates the power of white expectations of Indianness and how Native actions that run counter to these expectations are often read as mere anomalies—so exceptional that their noteworthiness proves the general rule of the dominant trope.

In other words, an Indian engaging in a "modern" activity is thought to be remarkably abnormal, because Indians are still coded as normatively premodern.[2] Deloria calls this Indian an anomaly and makes the distinction between an "anomaly" and something that is "unexpected." The former runs counter to expectations but does so in a way that reinforces rather than subverts expectations. The latter is distinguishable from an anomaly because it unsettles expectations by "resist[ing] categorization" and thereby clearing the way for a change of categories (Deloria 2006:11).

Increasingly, the barbaric and noble savage is being replaced by the new trope of the "rich Indian." Driven for the most part by the perceived success of Indian tribal gaming, the rich Indian idea is the notion that Indians are no longer poverty stricken. This trope has swiftly pervaded the news media, popular culture, and nearly all the classrooms in which I have taught.[3] Part of what is so powerful about this trope is the expectation of poverty among indigenous peoples.[4] Furthermore, what is interesting about the rich Indian is not just the idea's newness but also how it can abut, run counter to, and be completely separate from the prevailing notions of noble savagery. What does it mean when Indian communities have money and control industry? And how does this situation affect labor relations?

To some, the idea of a rich Indian is an oxymoron. The two categories are mutually exclusive: Indians do not have money; if they do, they are no longer Indians. Jessica Cattelino notes:

> The discourse of money...entails racial associations, with punishing consequences for indigenous people who simultaneously wish to inhabit their indigeneity and to escape poverty. Indigenous peoples worldwide generally are imagined to be poor, and their economic status and practice are constitutive of the very conditions of indigeneity. (2008:119)

Because the notion of poverty is inherently linked to indigeneity—either through material consequences of colonial exploitation or through the trope of the noble savage, which codes Indians as antimaterialist and outside monetary systems—Indians must forfeit either their money or their cultural identity. The rich Indian is Deloria's "anomaly" that proves the expectation that Indians are poor. In this regard, the idea of the rich Indian does not lie outside the common trope of noble savagery; rich Indians are just aberrations.

However, the rich Indian trope is being used in a more problematic and threatening way as white backlash against the success of tribal governmental gaming (Bruyneel 2007; Cattelino 2008; Spilde 1998, 1999). In the political realm, the concept of the rich Indian can be used to suggest that if rich Indians are not really Indians (because of their accumulation of wealth), then once their community amasses a certain amount of wealth, they should no longer maintain their unique legal and political identity (Spilde 1998, 1999). As Cattelino (2008:119–120) puts it, "American Indians enjoy political autonomy under conditions of economic dependency, but indigenous economic power undermines their political status." This attack on tribal sovereignty comes from external fear of the potent combination of economic power and political power (Bruyneel 2007; Kamper 2000). In this way, the rich Indian trope is Deloria's "unexpected," lying outside the dominant tropes of Indianness by being both modern and indigenous. Moreover, it is the difficulty of categorizing rich Indians as unexpectedly modern and indigenous that makes rich Indians so confusing and threatening to mainstream American political and economic systems. As Jack Campisi has trenchantly put it, "the only thing more despicable than a poor Indian is a rich Indian" (Pasquaretta 1994:712).

This growing stereotype has real-world consequences for non-Indians' perceptions of tribal labor relations. Contemporary versions of the noble savage flatten the political diversity of Indian Country and assume that Indians oppose "capitalist exploitation" as a larger part of Euro-American colonialism. But the stereotype of the rich Indian brings with it a whole new host of assumptions about Indians—both those that presume that rich Indians share the capitalistic neoliberalism of most wealthy Americans and those that construct tribal sovereignty as illegitimate. The trope of the rich Indian imports the notion of capitalism's adversarial labor relations to Indian Country to suppose that an Indian managerial class would be inherently antilabor. Moreover, the stereotype's skepticism toward tribal sovereignty suggests that rich Indians use sovereignty merely as a political shield to minimize the economic pressures of workers' rights and unionism.

If we think of the rich Indian in Deloria's category-challenging terms of the unexpected, then tribal labor relations have the potential to be spaces where modern economic processes can be used in conjunction with and to sustain the values and goals of indigeneity.[5] For nearly as long as Indians have had contact with Europeans, they have had to deal with the social, political, and economic consequences of white constructions of indigeneity in terms of barbaric or noble savagery. Now, Native communities must confront the trope of the rich Indian as they design economic-development strategies and tribal policy, because this trope threatens to create much of the larger legal, political, and social contexts under which tribal economic development will happen. The rise of the rich Indian trope does not come out of nowhere. It *is* directly correlated to a huge growth in tribal economies, but the semantics of the rich Indian trope express a non-Indian interpretation of this growth and this interpretative framework threatens to have negative consequences for tribal sovereignty.

Because of economic growth, labor relations in Indian Country are becoming acutely relevant. This chapter chronicles many of the social, political, legal, cultural, and economic forces—both within and outside Indian Country—that have aligned over the past fifty years to make tribal labor relations more important than ever. The exponential growth in tribal economies, the expansion of the capabilities and responsibilities of centralized tribal governments, the rise of grassroots activism in local Native settings, the growth in Native employment in industries dominated by labor unions, and the expansion of labor union organizing outside traditional job categories of membership have all combined in ways that make labor relations in Indian Country unlike those anywhere else. I follow the trends in Indian Country by examining the way the legal and political institutions that have a stake in tribal labor relations have responded to them. I do so for two reasons: first, to gauge the way interested parties have tried to use institutions such as tribal governments, federal labor law, federal Indian law, national labor unions, and tribal corporations to shape regulation of tribal labor relations, and, second, to quantify the real-world political consequences of these decisions on working conditions as mutually constituted by tribal corporate workers and managers. Invoked as the appropriate forums to govern tribal labor relations, these institutions vary in their constructions of how authority and responsibility are constituted in tribal labor relations.

The first part of this chapter focuses on the laws that shape tribal labor relations. These laws come from sources with diverse legal agendas, such as the federal government, tribal governments, and state governments. Among the most relevant pieces of legislation are the NLRA, the labor codes passed by specific tribal governments, tribal–state gaming compacts, tribal right-to-work ordinances, and federal Indian law. Some of these laws were enacted with employees of tribal corporations specifically in mind. But many others were not and thus deal with employees in only peripheral ways that are open to a great deal of interpretation. This interpretation is usually presided over by judicial systems and is the focus of the second part of this chapter: the importance and impact of rulings by the NLRB, tribal courts, and U.S. federal courts. These judicial bodies have directly and indirectly shaped policy determining the jurisdiction and regulation of tribal labor relations. Of course, legislation and legal decisions do not happen in a political vacuum. Various social, political, and economic forces, including tribal, state, and federal governments; tribal and nontribal corporations; labor unions; and tribal community-based labor organizations, have shaped the nature of tribal labor relations. Here I discuss the way non-Native notions of wealth and capitalist accumulation have adversely affected Native communities' right to determine the form and mode of their own economic development. Although I am highly critical of the way social, political, and economic forces have combined with legal interpretations to limit tribal sovereignty and Native jurisdiction over labor relations on Natives' own land and in their own businesses, I do not advocate for tribal management self-regulation or even the anti-union policies of right-to-work ordinances. Instead, I finish this chapter by discussing the potential of and urgent need for tribal labor relations codes that involve independent tribal judiciaries. These would create a regulatory system over tribal labor relations that preserves and enhances tribal sovereignty.

Tribal Labor Relations and Federal Law

Much of the debate about jurisdiction over tribal labor relations revolves around the issue of applicability: whether federal law concerning labor relations applies in Indian Country. For most of the past fifty years, rulings have focused on the characteristics of the economic enterprise in question by examining where the enterprise is located, who operates it, and whom it employs. Because these three factors can combine in multifaceted ways, legal interpretations of tribal labor relations have accrued through the common law of judicial decisions. Recently, however, the terms of the debate have shifted, and these three factors are not as important as the legal notion of the general applicability of federal laws. This legal theory suggests that laws of general applicability pertain to all Americans unless expressly exempt. Now courts place more emphasis on the nature of the federal laws controlling labor relations than on the nature of the enterprise in question. Under this legal formula, the baseline of argumentation is that federal labor laws by default apply to Indian Country and that tribal entities have to demonstrate the case for exemptions. This is a significant reversal from previous cases, in which the baseline was nonassertion of federal law and a legal argument had to be made to assert jurisdiction. The departure from previous legal standards can be attributed to the dramatic growth of tribal enterprises and an inability of the federal court system—and the American general public—to reconcile tribal wealth with conventional notions of Indianness and the jurisdictional liberty assumed by tribal self-governance.[6]

The NLRA is the cornerstone of the debate about legal jurisdiction over tribal labor relations. Established in 1935 to promote formalized relations between employers and employees, the NLRA was a response to the disruptive and often violent strikes and strikebreaking that had become the primary—often the sole—means by which labor disputes were solved. The NLRA provided an institutionalized and diplomatic way for labor and management to discuss and negotiate their relations, in the form of collective bargaining—delineating various legal guidelines for establishing union representation, negotiating contracts, and resolving disputes. The act also created the NLRB as an impartial administrative judicial body to help mediate this relationship. Since the original passage of the NLRA, several states have passed labor codes and established labor boards similar to the NLRA and NLRB, but most of the provisions in the NLRA still take precedence when it comes to labor relations.

The NLRA is not the indisputable determinant for how labor relations are to be negotiated and regulated in Indian Country. The inherent right of political sovereignty possessed by Native nations and the nature of federal Indian law provide a basis for limitations on applying the NLRA in Indian Country. This application must be understood in the context of tribes' ambivalent legal relationship with the federal government. The voluminous, complicated, and often contradictory body of law commonly known as federal Indian law has provided arguments both for a government-to-government relationship between tribes and the federal government, wherein tribes have sovereign status nearly equal to that of the U.S. government, and for wardship/guardianship relations, wherein the federal government recognizes limited governmental power of tribes but also subordinates them by considering them entities needing and necessarily under federal protection (Wilkins and Lomawaima 2001). The government-to-government relationship is based on the existence of Native communities as fully functioning and socially, culturally, politically, and economically integrated bodies long before the arrival of Europeans and long after the advent of European and U.S. colonialism. Because of this, they have reserved rights to self-governance and a quasi-independent status described as tribal sovereignty. Ever since the founding of the United States, treaties, the Constitution, congressional legislation, and executive actions have sustained this status and these rights. Tribal sovereignty is a fundamental part of federal law, but its exercise has been in no way uniform or consistent (Wilkins and Lomawaima 2001; Wilkinson 1987; Williams 2005). Tribal sovereignty has survived numerous political, social, and economic attacks from state and federal governmental entities and non-Indian interests. These attacks have been fended off as a result of tribal communities' bold and proactive insistence on sovereignty and the federal government's willingness to employ the notion of wardship—later described as guardianship (Deloria and Lytle 1983, 1984; Wilkinson 2005). Although guardianship may have protected tribes from state government power, the federal government has not always acted the in tribes' favor. Guardianship has led to notions of limited sovereignty, wherein Native communities are under congressional plenary power (Aleinikoff 2002; Wilkins and Lomawiama 2001). This has often meant that Indian Country is treated, in the eyes of the law, as federal land. In a legal, pragmatic sense, it makes tribes answerable to federal laws but at the same time allows tribes to fill in the gaps of federal law with their own codes, regulations, and jurisprudence.[7]

The ambivalent legal relationship with the federal government provides the context for understanding application of the NLRA in Indian Country. Any application of labor law has to be measured against this reliance on and support of the legal ideals of sovereignty. From a legal perspective, sovereignty and the whole idea of Indian Country are articulated through the concept of jurisdiction. American Indian law and government scholar Sharon O'Brien (1989) identifies three fundamental types of jurisdiction: territorial, personnel, and subject matter. Territorial jurisdiction is the geographic space over which tribal governments have jurisdiction; personnel jurisdiction is the demographic composition of tribal governmental jurisdiction; and subject matter jurisdiction refers to the kinds of regulatory issues over which tribal governments have jurisdiction. The ideas of territory, personnel, and subject matter combine in complicated ways, because no one type has unequivocal dominance over the others. For example, tribal governments have authority over nontribal members living on reservations regarding some issues, such as hunting and fishing, but not others, such as taxes. Conversely, some crimes committed by tribal members are under federal (in some cases, state) jurisdiction, not tribal jurisdiction. Lastly, through the acts of membership and voting, tribal governments do have authority over tribal members who live outside the territorial space of Indian Country. Until recently, jurisdiction over tribal labor relations was determined by the interrelationship between territorial and personnel jurisdiction, rather than subject matter jurisdiction. The location of the economic enterprise, the employees who worked there, and the company's management were more legally significant than the work done by the company. This legal convention can be traced by piecing together the handful of cases concerning the NLRA and

Indian Country. A juridical genealogy reveals how the law has attempted to structure the broad range of labor relations in Indian Country.

NLRB Regulation of Tribal Labor Relations

The first of the NLRB cases was initiated in 1960. In this case (*Texas-Zinc Minerals Corp.*, 126 NLRB 603), the steelworkers, operating engineers, and hod carriers unions all sought to represent workers employed at a uranium concentrate mill on the Navajo Nation. All three unions petitioned the NLRB to collectively bargain with Texas-Zinc Minerals Corporation, which was headquartered off the reservation. The Navajo Nation, acting as an interested third party because of its extraction contract with the mining company, opposed the NLRB's right to hold a representation election on the reservation. The Navajo Nation lost this case but in 1961 appealed to the D.C. Circuit Court (*Navajo Tribe v. NLRB*, 288 D.C. Circuit). Here its lawyers argued that the tribe's treaty gave it exclusive self-governance over the reservation, which meant that it could bar certain nonmembers and their activities from its land if it so pleased (Buffalo and Wadzinski 1994–95; Grez 2005; Kemp 1995; Limas 1993, 1994). This is exactly what the Navajo Nation had done. It had exercised its sovereign right of self-governance by passing a tribal code that barred "trade union activity on reservation land," threatening hard labor for Navajo workers who participated in union activity, and even evicting some union organizers from the reservation (O'Neill 2005:128). But this attempt to assert the tribe's own laws, dictating what it felt to be acceptable forms of labor relations, failed.

The NLRB ruled—and the D.C. Circuit Court agreed on appeal—that in this instance, the NLRA trumped and nullified the Navajo tribal code. The courts contended that fair labor relations, as defined by the collective bargaining principles in the NLRA, were more important than the Navajo Nation's legal right to self-governance. Much of the reasoning for these decisions was based on the issue of personnel jurisdiction (Buffalo and Wadzinski 1994–95; Grez 2005; Kemp 1995; Limas 1993, 1994). Although the work was taking place in the territorial space of Indian Country, the employer and many of the employees were not tribal members, so the courts argued that labor relations should be decided in the same way they would be anywhere else in the United States—following the processes set out in the NLRA.

Sixteen years later, the applicability of the NLRA to Indian Country came up again at the White Mountain Apache Reservation, but this case (*Fort Apache Timber Co.*, 226 NLRB 503 [1976]) was significantly different from the Navajo case. The White Mountain Apache Tribe was running a tribal lumber corporation called the Fort Apache Timber Company. Its employees were requesting union representation from an affiliate of the International Brotherhood of Teamsters. The employees and the union argued that, just like the millworkers at the Navajo Nation, they deserved collective bargaining rights under the NLRA. The NLRB ruled, however, that the White

Mountain Apache situation was distinguishable from the Navajo case on the grounds of personnel jurisdiction (Buffalo and Wadzinski 1994–95; Grez 2005; Kemp 1995; Limas 1994). In both instances, the corporate activity was taking place within the territorial jurisdiction of Indian Country, but the White Mountain Apache case involved a tribal corporation. As a tribal enterprise, the Fort Apache Timber Company was owned and operated by the tribal government and thus was found to be outside the jurisdiction of the NLRA. Moreover, most employees were tribal members, which dissuaded the NLRB from asserting its jurisdiction.

Nearly twenty years after the White Mountain Apache case, the NLRB refined its ruling in a case involving the Sac and Fox Nation (*Sac & Fox Industries*, 307 NLRB 241 [1992]). Here the tribe owned and operated Sac & Fox Industries outside reservation land. Even though the tribe had purchased the land where Sac & Fox Industries did business, the NLRB ruled that the act of moving the company off the reservation nullified its exemption from the NLRA (Grez 2005; Kemp 1995; Limas 1993, 1994). Territorial concerns—where the corporation was located—were thought to outweigh issues of personnel—the makeup of corporate management.

For several years, these three cases, interpreted together, set precedents for regulating labor relations in Indian Country. Tribes were given a certain amount of leeway to exercise sovereignty and maintain jurisdiction over the corporations they ran, but jurisdiction over nontribal corporations operating on reservation land and tribal corporations operating off-reservation was severely limited. The cumulative effect of the rulings was an emphasis on territorial and personnel jurisdiction. Furthermore, in terms of the latter, the focus was more on the makeup of corporate management than on the makeup of employees. In the Navajo case, the fact that management was from off the reservation was central to the decision to assert jurisdiction, and in the White Mountain Apache case, jurisdiction was abdicated because a tribal entity was running the corporation. Even in the Sac and Fox case, the debate centered more on what happens when a tribal corporation moves off the reservation than on whom the corporation employed.

Moreover, two minor cases also have stressed the importance of the composition of corporate management when trying to determine the appropriateness of the NLRA for Indian Country. In *Devil's Lake Sioux Mfg. Corp.*, 243 NLRB 163 (1979), the NLRB ruled in favor of asserting jurisdiction over a tribal enterprise that operated on the Devil's Lake Sioux Reservation, 51 percent of which was owned by the tribe. The board decided that it was more determinative that the minority ownership—the non-Indian Brunswick Corporation—had appointed five of the company's nine directors (compared with the tribe's four) and had also set most of the labor relations policies. Conversely, in *Southern Indian Health Council*, 290 NLRB 436 (1988), the NLRB abdicated jurisdiction over a health-care facility, even though it was not run by one specific tribe. Judges ruled that because each of the seven directors was appointed by each of the seven tribal governments party to a health-care consortium, these directors all had to be tribal members and that because they alone formulated labor relations policies, the health-care facility was exempt from the NLRA.

This juridical analysis of the many interrelated parts of tribal labor relations and their connection to one another is not uncommon to employment law in general. In examining how courts define "employee" in the context of prison labor, Noah Zatz (2008) argues that this relational analysis is critical to understanding how courts interpret and create employment law. In adjudicating employment issues, courts try to balance many factors that Zatz (2008) calls "relational markers," such as who does the work, who pays the workers and how, where the work is done, and within what markets the work circulates. However, Zatz finds that sometimes a single relational marker can outweigh the others in judges' minds.[8] He notes that

> courts engage in relational work...invoking the presence or absence of various relational markers and assembl[e] them into a coherent picture of [a given kind of labor]. The premise throughout is that employment exists as a relational package, that these markers clump together, and that when one is absent, it indicates something about the relationship as a whole. (Zatz 2008:936)

The different elements (or relational markers) that define a category of work gain their significance in their interrelationship to one another, and therefore a change in opinion about the importance of one element can change the whole. This is what recently happened with tribal labor relations as courts changed course and put more emphasis on the kinds of markets in which tribal enterprises were engaging—that is, how tribal businesses might affect interstate commerce.

This change began when courts' interpretations of personnel jurisdiction shifted toward a consideration of the composition of employees rather than just employers. When deliberating tribal labor relations, courts began to pay more attention to where workers in Indian Country came from. This new emphasis should also be contextualized within a broader trend of federal Indian jurisprudence that has attenuated tribal jurisdiction over nonmembers and often based opinions on outdated and sometimes even racists notions of Indian governments and their ability to provide justice (see Aleinikoff 2002; Frickey 1999; Williams 2005). More importantly, the shift in attention to the makeup of employees has opened the door to a greater change in the legal consideration of tribal labor relations: a shift toward subject matter jurisdiction. The shift toward subject matter jurisdiction when adjudicating tribal labor relations has created certain expectations of Indianness that are in large part based on non-Indian notions of the commensurability of wealth and Indianness. This situation in effect has forced tribes to exchange economic success for political rights.

The most recent court cases dealing with tribal labor relations have emphasized subject matter jurisdiction over territorial and personnel jurisdiction by focusing on the legal issue of general applicability. This theory suggests that a law of "general applicability" applies to everyone in the United States equally, unless a particular group or locale is expressly exempted. Here the subject area that a given law codifies and regulates takes precedence over geography and population because these two aspects of jurisdiction are deemed to be as broad as possible—that is, everyone within the United States. Conventionally, in most labor relations cases, the NLRA is treated as a law of general applicability. When applying this legal theory to tribal labor relations, questions of where a tribal enterprise is operated, who is running it, and whom it employs are less important than the fact that the NLRA, as a federal statute, should cover all cases of labor relations, including tribal labor relations.

The shift toward subject matter jurisdiction in tribal labor relations coincides with the expansion of tribal enterprises, particularly those that employ nontribal members, such as casino gaming. The change in employee personnel has had significant consequences for labor relations in Indian Country, mainly in terms of aggressive political and legal strategies on the part of unions and, in response, equally strong actions from tribal leaders. Some of these consequences can be attributed to the fact that nontribal employees are not tribal citizens; they do not have preexisting political allegiance to or participate in the tribal governments that run tribal corporations. Nor do tribal leaders have the sense of political responsibility to nontribal employees that they might have toward employees who are tribal members. Moreover, unions have acted aggressively because in most instances they seek to represent nontribal employees. Under these circumstances, organizers do not have to worry that their aggressive tactics toward and criticism of tribal governments and tribal corporations might offend employees and potential supporters. In contrast, when organizing Native employees in Indian Country, unions must be cautious that a proactive stance in favor of federal regulation of labor relations not be interpreted by Native employees as an attack on their tribe's sovereignty. Lastly, the changing landscape of employee personnel has also opened the door for expanding the jurisdiction of the NLRA under the auspices of general applicability. With the increase in nontribal employees, lawyers have argued and judges have concurred that a tribal workplace is like any other workplace in America and should therefore be regulated accordingly. The outcome of these cases is that tribal corporations and labor relations are becoming less and less unique legally.

As previously mentioned, this process has followed a strong trend in jurisprudence of federal Indian law limiting tribes' jurisdiction over nonmembers (Aleinikoff 2002; Frickey 1999). Aleinikoff (2002) argues that the Supreme Court has significantly limited the jurisdiction of tribal courts and governments over nonmembers in large part because of its concern for what he calls a "democratic deficit." He illustrates that the Court is very sensitive to what it perceives as limiting the justice that nontribal members can get in tribal judicial systems. It is important to note that the fear of a democratic deficit is not necessarily based on instances of miscarriage of justice, but rather on the Court's conviction that rights be founded in notions of citizenship as opposed to racial categories (Aleinikoff 2002).[9] The Court locates the democratic deficit for nontribal members in the fact that they do not have the electoral rights, responsibilities, and protections that come along with participatory and legal notions of citizenship (particularly in comparison with tribal citizens). Because of this democratic deficit, it is argued that U.S. laws should intervene in behalf of U.S. citizens acting in Indian Country. In other words, citizenship protections should not have to be checked at the border of Indian Country. Nowhere is this belief in the intervention of federal law more apparent than in debates over California tribal labor relations. In California, the fear of the democratic deficit is coupled with the argument that tribal gaming enterprises are just like any other corporation. The two arguments join to form a new version of rich Indianness that circulates around the regulation of labor relations in California tribal casinos.

California, Unions, and Indian Gaming

With the growth of casino gaming, nontribal workers have played an unprecedented role in California tribal economies. California tribal casino operations are generally situated at the nexus of some unique demographic and economic forces that have led to significant labor tension. First, most California tribal casinos are located among small tribal populations near much larger, non-Indian population centers. The proximity to nontribal members and the high number of jobs that cannot be exclusively staffed by tribal members have greatly increased what might be called the in-sourcing of labor to tribal communities. Statistics from 2003 suggest that of the 41,400 workers that tribal governments employ, 90 percent are non-Indians (Spilde 2003). Second, the work that is being in-sourced is mainly resort-oriented service industry and casino floor work. Not only are these jobs ones that unions traditionally have had success organizing, but also the timing of this growth in job opportunity is significant. The boom in California casinos has directly coincided with the dramatic rise in strength of three unions in California: the Hotel Employees and Restaurant Employees International Union (HERE), the Service Employees International Union (SEIU), and the Union of Needletrades, Industrial, and Textile Employees (UNITE). In the 1990s, HERE, SEIU, and UNITE seized the opportunity created by the shift in the U.S. domestic economy from manufacturing to the service industry. With the increase in service-industry jobs, HERE, SEIU, and UNITE initiated highly progressive and aggressive organizing campaigns throughout the country, with their California campaigns generating the most attention, intensity, and success (Milkman 2000, 2002, 2006).[10] They combined three organizing strategies—workplace actions that directly challenged management's authority, active recruitment of immigrants, and highly visible protest and boycott campaigns—to become by far the most successful American unions in the past fifteen years.[11]

The first of the strategies was a return to classic, direct organizing campaigns. A direct campaign is a worker-centered model of organizing that relies on face-to-face contact with as many workers as possible in a given collective bargaining unit, regardless of their proclivities toward unionism. It also prioritizes volunteer activism, in which workers help paid organizers to mobilize coworkers. Within HERE, SEIU, and UNITE, progressive factions were able to persuade leadership that the unions' resources were better spent organizing new members than predominantly servicing the contracts of current members. Many locals shifted resources away from representation and toward direct organizing or required international representatives to spend equal time organizing and servicing members of a given local.

The second organizing strategy was a direct result of demographic shifts that led to a huge influx of immigrant employees in the service industry; in California, these workers predominantly immigrated from Latin American, the Philippines, and South Korea (Milkman 2002). Rather than fall back on the nativism and racism all too common in the labor movement in the middle of the twentieth century, HERE, SEIU, and UNITE proactively recruited immigrants to be members, activists, and even paid organizers. Much of the recruitment was done irrespective of the immigrants' legal status. Not only did the unions make a conscious decision that workers' rights ought to supercede immigration regulations, but they also began to publicly support and collaboratively organize with immigrants' rights campaigns.

The third strategy harkened back to the secondary boycott campaigns used with great success by the United Farm Workers in the 1970s. These were designed to indirectly attack management, at the point of consumption—not just production—and through media attention and public shaming. For HERE, SEIU, and UNITE, secondary boycotts took the form of public protest in front of the hotels, office buildings, and clothing retailers that utilized subcontractors whose employees the unions were attempting to organize. Targeting corporations that hired subcontractors, in addition to the subcontractors themselves (the direct employers of the bargaining unit), lessened pressure on the direct subcontractors from those hiring them, who were concerned about and aggravated by the bad press and disruption of daily operations brought on by public protest. Indirect tactics also included the lobbying of public officials and religious leaders to further pressure management to come to a collective bargaining agreement.

It is within this context of proactive, aggressive, and innovative labor organizing strategies in California that we must view California tribal gaming as accelerating developments in tribal labor relations as a whole. With the advent of gaming, tribal economies grew at a dramatic pace in California. As a result, service-industry labor unions insisted on being involved in tribal economies to a degree previously unseen in Indian Country. These unions brought their proactive organizing strategies to bear on the issue of tribal labor relations, but tribal governments remained staunch defenders of tribal sovereignty. Indeed, during the revitalization of social movement unionism in California, tribal sovereignty was experiencing its own renaissance. A long period of indigenous political activism, relatively favorable federal Indian policy, and an expansion of tribal economies led to bold assertions of tribal sovereignty (see Barsh and Henderson 1980; Goldberg and Champagne 2002; Smith and Warrior 1996; Wilkinson 2005). The combination of swift economic growth, proactive unionism, and the defense of tribal sovereignty thrusts questions of tribal labor relations to the fore in public debate over California tribal casinos.

Of the proactive tactics that brought great success for service-industry unions in the 1990s, political organizing and public media campaigns translated best to the context of California tribal casinos. In California Indian Country, unions relied less on face-to-face organizing of casino employees than on the indirect tactics of lobbying legislators and public opinion about the issue of tribal gaming. And when needed, they were willing to resort to legal strategies. Under the Indian Gaming Regulatory Act of 1988 (IGRA), tribes and states must come to a negotiated agreement—a compact—over what kinds of gambling will be allowed in tribal casinos and over the process of joint regulation of tribal gaming enterprises. Because tribal–state gaming compacts were required, the process of creating compacts gave unions a unique opportunity to make their cases to politicians and the general public. This was especially the case in California, where decisions in the compacting process fell not only on the shoulders of state politicians but also on those of the general public. Because Republican governor Pete Wilson was unwilling to negotiate in good faith a compact that was acceptable to most California tribes, a significant group of tribes took advantage of California's healthy initiative process to circumvent Wilson's stonewalling (Contreras 2006; Goldberg and Champagne 2002; Gordon 2000; Lombardi n.d.).[12] Through two referendums, California Native nations took their case to the general public. But this process also gave unions a public venue in which to stake out their position on gaming and to pressure tribes into prolabor business practices.

In 1998 and again in 2000, Californians voted on tribal governmental gaming through propositions 5 and 1A. The basis of these propositions was whether or not California Indian tribes could conduct high-stakes casino gaming on their reservations. While both referendums went overwhelming in favor of Indian gaming (63 and 65 percent, respectively), the first referendum was more hotly contested. More money was spent on the Proposition 5 campaign than had previously been spent in the United States on any state referendum—both sides spent in total more than $90 million (Goldberg and Champagne 2002; Gordon 2000). Some of the strongest opposition came from labor unions, and HERE was the fiercest and most outspoken. Throughout the referendum campaign, HERE attempted to employ some of its previously successful tactics of indirect pressure. In this instance, it attempted to use the referendum campaign to sway public opinion and thus pressure tribes into enacting prolabor policies. With television ads, rallies, and public forums, HERE fought Proposition 5 by suggesting that gaming in Indian Country would be an unregulated business and therefore dangerous to casino employees. The union argued that workers would not have the standard protections that any other worker in the state of California would. This argument was often advanced through anecdotes of and testimonials from immigrant laborers who purportedly had been taken advantage of by tribal casino management.[13]

While other groups opposed tribal gaming propositions, the union's anti–Indian gaming tactics were distinguishable from those of the other gaming opponents. These other opponents—Christian organizations and NIMBY-ites—attacked Indian gaming on moral grounds or suggested that casinos would bring an influx of traffic, pollution, and crime to neighboring communities. Unions did not assail the gaming industry as a whole but rather focused on what they saw as flaws and loopholes in Indian Country business practices. This distinction is important because it illustrates the extent to which union tactics and referendum campaign discourse can be read as an effort to apply pressure and gear up for later legislative and legal battles. Unlike the religious fundamentalists and NIMBY-ites, whose arguments were purely ideological, unions saw the referendum campaign as part of a long-term strategy and realized that legislative and legal forums would be key in determining the regulation of tribal casino management.

Just as HERE claimed to be pro-union but not anti-Indian, leaders of California Native nations who favored Proposition 5 stressed that they were prosovereignty and not anti-union. To counter HERE's criticism of tribal gaming, some tribal leaders publicly touted their own working-class credentials and participation in unions. For example, at a Prop 5 debate, Mark Macarro, longtime chairman of the Pechanga Band of Luiseño Indians and key spokesman for Proposition 5, talked about his and his family's history of active participation in unions. He adamantly asserted, "It's not like we're anti-union here, we are the same universe of people. That's an important thing to regard" (UCLA Office of Instructional Development 1998). On the same debate panel, Ken Ramirez, vice chair of the San Manuel Band of Mission Indians, echoed Chairman Macarro's assertion as he talked of his tribe's negotiations with the Communications Workers of America (CWA) over collective bargaining rights. He did so to illustrate that his tribe was not anti-union; rather, it sought to exercise its sovereignty in a way that gave it a choice as to which union to deal with.

In an interview I conducted with Deron Marquez, tribal chairman of the San Manuel Band of Mission Indians from 1999 to 2006, he reinforced this point and explained how hard it was to communicate this idea to union leadership. He said that some union leaders try to make tribes appear antilabor, to which he responds: "It's not so much that we're anti-union. [It's] more that we're prosovereign by saying, 'Let us make those determinations [about collective bargaining and which unions to deal with].' And it's hard for people from the union to see that." He thinks that the question is not *whether* tribes should accept unionism—indeed, his tribe did—but rather *who* should make the decision. The choice should come from within the tribal community, he says, not be forced on Native nations by outside entities such as the state and unions through compacting. Moreover, from Chairman Marquez's perspective, tension over this issue could have been diffused if unions had recognized many Native people's past participation in unions. Similarly to Chairman Macarro, Chairman Marquez noted:

> A majority of tribal communities per household belong to unions.... [If HERE] went back and did it different, if they'd went back and did their research and said, "Look, many of you who are from the tribal communities either belong to or have belonged to unions. And so something good about a union was there for you," and approach it from that standpoint, they probably

wouldn't have had and wouldn't still have a lot of this back-and-forth [tension] that we have now. (personal communication, November 14, 2008)

From this strongly indigenous perspective, it was offensive that unions such as HERE were asserting that labor relations in casinos should explicitly follow the models established by the NLRA without consulting and respecting indigenous people's understanding of labor relations in Indian Country.

The tension between tribal leaders and California politicians and union leaders belies what some have argued is a practical reality of Indian gaming, that its economic benefits have come at the cost of tribal sovereignty (Corntassel and Witmer 2008; Light and Rand 2005). To make gaming acceptable to non-Indian governments and the public that those governments represent, Native nations have had to relinquish some aspects of their political sovereignty.[14] Indeed, IGRA allowed for a massive opening of Indian Country to outside oversight because the compacting process created joint regulation with tribal, state, and federal entities. Labor unions in California seized this opportunity by lobbying legislators to secure pro-union language in gaming compacts. Using lobbying and an intensive public media campaign, they were able to leverage their traditional support of and from Democratic legislators to gain pro-union language in tribal–state compacts.[15] In the end, at the behest of Governor Gray Davis and in exchange for Democratic legislative support of the Las Vegas–style gaming that most tribes sought, provisions to regulate tribal labor relations were included in every gaming compact (see chapter 3 for a more thorough discussion). It took a huge political effort to get tribes to agree to these labor regulations, but some unions sought even greater labor security than these compacts provided.

Tribal Labor Relations in Federal Courts

Despite public opinion and political lobbying campaigns, labor did not achieve all it had hoped for in the California tribal gaming compact process. As a result, it turned to the courts to press its concerns about jurisdiction over tribal labor relations. One legal maneuver was to file an unfair labor practice (ULP) charge with the NLRB. Filing a ULP claim was not just about redressing specific wrongdoings by certain managers against specific employees (or unions). More significantly, the process also forced the legal hand of tribally run casinos by drawing management and tribal leaders into a legal battle over whether the NLRB/NLRA had any authority over Indian casinos. The issue, then, was not just about where unions could picket, whether they could strike, or even whether management had treated certain employees unfairly. Rather, it became a question about the entirety of tribal labor relations. A ruling that tribal casino labor relations had to be regulated by the NLRB/NLRA would achieve nearly all the unions' goals in one fell swoop. More importantly, it would be a dramatic change from how the NLRA had been applied in Indian Country for the previous thirty years.

Such a ruling was handed down in 2004 in a test case known as *San Manuel* (341

NLRB 1055). The case was initiated by UNITE-HERE![16] in an attempt to represent employees of the San Manuel Band of Mission Indians' casino in southern California. UNITE-HERE! filed a ULP against San Manuel's tribal casino because the union felt that it was not being granted equal access to casino employees. The union argued that casino management granted access to another union (the CWA) but not to UNITE-HERE![17] Lawyers for San Manuel countered by arguing that the ULP was moot, because the NLRA did not apply to the management of the tribe's casino. The NLRB sided with UNITE-HERE!, and in *San Manuel v. NLRB* (2007), the San Manuel Band appealed to the D.C. Circuit, U.S. Federal Court of Appeals. The appellate-level case, like the NLRB case, is known as *San Manuel*. In both *San Manuel* cases, the broader issue of the NLRA's applicability dominated the legal proceedings, not the more limited issue of UNITE-HERE!'s access to casino employees. In the end, both the NLRB and the D.C. Circuit Court ruled against the San Manuel Band on grounds of the general applicability of the NLRA.

Until the *San Manuel* cases, courts had conventionally addressed the applicability of the NLRA in terms of its territorial and personnel jurisdiction, making decisions based on whether the worksite was on tribal land and whether the tribal corporation was the employer. The *San Manuel* cases dramatically diverged from this path by focusing instead on the issue of subject matter jurisdiction and the extent to which the NLRA, as a law of general applicability, applied to labor relations—irrespective of the location or parties involved—throughout the United States, including Indian Country. In taking up the mantle of general applicability, *San Manuel* followed previous rulings that had decided how other areas of federal law applied to Indian Country. In particular, the *San Manuel* cases drew from the Supreme Court's statements in *Federal Power Commission v. Tuscarora Indian Nation* (1960) and the Ninth Circuit's U.S. Court of Appeals ruling in *Donovan v. Coeur d'Alene Tribal Farm* (1985). These decisions put strict limits on the conditions under which tribal communities are exempt from federal laws that are meant to be laws of general applicability, and they placed "the burden on tribal parties to prove that their conduct fits the exception" (Singel 2004:706). Taken together, the rulings are symptomatic of a shift in interpretation of federal Indian law—a move from applying federal law in Indian Country only when the law explicitly mentions Indians to always applying federal law in Indian County unless the law explicitly exempts Indians. This shift is certainly a challenge to Native communities and their sovereignty, because it puts them in a legally defensive position; they must prove that Congress did not intend a law to apply to Indian Country, instead of an outside party having to prove that a federal law ought to apply to Indian Country (Singel 2004).

Indian law scholars have criticized the interpretive shift as inconsistent with a fundamental principle of federal Indian law, the canon of construction (Limas 1993; Singel 2004; Wilkinson 1987). This foundational legal theory has been in place at least since the trilogy of Supreme Court decisions authored by Chief Justice John Marshall in the early nineteenth century and was further buttressed by the seminal work on federal Indian law by Felix Cohen in the first half of the twentieth century. Native legal scholar Wenona Singel explains the principle this way:

> This canon of construction has been applied in several cases to prevent ambiguous statutes from creating an implied diminishment of tribal rights. The Indian canon of construction also counsels that tribal self-governance rights should be upheld unless Congress has made its intent to abridge them "unmistakably clear." (2004:700)

Tuscarora–Coeur d'Alene, and *San Manuel* all rely on judicial logic that undercuts this legal philosophy and in turn undercuts tribal sovereignty. More specifically, they hinder tribal economic development strategies and goals by limiting ways in which tribal governments can use their political sovereignty and economic development in a mutually reinforcing dialogue: using the uniqueness of sovereignty as a resource for economic development, and vice versa, using economic development plans to sustain independent self-governance.

As is typical in U.S. common law, *Tuscarora–Coeur d'Alene*, and *San Manuel* build upon one another—the latter two are informed by and in turn refine the former. In the *Tuscarora* case, the Supreme Court ruled in favor of an easement of tribal land for construction of federally funded power lines. A small but crucial component of the written decision was a dictum about the extent to which federal laws of general applicability apply to Indian Country when Indians are not mentioned in the statute.[18] It stated, "A general statute in terms applying to all persons includes Indians and their property interest." Running counter to the Indian canon of construction, this dictum created some confusion and a great need for clarification in the lower courts.

The Ninth Circuit has played a large role in trying to elucidate the issue and questions created by the *Tuscarora* dictum. The Ninth Circuit attempted to resolve the "incongruity of the '*Tuscarora* test' with established principles of federal law governing treatment of Native American tribes" by delineating exceptions to the test (Limas 1994:698–699). The *Coeur d'Alene* decision played a key role in codifying these exceptions. The issue in this case was whether the Occupational Safety and Health Act (OSHA) applied to a farm owned and operated by the Coeur d'Alene (Schitsu'umsh) Tribe. In the *Coeur d'Alene* case (and a few others), the judges put forward three general circumstances under which general statutes did not apply to Indians:

> If (1) the law touches "exclusive rights of self-governance in a purely intramural matter"; (2) the application of the law to the tribe would "abrogate rights guaranteed by Indian treaties"; or (3) there is proof "by legislative history or some other means that Congress intended [the law] not to apply to Indians on their reservations." (*Coeur d'Alene* 1985:1116; alterations in original; quoting *United States v. Farris* 1980)

The language in this ruling was an attempt to clarify and standardize when to consider a federal statute applicable to Indian Country. If a federal law did *not* meet any of these three conditions, then it ought to apply in Indian Country. Read alongside the opinion from *Tuscarora*, the three conditions are collectively known as the *Tuscarora–Coeur d'Alene* test or the *Tuscarora–Coeur d'Alene* exceptions. The overall goal of this judicial test is to "balance" tribal rights—both the inherent sovereignty of the canon of construction and treaty rights—against the principle of the general applicability of federal statutes.

Despite the intentions of the Ninth Circuit justices, the *Tuscarora–Coeur d'Alene* test has done anything but clarify the issue of general applicability in Indian Country, particularly in labor and employment law—in large part because of significant inconsistencies in the way courts have applied the *Tuscarora–Coeur d'Alene* test, not just between different circuit courts but also in cases within the same circuit court (Buffalo and Wadzinski 1994–95; Limas 1994). Additionally, the Supreme Court has never reviewed the fusion of these two rulings as a viable analytical method for interpreting federal Indian law (Singel 2004). Consequently, there is still great leeway in how lower courts apply the *Tuscarora–Coeur d'Alene* test.

Much of the leeway comes from the ambiguous language built into the test itself, particularly in the first two exceptions.[19] For example, with the first exception, different courts have differing opinions on what it means for a law to "touch" the right of self-governance. Judges have disagreed over how intrusive a federal law really is when it "touches" tribal sovereignty: can a federal law "touch" but not hinder self-governance and therefore apply to Indian Country? Similarly, there is inconsistent interpretation as to how a law of general applicability might "abrogate" treaty rights, which the second exception tries to guard against. The word *abrogate* seems to set a much higher threshold of interference than *touch*. Must a federal law potentially nullify a treaty before it is considered too much of a hindrance to apply to Indian Country, or is the mere potential of modifying a treaty enough to meet the second exception of the *Tuscarora–Coeur d'Alene* test? Some courts have chosen the latter and tipped the balance toward protection of treaties against any level of interference—using any modification to a treaty as grounds to block application of a federal statute in Indian Country (Singel 2004).

Moreover, there is significant debate over what exactly a "purely intramural matter" is. Indeed, to clarify this part of the first *Tuscarora–Coeur d'Alene* exemption, some courts have felt the need to establish an additional legal test, attempting to define a "purely intramural matter" as something dealing exclusively with domestic relations, membership, and inheritance. But not all courts have followed this model of interpretation. Similarly, there is significant debate about the meaning of "rights guaranteed by Indian treaties." Some courts have required explicit evidence that the federal law being considered would potentially abrogate a specific treaty provision; others have asserted that if a federal law would nullify rights that are merely implied by a treaty, then it should not apply to Indian Country (Limas 1994). Ultimately, much of the inconsistency in interpreting the *Tuscarora–Coeur d'Alene* test comes from the fact that these debates are mainly taking place at various appellate-level circuit courts and have yet to be taken up by the Supreme Court.

Some legal analysts, however, suggest that in certain circumstances the vagaries of the *Tuscarora–Coeur d'Alene* test are better left alone, to give courts some interpretive wiggle room. The ability to read these three exceptions expansively or restrictively allows courts to balance tribal rights with the federal code on a case-by-case basis. Helen Kemp (1995) and Kelly Grez (2005) argue that this flexibility makes practical sense when dealing with the issue of tribal labor relations and the NLRA. They suggest that the fairest way to balance tribal sovereignty against workers' rights is to have the NLRB use the *Tuscarora–Coeur d'Alene* test as a guideline to interpret the NLRA in terms of how it applies to specific tribally run corporations in specific employment circumstances. This is, in fact, exactly what the NLRB—with subsequent endorsement from the D.C. Circuit—did with the *San Manuel* case.

The first time the NLRB considered using the *Tuscarora–Coeur d'Alene* test to make a decision on labor relations was in the *Sac & Fox Industries* case in 1991. The Sac and Fox Nation owned a manufacturing facility that produced chemically resistant garments and was located off tribal land. In an attempt to represent the employees at this facility, the United Garment Workers of America asked the NLRB to assert its jurisdiction; the tribe claimed to be beyond the NLRB's jurisdiction. The NLRB applied the *Tuscarora–Coeur d'Alene* test in a limited fashion to make a decision as to which labor relations codes apply when tribally controlled corporations operate outside Indian Country. Despite the decision that the NLRA did apply to tribal corporations in this instance, it was exclusively the "off-reservation" instance that applied—still preserving the distinction of an "on-reservation" abdication of NLRB authority over tribal enterprises, established by *Fort Apache Timber Co*. However, some legal scholars read the mere use of *Tuscarora–Coeur d'Alene* as opening a new avenue of jurisprudence and signaling the NLRB desire to make a significant shift from how it previously handled tribal labor relations (see Kemp 1995; Limas 1994). The shift came to fruition twelve years later in *San Manuel*, when the NLRB decided that nothing was stopping it from asserting its jurisdiction over labor relations *in* Indian Country, regardless of who controlled management. And in early 2007, the D.C. Circuit Court upheld the application of the *Tuscarora–Coeur d'Alene* test to the NLRA, further confirming the NLRB's discretionary power. This expansion of power is significant because it gives the NLRB authority over not just tribal labor relations but also, more importantly, the contours of tribal economic development and tribal sovereignty.

With this expanded power, however, the NLRB stated that it would exercise discretion in asserting its jurisdiction. To preserve some aspects of tribal sovereignty, the NLRB ruled that although there were no existing legal grounds to prohibit applying the NLRA to Indian Country, it could also decline to assert its authority when it deemed this assertion of power to be too encumbering on tribal self-governance. Still, the NLRB reserved the right to be the sole decision of whether to assert jurisdiction and decided to use an expanded version of the *Tuscarora–Coeur d'Alene* test to make this determination. This was made manifest in an NLRB ruling handed down on the same day as the *San Manuel* ruling. The decision, known as *Yukon II*, involved the Yukon Kuskokwim Health Corporation, operated by a board of directors comprising individuals elected to represent the fifty-eight sovereign Native Alaskan communities that owned the health-care corporation.[20] The Teamsters petitioned the NLRB to hold a representation election for the facility's employees, but the Native health-care consortium claimed that the NLRB had no jurisdiction over its labor relations.[21] In writing this decision, the NLRB judges meant it to be read explicitly in conjunction with and as a clarification of *San Manuel*. They maintained their position that the NLRA authorized the NLRB's jurisdiction over the tribally run health-care corporation, yet "under its own discretionary analysis the Board [NLRB] found that providing free health care to Indians weighed against asserting jurisdiction" (Grez 2005:1162). As a foil for *San Manuel*, the *Yukon II* opinion illustrates that the NLRB is willing, in certain circumstances, to abdicate jurisdiction when judges believe that their intervention would hinder tribal sovereignty.

Taken together, these cases established a new, two-step analytic formula for considering tribal labor relations. First, the NLRB will use the *Tuscarora–Coeur d'Alene* test to decide whether anything would prohibit its jurisdiction. If not, the NLRB will use the *Tuscarora–Coeur d'Alene* test to decide whether any special circumstances and attributes of tribal self-governance might persuade it to voluntarily abdicate its jurisdiction. Despite the NLRB's apparent respect for the principles of tribal sovereignty, these joint rulings sustain its authority at the expense of Native self-governance and tribal economic development. The lasting effect of *San Manuel* and *Yukon II* is that in applying the *Tuscarora–Coeur d'Alene* test to the NLRA, the NLRB has taken cues from the circuit court opinions that read the *Tuscarora–Coeur d'Alene* exceptions in the strictest of ways—that is, interpretations that are most limiting to tribal sovereignty and most expansive to federal statutes. This interpretation creates such a low hurdle for the NLRB to assert its jurisdiction that almost all cases will end up in the second step of the NLRB's analytic formula for tribal labor relations and thereby under the purview of the board's discretion (Grez 2005). What is particularly troubling about the NLRB's strict application of the *Tuscarora–Coeur d'Alene* test to expand its jurisdiction over tribal labor relations is that the test itself has a kind of ambiguity that does not seem to sustain such a strict application.

In spite of this ambiguity, the NLRB's decisions have provided it with significant power to make policy decisions affecting Native communities. Above and beyond applying expertise to the issue of labor relations, the NLRB is now assuming authority over matters of Indian policy. U.S. legal policy affecting Indians has a long and complicated history, and tribal communities are rightfully wary of an administrative judicial body that was not created with the intention of handling Indian affairs becoming such a considerable player in Indian affairs. Singel has argued:

> [Tribes] are forced to submit the legitimacy of tribal governance to a largely homogenous pool of non-Indians at the bench. Since many judges and other

> tribunals, such as the NLRB, lack familiarity with tribal law and tribal institutions of self-government, these arbiters are poorly equipped to recognize when conduct in Indian Country implicates tribal self-government interest. (2004:714)

Indeed, the factors that the NLRB uses to make decisions about the practices of tribal corporations betray a bias toward considering only economic characteristics and not governmental and community-based aspects of tribal corporations.

In both of the *San Manuel* cases, the NLRB and the D.C. Circuit Court spoke to the concern that in the NLRB's asserting its jurisdiction over tribal labor relations, it might overstep the boundaries of its legal expertise. Both opinions tried to minimize this concern by arguing that overseeing labor relations would only minimally affect the practice of tribal sovereignty and self-governance. The NLRB's opinion argued:

> [Its] mandate is to "protect and foster interstate commerce," and assertion of discretionary jurisdiction over Indian tribes acting in these circumstances would effectuate the policies of the Act while doing little harm to the Indian tribes' special attributes of sovereignty or the statutory schemes designed to protect them...assertion of jurisdiction would not unduly interfere with the tribe's autonomy [because] the Act would not broadly and completely define the relationship between the [tribe] and its employees. Nor would the Act's effects extend beyond the tribe's business enterprise and regulate intramural matters.... Contrary to our dissenting colleague, the collective-bargaining process will not impair the Respondent's ability to hire as it wishes. An employer is not obligated to agree in bargaining to hiring restrictions, and the Board cannot impose any agreements. (341 NRLB No. 138:39–44; n. 23)

And the D.C. Circuit Court ruled:

> The total impact on tribal sovereignty at issue here amounts to some unpredictable, but probably modest, effect on tribal revenue and the displacement of legislative and executive authority that is secondary to a commercial undertaking...the NLRA does not impinge on the Tribe's sovereignty enough to indicate a need to construe the statute narrowly against application to employment at the Casino. (*San Manuel*, D.C. Circuit 2007:15–16)

In these passages, the judges suggest that the court is not forcing tribes to unionize per se or giving undue power to employees of tribal enterprises but rather is mandating that tribes follow the model of labor relations laid out for the United States as a whole.

However, what this interpretation neglects is what Zatz (2008) calls the constitutive function of employment law. Extrapolating from legal theory in general, Zatz notes that a large part of what employment law does is to provide a forum wherein interested parties seek to fit themselves within economically defined categories established by law and judges interpret how to regulate the relationship between the economically defined and interested parties. In this sense, "employment law's job is to identify correctly the real relationships out there in the economy, relationships that exist exogenously but require regulation" (Zatz 2008:940). But Zatz (2008:941) asserts that employment law does much more than this; it also has a "constitutive operation." This comes not just from the way courts and the law authorize certain parities as fitting certain definitions, powers, and exemptions but also from how interpretation of "employment law influences the 'facts on the ground' to which legal classification responds" (2008:942). Therefore, employment law does not just regulate employment relations but also influences how various aspects of employment relate to one another and can influence legal, economic, and political social relations outside employment.

This is the case with the *San Manuel* rulings. On its face, asserting jurisdiction over tribal labor relations seems to primarily affect how tribal enterprises relate to their employees, but these rulings also have a broader influence. This impact beyond labor relations comes from the *San Manuel* application of the *Tuscarora–Coeur d'Alene* test. As described above, this legal test puts supporters of tribal sovereignty in the precarious position of having to prove why they should be exempt from federal laws of general applicability that do not mention Indian Country, instead of requiring that federal laws explicitly denote their application to Indian Country. Not only does this test significantly expand the plenary power of Congress, but also it does so from the judiciary through implied congressional intent, not through the express statements of Congress (see Frickey 1999). In other words, judiciaries are implementing the plenary power over Indian Country that our federal system has assigned to Congress, by imputing the potential plenary power that Congress has regarding issues on which Congress has never explicitly commented. Parallel to the trend of asserting jurisdiction over Indian affairs from the bench, administrative judges appointed to the NLRB have been practicing "judicial activism" with regard to labor law. James Gross (1995:x) illustrates how over the past fifty-some years, "labor policy [has been] made without legislative changes through presidential appoint[ees] to the NLRB…[who engage] in lawmaking by giving specific meaning to broad statutory language and by filling in gaps in the legislation." In both judicial currents, judges act from silence in the law, not an enunciation of law. The two trends come together in *San Manuel* in a dramatic fashion for indigenous communities as the NLRB uses the *Tuscarora–Coeur d'Alene* test and the NLRA to cordon off another realm of tribal self-governance. Every time a judicial body rules as the NLRB did, it justifies the *Tuscarora–Coeur d'Alene* test as sound jurisprudence for any court to use in a variety of contexts in relation to a variety of federal laws. Thus, *San Manuel* has a broad impact on Native communities and tribal sovereignty, far beyond regulating the relationship between tribal governments and their employers.

As I illustrate in the next section, the *San Manuel* rulings also legitimate the trope of the rich Indian by constituting some tribal entities as commercial, not governmental, thereby assimilating a uniquely tribal entity into a mainstream market, further trivializing the value and goals of indigenous self-determination.

Commercial versus Traditional Tribal/Governmental Enterprises

On May 24, 2008, the NLRB simultaneously released its rulings on the *San Manuel* and *Yukon II* cases so that they could be read as companion cases, jointly charting the new path that the NLRB intended to employ to regulate tribal labor relations. With these cases, the NLRB declared that it would determine the line between tribal sovereignty and federal regulation of labor relations. The line was conspicuously drawn around the most economically successful tribal enterprises, tribal governmental gaming. It is not at all coincidental that the *San Manuel* and *Yukon II* cases were conjoined in order to dramatically shift the NLRB's policy on tribal labor relations. Indeed, each case represents an opposite end of a legal distinction that the NLRB put forward as the key determinant of whether to assert its jurisdiction.

Eschewing the importance of operating on reservation land, the NLRB instead drew a distinction between tribal corporations acting in what it describes as a traditionally tribal or governmental capacity and those functioning as commercial enterprises. In the opinion of the NLRB, a tribal casino plainly represents a commercial entity and is therefore in need of federal regulation, whereas a Native Alaskan healthcare corporation more clearly involves the function of a tribal government. The focus on the function of an economic enterprise marks one of the critical shifts in the way the NLRB conceptualizes tribal labor relations. A key provision in the NLRA is section 2(2), which exempts "the United States or any wholly owned Government corporation, or any Federal Reserve Bank, or any State or political subdivision thereof, or any person subject to the Railway Labor Act" from the definition of employer. This exemption was included out of concern for the way union negotiations and job actions could potentially disrupt critical public services of governmental entities.[22] Before *San Manuel*, the NLRB was inclined to consider tribal governmental enterprises as analogous to the other governmental entities of section 2(2) and therefore as exempt from the NLRA; however, this was never the sole grounds for not applying the NLRA to Indian Country. As mentioned above, the geographic location of the tribal enterprise in question mattered just as much as whether it was an arm of the tribal government.

Part of *San Manuel*'s dramatic shift in the course of tribal labor relations is how it deals specifically with the governmental exemptions found in the NLRA. The *San Manuel* decision explicitly vacated previous NLRB interpretations by reading section 2(2) literally, not comparatively. Because section 2(2) does not explicitly mention tribal governments but does mention other kinds of government and subunits of government, the *San Manuel* decision declared that tribal governmental entities could not qualify under section 2(2) exemptions.[23] Reading section 2(2) so strictly (and the D.C. Circuit Court's upholding of this interpretation) is in large part what allowed the NLRB to claim jurisdiction over Indian Country under the principles of the general applicability of federal law. However, once it asserted its jurisdiction, the NLRB was not done considering the governmental function of tribal enterprises. In deciding whether to conditionally abdicate its newly asserted jurisdiction, the NLRB attempted to weigh the importance of certain tribal enterprises against principles of tribal sovereignty. This calculation had nothing to do with exempting a tribal entity from the NLRA because it was exempt as a governmental entity per se, à la section 2(2), but rather was purely based on the NLRB's discretion as to whether a tribal economic enterprise could also serve a key governmental function. This interpretation gives the NLRB tremendous constitutive power over tribal economic enterprises by claiming for itself (not Congress or tribes) the authority to legally define the nature of enterprises. The NLRB seeks to establish this legal definition by trying to distinguish commercial from governmental functioning of tribal enterprises.

Much of the distinction seems to rely not on what *is* a governmental function but rather on what *is not*. Commercial activity is intrinsically defined as not governmental (or at best, as the D.C. Circuit puts it, "extra-governmental" and merely "ancillary" to the function of tribal governments). It should come as no surprise that the NLRB focuses on commercial activities. This is, after all, its area of expertise. But this focus also speaks to the problem of an administrative law court determining Indian policy and charting the limits of tribal sovereignty (Singel 2004).

In applying its expertise to a case of tribal labor relations, the NLRB bases much of its discretion to assert jurisdiction on a modified usage of the first of the three *Tuscarora–Coeur d'Alene* exceptions—abdicating federal jurisdiction over purely intramural matters or those thought to be wholly self-contained within a tribal community. But it is not easy to decipher how the notion of a "purely intramural manner of self-governance" relates to economic development and labor relations. Certainly, developing one's economy is a critical act of self-governance, but to do so purely in an intramural fashion and still be relevant or successful in a global economy may be impossible (Buffalo and Wadzinski 1994–95; Limas 1993, 1994; Pacheco 1994; Singel 2004). The NLRB has tried to weigh the extent to which a given tribal corporation is or is not functioning in a "purely intramural manner" against accommodating the federal Indian policy of promoting tribal self-determination and self-governance. In making this determination, the NLRB has drawn a distinction between a tribal corporation acting in a "traditionally tribal or governmental capacity" and one functioning as a "commercial enterprise" (341 NLRB No. 138:40). However, this distinction is far from a bright line.

Indeed, determining the distinction between essential governmental functions and commercial enterprises operated by a government entity is, in general, not easily done through the law. Ellen Aprill (1992:421) notes that courts and the IRS have consistently had trouble maintaining the commercial-versus-essential/traditional-governmental-function distinction because of the wide variety of income-earning activities in which state governments engage, such as "liquor stores, insurance companies, waste disposal services, transportation companies, investment funds, parking lots, lotteries, and utilities." At first, courts and the IRS tried to use a commercial-versus-essential/traditional-governmental-function distinction to decide whether to tax these various income-earning activities. But the overlaps were so great and the discrepancies so minor among the functions and purposes of these entities that it proved unfeasible to maintain the distinction. Given the difficulty of sustaining this distinction and given the confusion caused by it, the IRS ended up exempting almost all governmental income-earning activities (Aprill 1992). And for the most part, the Supreme Court has upheld this acknowledgment of the chimera that is the distinction between the commercial and essential governmental activities of governmental enterprises. The majority in *Garcia v. San Antonio Metro Transit Authority* (1985) put it this way:

> We...reject, as unsound in principle and unworkable in practice, a rule of state immunity from federal regulation that turns on a judicial appraisal of whether a particular governmental function is "integral" or "traditional." Any such rule leads to inconsistent results at the same time that it disserves principles of democratic self-governance, and it breeds inconsistency precisely because it is divorced from those principles. (547)

Yet, as *San Manuel* illustrates, the NLRB is willing to brave these treacherous waters and call upon a jurisprudential methodology that other judges have abandoned.

The distinction between commercial and essential/traditional governmental functions has specific implications for economic enterprises in Indian Country as well. In employment law, the term *traditional governmental functions* is commonly used to talk about the actions of governments, as opposed to private entities. However, the NLRB explicitly describes its distinction as "traditionally tribal," thereby denoting a concept of indigeneity, not just "governmental"-ness. In general, notions of "tradition" are inherently linked to indigenous peoples, with the expectation that their indigeneity relies on a longevity of activities and cultural traits that can be described as traditional. Such notions of tradition frequently do not allow for change or modernization—they are seen as the antithesis of tradition. However, non-Indian economic enterprises are not held to the same expectations that modes of economic development will remain quaint, with innovation held in check. This is precisely at the root of the unexpected quality of rich Indians—that they use economic innovation to make money and, if they do profit, they forfeit a certain amount of traditional Indianness.

The NLRB knows what it is looking for when it evaluates commercial enterprises. Applying this expertise to a tribal context, it considers things such as the extent to which interstate commerce is involved, how many people are employed by the enterprise, what percentage of employees are and are not tribal members, the financial worth of the corporation, and whether the management is in partnership with a non-Native corporation. The analysis not only considers tribal corporations through the same lens as most other corporations in the United States but also implies that tribal corporations must be measured in terms of the effect they might have on competing neighboring, nontribal corporations. The latter consideration is addressed in both the *San Manuel* and the *Yukon II* decisions as a peripheral justification for either asserting or abdicating NLRA jurisdiction. On the one hand, in *San Manuel* the NLRB declared that its interest in regulating tribal gaming was high, "especially in light of the keen competition in the gaming industry—the non-Indian sector of which is subject to the Board's jurisdiction" (341 NLRB No. 138:45). On the other hand, it reasoned, the fact that the Native Alaskan health-care facility in question was not in direct competition with other local enterprises weighed in favor of declining jurisdiction.

However, the very act of measuring the "commercial" values of tribal corporations undercuts what might make tribal corporations unique and obscures the extent to which we can view tribal corporations as enacting traditional tribal or governmental functions. Not-for-profit and for-profit tribal corporations can be distinguished from other enterprises in the United States because they are operated at the will of and in the interest of the tribal community as a whole. Profits do not go toward individual accumulation or distribution to shareholders who have assumed risk in a company by making an investment. Rather, profits are meant to sustain tribal sovereignty and the self-sufficiency of tribal self-governance. John C. Mohawk (1991:499) argues, "Indian economic development may be less about creating wealth than it is about creating the conditions for political power in the context of socially responsible choices for the continued existence and cohesion of the Indian nation." And Duane Champagne sees tribal capitalism as an explicitly unique kind of capitalism:

> The tribal government accumulates profits not for private purposes but for the good and the future investment of the tribal community.... This model of tribal capitalism enshrines the tribal government as manager of economic enterprise for the well-being of the tribal community. Jobs and wealth are managed for the collective well-being, at least in theory, and therefore individuals participate wholeheartedly because they, too are contributing to the collective and future economic well-being of the community. Since the tribal government is in control of economic enterprise, community goals and values are protected, and accumulated wealth from capitalist enterprise is reinvested or redistributed with the well-being of the community in mind. (2004:323)

Under this formulation, tribal corporations are extensions of tribal governments and thus are different from other kinds of commercial enterprise and more akin to a nationalized enterprise (see also Buffalo and Wadzinski 1994–95; Limas 1994; Rice 1996). The NLRA statute does in fact recognize that governmental entities in general are different from other commercial ventures and thus are actually exempt from the NLRA. But when it comes to tribal enterprises that on the surface look like other commercial enterprises, their governmental function is overlooked and ultimately undercut by analyzing operating procedures. That is, the current interpretation of the NLRA emphasizes how these corporations create revenue rather than what they do with it.

Perhaps the *San Manuel* ruling best illustrates this emphasis. The NLRB considers a tribal gaming enterprise "too commercial" to rise to the level of a corporation functioning in a traditional tribal or governmental capacity. Compared with the health-care facility examined in *Yukon II*, this distinction may appear to be clear in that the health-care corporation in and of itself is directly providing a social service for the community. A gaming facility does not serve its customers the same way a healthcare corporation does. Nonetheless, the very existence of many civil and social services in most Native communities with casinos can be directly linked to tribal gaming corporations (Cattelino 2008; Goldberg and Champagne 2002; HPAIED 2008; Marks and Contreras 2007; Spilde 2004a, 2004b). Before gaming corporations, in most cases there were none to very few social and civil services for tribal communities, despite the trust responsibility of the federal government. Until tribal gaming took hold in the mid-1990s, many Native communities completely lacked basic infrastructure such as running water, sewers and sanitation, paved roads, adequate law enforcement, and educational resources. To consider tribal gaming enterprises as commercial in a capitalistic sense and thus as lacking a critical component of governmental functioning overlooks all that the enterprises do for their communities.[24]

Moreover, as Singel (2004) warns, the NLRB's interpretation of tribal ventures in terms of their commercial nature belies many of the political agendas of federal Indian policy. For example, *Yukon II* was in fact a reversal of *Yukon I*, an NLRB case that originally ruled in favor of asserting jurisdiction over the Yukon Kuskokwim Health Corporation. *Yukon II* was a result of the D.C. Circuit Court's remand of *Yukon I* under the stipulation that the NLRB take federal Indian policy, such as the Indian Self-Determination Act of 1975, into consideration. The premise of the act is to promote tribal self-governance by facilitating tribal governmental takeover of social services from the federal government. Taking this policy into account, the NLRB used its discretion to consider the tribally run Native Alaskan health-care corporation a direct product of the policy of Indian self-determination and thus an entity that was enacting a traditional tribal governmental function. However, the Indian Self-Determination Act is far from the only congressional expression of federal Indian policy that connects the exercise and maintenance of tribal self-governance to tribal economic development. IGRA in 1988 and even the Indian Reorganization Act (IRA) of 1934 were established, in large part, with this very issue in mind.

IGRA is popularly characterized as the law that paved the way for "legalized" Indian gaming. But it did not just distribute the regulatory framework for tribal gaming among tribal, federal, and state officials. It also explicitly crafted an agenda of tribal economic development, and it unequivocally connected tribal commercial activities to the sustainment of tribal self-determination. The first of its three stated policy agendas expresses the importance of gaming as a means for tribal self-sufficiency. IGRA is declared "to provide a statutory basis for the operation of gaming by Indian tribes as a means of promoting tribal economic development, self-sufficiency, and strong tribal governments" (25 USC § 2702 [1]). From this perspective, tribal casinos are not merely commercial enterprises that utilize the broader U.S. market economy to make money; rather, the financial success from Indian gaming is defined as inseparable from the successful exercise of tribal self-governance.

Furthermore, IGRA mandates the indivisible connection between Indian gaming proceeds and tribal governance by legislating how profits can be spent. It sets out strict guidelines that require profits to be spent on tribal governance and the community as a whole. Net revenues from tribal gaming enterprises can be spent in only five ways: "(i) to fund tribal government operations or programs; (ii) to provide for the general welfare of the Indian tribe and its members; (iii) to promote tribal economic development; (iv) to donate to charitable organizations; or (v) to help fund operations of local government agencies" (25 USC § 2710 [b][2][B][i–v]). It is the second category that allows for per capita payments of profits to every individual tribal member, but even those cannot be doled out until the tribal gaming enterprise can prove to the secretary of the interior that it has a comprehensive plan to allocate funds to all five categories (25 USC § 2710 [b][3][A]). This regime of wealth distribution further distinguishes tribal gaming from commercial enterprises whose net profits are distributed among specific shareholders. These legal economic factors make tribal casinos significantly different from corporations typically under the purview of the NLRB.

The NLRB *San Manuel* ruling underestimates the economic development and self-governance agenda of IGRA by strictly reading "purely intramural affairs" as excluding commercial activities. The NLRB is not exactly going out on a limb here. The *San Manuel* decision follows a noteworthy precedent of a handful of circuit court rulings asserting that commercial enterprises are categorically not governmental.[25] But as Singel (2004:702) notes, these rulings are all faulty in that "Congress has never pronounced a policy that tribal sovereignty does not extend to tribal commercial activities. On the contrary, the current congressional policy toward Indian tribes promotes tribal self-determination and recognizes that economic development is essential to this aim." The thread of legal logic justifying each of these rulings' strict interpretation of what is and is not "purely intramural" can be traced back to the *Coeur d'Alene* case itself. To define what the judges meant by "purely intramural," the ruling proposed three examples: tribal membership, inheritance rules, and domestic relations. Some courts have turned the examples into a conventional legal standard by relying entirely on them in making decisions. But there are no definitive guidelines for determining the boundaries of these categories. Moreover, it must be pointed out that they are not statutory or exclusive—Congress has never legislatively defined them, nor has the Supreme Court verified them (Singel 2004).

Nevertheless, as these examples approach the level of institutionalization through iterative common law usage, they draw stifling boundaries around tribal self-governance and economic development in a way that excludes tribal commercial enterprises. Singel points out:

> The examples of tribal membership, inheritance rules, and domestic relations did not exhaust the potential matters of tribal self-government. Yet their inclusion as apt examples has served as a gatekeeper, decreasing the possibility that tribes will successfully argue for a more expansive interpretation of the sort of conduct which is presumed exempt from general statutes that are silent as to tribes. (2004:709)

The circuit court and NLRB rulings that refer to the three *Coeur d'Alene* examples also classify tribal corporations as "commercial" by considering whom the enterprises employ and who their patrons or service populations are. Employing tribal membership is the deciding factor; courts concluded that if a significant percentage of employees and/or patrons were not tribal members, then a tribal enterprise was participating in the general U.S. market economy and ought to be considered a commercial operation. As the NLRB put it in the *San Manuel* decision, "the casino is a typical commercial enterprise operating in, and substantially affecting, interstate commerce," and therefore it does not meet the definition of something that is purely intramural (341 NLRB No. 138:42). The San Manuel Casino, and almost all tribal casinos for that matter, is the paradigmatic case for categorizing a tribal entity as a commercial enterprise. Tribal casinos (1) almost always employ very high percentages of nontribal staff members; and (2) rely on nonmember patrons, which is perhaps the most crucial part of their business plans. But the NLRB's predisposition to focus on the composition of employees and patrons isolates only certain aspects of a tribal corporation and then uses them to pigeonhole the economic enterprise.

By using commercial features as an identifying marker, the *San Manuel* decision (along with similar rulings) essentially suggests that when a tribal enterprise engages non-Indians in employment and commerce, it must do so on the legal terms expected of non-Indians. This assumption of commercial activity strips the governmental function from tribal enterprise. However, there are other ways to legally construe tribal enterprises, ones that do not rely on establishing a distinction between commercial activity and "traditional tribal or governmental functions" (341 NLRB No. 138:40). It is crucial to consider these other legal avenues, because in the realm of Indian Country and federal Indian policy, the commercial-versus-traditional/governmental distinction is a false dichotomy.

Rarely is there a clear-cut separation between economic development and tribal governance. As an alternative, Singel (2004) relies on a route based on the legal precedent that delimits the authority of tribal governments over nonmembers' actions in Indian Country. This way, law is not imported to Indian Country along with nonmembers' visits or business relations; rather, nonmembers' visits and business relations are subject to the conditions under which tribal law has control over anyone on the reservation, including nontribal members. Tribal jurisdiction over nonmembers is far from boundless. In fact, the Supreme Court has strictly limited it, but the circumstances under which tribal jurisdiction has been found to be allowable are still very instructive for considering issues of tribal interstate commerce and tribal self-governance.

Singel affirms that three critical Supreme Court rulings from the late 1970s and early 1980s have drawn strict and clear boundaries about when tribal law applies to nonmembers.[26] She specifies that the cumulative effect of these three cases is that tribes can "exercis[e] civil jurisdiction over nonmembers who are engaged in conduct that threatens the tribe's political integrity, economic security, or health or welfare, or who have formed a consensual relationship with the tribe" (Singel 2004:712). Under this logic, the act of accepting employment from a tribal enterprise and the act of frequenting it would qualify as "a consensual relationship." This legal formulation maintains that when a nontribal member agrees to do business in Indian Country, he or she needs to follow the laws of the tribal community. It delimits the power and jurisdiction of tribal governments in a way that is much more consistent with the Indian canon of construction and federal Indian policies that have been established to preserve tribal sovereignty and the exercise of tribal self-governance.

The NLRB, in the *San Manuel* decision, recognizes the unique political and legal position that tribes occupy in the United States and the challenges this position poses to interpreting labor law. However, the focus on the commercial aspects of a tribal enterprise ultimately works to assimilate tribal economies into the U.S. market as a whole and works against tribes by asserting a different kind of economic relationship. The tribal jurisdictional approach asserted by Singel, in contrast, seeks to maintain what is unique about Native communities. In so doing, it follows the ethos of tribal self-governance established by one of the most important federal Indian laws of the twentieth century, the IRA of 1934. The policy agendas of the IRA—which, incidentally, are not mentioned in the *San Manuel* decision—significantly challenge the commercial-versus-traditional/governmental dichotomy created by the NLRB.

The IRA sought to intricately combine and sustain the traditional, governmental, and economic lives of tribal communities (Deloria and Lytle 1984; Philp 1995). This effort was marshaled in the disastrous wake of the General Allotment Act of 1887 —a federal law passed to assimilate Indians into the U.S. market economy and cultural milieu by dispossessing them of their "surplus" land and forcing them to hold property and land in individual family allotments and to learn to be self-sufficient farmers. The IRA rejected these market and cultural assimilation tactics by promoting tribal nationhood, replete with tribal constitutions, tribal judiciaries, and tribal business councils. Its reorganization of tribal governance was an attempt to create self-sustaining tribal communities that stood parallel to the rest of the United States and thus were more capable of interacting with it on a government-to-government basis.

The IRA was not just about political development and stability; economic development was seen as critically linked to the success of tribal self-governance. The IRA attempted to advance tribal economic development in large part by encouraging tribes to establish or expand business councils. Many tribes already had business councils before the IRA was passed, but in many cases they handled only external economic relations. Also, they were often puppet councils, established at the behest of the BIA to facilitate local community approval for and lend an air of legitimacy to natural resource development contracts with off-reservation corporations that the BIA negotiated on behalf of tribal communities (Deloria and Lytle 1983, 1984).[27] Not surprisingly, most of these contracts heavily favored the off-reservation corporations. However, the IRA attempted to reverse this situation by empowering the business councils with the support of governmental institutions framed by tribal constitutions or articles of association, legal codes, and representative councils. Many business councils still used by contemporary tribal nations to determine the direction of economic development, including the management of tribal casinos, can be traced back to the IRA.

Perhaps most important to understanding the connection between tribal self-governance and tribal commerce is the IRA's statutory provision for tribal business corporations. Section 17 of the IRA allowed the secretary of the interior to issue charters of incorporation to tribes. The purpose of the charters was to establish tribal enterprises, and—similar to provisions in IGRA—the framers of the IRA conceived of these businesses as serving the interest of the entire community. Attaining a charter of incorporation required a petition signed by one-third of all adult tribal members; it had to be ratified by a majority of the adult population. Once established, tribal corporations had the benefits and responsibilities that are common to incorporation: securing loans, purchasing and managing property, transferring land, issuing shares of corporate property, electing corporate officers, drafting bylaws, bringing lawsuits and also being open to suit themselves (Deloria and Lytle 1984). This was a huge step to advance tribal economic development. Vine Deloria and Clifford Lytle note:

> the chartered corporation permitted tribes to engage for the first time in a number of business enterprises.... For all intents and purposes this finally put an Indian tribe in the position where it could not only compete economically with its neighbors, but it could also control the internal operations of the corporation as well. (1984:144)

But the IRA did not stop at merely establishing the structure for tribal corporations. As part of the IRA, Congress also authorized the appropriation of $10 million to start a revolving credit fund (Deloria and Lytle 1984). Tribal corporations could apply for loans and repay them into a fund that made loans to other tribal corporations. Although individual Indians could in turn borrow money from tribal corporations, the revolving credit funds were exclusively granted to tribal corporations.

The charter corporations certainly had the look of non-Indian commercial enterprises, in many ways operated like non-Indian commercial enterprises, and to some extent competed with neighboring non-Indian commercial enterprises. But a big difference was that the tribal commercial enterprises were routed through communal means toward collective ends. They are best understood in the context of the IRA, or as it was also known, the Indian New Deal. Indeed, it was called the Indian New Deal because, like the other federal policies of this time, its goal was economic improvement through heavy participation from the state. Just as other New Deal programs created state-supported economic development and infrastructure projects, the Indian New Deal provided tribal governments with the political and economic resources to stabilize their local economies and create jobs for community members. Although the policy shift was not explicitly labeled socialism, it was the complete opposite of the economic liberalization policies of the Dawes Act (and those later attempted during the termination era).[28] It is worth noting that the NLRA was passed during the height of the New Deal ethos in Washington, D.C. In fact, the two bills were enacted only thirteen months apart (although not in the same Congress). I bring this up not to suggest that the two laws are in direct conversation with each other but to point out that they were part of the same progressive congressional ethos. Indeed, the NLRA does not mention Indian tribes or give any indication in its legislative history of considering Indians—hence the ubiquitous need for judicial interpretation of the NLRA—but both laws address excess American capitalism with collectivized solutions.

The fact that both laws were passed during the same period and with the same executive and legislative agendas suggests that we should look for ways to reconcile the two laws rather than read them in ways that create obtrusive contradictions. For example, the IRA aimed at creating tribal nations that could use their governmental infrastructure for state-run, or in this case tribally run, enterprises. The NLRA established grounds for the state to intervene in commercial labor relations as a means to even the playing field between workers and private corporations. But it explicitly intended to exempt governmental entities and their employees. Therefore, courts should be particularly cautious in reading tribal governmental enterprises as commercial enterprises and thereby using the NLRA to regulate them as commercial enterprises anywhere in the United States.

The architects of the IRA were sympathetic to the idea of overtly using state intervention to improve depressed local economies, advance those thought to be economically downtrodden, and benefit those thought to be historically disadvantaged by overly powerful institutions. Perhaps the best example is Felix Cohen. A renowned legal philosopher and one of the key figures in crafting the IRA, Cohen was an avowed socialist. His socialist leanings are clear in his policy suggestions. Some betray a general naïveté and common preconceptions about Indians held by many people in his position, that Native communities practiced an incipient form of communism and were preternaturally inclined toward such a political economic system. While drafting the IRA, Cohen even quipped that the bill would "mak[e] 'Reds' of the Indians" (Tsuk 2001:212). Witty comments like this, on the one hand, do not prove that the authors and supporters of the IRA saw the legislation as fulfilling the promise of communism in America. On the other hand, Cohen's quip is a window into the mind of IRA drafters, and it certainly substantiates that they did not intend the economic opportunities created by the Indian New Deal to be commercial enterprises founded on the principles of free-market ideology.

From the founding of modern tribal nations with the IRA, tribal governments have been charged with the task of improving the economies of their communities. This has often involved operating corporate enterprises to fulfill the governmental function of sustaining the infrastructure of a community. Seen from the vantage point of the Indian New Deal, the commercial-versus-traditional/governmental dichotomy is even faultier. From the beginning, the two functions existed simultaneously and cooperatively. In fact, based on how the IRA structured tribal commercial enterprises, they carried out one of the main governmental functions of tribal nations. Moreover, an entity that is commercial is no less traditionally tribal. The IRA illustrates that as early as the late 1930s, tribal governments were incorporating commercial enterprise into tribal communities. Contemporary casinos may seem right out of the mold of Las Vegas, but the idea that a tribal government would establish a commercial enterprise to support infrastructure has been in place for at least seventy years.

In many ways, the very perception of "tribe" employed in popular imagination and the law is derived from the kind of legal, democratic institutions created by the IRA. This is certainly not to say that tribal traditions begin with the IRA or that IRA governments are the traditional form of Native political and economic structure. Indeed, the most significant criticism of the IRA is that its drafters did not fully understand the non-Western, Native political forms that had existed long before the IRA and that they failed to adequately incorporate these "traditional" forms into IRA governments (e.g., Biolsi 1992; Philp 1995; Wolfe 2001). However, given the current longevity, authority, and external legitimacy invested in IRA-style governments, it would be incorrect to say that these governments themselves are not now deeply entrenched in the traditions of tribes as political units. Additionally, accepting the IRA was one way in which Native communities were and continue to be officially recognized by the federal government. Given the longevity and dominance of IRA-style governments in many tribal communities—and the resulting tribal economic development—it is inconsistent and disingenuous on the part of a federal institution to assert that the act of engaging in commerce contradicts tribal traditions, and even more erroneous to assert that it contradicts governmental functions. It is in this way that the jurisprudence of indigenous issues is linked to popular imaginations of Indianness (also see Williams 2005). The NLRB's insistence on a distinction between commerce and traditional tribal/governmental function reiterates and reinforces the popular expectation that the more commercial success Indian communities have, the less Indian they become.

Rich Indian Backlash

Coined by Katherine Spilde (1998, 1999), the term *rich Indian* stems from a political and cultural backlash against tribal gaming. Opponents of gaming and tribal sovereignty use this discursive trope to suggest that with success, gaming tribes no longer need federal funding or deserve the unique legal status of sovereignty. Spilde asserts that the notion of the rich Indian

> assumes that all Native Americans are benefiting financially from Indian gaming, overlooking the fact that only one quarter of the tribes offer gambling and many tribal casinos are only marginally successful from a revenue standpoint.... The purpose of the Rich Indian image is to undermine tribal sovereignty...by insisting that gaming tribes no longer need sovereign rights...to be self-sufficient. This argument relies on the notion of surplus (as defined by non-Indians) and shows up in legislation in the form of "means testing" which requires tribes to prove that they still deserve their sovereignty. (1999:16)

These kinds of assumptions constitute precisely the same logic used by the NLRB in applying the *Tuscarora–Coeur d'Alene* test to tribal labor relations.

The NLRB's narrow interpretation of *Tuscarora–Coeur d'Alene* requires tribes to prove that the actions of their tribally run corporations fall within the limited and somewhat ambiguous exemptions for tribal sovereignty. The *Tuscarora–Coeur d'Alene* test—though not legislative in origin—is a "means test," suggesting that certain commercial activities of tribal enterprises move beyond the realm of a tribe enacting its rights of self-governance. Tribal sovereignty is not the presumed starting point when it comes to decisions on tribal labor relations. Instead, by employing the *Tuscarora–Coeur d'Alene* test, the NLRB creates a de facto rich Indian policy whereby tribes have to legally defend sovereignty rights that were established independently of and before the NLRA. Certain tribal economic enterprises are by default under the purview of the NLRA because the very engagement in them is interpreted as a forfeiture of the need for the staunchest protections of sovereignty.

Moreover, the very way the NLRB defines a tribal enterprise as commercial in nature is based on a non-Native notion of surplus. Indeed, one trait the NLRB has used to measure the commercial nature of a tribal enterprise is simply the gross revenue of the enterprise, implying that the higher the revenue, the more likely the enterprise is to be commercial, not governmental. Surplus is not understood in the context of tribal capitalism; rather, a tribal enterprise's revenue is seen merely as wealth, without distinction, without consideration of the communal purposes and collective agendas to which that wealth is directed. The same point is forcefully made clear by the research of Jessica Cattelino (2008). She finds a strong distinction between the ways Indians and non-Indians interpret the fungibility of money. The Seminole people she works with see the money created by their casino as an opportunity to increase the wealth of their community as a whole through more social services, infrastructure, and cultural heritage activities and by eradicating poverty. In contrast, non-Indians focus on the personal accumulation of wealth that casino money has brought to individual Seminoles—to the point of non-Indians' near obsession with the fancy cars that Seminoles now drive.[29] The NLRB's emphasis on revenue focuses on commercial accumulation without much regard for how, given the fungibility of money, revenue can go toward both traditional tribal and governmental functions.

The logic of the NLRB usage of *Tuscarora–Coeur d'Alene* also reiterates the rich Indian discourse by implying that if a business is able to compete in the larger U.S. market economy, then it must follow the legal parameters of the general U.S. market at the expense of sovereignty. Ironically, it is actually the unique legal and political context of tribal sovereignty that provides the economic opportunity for gaming in the first place. If states and municipalities did not have long-standing traditions of putting legal restrictions on casino gambling in general—restrictions that historically did not apply in Indian Country—then tribes would not have the market advantage in gaming that they enjoy today. In fact, it is highly likely that the success of tribal gaming would be dramatically and swiftly limited if states simply legalized casino gaming altogether.

Spilde identifies another way in which the rich Indian trope is used to undermine tribal self-sufficiency and self-governance:

> The second way that the "Rich Indian" image is used to deny Native claims to sovereignty is through the implicit assertion that while tribes do not *need* sovereign rights due to their wealth, they also do not *deserve* these rights because they are not really Indian anymore. In this usage, "authentic" Indian identity is equated with poverty or traditionalism (neither of which can be reconciled with casino success). Therefore, being "rich" erodes tribal claims to sovereignty on the basis that tribal members are no longer sufficiently different from other Americans to deserve discrete political rights. This authenticity argument is often combined with quasi-concern by non-Indians about the threat gambling presents to "traditional tribal values"—the notion that somehow having money will destroy tribal cultures when 400 years of assimilation tactics have not. This denial of political rights stems largely from the fear of a new ("reverse") colonialism wherein tribes reacquire the lands within their reservation (and place it in trust status) and/or expand their territory even beyond reservation borders. (1998:147)

The first rich Indian argument is most commonly used against tribal gaming in general, whereas the latter construction fits more specifically with the issue of labor relations. The notion that tribal sovereignty protections are no longer warranted for tribes not acting "authentically" Indian enough is overtly expressed in the NLRB's commercial-versus-traditional/governmental function. This distinction relies on a notion of Indian authenticity linked to a "tribal" economic activity and to the "traditional" functions of a tribal government. It does so both by asserting that commerce is not traditionally tribal and by strictly defining "purely intramural" as having to do exclusively with domestic relations, membership, and inheritance. Moreover, the character traits used to classify a tribal organization as commercial are specifically based on trying to decide whether a tribal enterprise is "sufficiently different" enough to "deserve discrete political rights."

Of course, this situation directly parallels mainstream racial and legal classifications of Indianness. Non-Indians expect Indians to be sufficiently racially (through physical characteristics) and biologically (through blood quantum) different from any other racial group (Cramer 2005; Deloria 2006; Garroutte 2003; Sturm 2002). In terms of the legal classification of Indianness, the federal government currently requires tribes to produce very detailed and complete evidence to prove that they deserve federal recognition (Cramer 2005; Garroutte 2003). The notion of "sufficiently different" is so powerful that it is often accepted by Native people themselves. For example, most tribes use some component of blood quantum to determine tribal citizenship. But indigenous critique of this logic is often grounded in indigenous notions of Indianness over white notions (e.g., Alfred 1999; Deloria 1995; Garroutte 2003).

Similarly, the NLRB uses distinguishing characteristics typical of non-Indian commercial enterprises—such as number of employees and financial worth—by way of comparison with tribal enterprises. Measuring tribal enterprises in this comparative fashion necessarily codes tribal corporate activities as nonauthentic, because they are judged within a non-Native cultural context. The traditions and historical developments of tribal corporations that are unique to the context of tribal sovereignty and directed toward a communal goal of tribal self-determination are not fully taken into account.[30] On the contrary, a concept such as tribal capitalism tries to conceive of tribal corporate engagement with market economies within the historically communal context of indigenous economies and communities.[31]

The role of "rich Indian" imagery in the policy affecting tribal labor relations can also be found very clearly in the D.C. Circuit's opinion on the *San Manuel* case. This ruling is the result of the San Manuel tribe's appeal of the NLRB's decision to assert its authority over a tribally run casino. Practically speaking, the ruling is important because it is the most recent decision about tribal labor relations (handed down in February 2007) and is from the highest federal court to handle the case so far. Equally important, the ruling both supports and adds commentary to the NLRB's position on tribal labor relations. The D.C. Circuit found no reason to overturn the NLRB's *San Manuel* decision—which in itself is noteworthy because the decision did remand *Yukon II*, a similar case. Ultimately, it agreed with the NLRB's application of *Tuscarora–Coeur d'Alene* and the board's distinction between commercial enterprise and traditional tribal/governmental functions by trying to chart a middle path between tribal autonomy and federal oversight of tribal activities: "[We recognize] that, in some cases at least, a statute of general application can constrain the actions of a tribal government without at the same time impairing tribal sovereignty" (*San Manuel*, D.C. Circuit 2007:11).

But this middle road can be charted only by accepting a form of rich Indian discourse that treats tribal commercial enterprises as ancillary to tribal sovereignty, not as a critical component of sovereignty. Hence, Indian communities with lucrative gaming enterprises are just "rich Indians"—not tribal nations with strategic and successful economic development plans. "Rich Indian logic" codes the enterprises as disconnected from the survival of sovereignty and as merely a way for tribes to make a profit as any other business might. Ironically, the rich Indian logic constructs tribal enterprises as ultimately compromising tribal sovereignty rather than supporting it.

In its ruling, the D.C. Circuit Court does acknowledge that governmental features of tribal corporations are not always clear-cut: "Many activities of a tribal government fall somewhere between a purely intramural act of reservation governance and an off-reservation enterprise" (*San Manuel*, D.C. Circuit 2007:12). But the D.C. Court does little to interpret what these activities might look like and instead suggests that a federal law can limit them as long as they are deemed to be "extra-governmental," assuming that this category is common sensical or self-explanatory (*San Manuel*, D.C. Circuit 2007:12). Ultimately, in a similarly perfunctory fashion, the D.C. Court concluded that the San Manuel tribe's casino was extra-governmental because it was "virtually identical to scores of purely commercial casinos across the country"; thus, the San Manuel Casino was "a purely 'commercial enterprise'" (*San Manuel*, D.C. Circuit 2007:16, 23, quoting 341 NLRB No. 138). The court also ruled that the fact that the casino "employ[ed] 'significant numbers of non-Indians and...cater[ed] to a non-Indian clientele' who live off the reservation" was determinative (*San Manuel*, D.C. Circuit 2007:23, quoting 341 NLRB No. 138). Thus, the D.C. Court's definition of "extra-governmental" entities—that is, tribal enterprises that are ancillary to tribal governments—was based on the enterprise's engagement with the market economy that surrounded the tribal community rather than on characteristics that might distinguish this enterprise as an exercise of tribal capitalism.

When a tribal casino is considered equivalent to other profit-making enterprises, the fact that it is a tribal entity becomes secondary and functionally irrelevant. This logic reiterates the logic of the rich Indian backlash by suggesting that once a tribal nation engages in commerce with the world outside Indian Country (even if this involves patrons visiting Indian Country), it is necessary to put significant limits on its sovereignty; with tribal commercial enterprise, tribal members are not acting like Indians, or at the very least not acting Indian enough. In fact, the D.C. Court deems these activities to be so inauthentically tribal that it does not consider that limiting the activities might impair sovereignty, because such commercial activities are not deemed primarily an action of tribal sovereignty.

It is not exactly clear why neither the D.C. Court nor the NLRB is unwilling to consider what activities that fall between purely intramural governance and off-reservation enterprises might look like or whether tribal casinos might actually fit within this distinction rather than purely at one extreme. One answer might be the hallmark of market economy capitalism: competition. The NLRB and the D.C. Court are not considering the tribal casinos' effects just on unionization and the labor movement, but also on neighboring enterprises with which tribal casinos might compete. Categorizing tribal casinos as "purely" commercial enterprises because they are "virtually identical to scores of purely commercial casinos across the country" implies that tribal casinos compete with non-Indian operations. In other words, if there is nothing tribally governmental about them or if there is no proof of impairment to tribal sovereignty, then such tribal enterprises ought to be held to the same rules that apply to any other private corporation in the United States. The implication is that tribes should not have an unfair economic advantage—exemption from the NLRA—over neighboring corporations. The issue of competitive advantage is explicitly addressed in the NLRB's *San Manuel* decision, affirming that its interest in regulating tribal gaming was high, "especially in light of the keen competition in the gaming industry—the non-Indian sector of which is subject to the Board's jurisdiction" (341 NLRB No. 138:45). Additionally, the logic of free market competition is negatively implicated in the *Yukon II* decision. Here one reason the NLRB decided to use its discretion and not assert authority over the Native Alaskan health-care facility in question was that the hospital was only serving a Native population and was not in competition with other hospitals in the area. The board put it this way: "As the primary health care provider in the area, [it] does not compete with other hospitals that are within the purview of the [NLRA's] jurisdiction." What is particularly noteworthy in this decision is that the hospital's lack of marketplace competition was at least as important to the decision not to assert jurisdiction as the fact that it is a nonprofit organization and an arm of local tribal governments.

Focusing on a tribal enterprise's relationship to neighboring corporate enterprises under the purview of the NLRA through the lens of competition, the NLRB completely disregards what makes tribal corporations unique—the fact that the governments of tribal nations sponsor them. Indeed, using marketplace competition as a metric to judge the commercial nature of a tribal corporation goes beyond simply analogizing tribal enterprises to "similar" non-Native corporations. With the latter mode of comparison, operational characteristics of a tribal corporation are deemed analogous enough to other corporations that a tribal enterprise can be judged to be "a typical commercial enterprise." But comparing tribal enterprises to non-Native corporations based on marketplace competition—"operating in, and substantially affecting, interstate commerce" (341 NLRB No. 138:42)—necessarily evaluates and defines tribal enterprises as purely commercial. More than just suggest that these two kinds of corporations are analogous, it claims that they are competitive peers in a common marketplace. If tribal enterprises are competitors with nontribal enterprises, which fall under the NLRA, then tribal enterprises must also fall under the NLRA. Rather than judge tribal corporations on their own, unique terms, the rulings argue the necessity of evaluating them in terms of how and with whom they compete economically.

The NLRB's *San Manuel* and *Yukon II* decisions imply that asserting jurisdiction over a tribal commercial enterprise is a corrective to competitive imbalance. This has the political effect of overriding the uniqueness of a tribal corporation operating at the behest and in support of a sovereign Indian nation, in order to maintain the free market ideology that economic competitors ought to interact on an "even playing field." In this way, the rulings give credence to a key part of the rich Indian stereotype: sovereignty leads to an unfair economic advantage and therefore should severely be held in check. Many federal and state politicians have leveled this criticism at tribal gaming, calling for financial offsets to equalize the competitive business advantage to tribes outside state and federal jurisdiction on issues such as taxation, environmental impact, and labor relations. Since federal law and IGRA do not allow states to tax tribes or their casinos profits, state politicians have had to get creative in calling on gaming tribes to share their revenues to counteract state and local expenditures that benefit tribal casinos.[32] Although not explicitly state taxation, revenue sharing has the practical impact of limiting the economic advantage that circumstantially comes with tribes' inherent rights of sovereignty—the ability to open casinos where others cannot.[33]

Perhaps the most public expression of resentment of perceived Native competitive advantage was Arnold Schwarzenegger's declaration during California's 2003 gubernatorial recall campaign that gaming tribes were "special interest groups" that did not "pay their fair share" to the state (Spilde 2003). Such rich Indian propaganda helped him defeat opponent Cruz Bustemante, whose campaign was financially supported by many gaming tribes and was thus characterized by his opponents as tainted by unfairly generated wealth (Bruyneel 2007). Once elected, Governor Schwarzenegger continued to push this agenda; in his gaming compact negotiations, he demanded that tribal casinos share a higher percentage of their revenues with the state—peaking in 2008 with a 25 percent revenue-sharing plan negotiated with four tribes. This was an unprecedented amount of "fair sharing" in California—nearly double the previous highs for revenue sharing in the state.[34]

As in the NLRB cases, these uses of rich Indian imagery in public discourse and to serve the agendas of state politics conceive of tribal sovereignty in singularly economic terms. They treat tribal sovereignty as though it is an economic advantage that was legally created to aid tribal communities but can be isolated and rescinded when deemed to be unnecessary to tribal economic success. The underlying logic of the rich Indian discourse is that it treats tribal casinos and tribal sovereignty as if they were reparations granted to tribes to make up for colonialism and to promote an affirmative-action type policy. As with the general attack on affirmative action, the rich Indian logic argues that economic success putatively proves that sovereignty is an outdated policy. But tribal sovereignty and all it can entail (and even tribal casinos themselves) are not reparations. Sovereignty, as well as any economic benefit that may come from the legal advantages of limited tribal sovereignty, exists because sovereignty is an inherent quality of Indian tribes. Tribal sovereignty precedes the current U.S. market economy and any market circumstance that tribes might be able to take advantage of to gain an economic benefit. Generally, changing market circumstances—initiated from within or outside the tribes—are what enable tribes to use tribal sovereignty to their economic advantage. Tribal gaming is the best illustration of this. In fact, tribal gaming is the best counterexample to claims that the rights and benefits that come with tribal sovereignty are reparations. The history of tribal gaming shows that to appease states and the federal government, tribes give up much of their sovereignty through compacting to establish casino gaming (Darian-Smith 2003; Goldberg and Champagne 2002; Light and Rand 2005; Spilde 2003). Instead of being granted special rights and exemptions to operate the tribal commercial enterprises that are Indian casinos, tribes give up a significant chunk of their own authority over Indian Country. Therefore, it is incorrect to suggest that a policy or ruling that diminishes tribal self-determination over tribal economic development is merely a retraction of a policy that has outlived its purpose; it is in fact a stripping away of tribes' inherent sovereignty.

From the antireparations perspective, tribal self-determination is much more comprehensive than the NLRB treats it—as an isolatable economic advantage to be granted and rescinded by federal courts and institutions. As practiced by Native communities long before colonialism and later reconstituted by IRA-style governments, self-determination is a complex notion that interlaces culture, politics, economics, and community-based decision making. However, because of the ongoing settler colonial situation in which indigenous communities are embroiled, this sovereignty is not unlimited, and the process of limiting tribal sovereignty is a fracturing process. Different governmental institutions have different determinations and jurisdiction over different parts of tribal sovereignty. This situation is particularly significant with the U.S. judicial system. Even if courts try to deal with a single issue or circumstance in terms of its relationship to tribal sovereignty in general, it is rare for a ruling about one aspect of tribal sovereignty not to have significant impact on the rest of tribal sovereignty. Courts, including the NLRB and the D.C. Circuit, try to take the larger impact on sovereignty into account when considering their decisions, but ultimately their focus is more on specialized interpretations of law, not policy making. But what holds sovereignty together is more than just institutionalized law, and this is the problem with an administrative court such as the NLRB having so much power to make determinations on sovereignty. Courts may be able to make strong legal arguments to assert control over tribal labor relations, but their decisions will have significant ripple effects on the way tribes can go forward in making decisions about economic development—a crucial component of tribal sovereignty and crucial to tribal sovereignty.

This power is what makes some tribal leaders nervous, considering that tribal sovereignty is far from the expertise of the NLRB and its willingness to abridge sovereignty when considering the nature of tribal economic development. The Supreme Court has anticipated apprehension when considering the sovereignty of states:

> The essence of our federal system is that within the realm of authority left open to them under the Constitution, the States must be equally free to engage in any activity that their citizens choose for the common wealth, no matter how unorthodox or unnecessary anyone else—including the judiciary—deems state involvement to be. Any rule of state immunity that looks to the "traditional," "integral," or "necessary" nature of governmental functions inevitably invites an unelected federal judiciary to make decisions about which state policies it favors and which ones it dislikes. (*Garcia v. San Antonio Metro Transit Authority* 1985:546)

Under the canon of construction, tribes have conventionally had the freedom, com-parable to that of states, to practice self-determination.[35] But by relying on a distinction between "commercial" and "essential" or "traditional" governmental functions and on rich Indian tropes, the NLRB has threatened the democratic processes of tribal communities.

The *San Manuel* rulings have sent significant shock waves through the public conversation about tribal economic development. The specifics of the rulings and now the issue of labor relations in general are key topics of discussion at many industry conferences on tribal economic development. Anti-union lawyers and consulting firms have increased their presence in Indian Country, more tribes are considering right-to-work laws, and the National Congress of American Indians (NCAI) publicly opposes the Employee Free Choice Act.[36] All these factors speak very clearly to the NLRB ruling's constitutive influence on "facts on the ground" in Indian Country, which in turn come under the purview of the NLRB (Zatz 2008:942).

Of course, the NLRB is not the only force trying to constrain tribal sovereignty and the power it grants to tribal governments to oversee tribal labor relations. Labor unions have also initiated the debate over jurisdiction of collective bargaining in Indian Country. Unions have not been above employing a version of the rich Indian discourse to their advantage. Spilde (1998, 1999) notes that one form of backlash against the success of tribal gaming stems from non-Native fears that with newfound wealth, tribes will threaten non-Indian land and property holdings (see also Bruyneel 2007; Darian-Smith 2003). Labor unions fear the effect of tribal economic growth on labor markets. Unions have a valid concern: if regulation of tribal labor relations were nonexistent, tribal casinos could easily undercut a unionization effort. And, of course, service unions in states such as California have to be wary of how the growth of nonunionized labor could undermine their hard-won struggles to build the labor movement. For these reasons, unions opposed tribal gaming in California in the first place and later tried to hold up negotiations in order to secure pro-union language in the compacts. These are also among the main reasons why UNITE-HERE! filed its ULP against the San Manuel Casino.

However, unions' confronting of tribal gaming should not be read in purely politically strategic terms as a battle to maintain their foothold in the labor market. This reading oversimplifies and obscures genuine concerns of social justice. Although the stories of worker abuse at tribal casinos are at this point mainly anecdotal, unions cannot be blamed for wanting to make sure that abuses do not become systemic—something that is not out of the realm of possibility with zero oversight of tribal labor relations. The majority of people who work at tribal casinos come from the most vulnerable labor pools. Whether or not they are tribal members (most are not), most seeking employment in tribal casinos are either immigrants or longtime residents of areas that border Indian Country. They seek work in casinos because of massive global economic shifts and upheavals that have produced economic refugees abroad and ravished the manufacturing sector in the United States. Many available jobs are low-skill service-sector jobs, and tribal casinos—to their credit—do provide work in regions where there is generally very little.[37] But this same labor market, in which people have few places to turn, can add to the vulnerability of tribal casino employees. Moreover, some union organizers have expressed tangential concerns about gaming as an industry in general; it appears to them that tribal casinos achieve their financial success at the expense of working-class bettors. This frustration and generalization is at best purely anecdotal; at worst it heavily limits the agency of working-class bettors.

Still, many labor leaders affiliated with the unions most interested in organizing tribal casinos in southern California (and beyond) have helped build a newly progressive labor movement around battles for social justice (Brodkin 2007). Their commitment to making unions part of progressive social movements that actively seek coalitions and alliances among people who represent multiple marginalities is clear. As Karen Brodkin explains, these new labor leaders, who tend to come from marginalized backgrounds, foreground the racializing assaults on their families, communities, and culture by the dominant culture. They redefine working class issues as racial, gendered, and about immigration as well as about economics. Their stand is the public face of a progressive working-class movement. Their construction of a working-class political actor does a great deal of ideological work in defining what social justice means and how to practice it. But it is also a work in progress. (2007:176)

Indeed, the new progressive labor movement does seem to be a work in progress when it comes to Indians. With other marginalities, the economic is tempered by a critique of other social forces of oppression, but with indigenous communities, financial success remains the prime mover. Rather than recognize how tribal economic success can be a key part of decolonization and political transformation for tribal communities, some unions have merely reified Native financial success as evidence that tribal leaders/managers' newfound class position will necessarily lead them to oppress workers.[38] Instead of collaborating on modes of labor relations that help tribes maintain the political success generated by tribal gaming, which in turn has brought tribal sovereignty from the colonial margins to a place of potentially genuine self-determination and self-governance, some unions have turned to rich Indian discourses that paint tribes as the enemy of social progress, not models for how to achieve it. Efforts such as UNITE-HERE!'s public relations campaign and legal argumentation before the NLRB have highlighted the financial success of tribal casinos implying that tribal decision makers are the beneficiaries of tribal gaming corporate wealth and therefore that the commercial success of casinos will lead tribal corporate management to act in the anti-union fashion of conventional non-Indian corporate leaders. So far, judges have bought this portrayal of rich Indian–run commercial enterprises, and they have moved to protect the rights of employees of tribal economic ventures. However, we must also recognize the indigenous legal alternatives to administering tribal labor relations. These may prove to be the best way out of the growing stalemate between tribes and unions.

Conclusion

The main legal result of the *San Manuel* rulings is that the regulation of tribal labor relations is now under the purview of the NLRA and its administrative judicial body, the NLRB. While asserting its absolute regulatory authority over tribal labor relations, the NLRB has also attempted to establish a framework whereby it can make case-by-case decisions to abdicate its jurisdiction if its judges see the interest of tribal sovereignty as outweighing the NLRB's interest in regulating labor relations. On some level, the NLRB should be applauded for trying to establish a method that is sensitive to the current importance and historic relevance of tribal sovereignty (see Grez 2005). The board can be commended for its restraint in *Yukon II*, with the decision that asserting its jurisdiction would get in the way of the principles and operation of tribal self-determination. However, praise should be tempered by the fact that even the NLRB still retains ultimate discretion over how and when to apply this case-by-case method. Moreover, if the *San Manuel* ruling and the way it employed rich Indian tropes are any indication, the NLRB also is more than willing to further the assimilative efforts that Wolfe (1998, 2001) identifies as the hallmarks of settler colonialism. The most striking end result of *San Manuel* is how it seamlessly and uncritically assimilates tribal governmental gaming into conventional U.S. commercial market activities, nullifying its attributes as an expression of tribal capitalism and indigenous economic self-determination.

The shock waves that *San Manuel* sent throughout Indian Country illustrate how tribal gaming dominates the conversation about how tribal labor relations ought to be defined and regulated. The rulings will likely have a significant effect on tribal enterprises, particularly those enterprises that are not gaming based but can be categorized as commercial. This is one very practical way in which tribal labor relations suffer from what is at the core of the rich Indian discourse: many tribes are currently making a lot of money. Along with the benefits of revenue comes public and legal attention that tribal enterprises would not usually receive. But the questions remain: Is large revenue enough of a reason to limit tribal self-determination and regulate how this revenue is produced? Would there be such a strong push for federal regulatory intrusion into Indian Country if there were not so much money involved? And what if the money were not made in gaming?[39]

These questions of high-profile profit making and how it relates to labor relations indicate where the notion of tribal capitalism breaks down. As much as tribal communities can make a strong argument for the uniqueness of tribal capitalism, the court does not consider the act of making profits, particularly through casinos, traditional or tribal enough to be different from profit making anywhere else in the United States. This is one reason tribal labor relations are so important: a Native version of labor relations coupled with a Native version of capitalism strengthens the argument that tribal capitalism is about economic development that is responsible to a broad notion of community, not just shareholders or investors.

This is also where tribal casinos create such a conundrum for the issues of tribal enterprise and labor relations. Not only do the profits of tribal casinos bring outside skepticism about whether tribal communities and leaders are responsible about their economic development, but also non-Natives are heavily imbricated in the tribal casino industry as patrons, employees, and neighbors. This interaction makes casino gaming an anomaly as a tribal enterprise. Despite this fact, because of tribal governmental gaming's high profile and success, it promises to set an Indian Country–wide norm for limitation on tribal self-determination of labor relations. Indeed, in many regards, *San Manuel* is a perfect test case for the cause of unionization and those who seek to limit tribal sovereignty, but it presents the worst possible set of facts for those who want to defend sovereignty—much the same way that *Oliphant v. Squamish Indian Tribe* (1978), as Frickey (1999) argues, was the perfect test for those who detested the idea of tribal criminal jurisdiction over nonmembers. Economic development through gaming and its reliance on a non-Indian population is not the norm for tribal enterprises throughout Indian Country. Is *San Manuel,* then, really the best test case for how to regulate tribal labor relations? The tribal gaming industry is a double-edged sword. On the one hand, the economic success of gaming is a beacon and a model for how to engage in an economic enterprise in a way that can create exponential growth for tribal sovereignty and sustain Native communities' self-rule. On the other hand, economic success exposes tribal communities to outside intrusions that would likely not exist to the same extent without this success.

The ambivalence toward Native economic success and tribal sovereignty also has a very practical aspect that is reflected in the adjudication of Indian Country employment law. That is, there is significant inconsistency in how federal appeals and circuit courts apply the Indian canon of construction to federal labor laws. Mainly, four circuit courts have heard cases that deal with tribal employment and federal labor laws. The Seventh, Eighth, Ninth, and Tenth circuit courts have all heard cases on a variety of employment-related laws, including the NLRA, the Fair Labor Standards Act, OSHA, the Employee Retirement Income Security Act (ERISA), the Family Medical Leave Act, the Americans with Disabilities Act (ADA), and Title VII of the Civil Rights Act of 1964. Despite the variety of cases, with regard to Indian Country, the Seventh and Ninth circuits have tended to interpret the law similarly, as have the Eight and Tenth circuits. The latter two courts "have followed well established principles of tribal sovereignty and tribal self-governance and required a showing of express congressional pronouncement or clear legislative intent to curtail tribal rights before holding that these statutes are applicable to tribes" (Buffalo and Wadzinski 1994–95:1370). At the same time, the former two courts have elected to chart a new course by using the *Tuscarora–Coeur d'Alene* method, which significantly limits tribal sovereignty. Evidently, with the *San Manuel* decision, the D.C. Circuit also falls into this camp. These two diametric judicial approaches clearly point out significant disagreement in how federal courts view a tribal government's function as an employer and where the authority to regulate employment in Indian Country lies.[40] Given the lack of consistency in how to handle labor law in general in Indian Country, the NLRB's self-appointed discretionary powers over tribal labor relations might be justified in that the board is trying to chart a course that works for the NLRA. But, by the same token, the multiple and contradictory precedents make the NLRB's discretionary decisions much more subjective and potentially problematic. Irrespective of what impact this judicial disagreement over application of the *Tuscarora–Coeur d'Alene* method has on tribal labor relations cases before the NLRB, the inconsistency itself might lead to a Supreme Court review with a more definitive and a lasting effect on tribal labor relations.

This is where we must return to the agency of indigenous communities and their leadership. As it currently stands, the San Manuel Band of Mission Indians must decide whether to push its case to the Supreme Court. Given the current composition of the Court and its apathetic and downright negative attitude toward tribal sovereignty (see Aleinikoff 2002; Frickey 1999; Williams 2005), it is unlikely that San Manuel leaders will take the risk at this point. But other tribes, which now will be increasingly open to union activism and representation campaigns—because of the *San Manuel* rulings—might be willing to engage in legal battles challenging the rulings all the way to the Supreme Court. Finally, another proposed option is a legislative fix. Former congressional representative J. D. Hayworth of Arizona held more than one hearing on legislation to effectively reverse the NLRB decision and establish a tribal governmental exemption from the NLRA. However, these hearings never progressed to the point of full congressional consideration of a bill, and Hayworth is no longer in Congress. It is unlikely that the NCAI has ended lobbying efforts to achieve some sort of legislative fix. Indeed, as of the completion of this manuscript, the NCAI and the National Indian Gaming Association (NIGA) have teamed up to advocate that an explicit Indian Country exemption from the NLRA be added to Employee Free Choice Act legislation. They have already convinced Senator Daniel Inouye of Hawai'i to propose such an amendment. Stay tuned!

three
Tribal Structuring of Labor Relations

During late winter of 2004, I attended a meeting of concerned health-care employees of the Navajo Nation–run hospital in Tuba City, Arizona. Gathering in an unused classroom in a Tuba City boarding school, the employees expressed their frustration with what they perceived to be unfair and unresponsive labor relations with the tribal managers of their hospital. They sought union representation to establish collective bargaining with the tribal health-care corporation that managed the hospital but were repeatedly rebuffed by the corporation's board of directors. Adding to the workers' frustration and concern was the fact that a handful of their coworkers had recently been fired for questionable cause. Work conditions at the hospital were so problematic that many employees had recently picketed in front of the hospital, which is on one of Tuba City's main streets. Some of the employees' charges against the hospital certainly could have qualified as potential violations of the NLRA. But the workers at Tuba City had been following tribal labor relations cases at the NLRB; they knew that there had been no definitive decision on how to adjudicate labor relations in Indian Country.

A few months later, in May 2004, the NLRB jointly released its *Yukon II* and *San Manuel* decisions. The *Yukon II* decision made the NLRA unavailable to Tuba City workers, because the NLRB ruled that tribal enterprises providing health care did not fall under the regulation of the NLRA. Had these employees been tribal casino workers, the *San Manuel* decision would have brought them under the purview of NLRA regulation. A large part of whether the NLRA would apply to these two kinds of workers relied on the NLRB's determination as to whether the tribal enterprise that employed them either was in competition with non-Indian businesses or could be considered indistinct from typical "commercial" enterprises. According to the *San Manuel* opinion, not having to follow the NLRA would give an unfair advantage to tribal enterprises that were in competition with or indistinguishable from NLRA-regulated, non-Indian commerce. But in *Yukon II*, the fact that the tribal enterprise in question did not compete with other health-care providers significantly weighed against asserting NLRA regulation. Read jointly, these two rulings represent an attempt by the NLRB to create a level economic playing field between nontribal and tribal corporations that might appear to operate in the same market. *San Manuel* presumes that enterprises that do not have to follow a baseline regulation of labor relations have a competitive advantage over those that do—so they need regulation—whereas *Yukon II* implies that the converse is true: absent market competition, there is less economic advantage in being exempt from NLRA regulation and therefore less reason to assert NLRB jurisdiction. This emphasis on how regulation of labor relations affects market competition between corporations can obscure other, more important reasons for regulation of labor relations. Competitive market relations should not be more important than relations between employees and management and the need to ensure workplace rights and democracy in any enterprise.

The Navajo health-care workers in Tuba City provide an example of this necessity. Their dissatisfaction with and desire to change their labor relations go a long way toward undermining the NLRB's distinction as to whether a tribal enterprise is engaging in interstate commerce and competing with non-Indian enterprises. The absence of a competitive market advantage did not provide the workers with any more favorable labor relations. Moreover, given that most of the workers were Navajos who had an interest in the sovereignty and self-governance of their Native nation, the overall effect of calling on the NLRB and its willingness to undercut tribal sovereignty may have been unsatisfactory.

Considering the Navajo health-care workers in relation to how the NLRB applies the notion of competition to tribal labor relations shows that the NLRB seems equally concerned with how its ruling will affect employers and markets and how it will affect employees. This should not be too surprising. It is well documented that in the second half of the twentieth century, the NLRB and labor relations in general turned decidedly toward favoring management. This move had its genesis in the Taft-Hartley Act of 1947 and blossomed through several other political, economic, and social forces from within and outside the labor movement (see Gross 1981, 1995; Lichtenstein 2002; Milkman 1997; Tomlins 1985). More recently, the NLRB and lax enforcement of labor law in general have so favored employers that progressive labor unions have sought to organize employees outside and around the NLRA. Despite the worker protections built into NLRB representation elections, the NLRB has been so stifling to, and in some cases unwilling to enforce, these protections that some unions have forgone sanctioned representation elections and have tried to pressure management to recognize and bargain with them through direct actions that in many cases are not protected by law (see Bronfenbrenner and Juravich 1998; Clawson 2003; Lichtenstein 2002; Sharpe 2004; Sherman and Voss 2000; Tait 2005). Thus, given this promanagement bent, even if the aggrieved Navajo health-care workers from Tuba City could have turned to the NLRB, nothing guaranteed that the judicial body would have helped them solve their workplace problems.

Above all else, the example of the Navajo Nation health-care workers speaks to the need for indigenizing tribal labor relations—both in terms of establishing independent tribal entities to adjudicate and mediate tribal labor relations and in terms of unions responding more effectively to the specific needs of Native workers who are fully supportive of tribal sovereignty but also demand just labor relations. I believe that the groundwork for indigenizing tribal labor relations already exists in Indian Country; it is just a matter of pulling several forces together in a constructive and cooperative fashion. One place to start thinking about this goal is the perception of unions in Indian Country.

In 2002, *Indian Country Today*, the nation's leading Native newspaper, conducted a survey on tribal labor relations. The survey asked "American Indian Opinion Leaders" their feelings about unionization in Indian Country.[1] The survey found that "71 percent of respondents indicated that tribal enterprises and casinos should not allow labor unions to unionize tribal employees on Indian lands," as opposed to the "[20] percent of respondents [who] thought that labor unions should organize tribal employees while 9 percent indicated they did not know." Moreover, "79 percent of respondents also indicated that tribes should be protected from entering into coerced agreements to accept unionization of their enterprises and casinos" (White 2002). This sentiment seems to have solidified only after the *San Manuel* decisions markedly expanded the NLRA's authority over Indian Country.

It is no surprise that these decisions emboldened unions' efforts at organizing in Indian Country; there has been a significant uptick in union petitions for the NLRB to hold representation elections for tribal employees. The tribal response to *San Manuel* has been equally if not more fervent. Many indigenous leaders have used public forums and Native advocacy groups—such as *Indian Country Today*, the annual meeting of the National Indian Gaming Association (NIGA), the NCAI, and the Native American Rights Fund—to denounce the erroneousness and arrogance of courts' decisions in *San Manuel*. Frustration with the courts has also led some indigenous leaders to direct their ire toward labor unions, creating a strong current of unabashed anti-unionism in Indian Country. There has been an increase in the deployment of legal and political strategies to indirectly and directly confront unionization in Indian Country. These actions include introducing congressional legislation to reverse the *San Manuel* rulings, passing tribal right-to-work ordinances, employing anti-union lawyers and consulting firms, and even challenging the legitimacy of NLRB elections in spite of the *San Manuel* rulings.[2]

But not all indigenous public sentiment is against unionization in Indian Country. For example, even Ernie Stevens Jr., the chairman of NIGA, has taken a more conciliatory stance on unionization. In his prepared address at the 2008 NIGA Annual Conference, Stevens said, "It saddens me that tribes have to battle with union organizations that have been instrumental in securing worker rights" (Merina 2008). Some tribes and tribal leaders have not seen this clash as being as inevitable as Stevens laments. For example, in 1998 the Menominee Indian Nation of Wisconsin signed a neutrality agreement with four unions before opening its casino (Krerowicz 1998). The agreement ensured that the tribe and its gaming enterprises would not actively oppose unionization, would agree to unionization if a majority of employees signed union membership cards, and would agree to binding arbitration for disputes. As part of the agreement, the union used its organizing resources to help win a referendum to allow the Menominee Nation to build its casino on land purchased in Kenosha, Wisconsin, outside the reservation.[3]

The Cabazon Band of Mission Indians fostered a similarly positive relationship with labor unions in California. In 1999 it met with the Laborer's International Union of North America to collaboratively discuss tribal labor relations. These discussions were meant to build on a labor relations ordinance that the Cabazons' Tribal Business Committee had passed six months earlier (Apfelbaum 1999). The tribe felt that maintaining a productive relationship with unions was important. The tribal chairman put it this way: "It's important that we dispel the lie that tribes are anti-employee because it's always been about opportunity and living wages" (Apfelbaum 1999). This prolabor stance came about for many reasons, not the least of which was that both the tribal chairman and the second vice chairman had been members of the CWA—the former a one-time shop steward (Apfelbaum 1999). The CWA itself also managed positive relationships with a few other California Native nations by signing collective bargaining agreements with casino enterprises owned and operated by the San Manuel Tribe and the Viejas Band of Kumeyaay Indians.

Despite the strong opinions of many surveyed by *Indian Country Today*, opinion columnist Scott Lyons views the pro-union actions by tribes such as the Menominee, Cabazon, San Manuel, and Viejas as steps in the right direction. Lyons (2004) argues that instead of being a challenge and potentially detrimental to tribal sovereignty, unionization can strengthen sovereignty. Lyons acknowledges that the *San Manuel* rulings were certainly an assault on tribal sovereignty and just another example in a long line of judicial culling of tribal jurisdiction. However, he distinguishes between judicial attacks generated by efforts at unionization in Indian Country and the actual principles and act of unionization. He argues that although some zealous union leaders have led a charge against the jurisdiction of tribal sovereignty, unionization is not anti-Indian. Indeed, he says, unionization is "the Indian way" because it promotes empowerment, not exploitation, of labor and because of its fundamental principles of collective decision making and third-party mediation (Lyons 2004). These ideals are consistent with indigenous views that work and surplus should go toward the common good and on how to maintain harmonious sociopolitical relations. Lyons says that rather than counterattack unionism and lament the NLRB, Native peoples and nations should work

> to head [the NLRB] off at the pass and develop even stronger labor laws and worker protections—that is, stronger unions—than what the Americans currently enjoy. Make Indian enterprises the envy of workers everywhere.... [Doing this] just might transform that nagging sense of having been hoodwinked once again into an exercise of real sovereignty. (2004)

Thus, labor relations in Indian Country should be viewed not as something that undercuts tribal sovereignty but rather as something that provides Native governments and peoples an opportunity to improve and strengthen practices of self-determination by creating indigenous policies of labor relations.

Lyons' (2004:5) proposal for handling tribal labor relations speaks to what Joseph Kalt and Joseph Singer have identified as de recto, de jure, and de facto tribal sovereignty: "sovereignty by moral principle or right, sovereignty by legal decree or legislative act, and sovereignty in practice." Recognizing that the *San Manuel* rulings limit Native nations' de recto and de jure sovereignty, Lyons calls upon tribes to employ their de facto sovereignty by indigenizing labor relations in Indian Country. Kalt and Singer (2004:5) note, "Tribes and their supporters can compellingly and articulately assert the [de recto], and petition and lobby for the [de jure], but what ultimately matters is the last form of sovereignty—the *de facto* exercise of sovereign powers." Enacting comprehensive tribal policies and laws is the most powerful way to sustain tribes' abilities to make decisions about labor relations.

Equally important, this approach is consistent with the "nation-building" economic development strategies advocated by Stephen Cornell, Joseph Kalt, and many others associated with the Harvard Project on American Indian Economic Development (HPAIED) (see Lee 2001). Nation building focuses on political solutions to economic problems and creating a tribal governmental infrastructure that will encourage and support economic development. This process requires "effective governing institutions" that provide "stable institutions and policies; fair and effective dispute resolutions; separation of politics from business management; a competent bureaucracy; and cultural 'match'" (Cornell and Kalt 1998:12). In the realm of labor relations, strong and clear labor codes and policies could go a long way toward providing the stability, efficacy, bureaucracy, and political insulation needed for "effective governing institutions" and thereby the exercising of a tribe's de facto sovereignty. Tribal labor codes can be even more helpful at meeting the goals of effective governance when coupled with independent tribal court systems that can adjudicate labor laws in ways that are fair to all parties concerned and justly resolve disputes.

That being said, not all tribes have independent judiciaries or the resources to establish them. But this situation is beginning to change as individual tribes gain more economic resources, which they direct toward tribal judiciaries, and pool their resources to establish and share intertribal court systems.[4] The growth in independent tribal judiciaries is part of a larger governmental reform movement in Indian Country to strengthen tribal legal systems in ways that make them more effective, independent, and culturally appropriate (see Lemont 2001–02, 2006; Porter 1997a, 1997b). The movement is motivated by indigenous communities' desire to address a combination of forces coming from inside and outside the communities: expansion of tribal economies and governmental responsibilities, decolonization of Western forms of governance, tribal constitutional crises and political infighting, worldwide market globalization, legal attacks on tribal jurisdiction, environmental degradation, and cultural change, to name a few. Duane Champagne (2006:11) comments that tribal communities realize that if they "want to assert greater control over their economic, political, and cultural lives, they will need more effective forms of government." They will need to fix old laws and governmental structures and add new ones.

The regulation of tribal labor relations ought to be viewed within this larger context of tribal governmental reform. Amid the pressure from outside legal, political, and economic forces and the internal desire to broaden economies and self-determination, adding tribal labor codes could help tribes maintain more control of their futures. Structured properly, these laws could take full advantage of the functions already existing in many tribal governments and at the same time expand tribal governance by covering new areas of tribal jurisdiction and using governmental services in innovative ways. New tribal labor relations laws would lead to new governmental departments in charge of regulating and enforcing these laws and increased responsibilities of tribal courts to resolve labor relations disputes. Although the growth in regulation and adjudication would certainly be bureaucratically taxing, it has the potential to greatly increase the stature of tribal governance. As in the tribal governmental reform movement, tribal regulation of labor relations would require an interweaving of Western governmental and regulatory structures with indigenous values and traditional forms of governance (see Lemont 2001–02, 2006; Porter 1997a, 1997b).

Of course, the structuring of tribal labor relations is not done in a vacuum. It must address the pressure from and seek productive relationships with outside legal and political forces. In this way, tribal labor relations is an expression of how tribal sovereignty should be best thought of in terms of an interdependent sovereignty (Cattelino 2008; Young 2001). Young (2001:39) argues: "Self-governing peoples ought to recognize their connections with others and make claims on others when the action of those others affect them, just as the others have a legitimate right to make claims on them when their interdependent relations threaten to harm them." Young's model of interdependent self-determination is based on the idea that sovereignty is not an autonomy in which sovereigns are free from outside interference, but rather a nondominant interrelationship of polities. For Young, domination is different from interference; domination is arbitrary interference without regard for the interest and opinions of those with whom the dominant interfere. In our world of dense political, social, and economic interrelationships, autonomous noninterference is a fallacy, particularly for indigenous communities that are part of a settler colonial history. Young (2001:37) asserts that indigenous "claims for self-determination...are best understood as a quest for an institutional context of nondomination." Regulating tribal labor relations will work best when it is done in an interdependent context of nondomination.

I argue that this means combining the desires and needs of workers—even non-tribal citizens—and labor unions with those of tribal managers, tribal political leaders, and an indigenous community as a whole. Tribal law and self-governance is best suited to handle tribal labor relations because it is more likely to establish a nondominant yet interdependent relationship. Tribal labor relations codes, created with outside input, can maintain tribal self-determination and indigenous values while treating workers fairly and giving them a voice in the nature of their work conditions. This voice should not undercut or override tribal sovereignty but should be a part of negotiation between multiple forces whose interdependence is critical for successful tribal economic development and self-determination.

The balance of this chapter explores how tribal governments have attempted to regulate labor relations using their own governing structures. This discussion takes into account current legal decisions that limit the full realization of tribal regulation and of tribal legislative decisions, such as right-to-work laws, that seek to regulate labor relations in ways that limit unionization. This chapter considers what has been done so far and what potentially lies in the future for tribal regulation of labor relations.

The Interdependence of Tribal Labor Relations

The *San Manuel* decisions to assert NLRB jurisdiction rely on the judicially created distinction of purely intramural activities of tribal governance. In practice, this distinction is quite ambiguous, particularly regarding jurisdiction over Indian Country and tribal sovereignty. Indigenous governments and lands do not fit squarely into a nested hierarchy of powers and jurisdiction in the American political system, creating constant debate over how tribes relate to the federal and state governments (Biolsi 2005; Kalt and Singer 2004; Wilkins and Lomawaima 2001).[5] Moreover, as Thomas Biolsi (2005:245) explains, "tribal homelands are regulated, under federal laws, to a condition of heteronymous political space in which different citizens are subject to different sovereigns in coterminous space." But trying to define powers and actions that are specifically and exclusively intramural constructs sovereignty as something that is autonomous from the rest of the United States. This judicial interpretation limits sovereignty to governance over things that can be separated out from indigenous people's interactions with the rest of the world—such as membership, probate, and domestic relations. Although many Native communities are geographically isolated, the practical reality is that Indian peoples and governments inevitably interact with the political and economic communities that surround them (Limas 1993; Singel 2004).

The *San Manuel* rulings ignore the many ways in which indigenous self-determination

—and self-determination in general (see Scott 1996; Young 2001)—relies on interdependent relationships. Craig Scott (1996:819) asserts that "self-determination necessarily involves engagement with and responsibility to others." This interdependent self-determination is particularly apparent in the current structure of tribal gaming. Tribes must negotiate with states to structure gaming regulations; rely on non-Indian patrons and workers; contribute huge amounts of money to non-Indian charities, civil infrastructures, and political campaigns; and sustain local and state economies (Cattelino 2008; Spilde 2003, 2004a). But interaction with non-Indians has also led to negative consequences for Indians. Indigenous peoples who previously were relatively invisible to the rest of the United States have increasingly been thrust into the spotlight, along with their economic success. The rich Indian backlash illustrates that not all of this attention has been positive.

The rising prevalence of rich Indian imagery in popular discourse, court rulings, and federal policy can be interpreted as a backlash, not only against the success of tribal gaming but also against what tribes can potentially do with that financial success. The potential of tribal self-determination has rarely been perceived as being as powerful as it is currently, now that tribes have huge revenue sources to back their political and legal agendas. It is clear that this potent combination has made many non-Natives nervous as tribes become players in state and national politics through lobbying and financial support of candidates (see Bruyneel 2007; Light and Rand 2005). The rich Indian backlash is a combination of racialized class expectations of Indians, guilt over the way U.S. colonialism has marginalized Native communities, and fear of the potentially drastic and revolutionary forms that indigenous decolonization might take (Darian-Smith 2004; Kamper 2000; Spilde 1998, 1999). IGRA and the public media surrounding state referendums and compacting promoted tribal gaming as uplift for neglected and downtrodden Native communities. Tribal leaders significantly contributed to this discourse by highlighting the local political and economic benefits of gaming and not emphasizing the simple fact that their inherent tribal sovereignty ought to be argument enough to justify tribal gaming. This was particularly the strategy with the California gaming referenda. Tribal leaders and campaign managers astutely recognized what would appeal to and what might threaten the non-Indian public about Native financial success and how the legal complexities of sovereignty might confuse voters (Goldberg and Champagne 2002; Lombardi n.d.). But counting on the appeal that the theme of "community uplift" might hold for the non-Indian public also means that anything perceived to be beyond uplift is closely scrutinized, is labeled non-Native (or nontraditional), and plays into the rich Indian backlash. This response has been acutely the case with some labor unions' efforts to gain more control in tribal labor relations.

Labor union criticism of Indian gaming uses the rich Indian discourse to set up a labor conflict between casino employees and gaming tribes by implying that the accumulation of wealth inherently leads to anti-union policies—policies above and beyond the notion of community uplift. In discussing tribal labor relations, the question that organized labor wants to ask is whether tribes will be pro- or anti-union. But to tribal leaders, there is more to this issue: tribal labor relations are just as much about jurisdiction and tribal sovereignty as about unionism. Most criticism of the *San Manuel* rulings is not launched from an anti-union position per se, but rather from a pro–tribal sovereignty position. There is a sense that labor unions initiated the tension between tribes and unions and that tribes are just acting defensively to protect sovereignty. However, this defensive action does threaten to spill over into outright anti-union policies and tactics. Indeed, being pro–tribal sovereignty does not equate to being anti-union, but it does not necessarily equate to being pro-union either. Here is where the issue of the rich Indian backlash resurfaces. Tribes must be keenly aware of how their interactions and dealings with labor unions and their workforces might be negatively perceived, even if these are not that dissimilar from those of other American corporations. The rich Indian discourse makes it more likely that tribes will be publicly criticized for the way they handle labor relations. The consequences of even perceived injustices are more acute in Indian Country than in most other polities because always looming is the specter of federal institutions, such as the NLRB, that could seize the opportunity to intervene and further limit tribal sovereignty.

Arguably, the *San Manuel* case itself provides a textbook example of the delicate situation in which tribal corporations and tribal leadership find themselves as they balance their business decisions with outside perceptions. The NLRB's consideration of a singular instance of UNITE-HERE! arguing that it was being treated unfairly by the San Manuel Tribal Casino, because it was not given equal access to casino employees, turned into a comprehensive reordering of jurisdiction over tribal labor relations. As this case illustrates, in many ways the willingness of outside forces to interject themselves into tribal affairs is based on the perception that tribal corporations are not following acceptable standards and behaviors of labor relations. Of course, the notion of what is acceptable is subjective, highly contextual, and seldom consistent. But tribal sovereignty by no means gives tribes carte blanche in their treatment of employees. Indeed, it is when outsider forces perceive tribes to be "hiding behind sovereignty" that these forces are most likely to aggressively push for legal intervention. This is where Scott's (1996) declaration of self-determination being not just an engagement with others but also a responsibility to them is relevant.

In a case out of Wisconsin, for example, a multitribally run wildlife commission used sovereignty and treaty rights to prevent paying overtime to its employees.[6] In this instance, the Great Lakes Indian Fish and Wildlife Commission went so far to affirm its self-governmental decision-making rights that it was willing to contest a Department of Labor subpoena for tribal records needed to prove whether game wardens were being paid time-and-a-half. In other examples, tribal employees have been fired for attempting to unionize or strike, and tribal corporations have refused to bargain after union recognition (see Kemp 1995). However, these examples appear to be more anecdotal than systemic and do not indicate an antilabor predisposition among tribal enterprises.

Nonetheless, legal maneuvers and management decisions such as these threaten to stretch the limits of what the general public might interpret as fair behavior of a legitimate government. It is a perception of illegitimacy that most often leads non-Indians to doubt the worthiness and even authenticity of tribal sovereignty (see Kalt and Singer 2004). At the heart of the rich Indian backlash is the same skepticism about the legitimacy of sovereignty, and this is the backdrop against which tribal communities must make decisions about tribal labor relations and how to regulate them. Ultimately, tribal corporate leaders, political leaders, and community members need to decide the political costs of protecting one aspect of tribal sovereignty at the expense of other aspects of sovereignty. In other words, from a perspective of jurisprudence, it is critical to stave off any attack on the rights to self-determination and self-governance, but to what end do these serve if the very policies enacted with these rights might in turn threaten them?

Evidently, the whole idea of sovereignty is that a tribal nation should make its own decisions and laws about issues that the community collectively thinks are important. But these decisions cannot be made in a vacuum—particularly not in the quasi-colonial context in which Native communities still find themselves. That is, tribal leaders need to take into account outside perception and its political consequences when determining policies, particularly labor relations regulation. The good news is that just as perceived illegitimate forms of self-governance lead to attacks on sovereignty, self-governance that is and is perceived of as upstanding, fair, and effective can go a long way to help protect tribal sovereignty rights. As Young (2001:38) puts it, "in a densely interdependent world, people require political institutions that lay down procedures for coordinating action, resolving conflicts, and negotiating relationships." There is little chance that federal courts and states will yield to the authority of tribal jurisdiction without effectual tribal legal and governmental institutions. Creating the perception and reality of good governance is an important part of the move to reform and expand tribal governments.

Outside political and economic pressures have had a significant impact on how tribes regulate their labor relations and formulate their labor relations codes. This was particularly the case in California in 1998 when UNITE-HERE! lobbying of Democratic governor Gray Davis and Democratic state legislators led Davis to negotiate labor relations provisions in gaming compacts. Recognizing the political power of the labor unions, most tribes agreed to establish labor relations ordinances (Goldberg and Champagne 2002). In exchange, unions agreed not to oppose a public referendum to change the state constitution to allow for high-stakes casino games. Attending to outside perception of labor relations to complete compact negotiations and ensure that the constitutional amendment would pass may seem to be a capitulation on the part of California Native nations. But the tribal labor relations ordinances that resulted from these negotiations are better understood as a product of the interdependent sovereignty that institutionalized legitimate and equitable protections for the rights of tribal employees and for tribal rights to govern labor relations.

California Gaming Tribal Labor Relations Ordinances

The tribal labor relations ordinances (TLROs) used by many California Native nations with gaming enterprises are good examples of interdependent self-determination, in large part because most TLROs ostensibly come out of gaming compact negotiations. As of 2000, California tribes that sign a gaming compact agree that the compact will be null and void if the tribe does not provide a labor relations procedure acceptable to the state. This provision does not mandate specific labor relations procedures. However, to create uniformity and expedite the process, the state and tribes negotiated a model TLRO. The boilerplate document created an acceptable baseline; individual tribes have some leeway to add to but not subtract from the model ordinances mandated by the compact. Although mandated by gaming compacts, such ordinances are tribal law because they do not take effect until tribal governments officially approve them through their legislative processes. Moreover, each TLRO bears the name of one of more than sixty individual tribal nations that have passed TLROs. Because they were created as part of negotiations between tribal leaders and state leaders, the TLROs represent a nondominant form of interdependence.

Still, some tribal leaders feel that the TLROs were all but forced upon the tribes as a precondition to tribal governmental gaming (Deron Marquez, personal communication, November 14, 2008). The leaders' frustration speaks to the fact that it is an oversimplification to think that nondominant forms of interdependence can be divorced from power dynamics. Not all interdependency is the same. In the context of California, state leaders were able to include TLROs, and although some tribal leaders were unhappy about their inclusion, they ultimately agreed to these because they wanted to accomplish the overall goal of tribal gaming compacts. We must remember that tribes agreed to TLROs before the *San Manuel* decision, so at the time, they believed that they would be conducting tribal regulation of labor relations based on the model they had agreed to with the state rather than on the NLRA framework that was later forced upon them. Indeed, interdependent relations should not be divorced from the contexts of negotiation; these contexts contribute to differences in nondominant interdependencies.

For example, the compact that the Pala Tribe originally negotiated with Governor Wilson in 1998, before propositions 5 and 1A, had labor provisions more favorable to unionization than the ones with mandated TLROs that most California tribes signed in 2000, after Proposition 1A. At this point, Pala re-agreed to a 2000 compact that included TLROs, but not the more labor-favorable provisions of the 1998 compact. The difference was that California tribes had gained much more power in the negotiating process within those two years (because of a new governor and the public support manifested by the propositions) and Pala took advantage of this. By 2007, when a handful of other California tribes began to renegotiate their compacts, power dynamics and political winds had changed even further. During negotiations for compact extensions, some unions and legislators tried to push even further for more labor-friendly provisions in the TLROs, such as card-check neutrality (see Sweeney 2007).[7] But at this point (with another new governor, Arnold Schwarzenegger), unions did not have the political clout to get tribes to agree to these changes. Moreover, California was the only state that was able or even desired to include TRLOs in compact negotiations. In most other states, labor unions did not have the political power to force tribes to negotiate over this issue.

However, other states have certainly pushed the envelope on other issues in the compact negotiating process, to the point that the process no longer resembles nondominant interdependency. As Young (2001) argues, nondominance is based on lack of arbitrary interference. Some states have refused to negotiate compacts in good faith and have left tribes with few options or grounds on which to negotiate. Others have tried to include nongaming issues in the compacting process, such as trying to limit hunting and fishing rights that tribes already have by treaties and federal law (Corntassel and Witmer 2008). These examples are far more arbitrary than including discussions of labor relations—which are relatively central to the operation of tribal gaming—in compact negotiations. Moreover, despite some California leaders feeling frustrated that they had to compromise their stance on regulation of labor relations to get a gaming compact signed, this *was* a process of negotiation and therefore certainly far more nondominant than the NLRB's blanket usurpation of regulation through the *San Manuel* ruling. California's gaming TLROs still based the regulation of tribal labor relations within an indigenous context, not a federal one.

The TLROs take their cues from federal and state labor law but are written to specifically govern tribal casino labor relations, so they are sensitive to both the rights of tribal sovereignty and the specific circumstances of the tribal casino industry.[8] In some cases, they go beyond the NLRA, but in others they do not offer workers the same protections (cf. Goldberg and Champagne 2002; Gordon 2000; Herman 2000). The California gaming TLROs recognize not just casino employees but also those working in "related facilities" such as hotels, restaurants, and golf courses. However, TLROs are applicable only to tribal casinos with more than 250 employees. Like the NLRA, the TLROs include fundamental workers' rights, such as the rights to join a union, negotiate collective bargaining contracts, and strike. They also give unions access to employees in the workplace during "non-work time in [a] non-work area" and to a list of names and addresses of employees. They allow for representation election after proof that 30 percent of the bargaining unit supports the union. The TLROs also establish a set of ULPs that lay out prohibitive guidelines for both casino management and labor unions. The ULPs are similar to nontribal labor law: securing workers' right to support a union and prohibiting tribes from financially supporting unions, refusing to bargain with unions, and discriminating against employees who support unions. But one provision that significantly differs from the NLRA is that in an effort to fit the unique situation of tribal communities, TLROs permit Indian preference in employment decisions, such as "promotion, seniority, lay-offs or retention."[9]

As for union ULPs, TLROs also prevent unions from refusing to bargain and from interfering with the right of employees who choose not to support the union. Another union ULP unique to the context of Indian Country is prohibition "to attempt to influence the outcome of a tribal government election, provided that this section does not apply to tribal members." This rule is clearly designed to respect the uniqueness of tribal political processes.

Lastly, California gaming TLROs have exceptional provisions concerning strikes. They allow for strikes only after an impasse in contract negotiations, but at the same time, most do not allow picketing on tribal land, which can limit the efficacy of strikes. However, unlike all other California Native nations, Los Coyotes Indian Reservation of the Cahuilla Nation has modified its TLRO to allow unions to picket and leaflet "adjacent or leading to, but not inside, the Tribal Casino." To strike only after impasse is not an uncommon provision for labor relations meant to promote peaceful resolution to disputes. What is unordinary is that these TLROs do not prevent secondary boycotts—strikes that the NLRA outlaws because they target not the corporation with which the union is negotiating a contract but a secondary company that does business with the negotiating corporation (Goldberg and Champagne 2002; Herman 2000). This was a significant concession for UNITE-HERE! to gain from compacting, because UNITE-HERE! had been very successful in staging public protests against secondary corporations.

A few other provisions that individual tribes have added have to do with making union recognition easier in exchange for putting some limits on certain union activities. For example, the Pauma Band of Mission Indians' TLRO states that if the union says in writing that

> it will not engage in strikes, picketing, boycotts, attack websites, or other economic activity at or in relation to the Tribal Casino or Related Facility...that it will not disparage the Tribe for purposes of organizing Eligible Employees, and it and its local affiliates will agree to resolve all issues, including collective bargaining impasses, through binding dispute resolution...

then the tribal government will remain neutral during the union's organizing drive and will grant union recognition through a card check, not a representation election. The last provision is significant because card-check recognition is based on convincing a majority of employees to sign a card supporting the union, which is much easier to accomplish than an election. Card checks take place over a longer period of time than elections and give organizers more opportunity to convince workers to support unionization. Los Coyotes' TLRO has a card-check provision that takes effect if the union agrees to a no-strike clause.

A further expression of the interdependent spirit of California gaming nations' TLROs is the provision to establish a Tribal Labor Panel. This statewide agency comprises ten arbitrators who are charged with overseeing disputes revolving around representation elections and ULPs. As Herman (2000) points out, it is not exactly clear how these people are chosen; the TLROs state that they will be mutually chosen by the "parties" involved and that each member "shall have relevant experience in federal labor law and/or federal Indian law." The Tribal Labor Panel is meant to be the second level in the dispute resolution process. The first is the tribal council or a tribally designated committee. Decisions at the first level are binding but can be appealed to the Tribal Labor Panel. Decisions by the Tribal Labor Panel in turn can be appealed to a tribe's court system. But the final authority is the state and federal court systems, at which point the tribal government must waive its sovereign immunity.

This last provision is a clear illustration of tribes' willingness to compromise. Tribal judicial systems significantly participate in the dispute resolution process, but the fact that they are not the ultimate arbiters is a blow to tribal sovereignty. If tribal (and intertribal) court systems are ever going to be given the respect and legitimacy they deserve, they ought to be given the full responsibility of determining justice in Indian Country. Full-service, independent tribal judiciaries are no less impartial than federal or state judicial systems (Kalt and Singer 2004). Of course, those from outside a Native community, such as unions and nontribal employees might be more comfortable in state and federal rather than tribal courts. But they should not expect their court systems to follow them with their employment choices any more than if they were working in another state or a foreign country. Perhaps the best solution would be a dispute appeals system that ends in tribal courts, provided that tribes, when acting as employers, waive their sovereign immunity in tribal court. This way, tribal judiciaries could hand down justice and at the same time preserve the sovereignty of Native communities vis-à-vis external court systems.[10]

Another way to improve the spirit of interdependence and compromise in TLROs would be for more tribal governments to follow the Pauma's and Los Coyotes' lead in allowing for neutrality agreements and card checks to establish union recognition. This system could foster much more positive and productive relations with labor unions. Moreover, I would argue that this should be a standard part of TLROs, without requiring any concession of no-strike clauses. Although in many cases this arrangement goes beyond state and federal law, card-check neutrality is in many ways an optimal way for workers to choose fairly whether they want unionism.[11] As Lyons (2004) advocates, tribal labor relations can be an opportunity for indigenous communities to demonstrate a responsibility and morality that is above and beyond what is generally expected in America. Card-check neutrality would do so by making a significant public statement about workers' rights and representing a strong alternative and counterbalance to the anti-union tendencies found in tribal right-to-work ordinances and the growing participation of union-busting consulting firms in tribal labor relations.[12]

Despite the benefits and potential of the California gaming TLROs, the current *San Manuel* decisions cast doubt over their authority and their reason for existence in general. These decisions leave little wiggle room for anything other than NLRA jurisdiction. By the same token, they have not specifically outlawed TLROs. There are two conditions under which the authority of TLROs might not be vacated by the *San Manuel* decisions: first and foremost, when the industry in question falls under the "purely intramural" definition, such as the Native Alaskan health-care facility in the *Yukon II* case. In this context, a tribal government could very likely pass a TLRO to deal with "governmental employees." The process could address the intramural issue by providing collective bargaining rights and significant protection for workers above and beyond workers having to rely merely on internal tribal corporate human resources policies.

The second condition is more theoretical than the first: theorizing TLROs as an illustration of how tribal self-determination is a matter of interdependence—not autonomy—would work toward expanding the notion of "intramural" by interrogating what is and is not "purely" domestic. This follows Singel's (2004) critique that the *Tuscarora–Coeur d'Alene* test arbitrarily limits what is considered to be a "purely intramural" act of self-governance and that the limits, in fact, are not statutory. It is worth considering how the very act of legislating a TLRO might be construed as a legitimate act of tribal sovereignty that is not in need of federal oversight or at the very least could constitute some form of joint jurisdiction. Legislating a TLRO is much more an act of governance than merely creating human resources policies for individual tribal corporations as part of a specific tribal government–sponsored economic development plan. Federal courts might be more willing to err on the side of tribal sovereignty if it were deemed that the NLRA was not serving a regulatory function that is missing from Indian Country but rather duplicating a function that could just as well be served by tribal governmental institutions.

Indeed, one of the arguments attorneys for the San Manuel Tribe made against NLRA regulation was that the tribal government had already established a TLRO. The NLRB, the attorneys claimed, threatened to undercut this act of self-governance and tribal sovereignty by overriding tribal jurisdiction. The D.C. Circuit responded by opining:

> The Supreme Court's concern for tribal sovereignty distinguishes among the different activities tribal governments pursue, focusing on acts of governance as the measure of tribal sovereignty. The principle of tribal sovereignty in American law exists as a matter of respect for Indian communities. It recognizes the independence of these communities as regards internal affairs, thereby giving them latitude to maintain traditional customs and practices. But tribal sovereignty is not absolute autonomy, permitting a tribe to operate in a commercial capacity without legal constraint. (*San Manuel*, D.C. Circuit 2007:15)

Here the D.C. Circuit's argument clearly parallels the logic of the rich Indian mentality, asserting that acting in a "commercial capacity" is not on a par with and is therefore distinguishable from "traditional customs and practices." It also resembles the way *Tuscarora–Coeur d'Alene* narrowly interprets what "purely intramural" activities are and thus severely limits the ability to enact self-determination. Lastly, and most important, the argument reiterates the NLRB's commercial-versus-traditional/governmental dichotomy as a way to say that tribal commercial activity does not enjoy the lack of infringement that other (more "traditional") governmental functions of tribal sovereignty might. The justices state that tribal commerce cannot "operate...without legal constraint." But the question is not whether the San Manuel Casino was operating "without legal constraint"; rather, it is who will do the regulating: a tribal entity (a TLRO) or an outside entity (the NLRA)? In this specific circumstance, regulation did exist because San Manuel had already established a TLRO as a part of its gaming compact. Like almost every other California gaming tribe, the San Manuel tribal government legislatively approved its TLRO, thus officially making it an act of tribal governance. Indeed, in regard to "legal constraint," San Manuel's TLRO even gave state and federal courts authority to overturn the dispute resolution decisions made by tribal courts.[13]

The D.C. Court tried to specifically address the issue of San Manuel's already existing TLRO:

> Certainly [San Manuel's] enactment of a tribal labor ordinance to govern relations with its employees was a governmental act, as was its act of negotiating and executing a gaming compact with the State of California, as required by IGRA.... Moreover, application of the NLRA to employment at the Casino will impinge, to some extent, on these governmental activities. Nevertheless, impairment of tribal sovereignty is negligible in this context, as the Tribe's activity was primarily commercial and its enactment of labor legislation and its execution of a compact were *ancillary* to that commercial activity. The total impact on tribal sovereignty at issue here amounts to some unpredictable, but probably modest, effect on tribal revenue and the displacement of legislative and executive authority that is *secondary* to a commercial undertaking. We do not think this limited impact is sufficient to demand a restrictive construction of the NLRA. (*San Manuel*, D.C. Circuit 2007:15; emphasis added)

Despite this rejection of the overarching authority of San Manuel's TLRO, there is a significant amount of equivocation in this opinion and arguably room to distinguish between San Manuel's TLRO for the purpose of its gaming compact and TLROs in general. Following the court's (and the NLRB's) concentration on the commercial activities of the tribal corporation, the governmental act of passing the TLRO is seen as secondary to and contingent upon the operation of the casino. Given California gaming compacts' mandates for TLROs, and for that matter IGRA's mandate for a tribal–state compact, interpreting the San Manuel tribal government's actions as primarily commercial and secondarily governmental is understandable. Of course, this again presupposes the dichotomy between commercial activities and tribal traditional/governmental functions.

But perhaps even more offensive to tribal self-governance is the way this decision underestimates the true governmental nature of tribal legislatures and executives by treating them more like corporations than nations. The judges assume that acts of tribal legislation—such as TLROs and the tribal gaming ordinances mandated by IGRA—are being passed only to support a commercial agenda. These are somehow "ancillary" and "secondary" to an economic agenda rather than part of a comprehensive policy-making body that makes decisions and laws concerning economic development as any state or national legislature or executive would. Instead, the ruling constructs TLROs as a corporate policy or part of the business model of an enterprise whose only goal is economic, not governmental. This interpretation limits what is conceivably an intramural function of a tribal government. Moreover, it disregards the way IGRA constructs tribal gaming as something meant to support the self-sufficiency of Native communities—in terms of both economic and political stability. Tribal gaming supports the ability of a tribal government to function, just as tribal (and federal) legislation allows for and undergirds the commercial enterprise of a casino. The two are mutually constitutive, not subordinate.

In terms of the D.C. Court's specific rejection of the San Manuel Tribe's TLRO, it is conceivable that a tribal government could pass a TLRO independent of, before the existence of, or in the absence of a casino gaming operation. In this case, it seems that the question of whether the NLRA ought to supercede such a TLRO is still open. Under these circumstances, it would be hard to argue that a TLRO was merely ancillary to a commercial enterprise and not an act of tribal self-government trying to regulate labor relations within its sovereign boundaries. Indeed, the Mashantucket Pequot Tribe did try to make a similar argument twice before a regional panel of the NLRB. In 2007 and again in 2008, the tribe appealed two different orders for representation elections for employees seeking to be represented by the UAW and then the Operating Engineers. Lawyers for the Mashantucket Pequots argued that the UAW's and the Operating Engineers' collective bargaining rights should be regulated under the tribe's own labor codes—the Mashantucket Pequot Labor Relations Law (MPLRL)—not under the NLRA. Before going to court, the tribe had asked the unions to use the MPLRL; the unions' rejection of this request is what put the cases before the NLRB. Once in court, the Mashantucket Pequots argued that the NLRA should not supercede the MPLRL, because the MPLRL was an act of tribal governance. The difference between the MPLRL and the TLROs of California gaming tribes was that the Mashantucket Pequot government passed the MPLRL independent of its gaming compact. However, it was clear that this law was passed specifically after the *San Manuel* decisions and in a direct effort to deal with attempts to organize the casino that the tribe owned and operated: the Foxwoods Resort Casino.[14] The NLRB rejected the Mashantucket Pequots appeal, in large part following the *San Manuel* rulings' distinctions between commercial and governmental functions. The MPLRL's apparent connection to the commercial endeavors of the casino again seemed to undercut the full legitimacy that the NLRB would grant to tribal regulation of labor relations.

The distinction between commercial activities and governmental ones might be harder to legally sustain if a tribal relations ordinance was not created to deal directly with gaming. Tribal gaming in this regard is the context for setting the legal precedent, but the industry's overwhelming vulnerability to the rich Indian stereotype makes it hard for unions, the courts, and the general public to see anything other than a commercial enterprise in tribal gaming. Although not yet challenged in court, TLROs established in a nongaming context may hold up better to the scrutiny of outside pressure.

Navajo Nation Tribal Labor Relations Codes

Some TLROs have been created in the absence of tribal gaming. The foremost example is the Navajo Nation's collective bargaining codes and Office of Navajo Labor Relations (ONLR). They provide an exemplary model for regulating general tribal labor relations without privileging one specific type of industry. The TLRO and the office created to regulate it were established in 1994 in a context completely unrelated to tribal gaming.[15] Rather, it was part of a larger effort by the tribal government to codify and strengthen its labor law.

The effort was an attempt to create a work environment that balances the protection of employees and sovereignty. The tribe's labor code is structured similarly to labor laws in other parts of the United States. For example, the child labor code defers to codes of the four states that border the Navajo Reservation, stating, "The Navajo Nation shall adhere, as nearly as possible, to the applicable child-labor laws of the states Arizona, Colorado, New Mexico, and Utah" (T. 15, Ch. 7, § 801); however, the tribe does retain the right to add protections as the president sees fit (see T. 15, Ch. 7, § 802). This section of the code is typical of how the Navajo Nation has attempted to develop laws that draw from both Euro-American and Navajo traditions to find a system that works in the unique social locale of the reservation (e.g., Lemont 2001–02; Wilkins 2002).

An important part of Navajo Nation labor laws is a set of codes regulating labor relations. These collective bargaining codes were also passed in 1994, and they reflect the development of both the Navajo Nation's economy and its tribal government.[16] Although in 1961 the Navajo Nation failed in its attempt to bar unions from its reservation (*Navajo Tribe v. NLRB*, 288 F.2d 162 [D.C. Cir.], *cert. denied*, 366 U.S. 928), it took until the mid-1990s to create a formal policy dictating the tribal government's role in regulating collective bargaining on the reservation. The collective bargaining codes are clearly based on the NLRA and state labor law. They set up frameworks for representation elections, union recognition, contract negotiation, mediation, and decertification. These frameworks generally reflect the formulations of labor relations common in the rest of the United States. They also reiterate federal law by establishing collective bargaining rights for all nontribal governmental employees on the reservation; however, they go one step further by incorporating jurisdiction over the bargaining rights of employees of the tribal government or tribally run corporations. They are very explicit about the tribal government's and managers' neutrality in regard to union representation and offer recognition through a card-check procedure if more than 55 percent of the employees request union representation. If between 35 and 55 percent of employees seek union representation, recognition can be gained through a representation election. Lastly, like many state and federal labor laws, the Navajo Nation collective bargaining codes prohibit tribal governmental workers from striking.

Establishing these codes was a progressive act meant to advance both the rights of workers and tribal sovereignty. Indeed, their stated purpose "is to promote harmonious and cooperative relations between the Navajo Nation, its agencies and enterprises and Navajo Nation employees" (§ 1). The choice of the word *harmonious* appears significant, at least in theory, considering Navajo cultural emphasis on balance and harmony, traditionally known as *hózhó* (e.g., Witherspoon 1977).[17] By establishing its own law, the Navajo Nation asserts its authority and its cultural values in this area of contemporary reservation life. Labor relations become more than just systems to increase the security and productivity of an economic venture; they become a way for the Navajo tribal government to assert sovereignty by establishing another area of civil regulation. The Navajo government took the initiative in formulating these codes to provide rights for its tribal employees—neither the federal government nor the courts forced their creation—and thus it effectively codified what was at the time—before the *San Manuel* decisions—an open, ambiguous, and often contentious area of jurisdiction. Moreover, this act fosters and secures sovereignty by carving it out in advance of intervention from federal and state governments. Whether the act will survive the *San Manuel* decision remains to be seen. This is particularly true given that the Navajo Nation recently opened a tribal casino.

The Navajo Nation collective bargaining codes also institutionalize the interdependent nature of tribal sovereignty by allowing for an exterior, third-party mediation and arbitration. Through this process, the Navajo Nation involves the Navajo Nation chief justice by having him or her approve and select mediators and arbitrators. Moreover, entering into arbitration with a union could potentially compromise the tribal government's sovereign immunity. Navajo tribal leaders are distinctly aware of this conflict of interest. In a memo reviewing the codes before their approval by the Human Services Unit of the Navajo Nation, Assistant Attorney General Thomas Christie notes his concerns about the Impasse Resolution in section 7: "Any time 'arbitration' is used, if it is binding on the parties (as it would appear to be under the proposed rules), a government essentially gives up sovereign immunity; it allows a third person to determine its rights, responsibilities and course of action."[18] In anticipating these sorts of concerns, Limas (1993) suggests, tribes should engage with the notion of limited abdication of sovereign immunity. She suggests that if tribes relinquish sovereign immunity in labor disputes and limit the amount of damages to be paid out, they will help secure sovereignty by appearing fairer to all interested and external parties—unions, corporations, and the federal government.[19] Ultimately, the Navajo Nation Council decided to accept language in the code that did allow for arbitration.

Still, the judicial branch of the Navajo Nation would arguably be an even better venue to resolve disputes. The Navajo Nation Supreme Court is one of the most respected tribal courts in the country and is fully qualified to be an impartial determiner of justice in Navajo tribal labor relations, in the same way the NLRB rules over the NLRA. Additionally, within the Navajo Nation judiciary is a highly organized peacemaker court system. Diné peacemakers and the Navajo Nation peacemaker courts indigenize the process of mediation and arbitration. Most importantly, using the Navajo judiciary would set an example that would greatly enhance tribal self-determination not just in the Navajo Nation but also in Indian Country in general.

As the Navajo Nation example illustrates, TLROs are best understood as a Native alternative to the NLRA. Even if the legal language of TLROs is similar to federal and state labor laws, what matters is that with TLROs, tribal communities are established and adjudicate these laws. As tribal laws established within a system of tribal governance, TLROs are more likely to be exercised and interpreted in ways that are consistent with community norms and local values. Local exercise and interpretation are fundamental to indigenous self-rule. Scholars of tribal economic development argue that this is also what tribal capitalism is about—reinterpretation of a non-Native economic system through local indigenous values. But the fact that tribal capitalism is directed toward the community does not mean that tribal managers are necessarily more prolabor or that all participants are equally invested in the community—particularly if some participants are not tribal members. It would be foolish and romantically naive to think that tribal capitalism is immune to greed, that there is no potential for corruption with TLROs, or that TLROs always work as effectively as they are written. In fact, even the Navajo health-care workers had trouble finding protection and resolution through the well-crafted Navajo Nation collective bargaining codes. (See chapter 6 for a more thorough discussion of this issue.) As with any law, how it is implemented and enforced can be just as important as how it is crafted.

There is also no real reason to think that labor relations in tribal capitalism are any more open to corruption than the general American capitalist system or labor laws. Nor is there any reason to think that the NLRA is better equipped than TLROs to handle indiscretions and disagreements. Indeed, many unions have moved away from relying on the NLRA for much of their organizing campaigns because of potential biases in NLRB adjudication. Even UNITE-HERE!, the biggest proponent of NLRB intervention into Indian Country, frequently does not rely on the NLRB (apparently, Indian Country is an exception). Instead, TLROs can provide a balance to tribal capitalism in a way that sustains tribal sovereignty. Furthermore, researchers with the HPAIED have consistently found that promoting policies of self-rule leads to economic success, in large part because self-governance creates an increased sense of responsibility and accountability in indigenous communities (e.g., Cornell and Kalt 1998; HPAIED 2008; Kalt and Singer 2004). Promoting TLROs would very likely create a similar atmosphere, wherein tribal leaders and community members feel an added investment in maintaining positive tribal labor relations.

Tribal Employee Rights Ordinances

In addition to the labor relations codes of the California gaming tribes, the Navajos, and the Mashantucket Pequots, another model of tribal labor law might provide a paradigm for regulation of tribal labor relations. The Tribal Employee Rights Ordinance (TERO) was established in Indian Country in the 1970s to preserve and strengthen hiring practices that gave preference to Natives. A handful of legal and Native labor activists (mostly from the Navajo and Blackfeet nations) created TERO as a prototype tribal code that tribal governments could use as a model to ratify their own laws ensuring that their tribal members were hired for on-reservation projects (O'Neill n.d.). At this time, there was a boom in reservation economic activity in the extraction, energy production, and construction industries. Federal Indian-hiring-preference laws had been on the books since the nineteenth century, but there was no institutional enforcement of these laws and it became very hard for indigenous people to get jobs with non-Indian corporations that were taking advantage of tribes' resources. As an indigenous-based strategy for protecting the rights of Native workers, TERO programs quickly sprang up on several reservations. These held nontribal corporations accountable to contractual agreements they had made with tribal governments and the BIA to hire tribal members. One reason TERO programs became ubiquitous so quickly was that, early on, the founders of this movement worked collaboratively across several tribes, sharing ideas and strategies for dealing with nontribal employers (O'Neill n.d.). To this end, they also established the Council for Tribal Employment Rights (CTER; http://www.ctertero.org/history.html), which has had annual (and biannual) meetings for the past thirty years and now boasts the representation of more than three hundred tribes with TERO programs.

Although TERO programs share resources and strategies through CTER, each one is set up at the tribal governmental level; the programs become a part of tribal law and have their own local variations of agenda and services. Many TERO offices have expanded beyond employee preference to include acting as hiring agents and fighting anti-Indian racism in and outside the workplace, on and off the reservation (O'Neill n.d.). Colleen O'Neill's (n.d.) excellent activist-centered history of TERO programs gives voice to these relatively unheralded tribal institutions and recognizes the important role that TERO officers have played during the self-determination era, not only in securing many jobs for tribal members but also in asserting the sovereignty rights of tribal governments to dictate the terms of employment in Indian Country. Many Native workers recognize the value of TERO programs and often compare them to an indigenous union that does many things that trade unions do but specifically looks out for tribal members (O'Neill n.d.). Labor unions themselves have recognized their importance and have worked collaboratively with individual tribal TERO programs and CTER, as a national organization, to help with job training and job placement and to create a workforce of Native laborers to fill positions created by Indian preference programs. Unions have also reaped the benefit of these collaborative projects, because these have brought in Native members who appreciate the way unions have worked with TERO programs and CTER. In certain tribal labor markets, unions have bolstered their own position by seeing to it that jobs guaranteed to tribal members also become union jobs.

These labor union–TERO collaboratives make TERO programs a potential option for nonantagonistic tribal labor relations grounded in tribally based institutions. However, to date, most TERO programs have been concerned with enforcing hiring provisions in contracts between tribal governments and companies doing work in or near Indian Country, not with facilitating the negotiation of labor contracts or collective bargaining. Moreover, as more and more tribes have become employers in their own right, TERO offices have been placed in an ambivalent position, because their conventional role has been to watchdog nontribal corporations and advocate for tribal-member employees, not to regulate tribal companies or advocate for the right of tribal (enterprise, not necessarily member) employees (O'Neill n.d.). At a CTER meeting I attended in fall 2007, this tension was palpable as the *San Manuel* decisions were being discussed. Some attending the conference were interested in ensuring that tribal members got union construction jobs associated with building tribal casinos and at the same time wanted to safeguard against union organizing of nontribal service employees once a casino was up and running. However, those with strong backgrounds in the labor movement sought to use TERO programs to establish TLROs as a tribal solution that balanced sovereignty and unionism. One CTER leader proposed to help tribal leaders write TLROs, just as he originally had with TERO ordinances; it is not clear how many tribal leaders took him up on the offer.

Tribal Right-to-Work Laws

The whole idea of tribal self-governance involves Native communities making local decisions and laws that best suit local needs, issues, and values. Of course, a tribal government can decide that unionism is not necessarily in the best interest of the community. This is the case with another kind of tribal ordinance enacted to regulate labor relations: a tribal right-to-work law. Whether prolabor or promanagement, most people agree that right-to-work laws are designed to undercut the strength of unionism. The rationalization for such laws is that unionism can stifle business and therefore capital investment. Desiring to make their reservations more marketable to outside investment, a handful of tribal governments have passed right-to-work laws. Since the *San Manuel* ruling, there has been a growing interest in these laws, and they have taken on an additional meaning. Many tribes that recently considered and passed right-to-work laws already had vibrant economies—in most cases because of tribal gaming. In these situations, the tribal ordinances can be seen as a reaction to how the NLRB's change in interpretation of labor law jeopardized tribal sovereignty. The ordinances bespeak a willingness to use tribal self-governance to directly strike back at union activism that has challenged tribal sovereignty rights, and they connote an aggressive (re)assertion of the remaining legal jurisdictional powers tribes have after *San Manuel*—a federal appellate court has already sustained tribal authority to pass right-to-work laws. Ultimately, this exercise of tribal self-determination threatens to compound the tensions between unions and indigenous communities.

The legal concept of a right-to-work code is a direct response to labor contract provisions known as union security agreements. Under collective bargaining procedures established by the NLRA, labor unions and management can negotiate union security agreements mandating that, as a condition of employment, workers join the union (or at least pay a portion of membership dues to the union) that represents their job classification. This provision is meant to protect the strength and existence of the union as a counterbalance to management's right to make hiring decisions—protecting a union from a management ploy to hire only people who oppose unions. There is an exception to the union security provision of the NLRA. State governments are allowed to pass laws prohibiting union security agreements, hence the term *right-to-work*, because these laws are thought to open the job market to anyone, regardless of his or her feelings about unions or willingness to join them.

The question of whether right-to-work laws are allowable in Indian Country was reviewed in 2002 by the Tenth Circuit of the U.S. Federal Court of Appeals in *National Labor Relations Board v. Pueblo of San Juan*. In this case, the tribal government had leased tribal land to a non-Indian timber company, which in turn negotiated a union security agreement with the union representing its employees. Enacting its rights of territorial sovereignty, the San Juan Pueblo Tribal Council then passed a right-to-work law outlawing the union security agreement; the union in turn sought an injunction against the tribe's right to pass this law. The union claimed that tribal governments did not qualify as the kind of governmental institutions outlined in the NLRA that are allowed to prohibit union security agreements. The NLRA decrees that "any State or Territory" can pass laws preventing union security agreements, and thus the question becomes whether a tribal government fits the categorical definition of "State or Territory" (29 U.S.C. § 158[a][3] 1994). Despite arguments to the contrary—that if Congress meant to put tribal governments on the same level as states and territories for this exemption of the NLRA, it would have specifically included them in this clause—tribal sovereignty prevailed.

Here, unlike the NLRB's and D.C. Circuit's *San Manuel* decisions, the Tenth Circuit ruled that the importance and precedence of tribal sovereignty were so significant that there was no basis for impinging on tribal governments' authority and their jurisdiction to make a law on this key aspect of labor relations on tribal land. Contrary to *San Manuel*, the *San Juan Pueblo* decision upheld the Indian canon of construction and explicitly rejected the *Tuscarora–Coeur d'Alene* test. This ruling is hugely significant for tribal self-governance because the *San Juan Pueblo* court takes the opposite approach of the *San Manuel* courts by placing "the burden of proving that Congress has [intentionally] abrogated tribal sovereign powers squarely on the [NLRB]" rather than forcing tribes to prove that Congress did not intend a federal law to apply to them (Singel

2004:728). The Tenth Circuit decision states: "Congress' silence as to the tribes can therefore hardly be taken as an affirmative divestment of their existing 'general authority, as sovereigns, to control economic activity' on territory within their jurisdictions." (*NLRB v. Pueblo of San Juan*, 276 F. 3d 1198, 2002 [10th Cir.]; quoting *Merrion v. Jicarilla Apache Tribe*, 455 U.S. at 137). Of course, this statement chronologically precedes but also significantly contradicts the logic of the NLRB's *San Manuel* decision on the applicability of the NLRA to Indian Country. But in deciding *San Manuel*, the NLRB attempted to minimize this contradiction by suggesting that at issue in *San Manuel* was a complete exemption from the NLRA whereas the authority to pass a right-to-work law concerned an exemption from only one provision of the NRLA. This is certainly not the strongest argument—attesting to inconsistencies in the NLRB's application of labor law (see Gross 1995; Zatz 2008, 2009). It seems pieced together to preserve the overall opinion on the general applicability of the NLRA and usefulness of the *Tuscarora–Coeur d'Alene* test. Although the D.C. Circuit has backed the NLRB's *San Manuel* opinion, the Tenth Circuit's decision in *San Juan Pueblo* may pose potential challenges for how the NLRB has decided to treat tribal economic development and labor relations.

The unpersuasive and equivocal way the NLRB squares *San Manuel* with *San Juan Pueblo* comes in part from the way union security agreements uniquely map onto tribal economic development. The NLRA delimits the notion of what is an acceptable union security agreement in a way that spans the functional breadth of a tribal economic enterprise: as something that functions both as a corporation and as a governmental entity. In codifying union security agreements, the NLRA states: "Nothing in this subchapter, or any other statute of the United States, shall preclude an employer from making an agreement with a labor organization to require as a condition of their employment membership therein" (29 U.S.C. § 158[a][3] 1994). This section recognizes the right of a corporation to establish a collaborative policy with unions that helps preserve unionism. The NLRA subsequently delimits this right by declaring: "Nothing in this subchapter shall be construed as authorizing the execution or application of agreements requiring membership in a labor organization as a condition of employment in any State or Territory in which such execution or application is prohibited by State or Territorial law" (29 U.S.C. § 164[9][b] 1994). This section allows regional legislative bodies to outlaw union security agreements. Tribal governing bodies effectively parallel both definitions. Under the latter section, they can outlaw union security agreements; under the former section, they can authorize tribal corporations to establish security agreements with labor unions. This example runs the gamut of tribal economic enterprises; they are simultaneously commercial and governmental exercises. That they are not readily divisible into separate commercial and governmental parts betrays the logical strain in the NLRB's attempt to reconcile governmental power to pass right-to-work laws with what it also calls the "typical commercial" features of tribal gaming corporations.

Moreover, the complexities of regulating the labor relations of tribal economic enterprises illustrate the limited, paradoxical, and often contradictory way in which the NLRB has tried to balance tribal sovereignty against its own authority. On the one hand, the "tribalness" of tribal corporations does not meet the NLRA definition of a government employer or what is termed a political subdivision, which is exempt from the NLRA. On the other hand, tribal governments are considered to meet the definition of a state or territory, which allows them to pass right-to-work laws. To some extent, this apparent contradiction does fit the liminal status the NLRB has designated to the economic activity of Native nations. A tribal economic enterprise is created by, maintained by, and in turn used to fund tribal governments, and in this respect it is the economic development arm of the tribal government—a fundamental part of the government. But in addition to a Native nation's ability to set up an economic development corporation, a tribal government can pass laws that regulate union security agreements. In considering these different functions of tribal governments, the (recent) NLRB has been committed to treating tribal labor relations like labor relations anywhere else in the United States. It has done so by focusing its rulings on the commercial aspects of tribal economic enterprises at the expense of their governmental functions. The Tenth Circuit's *San Juan Pueblo* ruling in favor of tribal right-to-work codes treats tribal governments like governmental entities, not like commercial entities. Again, this ruling might appear to directly contradict the logic of the NLRB's *San Manuel* ruling; however, the NLRB has reconciled its position with the Tenth Circuit's position by incorporating right-to-work laws into the commercial enterprise versus tribal traditional/governmental function dichotomy that the NLRB itself created to judge tribal labor relations. For the NLRB, the technical legal exemption that allows tribes to pass a right-to-work law merely fits within the category of "governmental function."

Maintaining the commercial enterprise versus tribal traditional/governmental dichotomy in the face of the incongruity posed by the *San Juan Pueblo* decision has the effect of delimiting a tribe's jurisdiction over its labor relations almost exclusively to right-to-work codes. Given that the NLRB will abdicate its regulatory authority only when tribal traditional/governmental functions are involved, passing a right-to-work law—a governmental function—proves to be the only option left for tribal governing bodies to maintain authority over tribal labor relations. This outcome was predicted by Singel even before the D.C. Circuit upheld the NLRB's *San Manuel* ruling.

> The likely outcome of the *San Manuel* and *Pueblo of San Juan* decisions is that tribes will likely attempt to minimize the threat of unionization by passing right-to-work statutes. Although this strategy allows tribes to exercise some degree of self-governance over labor relations, this strategy is at bottom a reactive and insufficient approach that will thwart the ability of tribes to develop more progressive and comprehensive labor policies that satisfy the specific needs of the tribal community. (Singel 2004:728)

Tribal right-to-work codes are by no means pervasive in Indian Country, but they are certainly gaining more attention as a possible solution to the D.C. Circuit's support of the NLRB's position on tribal labor relations. Yet, as Singel also asserts, right-to-work statutes are only a partial solution, and they are far from a productive resolution to the issue of tribal labor relations.

Despite the euphemistic phrase coined to describe statutes outlawing union security agreements, right-to-work codes are, at base, anti-union laws—perhaps the most effective legal tool to prevent unionism. Union security agreements are meant to counteract the practical advantages and financial power that management has over worker collective action. They solve the "free-rider" problem created by the legal fact that a union must represent all employees equally, even if not all employees choose to join the union and pay membership dues. By outlawing union security agreements, right-to-work laws undercut a union's financial support and contribute to the free-rider situation. They also make it even easier for employers to hire people predisposed to oppose collective action. Statistics and research are inconclusive as to whether right-to-work laws make for more productive workplaces or just more corporate profits.[20] But these ordinances are undoubtedly touted as a kind of market liberalization capable of increasing corporate investment; this alone should illustrate how promanagement the statutes are.[21]

Despite the anti-union, pro–corporate revenue agenda of right-to-work codes, it is important to *not* read tribal right-to-work statutes in the vein of a rich Indian discourse. There is nothing inherent in financial success—as the rich Indian backlash would have us believe—that would compel tribes to pass right-to-work laws or to be anti-union. Instead, tribal right-to-work codes must be understood in the context of tribal sovereignty and tribal capitalism. Then we can see tribal right-to-work laws, as Singel interprets them, as "reactive" and defensive. The turn toward right-to-work ordinances is a Native backlash against the aggressive tactics of labor unions and the policy making of the NLRB, a deployment of the only apparent legal alternative left. However, this explanation is by no means an apology for the highly negative effect these laws have on workers' rights. It is important to consider right-to-work laws within the context of tribal capitalism and the extent to which laws such as these hinder responsible tribal economic development. Singel forcefully makes this point, arguing that

> the passage of a right-to-work ordinance is essentially defensive. Once confronted with the threat of NLRA enforcement, tribes are forced to divert their attention away from the pursuit of a vision for community labor relations that may in fact embrace unions and promote organizing activity but impose restrictions on bargaining tactics where the employer provides essential public services. (Singel 2004:728)

She insightfully notes that employing the overtly anti-union policy of right-to-work might be the quickest solution to the serious threats presented by *San Manuel* but that there is nothing to suggest that this is the most healthful for economic development or a community as a whole in the long run. In the short term, right-to-work ordinances might gain tribal leadership more control over an influx of non-Native influences, such as unions and non-Native employees, in local tribal communities. But in the long run, such policies do not promote healthy and balanced relationships between management and employees, because they seek to strengthen management at the expense of workers. Moreover, right-to-work laws are comprehensive ordinances affecting all tribal corporations, not just those whose predominant workforce might be non-Native. Thus, right-to-work ordinances could have the most adverse effect of dividing the community when both management and employees are tribal members. Rather than create productive negotiations with their employees, some tribal leaders have closed off conversation about unionism by conflating pro-unionism with antisovereignty or, even worse, anti-unionism with defending sovereignty. This attitude comes from the same fearful position that led unions to attack sovereignty as being anti-union in the first place. In the end, tribal right-to-work laws do little to resolve the current tension between labor leaders and directors of tribal economic development and, more likely than not, will exacerbate the situation.

Conclusion

Several indigenous scholars strongly caution against uncritically employing Western political and legal models as the basis for structuring or reforming Indian governments and communities (see Alfred 1999; Champagne 2006; Porter 1997a, 1997b). Much of their concern revolves around the incompatibility of Western representational democracy, adversarial legal systems, and attention to individual rights with indigenous consensus-based governance, peacemaking dispute resolution, and broadly conceived collective responsibility. This is not to suggest that Western models are untenable for Native communities, but rather that indigenous governance can be most successful when based on a synthesis of traditional-, colonial-, and U.S. constitutional–based systems of governance (Champagne 2006). Equally important is that each of the hundreds of indigenous communities in the United States decide on the mix that is most beneficial for its unique and diverse needs and circumstances. Accepting this diversity does not mean that we cannot talk about similar experiences and shared circumstances. Indeed, tribal labor relations are potentially such an experience/circumstance and one whose regulation certainly requires a combination of governing forms.

What is unique about labor relations is that, despite coming out of market economic relations, they present certain issues that indigenous communities are well situated to handle. For example, the process of union-recognition decision making is not necessarily based on a consensus of the workers a union represents, but the most successful unions and union actions are the ones with broad-based appeal that address the concerns of the most workers possible. Additionally, the process of collective bargaining is, itself, consensus based; labor and management make proposals and counterproposals and negotiate until there is a compromise agreement. Moreover, for the most part, labor relations are based on collective rights, not individual rights; workers bargain for their collective benefit and security. What is more, when problems in labor relations boil down to an issue of an individual worker's rights, they are frequently solved through arbitration or mediation. This is essentially a peacemaking process and is certainly a process that could be easily adapted to indigenous forms of peacemaking. Given the proclivities of labor relations and the importance of sustaining tribal self-determination, tribal government–based regulation of labor relations appears to have great potential.

This regulation would require tribal governments to enact and enforce strong and clear labor relations law. The model with the most potential for success appears to combine the structure of federal and state labor codes with indigenous jurisprudence. As Champagne (2006:11–12) notes, compared with Anglo-American governing forms that share the same functions, "many traditional Native forms of government and political processes are not suitable to managing markets, bureaucratic, and competitive relations with state and local governments." Combining conventional U.S. labor codes with local Native implementation and dispute resolution would balance what both Anglo-American and indigenous political systems do well. Legal structures of establishing union recognition and fair bargaining procedures have been in place in the United States for nearly seventy-five years. Although they have been far from perfect and have recently favored the employer side, in principle they set a solid baseline for equitable relationships between workers and their managers. The success of these structures, though, relies on how they are implemented.

Indigenous methods for resolving disputes in ways that build consensus and sustain communal relations have been in place for thousands of years. Of course, modern tribal communities have a far from perfect record in avoiding internal conflict, but a commitment to indigenizing labor relations will go a long way toward harmonious, responsible economic development in Indian Country. The lessons from indigenized labor relations could create new models for dispute resolution that labor unions could implement in their negotiations outside Indian Country. Given the failed promise of the NLRA, exporting indigenous forms of labor relations could even provide the greater equity that unions seek in labor relations in the United States. By approaching tribal labor relations with an open mind and the spirit of innovation, labor unions and tribal leaders can fulfill the mutually beneficial potential of interdependent self-determination.

PART II
Organizing in Indian Country
Navajo Labor Relations

"The goal of the union is to be a voice for the people. To be there to help the people who can't, or are unable to speak up for themselves." This is what Anita John, a Navajo health-care worker, explained in one of our discussions about union organizing in Indian Country. Her words reveal a straightforward truth about the goals of unionism worldwide: at base, unions exist to represent the collective needs and desires of workers. When we look at the complicated political and legal maneuvers that circulate around the regulation of tribal labor relations, it is easy to lose sight of this basic goal. At the same time, Anita's plainspoken commentary obscures the political intricacies of tribal labor relations that manifest themselves as aggressive and defensive actions taken by labor unions, state and federal governing bodies, and tribal leaders. We see these aggressive and defensive maneuvers in action when tribal leaders pass right-to-work laws, when federal and state governments insist on regulatory authority over tribal economic development, or when unions use their political power to legislate union recognition without first mobilizing the employees they anticipate representing.

These aggressive and defensive actions can be seen in the California tribal gaming compacting process. During the 1990s, some California union leaders sought language that would guarantee their positions as collective bargaining agents. Many state legislators supported such contract provisions to maintain their political relationships with organized labor, and tribal leaders lobbied vehemently against these provisions. Missing from the debate over tribal labor relations was the perspective of the people working in tribal casinos. Unions tried to assume representation of these workers primarily through legislative action, a relatively retrogressive, "top-down" action reminiscent of much maligned models of business unionism. A "bottom-up" campaign that mobilizes workers is a more progressive and, frankly, more legitimate way to gain union representation. Most importantly, it focuses on the workers themselves.

Emphasis on workers is central to Anita's describing unions as "a voice for the people." Focusing on the laws and governmental bodies that compete to regulate tribal labor relations, as I do in part 1, tends to mask the actual people who are the subjects of tribal labor relations. The next three chapters provide a case study of labor relations at the Navajo Nation as a way to locate workers' roles in tribal labor relations. This study involves a different kind of triangulation between workers, unions, and tribal governments—one that focuses less on regulation and antagonistic relationships between unions and Native communities and more on how unions and Native peoples can work collaboratively to participate in tribal governance. I look at a Navajo example of how tribal labor relations overlap and interact with Navajo tribal politics, law, and development strategies. Examining these issues from a worker-centered perspective forces us to view indigenous self-determination and economic development differently—not from a perspective that emphasizes the actions and policies of federal agencies and centralized tribal governments. In the following chapters, I consider how workers can use tribal labor relations to comment on and participate in the processes of self-determination and economic development.

The Navajo Nation example revolves around a proposal to enact tribal self-determination by taking over the delivery of health care to Diné citizens. This proposal and the eventual takeover engendered a strong response from Navajo Nation health-care workers and the union that represented them, in the form of a highly organized union campaign and community-based grassroots protests. I examine this worker-centered response in three ways: (1) in chapter 4, by contextualizing the union campaign within the history of Navajo Nation politics and labor relations; (2) in chapter 5, by locating workers' participation in the campaign through their co-articulation with union organizers of the meanings of unionism in this context; and (3) in chapter 6, by examining health-care worker and community collaboration in grassroots protests.

Before shifting an in-depth focus to the Navajo Nation, it is helpful to understand the basics of this indigenous community. The Navajo Nation has the largest land base of any reservation in the United States. Navajoland spans more than 27,000 square miles (making it larger than one-fifth the total area of all U.S. states combined) and extends into Arizona, New Mexico, and Utah. The U.S. government recognized this land as the Navajo Reservation through the 1868 treaty signed with Navajo leaders at Fort Sumner. Since then, the land base has quadrupled in size. The treaty signaled the end of a horrific five-year internment of Navajos at Bosque Redondo in southern New Mexico. Navajos had been forcibly removed from Diné Bikéyah to Bosque Redondo on what is known as the Long Walk—a traumatic on-foot journey that killed many. After signing the treaty, Navajos were able to return to their land, which "Navajo teachings hold [is where] Navajos emerged here into this [world], that the Holy People determined...was the proper place for them to live" (Iverson 2002:3).

The tribe has nearly three hundred thousand members, making it second only to the Cherokee in number of members. Nearly 60 percent of those members live within Navajo Nation borders, making Diné Bikéyah the most populous indigenous nation in the United States (see Arizona Cooperative Extension 2008 for a summary of these demographics). Window Rock, Arizona, is the capital of the Navajo Nation. Within the governmental structure, there are 110 chapters, or community-based governments. The chapters elect eighty-eight representatives to the Navajo Nation Council, which is the legislative branch of the Navajo government. The other two branches are the executive branch, headed by a popularly elected president and vice president, and the judicial branch, consisting of trial courts and a supreme court, with three appellate justices appointed by the president and approved by the legislature.

four
Navajo Nation Politics and Pragmatic Unionism

Early in 2001, LIUNA initiated an organizing campaign to secure union representation for employees of the Navajo Area IHS. Anita John played an integral part in this campaign. She was a Navajo clerical worker at the Crownpoint Health Care Facility in Crownpoint, Navajo Nation (New Mexico). At the time, Anita had recently agreed to be one of two union stewards of LIUNA Local 1376 for the thirty-two-bed hospital, which serviced about twenty thousand Navajos. Unlike the situation at the tribal gaming casinos discussed in chapters 2 and 3, the fact that Anita was both a member of the tribe and a member of the union was more the norm than the exception. In fact, at Anita's hospital in Crownpoint and throughout the Navajo Area IHS, most healthcare workers are indigenous. The percentage of Native employees (mostly Navajo but also members of the Hopi, Zuni, and Paiute nations) varies across the service units, from 75 to 95 percent. This situation creates a different labor politics dynamic within the Navajo Area IHS than in tribal casinos, where most union-eligible employees are non-Native.

Indigenous workers such as Anita have interests and priorities as both employees and tribal members. These overlap, combine, and contradict in ways that are different from those of nontribal employees, whose citizenship interests tend to revolve around the intersection of nontribal political entities, such as a state, the United States, or even a foreign nation. Labor unions and the NLRB have treated nontribal citizens employed by tribal enterprises in Indian Country in ways akin to what Kim Barry (2006:19) has labeled "emigrant citizenship." Barry flips the discussion of the transnational flow of immigrant labor on its head by looking at what "emigrant states" do to protect the interests of citizens working and residing abroad and to foster migrants' allegiance to their home nations. Similarly, labor unions and the NLRB have acted in an "emigrant-state" fashion by trying to assert the political and economic interests of nontribal U.S. citizens working in Indian Country. My application of Barry's term to describe the United States is tinged with a bit of irony in that the American public usually thinks of the United States not as an *emigrant* but as an *immigrant* state, which takes in migrant workers and expects them to abide by local laws.[1] However, when nontribal members come onto the reservation for employment, even though most do not actually immigrate or emigrate, they do enter the domain of a Native sovereign nation. Workers' journeys across the reservation border are often part of their daily commute. But in the eyes of labor unions and federal courts that assert regulatory jurisdiction over Indian Country, the border is virtual. This is yet more evidence of the devaluation of tribal sovereignty and the continuation of settler colonialism.

Tribal labor relations with nontribal members have largely been framed around concern for the workplace rights of the nonmembers—what Aleinikoff (2002:115) calls the fear of a "democratic deficit." But when workers are also tribal members, more localized political and economic interests can shape labor relations. These localized interests can lead to a pragmatic approach in which unionism is used not only as a tool to improve work conditions or economic status but also as a force in community-based politics. I found that Navajo health-care workers demonstrated a localized, pragmatic conception of unionism both at the local level of Navajo communities serviced by health-care facilities and at the broader tribal level of the Navajo Nation as a whole: workers used the health-care union campaign to voice their concerns about responsible and accountable tribal leadership. Although this was not purely an economic issue, the workplace became a key venue in which to express the political and social will of tribal members invested both as community members and as employees.

LIUNA began its health-care-worker organizing campaign after the Navajo Nation Council (NNC) made its controversial 2001 decision to take over administration of IHS health care. Consequently, the union campaign provided the opportunity for tribal members to continue the public discussion of whether and how the tribal government should run health care. From a tribal worker's perspective, unionism served as one of many political tools to meet local tribal political ends; it was not merely an economic concern that began and ended in the workplace, detached from social, political, and cultural life. This pragmatic construal of unionism resembles what some of the most progressive unions in the United States call community-based unionism. It seeks to be based at all levels in a community and conceives of workplace issues as part of larger community issues and of unions as potentially progressive forces to advocate for all sorts of community justice issues outside the workplace.[2] LIUNA, the union that represented the Navajo health-care employees, used this approach as it tried to work with community values of tribal sovereignty (both cultural and political), not against them, even though few of the organizers were Navajo. Moreover, a small but significant number of employees in the Navajo health-care facilities were nontribal, but they, too, worked to make unionism useful to the local community and to local social and political ends. This is not to say that what was at stake for the non-Navajo folks was the same as for the Navajo folks or that Navajo health-care workers saw the union's usefulness for anything beyond their immediate political and economic needs. But in this context—the Navajo Nation tribal government's attempt to take over administration of health care—the union's goals and non-Navajo employees' interests became enmeshed with those of Navajo tribal members. This is significantly different from a situation in which nontribal union organizers and employees work against sovereignty to maintain a mode that they believe best ensures rights for workers (as workers, not necessarily as community members).

Although the Navajo health-care workers' union campaign was not free of adversarial relations, conflict did not generally manifest in terms of tribe versus union, as it has in the legal regulatory battle over tribal labor relations (see part 1). Here the union and the workers consciously did not construct their campaign in opposition to the concept of tribal sovereignty. Instead, they worked within the structure and laws of the Navajo Nation government to enjoin a public discussion about tribal self-determination and how best to enact it. In so doing, the union campaign echoed the discourse on tribal capitalism as a tribal communal endeavor undertaken not merely for the benefit of individuals but also for the community as a whole. What this campaign adds to the notion of tribal capitalism as responsible political economic development is a notion of the tribe's special responsibility to tribal employees as the human resources of the tribe. Finally, the campaign was centered on employing the Navajo Nation's tribal labor relations ordinances, which had been established to ensure balanced labor relations. The success of the campaign proves the importance and the success of Navajo collective bargaining codes in the way that they, too, can provide, as Anita puts it, "a voice for the people."

Providing a voice for the people is part of the rhetoric and high-minded agenda of any union campaign. But when considering tribal labor relations, it is also important to attend to how the notion of a politicized and classed voice is indigenized—that is, how a union campaign is molded and characterized by workers, union leaders, and tribal leaders to fit an indigenous community's political, economic, and cultural milieu. The Navajo Nation has a history of political tension being manifested in public discussion and criticism of the role of the centralized tribal government in setting policy. NNC decisions often come under scrutiny from the Navajo Nation general public and can have broad-reaching and long-term effects on how rank-and-file tribal citizens view tribal leadership. The NNC's proposal to take over administration of health care reflected this tendency in Navajo politics. In reaction, LIUNA's campaign involved much more than issues of workplace rights; it was equally about Navajo workers' feelings about the politics of the tribal administrative takeover and self-determination in general.

Tribal labor relations are frequently articulated in the politics of indigenous self-determination and economic development. Relations between workers and management are inherently bound up with the collective decision-making processes of an indigenous community. At the Navajo Nation, this situation has led to pragmatic approaches to unionism. I borrow this framework from Colleen O'Neill (2005), who found that Navajos have had an ambivalent and shifting relationship with unionism. I use the notion of a "pragmatic approach" to unionism in contrast to what might be called an ideological approach to unionism. For example, a common refrain from those long steeped in the ideological approach to the union movement is to "never cross a picket line," no matter what the circumstances—the idea being that unions should be supported at all costs. Some individual Navajos might also subscribe to this belief, but on the whole, Navajos have tended to view unionism with much less ideological fixity. To this community, it is less about a grand historical struggle between labor and management than about using unionism pragmatically to meet the needs of the local community.

Navajos have tended to use unions strategically for contextualized political purposes, not necessarily for the greater end of participating in a larger union movement. For its part, the Navajo Nation government has variously opposed and supported unionism based on specific circumstances and political advantages. Similarly, in some cases Navajo workers have fully participated in unions; in others, they have withheld active participation but not necessarily opposed unions. This is not to say that unionism and participating in unions have not been meaningful to many Navajo workers. Rather, their involvement in unions has been characterized by a pragmatic approach that seeks not just to gain conventional workplace protections but also to use unionism to strategically participate in indigenous community–based politics. If it is not directly clear how a union can be instrumental in a given workplace or community political situation, Navajos tend to remain relatively indifferent to unionism. However, it is worth noting that some forward-looking Navajos have tried to establish an indigenous Diné labor movement by setting up organizations to meet the specific needs of Navajo workers (O'Neill 2005). Even these have a pragmatic quality, because they are thought of as distinct from the larger American labor movement and international unions. The local Diné labor organizations focus on localized issues and needs, which are not always strictly workplace issues, and ones that Navajo workers feel larger labor organizations are not capable of or interested in handling (O'Neill 2005). The Campaign for Union Recognition dovetailed with this pragmatic approach to unionism; it became as much about workplace issues as about the local politics of self-determination.

The success of the Campaign for Union Recognition can be attributed to the conjoining of two forces particular to the Navajo Nation: a pragmatic approach to unionism and tension between Navajo people and their centralized tribal government. Before delving into the specifics of the Campaign for Union Recognition and the on-the-ground actions and interactions of union organizers and workers (chapter 5), this chapter contextualizes the campaign by discussing the history of Navajo politics and Navajo engagement with unionism. These histories illustrate the shifting, intermittent, and strategic nature of Navajo politics and tribal politics in general. Despite intense political feelings and occasional flare-ups of political stalemate or violence, tribal politics is not, as outsiders have often portrayed it, characterized by intense political factionalism that can produce only unsophisticated, avaricious, and dysfunctional governments. I believe that tribal politics is more aptly characterized as a public debate engaged in the process of making tribal self-determination happen. Tribal labor relations can be an important way for indigenous people to participate in public discussions about the political process of enacting tribal self-determination.

Commencing the Campaign for Union Recognition

LIUNA has been representing health-care workers of the Navajo Area IHS for more than thirty years.[3] Before organizing on-reservation workers, LIUNA represented many Navajo and other Native workers in off-reservation employment in major cities in the Southwest. These were not health-care workers, but in most cases construction workers. This should not be surprising, given that construction workers are the mainstay of and the original workers organized by LIUNA. Nor should it be surprising that LIUNA is willing to represent indigenous people. Founded in 1903 to represent hod carriers and building laborers, LIUNA has long been an advocate for the rights of workers of color. The union was founded in part by African American construction workers; in the 1920s LIUNA denied membership to segregated locals; and in the 1970s the union advocated for Latino workers' rights. More recently, LIUNA has been among the progressive unions that use community unionism techniques to work for immigrant rights (Fink 2003; Gordon 2007). Despite its progressive agenda, LIUNA has not been free from scandal. In the late 1990s and early 2000s, the union's credibility was tarnished by allegations of connections to Mafia bosses in New York and Illinois and the conviction of some local union leaders. The controversy was resolved when the union brought in independent reviewers and investigators to help remove these leaders and then held elections for new leadership in the locals.

This happened in construction worker locals, not in the division of LIUNA that represents Navajo Area IHS employees. This division is known as the Public Employee Department; it consists of about 15 percent of the half million members of LIUNA. In addition to representing public (municipal, state, and federal) employees throughout the country, the Public Employee Department organizes tribal and federal employees all over Indian Country, today representing more than three thousand employees in jobs connected to more than forty tribal communities. Most, as at the Navajo Nation, are IHS employees. Representation of Navajo health-care workers has also not gone without bumps in the road. In 2000, because of accounting irregularities and potential embezzlement of union funds by local union leaders, international representatives from the Public Employee Department put the local under "emergency supervision of the international union." The international union sorted out the bookkeeping and removed offending union officers (Tohtsoni 2000). This situation generated some public tension.

Some local Navajos were concerned about intervention by the international union. Others understood the necessity for this action and that the international union was not interested in wresting local control from Navajo health-care employees. Within a few months, after reforms were made and new local leadership elected, local control was restored. On the heels of this incident came a potentially much more significant challenge to local representation of Navajo health-care workers.[4]

Early in 2001, the Navajo tribal government began in earnest to implement the long-proposed process of taking over management and administration from the federally run Indian IHS. The passage of Public Law 93-638 allowed tribal nation governments to more easily replace the federal government as administrators of social services. This process is commonly called "going 638" or "taking" a service 638. In taking the Navajo Area IHS 638, the NNC's stated goals were to improve the quality of health care and to enact the right of political and economic self-determination. The proposed change of administration would also end IHS employees' collective bargaining agreement with the federal government. Consequently, any collective bargaining rights or agreements would have to be renegotiated with the new management, the Navajo Health Care System Corporation, a tribal enterprise authorized by the NNC. Thus, in advance of final approval of the proposed takeover, LIUNA began a proactive campaign to preserve Navajo Area IHS workers' collective bargaining rights and to maintain its position as the workers' bargaining representative.

It is not uncommon for private-sector labor contracts to contain provisions that allow unions to retain representation rights after changes in management; however, in Indian Country, the situation was significantly different. There was not going to be just a change of corporate management, but also of governing and regulating bodies—from the federal government and federal labor relations authority to the NNC and Navajo Nation's collective bargaining laws. Under tribal labor relations codes, for union recognition to be granted, a union must prove that 55 percent of the workers in a given bargaining unit support collective bargaining (see chapter 3). Although it is easier for a union to accomplish a card-check recognition than to hold a representation election, this particular change in regulation of tribal labor relations would require significant work on the part of LIUNA, which would effectively have to start over the representation process from square one. LIUNA organizers believed that they needed to be well prepared for the potential change, so in March 2001, LIUNA kicked off the Campaign for Union Recognition, even though the tribal government had not yet approved the takeover of health care. Venturing into uncharted waters—the Navajo Nation's collective bargaining code had existed for more than fifteen years, but no union had ever employed it—LIUNA put together a petition for workers to declare their desire for union representation. LIUNA sent four organizers from its international offices in Sacramento and Phoenix to the Navajo Nation to work with the local's executive board, as well as with stewards and volunteer organizers at each service unit, to persuade Navajo Area IHS employees to sign a petition requesting collective bargaining rights from the Navajo Nation.

In five months, the professional organizers, along with many local volunteer employees, successfully convinced more than 55 percent of all Navajo Area IHS employees—working at more than twelve different facilities—to sign a petition declaring their support for collective bargaining and their desire for LIUNA to represent them.[5] The effort represented a significant endorsement of unionization for Navajo Area IHS workers. It was also a remarkable organizing effort. In previous campaigns in the Navajo Area and other IHS service units, LIUNA generally had convinced only about 30 percent of employees to make similar commitments to support union representation.[6] Because the Navajo labor relations code called for unions to garner support from 55 percent of a collective bargaining unit, LIUNA had to redouble its organizing efforts. And it was very successful in doing so. At certain Navajo Area IHS service facilities, support went above 55 percent, with 60 to 90 percent of workers signing the petition for union recognition. This was impressive, given that the union had recently received some unfavorable press about the faulty bookkeeping and trusteeship of the local only months before. Even more remarkable than LIUNA, increasing its support from 30 percent to 60 percent and more was the proportion of those willing to sign the petition supporting unionization, compared with those who explicitly declined to sign. I observed organizers talking to several hundred workers, and only five were unwilling to sign. The success rate impressed the leaders of the campaign and workers who participated in it as much as it did me.[7]

The principles of direct organizing formed the basis of the campaign. LIUNA ran a grassroots-style campaign that sought to talk to as many workers as possible through face-to-face interaction. Such labor-intensive campaigns often run for a short time and rely significantly on professional organizers, but they also necessitate local community support to supplement the work of professional organizers. In the Campaign for Union Recognition, the four professional organizers put many of their other union duties on hold during the six-month campaign. They came to the Navajo Nation in one-day to one-week stints, spending their time engaging employees in face-to-face conversations to mobilize support for unionization. Support was made tangible by the act of signing the petition. Although the legally binding threshold was signatures from 55 percent of employees, intensive campaigns such as this seek to contact every employee possible—both to gain future bargaining power by garnering as much support as possible and to create a percentage cushion for duplicate, illegible, or even illegitimate signatures. To meet the ambitious contact goal, local Navajo Area IHS workers were indispensable to the Campaign for Union Recognition. They circulated petitions, persuaded coworkers to sign, and introduced them to the professional organizers.

Throughout the campaign, LIUNA proactively tried to put workers in a position to claim union recognition under the Navajo Nation collective bargaining laws if Navajo health care did go 638. This forward thinking and advance planning turned out to be quite significant; it meant that the Campaign for Union Recognition overlapped with Navajo public debate over the direction of reservation health care. For the most part, the union remained on the sideline of the public debate, officially staying neutral about the issue of 638 and whether the tribe should take over health care. LIUNA was careful not to take a stance that could be perceived as being against Diné sovereignty and self-determination. Yet, the issue always loomed large in face-to-face organizing conversations between union organizers and Navajo health-care workers. Both parties implicitly and explicitly referenced aspects of the public debate. The issues surfaced in various interlocking forms, such as dissatisfaction with how the decision to operationalize the takeover was being made and perceptions of how tribal leaders should be responsible to the people they represented and served. A few workers even chastised organizers, saying that LIUNA should have taken a more proactive stance against the takeover despite the appearance of interfering with tribal sovereignty. Workers also expressed concerns about how 638 would change the delivery of health care for the community and how it could change work conditions. This dialogue in turn led to discussions of how union representation could provide employees with a voice after a tribal administrative takeover.

The Politics of Navajo Self-Governance and Self-Determination

The backdrop for the Navajo Nation's attempted takeover of health care is the 1975 passage of the Indian Self-Determination and Education Assistance Act. The goal of this federal act was to facilitate tribal self-determination by moving social services that were under the purview of federal agencies to local tribal management. The law was meant to increase tribal sovereignty both by putting control of social services in the hands of local people, who better understood local needs and values, and by expanding the operations and responsibilities of tribal governance. It is important to note that the act was not a federal award of sovereignty, but rather the enactment of a procedural system that made it easier for tribes to reclaim and put to use sovereign rights they had always possessed.

George Castile (1998:xv) maintains that the Indian Self-Determination Act was a critically important shift in federal Indian policy because it was an "acknowledgement of the permanency of Indian communities and encouragement of their self-governance." Much as, forty years earlier, the IRA had been a policy response to the General Allotment Act, the Self-Determination Act was a response to termination-era policies of the 1950s and 1960s, which attempted to completely sever tribal communities from the federal government's trust responsibility and to abolish the notion of Indian Country and tribal citizenship. Self-determination ushered in a renewed support for tribal self-governance under the trust and guardianship of the federal government. Under 638, tribal governments apply for contracts with the federal government that will maintain federal financial support for civil and social services but allow local tribal entities to administer the funds and manage the programs. The most common services to go 638, such as schools, health care, police, and firefighting, are those previously controlled by the BIA and the IHS. However, 638 has not transformed Indian Country social services overnight. To this day, most tribes employ a selective, not a comprehensive, approach to taking social services 638, and many tribes have not established 638 contracts at all—partly because of the BIA's bureaucratic reluctance to fulfill a policy agenda effectively meant to produce its own obsolescence.

An equally important factor is the mixed opinions about 638 from inside Indian Country (Castile 2006). For example, successfully taking over certain social services requires administrative and managerial capacities that, for various reasons, not all tribal communities possess. Moreover, some Native peoples believe that, on principle, their tribal government should not take given services 638. Many tribes have their services guaranteed by treaty rights; taking these services 638 could be interpreted as letting the federal government off the hook for its treaty responsibilities. In a similar vein, some Natives worry that 638 is a backhanded form of termination. They are concerned that tribes successfully administering their own social services would set a dangerous precedent, causing the federal government to declare that tribes no longer need aid and sovereign rights (Castile 1998, 2006).[8] This apprehension has increasing validity, given the growth of rich Indian discourse that seeks to undercut sovereignty (see chapters 2 and 3). Lastly, the Self-Determination Act has been criticized because it does not ensure complete sovereignty. Taking an entity 638 does not constitute complete independence from the federal government, because the money to run the civic programs still comes from the federal government (e.g., Ickes 1981). Dependency is further manifested by the fact that the federal government must approve 638 contracts and has complete control over the amount of money granted to tribes even after 638 contracts are in place (Barsh and Trosper 1978). However, rather than think of 638 as flat-out colonial dependency, it may be more practical to think of it as foreign aid and as an example of interdependent sovereignty.

Indeed, from the perspective of tribal communities and tribal governments, the Indian Self-Determination Act is about more than just increased local governmental functions; it is also about economic development. This perspective reflects the federal government's inspiration for creating the act. The founding principles of the Indian Self-Determination Act came out of President Lyndon Johnson's War on Poverty and the Office of Economic Opportunity's Community Action Program (Castile 1998, 2006). The former was particularly successful in creating new economic opportunities in Native communities, which likely would have never happened under the more conservative BIA. In practice, establishing a 638 contract can be very important to tribal economies because in most Native communities, the civil service is the largest job sector (Castile 2006). Thus, taking certain services 638 increases a tribal community's control over and opportunities for economic development. And often the process of going 638 can increase the money available to tribes to run the social services. Key here is that as a tribe controls how funds are spent and takes control of decisions about how governance connects to developing a tribe's economy, it is creating jobs, promoting certain industries, and prioritizing the use of the community's natural, human, and technical resources.

Yet, as Castile (2006:114) notes, this situation also can pose significant challenges to Native communities because "the vastly increased control of resources, particularly jobs, by tribal chairs has led to more to fight about." Whether the process leads to actual fighting or just contentious democratic debate about whether and how tribal governments should take certain services 638 varies from circumstance to circumstance. It suffices to say that there are multiple views on 638 within Indian Country in general and within each indigenous community.

Ultimately, these issues surfaced within the Navajo Nation during the NNC's bid to take health care 638. Promotion of and concern about going 638 appeared in multiple forms of public discourse as both formal and informal political debates. But before going into the details of this situation, it is useful to review some aspects of contemporary political debate in Indian Country and the Navajo Nation in general. Indigenous nation politics can be exceptional in that big-impact and far-reaching nationhood decision making is often done within the context of highly localized and relatively small demographic politics. This process more easily enables consensus-based decision making and at the same time can empower multiple small and competing opposition groups. Unlike mainstream U.S. politics, tribal politics is rarely party driven.[9] This is not to say that there are not durable and institutionalized political affiliations in Native communities, but these generally take the form of clan- or kin-based politics. The lack of party politics also does not mean that tribal politics is not ideological; rather, tribal politics in Indian Country does not necessarily follow the conventional ideological regimes of U.S. national politics, such as conservatives versus liberals, Republicans versus Democrats, or rural versus urban.[10] More commonly, perspectives within tribal political debates and electoral campaigns are situational, contingent, and episodic. This situation is thought to lead to a certain amount of political instability in indigenous communities. At the same time, contentious political debate "can be socially and politically healthy; it instills a vigor in tribal governments in the process of resolving [conflict]" (Bee 1999:286).

The most acrimonious, scandalous, and in some cases outright violent tribal political confrontations—such as the near civil war on the Pine Ridge Reservation in the 1970s, the Peter MacDonald standoff and removal at the Navajo Nation in 1989, and more recent battles over disenrollment with the Cherokee Nation of Oklahoma and some California Native nations—get the most public attention. But these are far from the standard in tribal political relations. Most political debates in Indian Country, like small-scale debates anywhere, are handled through civil debate, day-to-day political actions, or the ballot box. Nonetheless, a considerable amount of academic energy—particularly in the 1960s—has been spent describing tribal politics as disruptive or unresolvable "factionalism" (Fowler 2004).[11] Although Fowler notes that such studies were on the wane by the 1970s, the diametric oppositions reified by these studies—such as progressives and conservatives, mixed-bloods and full-bloods, and Christians and traditionalists—still die hard in the popular imagination, despite recent academic attempts to undercut them.

It is telling that the analytic terms used to label a faction usually express the faction's relationship to Europeans and Euro-Americans, not to its own community members (Kugel 1985). For example, the binary "traditionalist" and "progressive" labels designate factions according to how they relate to Euro-American culture, not how they relate to each other. Thus, not only have outside forces tried to manipulate differences of opinion in Indian communities for their own social, political, and economic ends, but also the terminology used to describe Native politics has a built-in foreign bias that obscures the complexity and diversity of opinion found in tribal communities (Lewis 1991). It is safe to say that internal contention in tribal politics is not merely a postcontact phenomenon. However, the looming presence of the federal government and the institutionalized power it maintains over Indian communities complicate and muddle tribal politics (Bee 1999; Biolsi 1992; Holm 1985; Kugel 1985). Before the colonial restrictions placed on tribal communities, extreme differences were solved by a subgroup of a community moving away and starting anew. But today "dissidents" cannot just leave and set up shop somewhere else. They are bound to the tribal government (and thus the federal government) for all official, financial, and institutional purposes—otherwise, Native groups have no recognized authority to enter into contracts or to sustain legal rights (Lurie 1976, 1986).[12] Tribal communities have to work through or live with disagreements over what constitutes appropriate behavior and what direction the community should move. Rather than factional binaries, this means multiple, intermittent political perspectives that can vary from issue to issue and even manifest in complete disengagement from tribal-level politics. Some even give up hope of salvaging any utility out of a centralized tribal government, which can lead to genuine problems of legitimacy for tribal governments. For all these reasons, it is important to focus on the nature of political contention in specific tribal contexts.

Political debate in Navajoland usually takes the form of tension between the people and the centralized tribal government concerning questions of the legitimacy of the tribal government and the actions of some of its leaders. This has manifested several ways throughout the modern history of the Navajo Nation and is still one of the most important aspects in the political life of the tribe as the Navajo body politic currently debates how to reform tribal governance. Much of the Navajo people's lack of investment in centralized government can be traced back to pre- and early reservation days, when a strong centralized government was never a fundamental feature of political life. Traditionally, the Diné thought of themselves as a cohesive community sharing common cultural, language, and territorial boundaries, "but their political organization, in general did not extend beyond local bands that were led by headmen" (Wilkins 2002:95). Periodically, the local leaders would have a regional meeting to discuss large political issues, but power clearly did not rest primarily in these more centralized forms of governance. European colonialism demands centralization of power: indigenous communities had to join for common defense against colonialism and to meet European expectations of political negotiation with a centralized leadership—even if the communities did not recognize the legitimacy of the centralized leadership. The Navajos were no exception. The Spanish and then Euro-Americans expected to deal with and negotiate treaties with a small group of leaders who would represent all Navajos, despite the fact that these leaders may not have been representatives in the way that Europeans conceived of political leadership (Denetdale 2007; Wilkins 2002). Although some Navajo leaders were held in high esteem for how they dealt with whites, the forced emphasis on centralized governance created political tension and resentment between Navajo people and their leaders.

U.S. settler colonialism in Navajoland intensified this tension, particularly with the advent of the modern tribal government. The first Navajo tribal council was not established by the will of the people, but appointed by forces outside the tribe. In 1923, at the behest of oil companies that wanted access to the natural resources at Navajoland, the Department of the Interior established and maintained strong control over a Navajo tribal council, which acted primarily as a business council to sign leases with resource extraction companies (Wilkins 2002). A decade later, when given the opportunity to establish a tribal constitution to further solidify a central government, the Navajo people rejected it and instead lived for years with a tribal code that established rules for running the tribal council and various other aspects of governance and tribal life. The more recent history of the centralized tribal government has at times been marred by political scandal and financial impropriety on the part of tribal leaders, leading to national attention and even some prison sentences. Other allegations did not produce convictions but created cynicism about leaders of the centralized tribal government.

Nonetheless, the Navajo Nation government is one of the most sophisticated and well-developed governments in Indian Country. Although Navajo people certainly have their frustrations with it, most still actively engage it as a viable political system and participate in the processes of refining governance in ways that make it more useful to the people and better fit commonly held Navajo values. For example, the Navajo have enacted several reforms in an effort to temper the political power of the centralized government and to distribute it across local communities, creating a political system in which, ideally, local and centralized governments can work in a complementary fashion. In the late 1980s, when it appeared that too much power rested in the hands of the tribal chairman, the tribal council took steps to further separate legislative and executive powers. Among the reforms was the changing of the tribal chairman to a president and the removal of the president's duty as speaker of the tribal council, instead creating a new position, the NNC speaker, who would be elected from the council body (not the population at large) and would share some key leadership duties with the tribal president (Wilkins 1999, 2002). Recently, some have suggested that these reforms give too much power to the legislative branch, and the current Navajo Nation president, Joe Shirley, has spearheaded an effort—supported by many tribal members—to give the president line-item veto power and to significantly decrease the size of the tribal council, from eighty-eight to twenty-four representatives, to make it more efficient and to make the representatives more responsible to their constituents (Begay 2009; Navajo Nation Office of the President and Vice President 2008a, 2008b, 2008c).

Perhaps most important for the issue of decentralized governance, the NNC passed the Local Governance Act in 1998 to strengthen the governing powers of chapters. The NNC sought to distribute power to local communities because it recognized that "Navajo Nation Chapters are the foundation of the Navajo Nation Government" (Wilkins 1999:146). Chapters, as local municipal forms of governance, retain power over local issues such as land rights and usage. Chapter houses, the local chambers of political life, are grassroots hubs of active political participation among Navajos, demonstrating the key value that Navajos place on decentralized governance (Wilkins 1999). Their popularity, along with other aspects of Navajo political life, illustrates that Navajo politics cannot be understood in the oversimplified political binary of progressive versus traditionalists. On the contrary, during the past seventy-five years, Navajo tribal politics has seen its fair share of political tension, most significantly, circulating around the centralized tribal government and the office of the presidency.

The two most dramatic political episodes since the territorial consolidation of the reservation arguably have been the events surrounding livestock reduction and Peter MacDonald's final presidency (Iverson and Roessel 2002; Young 1978). The contention in these episodes cannot be easily reduced to the progressive–traditionalist divide, in which the latter faction distrusts the former for "employing Western structures" and the former accuses the latter of "not being able to adapt with the times." Rather, centralized Navajo governmental authority makes a critical policy decision whose potential or actual adverse effect creates political tension around which oppositional factions can develop. In general, these factions, or "floating coalitions of interest," as Robert Berkhofer (Lewis 1991:140) puts it, are contingent upon the details of the policy decision, yet they can engender political resentment for a long time.

At the Navajo Nation, for example, the NNC cooperated with John Collier, head of the Office of Indian Affairs (OIA),[13] and his plan to drastically reduce the number of livestock throughout the reservation in the 1930s. The plan was a solution to erosion that was putatively being caused by overgrazing. On the one hand, the motivations behind this initiative can be interpreted sympathetically as an attempt to save Navajos from an impending ecological disaster. On the other hand, they can be read cynically as a selfish safeguard of the federal government's massive financial and political investment in the Boulder (Hoover) Dam, which was in danger of being rendered worthless by erosion-induced silt runoff (Iverson and Roessel 2002; Parman 1976). Irrespective of the policy's intentions of the policy, the result was nothing less than paternalistic colonialism—even Felix Cohen, John Collier's legal right-hand man, said as much at the time (Iverson and Roessel 2002).

Because livestock was a fundamental part of most Navajos' economic, religious, and cultural lives, many could not understand the purpose of the OIA policy. The early twentieth century saw a rapid increase in the number of Navajo sheep, goats, cattle, and horses, and the size of a herd equated to a family's wealth, community prestige, social position, and overall well-being (Iverson and Roessel 2002). Fred Nelson, a Navajo from the western part of the reservation, argued during an NNC debate over livestock reduction: "For the white people the good old dollar is where they get their substance of life and the Navajos get their substance of life from the goats and the sheep, so it would not be fair to the Navajo to give up their goats and not the white people part of their dollars" (Parman 1976:55). Nelson expressed the extent to which Navajos felt that the fundamental role of livestock in their community was not being respected and that the Navajos were being forced to suffer unequally the burden of overgrazing. The rapid growth of livestock had clearly led to an overextension of the carrying capacity of the reservation borders. The Navajo solution to this problem was an increase in the size of the reservation, along with a more modest, natural, and self-imposed reduction in livestock. But local white landowners neighboring the reservation would not hear of it, and not surprisingly, the federal government sided with them. Ultimately, feeling hemmed in by pressure from John Collier and the OIA and holding out hope for an increase in reservation size in exchange for agreeing to the federal government's plan, the NNC consented to livestock reduction. The trauma eventually caused by livestock reduction engendered significant resentment toward centralized Navajo authority and those who had approved the reduction plan. The political repercussions were felt in a polarization of the body politic over the issue and in the subsequent rejection of the IRA and its centralized tribal governance.

Implementation of the stock culling was a disaster from the perspective of the Navajo. In many cases, it amounted to more of a massacre than a systematic downsizing of herds. The range men responsible for the culling rarely spoke Diné or bothered to explain what was happening beyond stating that the animals were to be killed on John Collier's orders (Iverson and Roessel 2002; Parman 1976). There were many reports of animals being shot and left to rot (Iverson and Roessel 2002; Roessel and Johnson 1974). As implementation went on, resistance and opposition began to grow. Resistance ran the gamut, from mild forms of noncompliance, to signing petitions and lobbying Congress, to threatening range men and even kidnapping an OIA superintendent (Roessel and Johnson 1974). Opposition organized behind Jacob Morgan, who rose to prominence as a critic of the reduction program and the Navajo tribal council leadership that had approved it—particularly Chee Dodge and his son Tom, leading figures on the council and members of perhaps the wealthiest Navajo family at the time.

The political conflict over livestock reduction became bitter. It spilled into the IRA election and tribal governance in general. The way Collier had set up the IRA, each tribe could vote on whether it wanted to be organized under the law with a constitutional government. Tribal-wide referendums provided significant opportunity for the expression of political differences in indigenous communities throughout Indian Country—a little less than 60 percent of the tribes voting ultimately rejected an IRA constitutional government (Biolsi 1992; Kelly 1975).[14] Navajos rejected the IRA in a relatively close election, 8,197 to 7,679. Dodge offered lukewarm support for the IRA, and Morgan campaigned vehemently against it. This vote can be read not so much as a vote on the IRA but as "a referendum on the current state of Navajo affairs" and as an expression of distrust of the federal government and the NNC because of the livestock reduction debacle. The vote also helped increase Morgan's political power. Iverson and Roessel (2002:157) note: "The anger felt by many Diné about the heavy-handed tactics of the government naturally encouraged a groundswell of popular support for Morgan and antagonism toward federal officials." Eventually, Morgan parlayed this support into replacing Tom Dodge on the council.

Resistance to livestock reduction and the IRA grew extremely strong; OIA officials worried that political tension might divide the reservation in two (Parman 1976). But it is important to recognize that the differences between Morgan and the Dodges and their respective supporters stemmed from a specific issue. Each controversy had its roots in a specific policy decision; for example, how tribal resources such as livestock and oil revenues were to be managed, or whether Peyotism should be tolerated (Young 1978). The political tension was not the result of abstract allegiances to Eurocentric binaries such as progressives versus conservatives or Christians versus traditionalists.

Another influential episode of Navajo political contention revolved around the final administration of Navajo Nation chairman Peter MacDonald. Leading up to this episode, two men, Peter MacDonald and Peterson Zah, had dominated the Navajo political scene between 1970 and 1994. MacDonald held the office for three terms in the early part of this period, and then the two men alternated chairman election victories every four years, from 1982 to 1994. Both men had community activist backgrounds and had made names for themselves in the 1960s by participating in important community programs on the reservation that were offshoots of the Office of Economic Opportunity. MacDonald was the first director of the Office of Navajo Economic Opportunity—a grassroots program that, like other Office of Economic Opportunity initiatives, worked to uplift the community on several fronts, such as legal services, housing, cultural centers, youth groups, educational and job training, and addiction treatment. Zah helped start Diné Be'iiná' Náhiilna' Bee Agha'diit'aahii (DNA) Legal Services—a community-based legal-aid program.[15] The political rivalry between the two men generated passionate support across the Navajo Nation (Iverson and Roessell 2002). Much of the political tension and campaign sniping generated by the men revolved around differing opinions on how to run the centralized tribal government and its purpose. MacDonald was known as an outspoken and often combative leader who was admired for his aggressive defense of Navajo political and economic interests. He made it his goal to consolidate power in the tribal chairman's position, but ultimately this led to accusations of excessive behavior. The criticism came from Zah particularly in the 1982 campaign, when he first defeated MacDonald. Iverson and Roessell (2002:272) contend that "many Diné voters responded enthusiastically to his goals of decentralization and a less imperial chairmanship...[in] his triumph, Zah declared it to be the end of 'unbalanced, unresponsive government.'" But MacDonald did not disappear, and in fact he later would both replace Zah and be replaced by Zah yet again after similar political excess. Clearly, the tension between the two candidates reverberates a larger theme in Navajo politics: public debate over the power and role of the centralized government. This debate manifested in tension between the need for responsive, locally attuned government that effectively serves the people and a strong centralized power that can advocate for the people when confronting larger political and economic entities such as states, corporations, other tribes, and the federal government.

Much of the strong political feeling came to a head during MacDonald's last term as chairman. In 1986 MacDonald defeated Zah and soon began what would be the end of his professional political career. His term was marred by scandal that greatly intensified political contention on the reservation. Only months after being inaugurated, MacDonald had the tribal newspaper closed down, ostensibly for financial reasons but arguably because the paper had supported Zah in the election and had publicly criticized MacDonald (Iverson and Roesell 2002). This act was a portent of the political excesses to come. Half a year later, the Navajo Nation, under the recommendation and direction of Chairman MacDonald, completed its largest purchase of land ever. In addition to providing potential economic benefit for the tribe as a whole, the property proved to be a windfall for MacDonald personally—as well as his political downfall. It was revealed that MacDonald and his associates had received hundreds of thousands of dollars in bribes, kickbacks, and sweetheart contracts. As details of these deals came out over the next year and half, Congress began investigating MacDonald. Then the NNC put MacDonald and many of his staff members on administrative leave, and although he appealed, the Navajo Supreme Court upheld the council's actions. The political tensions reached their apex as the NNC started its spring term of 1989, when MacDonald supporters protested outside NNC chambers. A few months after these passionate demonstrations, tempers boiled over. Riots over who was in charge of the tribal police erupted outside tribal administrative buildings. When the dust settled, two people were dead and six more injured (Iverson and Roessel 2002). Ultimately, a federal grand jury convicted MacDonald for his role in the riot and sent him to federal prison. Zah was elected in 1990 to replace him.

Iverson and Roessell (2002:291) liken the tumult surrounding MacDonald's last term and summary removal from office to a massive earthquake whose aftershocks are still being felt in Window Rock and throughout the Navajo Nation as a whole: "The resulting turmoil in the summer of 1989 and the memories that remain from this troubled time are a bitter and lasting legacy of the most traumatic time in Navajo life since livestock reduction." Indeed, the two presidents following Zah were each removed for financial improprieties. Russell and Henderson (1999) and Wilkins (2002) note the impact that MacDonald and Zah still have on tribal elections and voting patterns, in terms of how people vote and suppression of voting. But the legacy of this period of intense political contention is not all negative.

Much in the same way Bee (1999) argues that contentious political debate can bring about positive change, the MacDonald political scandal directly motivated comprehensive reform to the Navajo political system and tribal code. MacDonald's administration made apparent the need to balance and distribute the power of the tribal chairman. Indeed, the subsequent resolution to amend the Navajo Nation tribal code opens by stating:

> Recent controversy involving the leadership of the Navajo Nation has demonstrated that the present Navajo Nation Government structure allows too much centralized power without real checks on the exercise of power. Experience shows that this deficiency in the government structure allows for, invites and has resulted in the abuse of power. (Wilkins 1999:App. G)

The key solution provided by this resolution was to split the power of the chairman into a legislative and an executive branch. The legislative branch would have a speaker of the council, nominated by the executive branch and elected by the council, who would run the operations of the NNC. The reform also transformed the chairman and vice chairman into the president and vice president, made them the top offices of the executive branch, and diminished their direct power over the NNC. Ironically, it was MacDonald's excessive use of the power of the Navajo Nation tribal chairmanship that resulted in a much more balanced distribution of political power and access to tribal resources. His political excess—epitomized in the riot that he and his supporters provoked—garnered the Navajo Nation a great deal of public attention from the non-Indian public. The public attention frequently took a patronizing form, playing upon primitivist stereotypes implying that Indian Country politics were inherently chaotic and corrupt and could not operate in a peaceful and rational fashion. The legislative response to the MacDonald episode proved just the opposite to be true.

Nonetheless, as Wilkins (2002) points out, there is still work to be done. He contends that as important as it was for the tribal council to amend the tribal code, "the Navajo people have still not had nor have they taken the opportunity via a referendum/initiative to express their collective will about what shape Diné democracy should be like, and this needs to be rectified" (Wilkins 2002:125). Until issues such as this do come before the people, political tension between the decision makers in the NNC and the people as a whole will continue. This same kind of tension resurfaced in the decision to exercise tribal self-determination over the Navajo Area IHS. Like the livestock reduction plan and the controversies surrounding Peter MacDonald's land dealing, the potential change in health-care administration brought out significant public debate over whether the change would benefit the Diné as a whole and how much power and authority should be granted to the centralized government.

Political debate in tribal communities is often rooted in questions about the supervision of tribal resources. In their most contentious forms, debates manifest in criticism of specific tribal leaders or the centralized government for perceived unfair distribution of and mishandling of resources (Bee 1999; Holm 1985; Lurie 1976, 1986). Robert Bee (1999:288) maintains that accusations of poor tribal leadership usually come in three forms: "1) nepotism in assigning paid positions in the tribal administration; or 2) misappropriation of tribal funds for personal use; or 3) actions that cut off some constituents' receipt of benefits" (see also Lurie 1976, 1986 for a similar formulation). These concerns could be applied to any tribal government policy decision, but they are particularly relevant to enacting self-determination contracts because of the way 638 takeovers combine local control of political and economic resources. The presence of these concerns in community discussions over things such as 638 contracting does not necessarily mean that tribal leadership is in fact guilty of the accusations. Rather, we can read these concerns as a discursive attempt to intensify public accountability of leadership and collectively work through the meaning of legitimate and responsible tribal leadership. Sometimes public criticism is effective and sometimes it is not, but this does not necessarily mean wholesale disbelief in the idea of tribal sovereignty expressed in the form of centralized tribal governments. Rather, it signifies an engagement in the "national" politics of the tribe, albeit a selective and contingent investment of political energy.

At the Navajo Nation, criticism of the leadership's attempt to take the Navajo Area IHS 638 reflected these three discourses about leadership decision making: people expressed suspicion that tribal leaders wanted to run the administration of health care to give contracts to families and friends; many were concerned that greed and desire to increase tribal coffers motivated the 638 takeover; and other community members were skeptical that 638 would improve health care—some even speculated that it would decrease the quality of health care and the availability of services. The tribal leaders proposing the takeover seemed to be cognizant of most of these criticisms and frequently attempted to prove that they had the best interest of the people in mind. Nonetheless, among the tribal members most concerned were those employed by the health-care facilities that the tribal council sought to take over. Many worried that their work conditions would adversely change under tribal management. For Navajo health-care workers, the issue of the 638 takeover became a concern in terms of both community health care and tribal labor relations. They began to actively express their concerns in terms of tribal labor relations when they used LIUNA's Campaign for Union Recognition to articulate their political frustrations with the centralized tribal government.

Public Debate over Self-Determination in Navajo Health Care

In 1995 the Navajo Nation government approved the formation of the Navajo Health Care System Corporation (NHCSC) and appointed a design team to propose a 638 contract for administration of reservation health care (Maniaci 2001d). However, little was done with the proposal until early 2001. Much of the renewed interest came from Navajo Nation president Kelsey Begaye, who made it a policy initiative to revive the effort to take health care 638. But President Begaye was not universally heralded for this decision. Hank Tomlinson, a non-Navajo physician's assistant, described how President Begaye got a firsthand taste of what some people thought of 638 for health care while visiting Hank's workplace, a small clinic in a remote area of the western part of the reservation. The clinic is not an easy drive from Window Rock; it is forty-five minutes off a major highway. Moreover, this small facility rarely has more than one doctor at a time, is closed nights and weekends, and often refers patients to larger regional facilities. Hank told me that as soon as President Begaye arrived, he was harassed by Navajo patients and some Navajo employees because of his support of 638. Hank chuckled that the harassment got so bad, Begaye had to return to the parking lot and "lock himself in his car." Although perhaps a bit exaggerated, the very act of recounting this story illustrates Hank's frustration with President Begaye. From my conversations with many Navajos and from stories in the local press, it was clear that Hank's frustration was not an aberration. The public frustration was as much in response to the idea of taking health care 638 as it was to the way the president and the NNC made the decision to go 638.

Early in 2001, the NNC began in earnest the legislative process to approve the takeover plan created by the design team. As the NNC got close to voting on the plan, complaints that tribal members where being left out of the decision-making process began to surface. Many people called for the issue to be put to a tribal-wide referendum; a grassroots committee formed to protest and challenge the takeover; and a majority of chapter houses voted against the proposed takeover. Criticism became so intense that the NNC had little choice but to at least consider opening the process to the general Navajo public (Maniaci 2001b, 2001e). In a close vote, the NNC approved a resolution to hold a nationwide referendum that allowed tribal members to express their opinions on 638 for health care (Maniaci 2001f).[16] However, this referendum did not come off without controversy.

The controversy stemmed from two specific aspects of the Navajo Nation tribal code that govern referendum elections. First, there could not simply be a referendum on whether to approve the NNC's 638 plan. As the NNC's attorney argued, since the NNC already had the authority—as an inherent part of its governmental powers—to take over health care, it legally did not need voter approval for this action (Shebala 2001a; Tohtsoni 2001). Therefore, he declared that the referendum had to be worded such that voters voted to *prohibit* the NNC from going forward on 638, not to *authorize* a tribal governmental takeover of health care. The ballot measure read: "Shall the following statute be added to Title 13 of the Navajo Nation Code.... The Navajo Nation shall be prohibited from contracting IHS Health Care Services for the Navajo people" (Shebala 2001a).[17] This wording created an awkward and often confusing polling situation; to be against the takeover, one had to vote yes in the referendum, and those in favor had to vote no.

Second, by law, all Navajo Nation general referendums require a majority of registered voters to pass. This threshold, rather than a simple majority of those voting, ensures that referendums reflect the electoral voice of the broadest Navajo population possible. But because of the high threshold, at the time of the 638 referendum, no referendum initiative had ever been successfully passed by Navajo voters. For the 638 referendum, there were 87,158 registered voters (Di Giovanni 2001b).[18] This meant that more than 43,500 people had to vote yes to prohibiting the takeover to prevent the NNC from taking action on health care. In the end, 16,431 people voted against a tribal administrative takeover, and about 3,750 voted in favor (Di Giovanni 2001b). Falling well short of the 43,500 votes needed to pass, the referendum failed. Tribal council supporters of 638 could claim by the letter of the law that it now was legitimate for the tribal government to go ahead with the 638 process. Opponents of 638 for health care instead relied on the spirit of the law and pointed to the four-to-one margin as justification to halt the takeover plans.

It is hard to interpret exactly what these electoral numbers mean and how they connect to the political voice of the Navajo people. Even the Navajo Nation vice president—who not only campaigned for 638 but was also on the design team that created the 638 contract—hesitated to declare outright victory. Instead, he publicly declared a week and a half after the election: "The meaning of the health care referendum is not absolutely clear, for we believe the results lend itself to a number of interpretations, but at the moment we are taking careful thought on the results of the referendum election" (McKenzie 2001). The more than sixteen thousand votes to prohibit the 638 takeover certainly do not represent the large percentage of voters needed to pass a referendum (43,580) or all eligible voters (87,158). At the same time, this is not an insignificant number, especially when coupled with the margin of victory.[19] The voter turnout for this special election was low. It was less than 25 percent, compared with a 54 percent turnout in the 1994 Navajo Nation presidential election (Russell and Henderson 1999), a 42 percent turnout for the 1998 presidential primary (Wilkins 2002), and a 55 percent turnout in the 2008 federal general election (Navajo Nation 2008). However, those were hotly contested, historic races, whereas the 638 takeover referendum was a special election in June, with only this issue on the ballot. Perhaps more comparable is the 2000 referendum vote on decreasing the size of the NNC from eighty-eight to twenty-four delegates. This vote happened in September (two months in advance of the federal general election), and 33 percent of eligible voters turned out.

It is difficult to get a sense of "normal" voter turnout at Navajoland because few comprehensive studies have been conducted on Navajo voting patterns. Russell and Henderson (1999) looked at statistical results from one presidential election (in 1994), and Williams (1970) did a qualitative study of local governance (chapter) voting, but no one has studied tribal-wide referendum voting. However, Williams's findings might shed some light on the 638 referendum. He noted that those who dissented from popular opinion chose to vote with their feet rather than their voices. That is, instead of risking public shame or political tension by voting against the majority, people chose not to vote. We might interpret the 638 referendum in this light, that the tens of thousands of nonvotes represent people not wanting to go against a perceived popular opinion in favor of 638. However, the smaller group dynamics that apply to chapter voting may not easily transfer to tribal-wide voting, especially considering that Williams (1970) looked at face-to-face, in-person voting in chapter house meetings, not the impersonal secret-ballot method used with tribal-wide referenda.

Furthermore, there is not much evidence that 638 was popularly supported. Indeed, on the contrary, much of the media attention and general buzz around the reservation going into the referendum was critical of 638 and the referendum process. This buzz, along with the sixteen thousand voting against the takeover, might be excused as merely a vocal but unrepresentative minority—as some tribal council members implied. But this very vocal minority became a significant opposition that fomented serious public debate on the politics of 638 for health care and ultimately derailed the plan. Thinking about the 638 referendum in these terms, the low turnout could represent a general protest against the referendum. A refusal to participate certainly might explain some people's nonvotes, but there was no publicly organized effort calling for a boycott of the referendum (a common strategy for oppositional groups worldwide trying to protest the very legitimacy of an election). Indeed, the opposition to 638 was not a singularly organized group with a uniform front. It was more of a confluence of many voices speaking out against the process of taking health care 638.

It is highly likely that the low turnout was due to the confusing ballot language. Before and after the referendum, local news media, personal interviews, and my observation of tribal council meetings and Navajo community life in general all revealed a great deal of criticism for the awkward and confusing nature of the ballot language (Ahkeah 2001; Anderson 2001; Beyal 2001; Shirley 2001; Yazzie 2001). Much of the confusion was about the legalese of the referendum ballot, which created a scenario in which no meant yes and yes meant no. One letter to the editor of the weekly tribal newspaper, the *Navajo Times*, protested:

> The grassroots people's vote will not be taken serious again.... The language for the referendum is just lawyer's jargon and confusion. How can our grandparents understand this language? Why can't it just be simply grassroots people language?... How about playing a fair baseball game with the voter or criticism will continue. (Ahkeah 2001)

This tribal member was most concerned with how the wording of the referendum made the important issue of what to do about tribal health care unclear to the average Diné. Even more questionable to the letter writer, the jargon made the referendum inaccessible to community elders, who traditionally hold a very important role as decision makers.

The confusing ballot language was compounded by referendum rules calling for the high threshold of votes for passage. Coupling the two nearly guaranteed that the NNC would be able to make its own decision about health care, because it was very unlikely that enough people would vote to prohibit taking health care 638. This situation gave the biggest critics of 638 and the NNC the opportunity to argue that the council intended the referendum to fail. First of all, in authorizing the referendum, the NNC had the ability to lower the threshold of passage to a simple majority of voters, but it chose not to do so (Maniaci 2001f)—some suggested, because it knew that lowering the threshold would mean the passage of the prohibition against 638. Skepticism was further fueled after the referendum failed, when, based on criticism of the 638 vote, some council members attempted to change the requirement for a majority of all registered voters to pass a referendum. Although energetically debated on the council floor, referendum reform garnered little support. A few opposing council members even explicitly argued against reform, asserting that the move was merely a "sore loser" ploy to stop 638 by changing electoral rules so that a second referendum preventing 638 could succeed. But most council representatives based their opposition to changing the high threshold—both before and after the 638 referendum—on the broad democratic principle of making sure that there was widespread support for electoral initiative action.

Other critics of 638 went so far as to contend that the ballot legalese was deliberately designed to suppress votes. They argued that many voters who were confused about what exactly they were voting for would simply not vote and that phrasing the initiative as a prohibition, not an authorization, ensured that the NNC, not the voters, would maintain authority over the issue of health care 638. This argument led to many people questioning the legitimacy of the referendum, suggesting that the NNC never really intended to take the people's voice seriously.[20] In a letter to the editor of the *Navajo Times*, the president of the Shiprock Chapter addressed the issue of mistrust and warned of damaging effects to tribal popular democracy:

> What is this business about "yes means no and no means yes?" Sounds like legal mumbo jumbo, Window Rock Style. The Window Rock "comedy of errors" is getting worse—a bad joke with potentially serious consequences.... The explanation that the legislative counsel gives as to why this ridiculous situation happens the way it has, is reasonable. The legislative counsel tells us they are bound by the dictates of law to present the referendum in this manner. Even so, the way this is perceived by the people is that, it is a deliberate and complicated strategy intended to deny the people their voice in this important issue.... It would behoove these highly trained and articulate lawyer types...and our Navajo leadership to step back and to see how deceitful and conniving this is appearing to be. They should be able to craft referendum language that the people can understand, such as, "Do you support the contracting of IHS—yes or no?" (Yazzie 2001)

The referendum over 638 was initiated to give the general public a greater say in deciding the future of tribal health care. However, as this local tribal official illustrates, the referendum left many people feeling that their collective political voice was even less relevant than before, when they had at least succeeded in demanding a referendum over the issue. Indeed, this was not the first referendum viewed as problematic and potentially undemocratic.[21] The 638 referendum became part of a larger debate on how the referendum process ought to work and how to use it to best empower the general public. This question in turn is part of a larger, perpetual discussion about how to balance the authority of the centralized tribal government against the accountability concerns of rank-and-file tribal members. One council representative summarized the frustration of many 638 referendum voters by chastising his colleagues on the floor of the NNC, declaring, "We have broadened the gap between the council and the people...we, the council...have made ourselves too untouchable." He urged the council to "give the government back to the people." This reprimand was made during an attempt to pass referendum reform, but it also echoes a common attitude of frustration among the Navajo general public and Navajo Area IHS employees.

Dissatisfaction over the tribal council's push for 638 was not just about frustration over the referendum process but also about people's suspicions of council members' motivations, which several tribal members suggested were financial. Tribal council members and other proponents of 638 acknowledged the financial aspect of 638 by proclaiming that it would bring more federal money into health care. What is more, they heralded the fact that the influx of money would be controlled locally—making health care more efficient and responsive to local needs (Maniaci 2001a, 2001c).[22] However, it was local control of money that made people nervous about the takeover. Many tribal members and Navajo Area IHS employees alleged that personal greed was part of the motivation.[23] This feeling varied, from subtle implications that "money has something to do with it" or it is "probably greed," to the more acrimonious and cynical suggestion that tribal leaders wanted to take more money from the federal government so that "they [could] pocket it and buy double-wide trailers and duallies and ride around and get everybody what they need."[24] A frequent criticism that followed a similar line of argument was speculation of cronyism and nepotism. Anita John jokingly told me that if she were related to a tribal council member, she would be happy about 638, but since she is not, she did not want it to happen.

These discourses were prevalent despite several public assertions from leaders of the NHCSC and Navajo Nation vice president Dr. Taylor McKenzie, himself a former IHS employee for more than twenty years, that the health-care corporation would be a separate entity from the tribal council and that its budget would come directly from the federal government, without arbitration and redistribution by the NNC (McKenzie 2001). The Navajo Division of Health's own publication (mainly distributed in Navajo Area IHS facilities) quoted Lydia Hubbard-Pourier, the CEO of the future NHCSC:

> "There is...still the idea that the Navajo Nation will run the health care system under the contract, but the Board of Directors is insistent that it will not." She added, "From the beginning, the plan has always been to establish a private non-profit corporation to run the health care system. That entity is called the Navajo Health Care System Corporation. It is not part of the Navajo Nation tribal government bureaucracy." If indeed a contract is approved, CEO Hubbard-Pourier believes the Corporation will be supported to keep the health care system separate from all kinds of government, including federal and tribal governments. (Louis 2001:1)

After the election, Hubbard-Pourier and her associates frequently made statements to this effect, a clear indication that even the leaders of the 638 transition realized that the general Navajo public was skeptical about how tribal leaders would handle and spend the influx of money generated by the 638 contract. However, rather than acknowledge these concerns as a problem of general trust in the centralized government, CEO Hubbard-Pourier and other boosters of 638 treated them as an information problem, suggesting that people did not fully understand the plans for 638. Indeed, a key part of the NHCSC's official response to dissent in the 638 referendum was to improve communication about its plans, to "help allay the fears of the Navajo people and the federal employees and their families" (Louis 2001:1). After all, even though the referendum had not prevented 638 from going forward, the plans for health care 638 had not been finalized or ratified by the NNC. The 638 design team knew that it still had a public relations campaign ahead of it to ensure NNC passage of its plan. Despite a concerted effort to clarify the proposed relationship between the health-care corporation and the NNC, criticism of the plan persisted.

The most vociferous and organized opposition came from a group of current and former IHS employees who called themselves Doo' Dah 638, which translates to No 638 or Against 638. This was a small group held together mainly by five people, who ran a weekly meeting at a restaurant in Window Rock. Meetings were open to anyone who was against health care 638 and wanted to discuss plans for public opposition to 638. Ironically, the restaurant that hosted these meetings in its back "private-party room" frequently also served the disparaged tribal government leaders lunch and hosted their business meetings.

The self-appointed spokespeople for opposition to 638 made their voices heard. They were frequently quoted in the paper, set up protest signs around Window Rock and the tribal governmental complex itself, and even entered a Doo' Dah 638 float in a Navajo Nation Fair parade. The group earned much of its legitimacy from the fact that it collected more than ten thousand signatures on a petition to put the issue of 638 for health care to a tribal-wide initiative. Although this number was well short of the 30 percent (more than twenty-five thousand) of registered voters required by tribal law to initiate a tribal-wide vote, it was an impressive feat for a small cadre of volunteers. Nonetheless, Doo' Dah 638 never quite became an institutionalized force on the reservation, in large part because, as a very small volunteer group, it lacked long-term mobilization capacity.

As the Shiprock Chapter president contended (Yazzie 2001), what was at stake with the referendum vote and the entire process of taking over health care was not whether Navajo elected representatives acted with the public's best interest in mind. Rather, a vocal segment of the Navajo public perceived itself to be disenfranchised by what it saw as an inadequate electoral procedure and decision-making process on health care 638 as a whole. To these people, the consequences of this disenfranchisement would mean an unfair distribution of tribal resources, both money and social services. Similar to contention around livestock in the 1930s and 1940s and Peter MacDonald's presidencies of the 1970s and 1980s, what was being publicly deliberated in the debate over the 638 takeover of the Navajo Area IHS was the relationship between the Navajo people and the decision makers of the centralized government.

Many were unhappy with the NNC's actions, but perhaps none more so than those who would be affected most by the takeover, the employees of the Navajo Area IHS. And LIUNA, with its Campaign for Union Recognition, provided a way for them to express their concern and displeasure. The campaign was beneficial to the union and the workers. Dissatisfaction about how the takeover plan was being carried out significantly increased support for and participation in unionism. Navajo Area IHS workers were able to use the union to meet their local needs for political expression. The next chapter details how this happened on the ground through face-to-face organizing by the union and workers. But before looking at this co-articulation of political and economic agendas, it is important to review the pragmatic approach toward unionism that the Diné have taken in the past.

Pragmatism in Navajo Tribal Labor Relations

As with the term *tribal labor relations* in general, when discussing Navajo labor relations, I am talking about how labor relations play out in the context and geographic locale of the Navajo Nation. However, interactions between workers and tribal management, and equally, Diné laborers' interactions with unions, are informed by labor relations that also take place off the reservation. Colleen O'Neill's (2005) groundbreaking history, *Working the Navajo Way*, provides by far the most detailed account of Navajo unionism both on and off the reservation. She notes that some of the Navajos' earliest encounters with unionism were indirect results of the 1930s livestock reduction. As the opportunity to support themselves through herding decreased, Navajos increasingly sought off-reservation work—frequently in the booming Southwest mining industry, particularly in mines that were close to Navajo Nation borders. At these sites, Navajos were given "Indian work," the less skilled, surface-level, and maintenance jobs (O'Neill 2005).

Going to work at mines did not always mean positive relations with unions. In many cases, it meant the opposite. During the 1930s, some Navajos worked as strikebreakers in mines in Madrid and Gallup, New Mexico, which undoubtedly soured unions against them. By the same token, unions were not necessarily seeking to turn around these workers. As O'Neill (2005) notes, unions actively used mining corporations' hiring of Navajos as a wedge issue against management in order to increase Mexican and Chicano membership. Navajo workers, for their part, had mixed views about unions. Some negotiated special short-term job appointments with management so that they would not have to join the union; others became proud union members (O'Neill 2005). Whatever Navajos' interactions were with off-reservation unionism, they certainly did not forge a social movement of unionism. Rather, it appears that Navajo laborers made their decisions on a case-by-case basis. Undoubtedly, these experiences informed how Diné reacted when unionism came to the reservation.

The earliest account of union activity within Navajo Nation borders is Gordon Strieb's (1952) observation of an attempted organizing campaign and strike among Navajo workers constructing a natural gas pipeline across the reservation in 1951. Using fictitious names for the community, company, and union, Strieb followed a failed attempt to organize the workers. For the most part, he blamed the Navajo laborers' illiteracy and lack of experience with unions, but from his account it seems just as likely that the Navajos took a pragmatic approach to the union and did not find anything overwhelmingly beneficial in the relatively radical strategy the lead organizer put forward—particularly in light of organizers' inability to construct the campaign in a way that attended to the local sociocultural and political milieu.

Strieb details the significant interest and support that the lead organizer obtained when he first talked to Navajo workers. The organizer argued that the union would fight in their behalf over jobs that these Navajos were qualified to do but were not being hired for. The company was not offering enough of these disputed jobs to Navajos, despite the fact that it and the tribal council had agreed that Navajo workers would be given preference. So many workers at the meeting expressed interest that the organizer ran out of authorization cards. But what is important is that these workers were not signing up for union membership; they were just authorizing the union to represent them. This authorization certainly demarcates support for unionism and the way in which the union might help them get jobs, but it does not indicate the level of support needed to convince someone to walk a picket line or go on strike. Indeed, the lead organizer had significant trouble persuading the Navajo workers to fully participate in the strategy that he believed would work (Strieb 1952). He could get very few, if any, Navajo workers who had already been hired to strike in protest of the company's hiring policies. After the company began to offer jobs to Navajos, he could not convince these individuals to reject the jobs and hold out until these became unionized jobs. He did have some success getting Navajos who wanted employment but had not been offered jobs to the picket line, but their numbers dwindled as the strike went on. Indeed, many came to the picket line early on, when the union offered lunch to picketers. The lead organizer almost admitted as much when he canceled the free lunches out of frustration. After the lunches were canceled, participation decreased.

Moreover, he could not get those who did turn out to picket to "fire up" in a sufficiently raucous and passionate way. Strieb (1952:28) reports that the lead organizer wanted the Navajos on the picket line to shout, "'Don't go to work!'" at those crossing the picket line. The organizer became frustrated at their unwillingness to shout and at his interpreters' unwillingness to ask the protesters to shout—so much so that he himself shouted the phrase in Navajo to communicate the force with which he wanted them to shout. But Strieb notes that the Navajos responded by silently staring at him. Strieb (1952:28) attributes this instance of low support for the union's tactics to an essential character trait of Navajos: "Had [the lead organizer] been better informed or more sensitive to Navaho ways, he would have realized that Navahos never shout or behave in a noisy manner, except when intoxicated." Clearly, the organizer had not crafted the most culturally attentive strategy, but there is likely more to the story here. Beyond just the failures of the campaign, Strieb (1952:30) goes on to suggest that Navajos' pastoral-agricultural life provided little opportunity for them to foster any sense of working-class solidarity. Moreover, he argues that Navajos' longtime reliance on the government and the living conditions that they believed the government owed them had created a situation in which "feelings of self-help and self-reliance [had] become almost vestigial" (1952:30). Strieb goes on to assert:

> There is little awareness—and quite understandably—of the necessity for responsibility and participation on the part of the [Navajo] people themselves towards achieving some future goal. It can thus be easily seen why a labor organization—a fundamental means for workers to achieve some control of their own destiny through concerted effort and sacrifice—might meet with Navaho indifference. (1952:30)

Strieb's interpretation of this campaign failure is clearly influenced by his own mid-century economic determination, cultural essentialism, and primitivism. But his assumption of an internalized Navajo wardship obscures important ways in which these Navajos were relating to—and even beginning to indigenize—unionism. It also understates the union's failure to implement a localized strategy as key to the campaign failure.

Strieb believes that Navajos had become too dependent to speak up for themselves and thus found the concept of a union and a strike foreign. He even cites "one far-sighted government employee" hypothesizing on the promise of unionization for Navajos because it "could make the Navahos realize that they can and must act together, without reliance on outsiders, if they are to move towards self-government and economic independence" (Strieb 1952:30). The irony of this statement is that, as Robert Young (1978) illustrates, during this same period the Navajo Nation tribal government was beginning its strong push for institutionalized self-determination. He chronicles how in the 1950s and 1960s, the NNC attempted to take over government functions and services despite (or perhaps because of) the climate of termination (Young 1978).[25] With increased tribal income from mining operations and royalties, the Navajo government sought to increase its control over negotiating leasing and extraction contracts; maintenance of wells, roads, and irrigation systems; and local law enforcement responsibilities and facilities. With increased tribal coffers and amid the general climate of federal Indian policy in the 1950s and 1960s, "Navajos were quick to take advantage of opportunities for independence short of termination" (Young 1978:145). The tribal council's push for local self-determination while maintaining important legal, political, and economic relationships with the federal government laid the groundwork for an interdependent but nondominant relationship.

Of course, Navajos had long shown this collective, defiant self-reliance. They publicly protested their treatment on the Long Walk and at Bosque Redondo. After returning from Bosque Redondo, they frequently appealed to the federal government to increase the size of their reservation. They petitioned to be excluded from the ravenous allotment policies of the Dawes Act. And most significant to the events described by Strieb, many actively and publicly protested livestock reduction policies—including assertive protests that Strieb claimed were un-Navajo. In fact, many Diné were so upset by these policies that they voted down the chance for an IRA constitution because of its connection to the same forces that had pushed livestock reduction. Moreover, standing against livestock reduction was not that far from an act of working-class solidarity. In essence, those who made their living working with livestock collectively protested a plan that would ruin their livelihoods.[26]

Protest against livestock reduction is a clear illustration of how Navajos willingly used whatever political avenues were open to them to make a political statement. We should view Navajo unionism through the same pragmatic lens, and the campaign Strieb discusses provides great examples—as long as we read between Strieb's lines. Indeed, this pragmatism infused the entire campaign. Navajos willingly and enthusiastically supported the union by signing authorization cards—and to some extent even showing up at the picket line—when it was clear that the union was trying to secure jobs for them. But after they got jobs, many no longer participated in protests. It appears that advocating for jobs was one thing but it did not make sense not to take a job once it was gained. For some, even showing up at the picket line was, at the most base level, a practical choice: Will I get a free lunch or not?

Moreover, Strieb notes what he considered to be a key instance that damaged the union's cause. After the union had gained some support, a Navajo supporter of the union (and interpreter for the lead organizer) openly criticized the Navajo Nation Tribal Council,[27] its advisers, and a local leader in a pro-union speech at a public dance. Strieb suggests that the public criticism of tribal leaders was offensive and culturally inappropriate and therefore turned people off to the union's methods, even if they agreed with its fundamental cause. I find this interpretation, that public criticism of leadership was an unacceptable cultural taboo, too simplistic. Twenty years earlier, during the crisis of livestock reduction, Navajos had publicly and vehemently criticized leaders and tribal council members who supported the reduction plan. It was more likely an unwise making of a political enemy than it was a problem of using the tactic of public criticism. Indeed, Strieb himself implies that the campaign suffered from a lack of assessment of the local political economic system. For example, he argues that the lead organizer underestimated the key role that white traders played in the community. Not only were these traders powerful economic forces as local, centralized hubs of commerce, but they also acted as labor agents for the company building the pipeline. On a broader scale, tribal council leaders also served the latter function. Given this complicated local political economic milieu, it is understandable that Navajos seeking work did not choose the union as their sole source of political economic power. The union was just one of many ways to secure a job and access financial resources. Moreover, a person had to question what level of support for the union might alienate him from other sources of power. Given the multiple forces and constraints, it is easy to see how an indigenized approach to unionism might rely on a pragmatic application of a union's tactics.

The same attitude could be seen twenty years later with Navajo mine worker participation in unionism on the reservation. In observing union activism at the Navajo Nation in the late 1970s, Susan Steenrod (1979) described Navajo employees using unionism to meet the local indigenous needs. Steenrod looked at strikes and activism by Navajo mine workers at Peabody Coal's Black Mesa mine and other on-reservation mines operated by the BMMC. She argues that in many instances, Navajo mine workers participated in and initiated the activism of their union, the United Mine Workers of America (UMWA), as much as Navajo community members as union members (if not more so). Many instances that provoked Navajo walkouts had to do with Navajos, combining workplace rights and civil rights. This process would manifest itself in both complaints of workplace discrimination and Navajo workers using labor relations to solve tensions in the community in general. "The union as an institution," Steenrod (1979:152) suggests, "merely provided the vehicle through which their displeasure could be voiced. The walkout provided an opportunity for all Navajos who felt they were involved to be heard...a display of the behavior values of group consensus, solidarity, and individual right to speak." Some strikes were provoked by Navajo workers who felt that management unfairly disciplined them because of their Navajo-ness. In other instances, Navajo workers used the tactics of unionism to protest the treatment of Navajo mine workers outside the job site.

In the latter instances, terms and conditions of employment had very little or nothing to do with what the workers wanted to protest. For example, Navajo mine workers had a confrontation with a white mine employee, off the job site and after work hours, about receiving help with a broken-down car. Despite this minimal connection to the mine, Navajo workers sought to redress the affront through labor relations and the union. To them, the union was a pragmatic tool with which to make their concerns heard.

> Navajos were protecting their own, as unions have always done. They were acting within a political and cohesive framework to protect relationships and "Navajoism." The union provided an immediate and effective vehicle with which to express Navajo dissatisfaction over personal relationships, job conditions, and anything else pertaining to jobs at BMMC. A caveat must be interjected at this point. Navajos have always effectively and pragmatically adapted non-Navajo ideas and concepts to the Navajo way of life. There is no reason to assume that a Navajo union will act, nor will Navajos expect it to act, along the familiar and traditional lines that Anglos are accustomed to. Navajo unionism will probably be manifested in a way that is uniquely Navajo in function and role. (Steenrod 1979:202–203)

The Navajo experience with unionism that Steenrod describes is not all that dissimilar from that of other communities of color that have participated in unions both to strengthen their workplace rights and to secure power in the larger community and society.[28] However, Navajo unionism is characterized more by the pragmatism of utilizing unions intermittently for discrete political ends than by the ideological basis that generally comes with social movement unionism.

Although the Navajo approach to unionism appeared to be more pragmatic than ideological, this does not mean that support for unionism as a useful political strategy did not take hold among Navajo workers and community members. Lynn Robbins (1975) traces the growth of Navajo support for unions throughout the 1970s, until Navajo workers made efforts to indigenize unionism by creating associations of workers outside and parallel to unions. Robbins locates much Navajo participation in unionism in the push to make sure that Navajo-preference laws were enforced. Provisions that give preference in hiring to Navajos and provide for laying them off last are included in most agreements and leases the NNC has negotiated with off-reservation corporations that seek construction and mining projects at the Navajo Nation. In the past, unions and union workers were not particularly fond of these agreements, believing them to be unfair (Robbins 1975). Despite the existence of such preferential employment laws, Navajos had to go through unions and union halls to secure work. This process proved to be a significant impediment for Navajo workers. In some cases, they had to drive long distances to cities off the reservation to get jobs in their own backyards. Navajo workers became fed up with this and what they saw as other acts of discrimination and unjust firings. In May 1972, Navajo members of the carpenters union decided to protest their treatment and go on strike (Robbins 1975). During this wildcat strike, Navajo workers were able to shut down construction of the Navajo generating station. However, the strike lasted only two days because it did not have the support of the international union. Ultimately, many non-Navajos crossed the picket line.

Despite the limited success of this action, it illustrates a willingness to engage in proactive labor relations and to use the tactics of unionism, even if the union does not fully support the action. Moreover, it illustrates a practical approach to the union in that the strikers were union members; because the union was not willing to take on their cause, they acted on their own. They used the union when it benefited them and were willing to go above and beyond it when it would not. Robbins (1975) argues that as a result of the wildcat strike, Navajo workers were able to further infuse tribal labor relations with their own indigenous workplace needs. The workers who were ultimately undercut by their union realized that they needed another option and formed the Navajo Construction Workers Association. This organization, headed by Navajo union members, advocated for the unique needs of Navajo workers by coordinating unions, foreign corporations, and the NNC. By 1974 the union had more than two thousand members, which was about 11 percent of Navajos employed on the reservation (1975). More importantly, its existence helped push the tribal government to establish the ONLR, whose charge was to advocate for Navajo workers by making sure that Navajo-preference codes were being followed and that off-reservation companies dealt with Navajo employees appropriately. More recently, a collective of Navajo workers from several different industries created Naalnishí, or the Navajo Central Labor Council, a grassroots organization that advocates and provides mutual aid for Navajo workers independent of the tribal government and international labor unions, although Naalnishí members are generally represented by these entities as well. These three uniquely Diné institutions are lasting illustrations of Navajo workers' pragmatic approach to unions and tribal labor relations. Navajos used unions when these were beneficial for their jobs. When unions reached the limits of their effectiveness, Navajos indigenized unionism to meet their community and workplace needs. Moreover, one last key aspect of this pragmatic approach to unions meant that Navajos were just as likely to engage in workplace activism and advocacy through channels that ran outside unions. This was not done to undercut unions, but to act in a parallel fashion to them. Indeed, the power and purpose of unionism were well recognized, along with its limitations. Navajo workers have shown a willingness to inventively indigenize Indian Country labor relations in ways that parallel conventional Western models of labor relations and that rely on NLRA-style negotiations and collective bargaining. The grassroots activism at Tuba City discussed in chapter 6 provides a perfect example of how Navajo workers have sought to simultaneously engage in multiple methods of workplace and community-based collective action to gain an institutionalized voice in local tribal labor relations that is not necessarily based on collective bargaining.

Conclusion

Given that Navajo workers have expressed a pragmatic attitude toward unions, it may be no surprise that the Diné tribal government has taken a similar approach. The establishment of the ONLR in the early 1970s was a significant about-face from the late 1950s and early 1960s, when the NNC did as much as it could to prevent unionism within the boundaries of the Navajo Nation. In 1958 the council passed a law strictly forbidding unions on the reservation—including threats of hard labor, imprisonment, or expulsion from tribal land for organizers who broke this law (O'Neill 2005; Robbins 1975). In 1961, when two unions tried to organize mill workers, the Navajo government appealed to the NLRB and then the D.C. Circuit Court to try to prevent representation elections and unionization on the reservation. In this landmark case for tribal labor relations, *Navajo Nation v. NLRB*, the tribe argued that its 1868 treaty allowed it to prohibit any non-Indians from the reservation, including labor unions. When the tribe lost its appeal, its press release declared "Unions to Invade Reservation Land" (Robbins 1975:3), a clear effort to code unions as outsiders (O'Neill 2005). Yet, nearly fifteen years later, the tribal government established the ONLR to deal fairly with unions and in some instances in the late 1970s and 1980s even spoke out in favor of striking Navajo laborers in efforts to end strikes in ways that would benefit workers (Steenrod 1979). Similarly, in 1973 Thomas Brose, then director of the ONLR, explained to the U.S. Commission on Civil Rights at a hearing in the Navajo

Nation capital that the tribe no longer sought to enforce its right-to-work policy outlawing unions. Instead, its strategy was to appeal to unions to negotiate Indian-preference clauses in their collective bargaining agreements (O'Neill 2005).

The Navajo pragmatic attitude toward unionism seems the best lens through which to understand the NNC change of course in labor relations. In part, the NNC's original objection to unions was an economic liberalization policy meant to increase outside investment, following the model of the State of Arizona's right-to-work law (O'Neill 2005; Robbins 1975). Moreover, this action was a way for the NNC, still suffering from low Navajo public opinion of how livestock reduction was handled, to prove that it could make a bold stand against outsiders. O'Neill (2005:139) argues that by characterizing unions as outsiders, the NNC was "naming what was *not* Navajo, thereby stressing their autonomy from the institutions that characterized U.S. culture." Thus, resistance to unionism was not necessarily an ideological decision about Navajo tribal labor relations, but a politically pragmatic response that later could be reversed given changes in economic and political conditions. When the infusion of foreign investment in the reservation did not fulfill the promise of Navajo jobs in the way the NNC had anticipated and negotiated, off-reservation corporations could more easily be characterized as outsiders, and labor unions could be characterized as allies to help secure Navajo-preferential employment and limit discrimination. When even this did not fully work, Navajo laborers and then the NNC itself created their own institutions to establish labor relations that were responsible to the community's needs and desires. The shifting politics of Navajo economic development and labor relations necessitated that the NNC take a pragmatic approach to unionism.

Navajo tribal labor relations are best understood within the context of Navajo tribal governmental politics. The NNC has the institutionalized authority to make decisions on tribal self-determination and economic development. However, as history shows, this centralized authority does not go unquestioned by rank-and-file tribal citizens. The combination of the NNC's attempt to take health care 638 and LIUNA's subsequent Campaign for Union Recognition presents a striking example of Diné people's willingness to publicly debate the processes of government in ways that cannot be reduced to dysfunctional ideological factionalism. Rather, Navajo workers and community members employed a political pragmatism, using whatever options were open to them to make their political economic voices heard.

Understood in terms of Navajo political history, tribal labor relations become much more than an issue of negotiating working conditions; they become part of the local political milieu. In this way, tribal labor relations cannot be oversimplified into a debate between union rights and tribal sovereignty rights. Indeed, commerce, tribal governance, and unionism intertwine in complicated ways—particularly where employees' and union organizers' discussions about unionism and self-determination overlap and run parallel. Unionism can become a useful means of articulating people's feelings about how tribal sovereignty should be enacted. And tribal self-determination of Navajo health care does not happen only on the tribal governmental level. The Diné people need to be invested and involved in the process. When the referendum over 638 proved insufficient to many people, they turned to other avenues of political expression. One key way was through their position as workers, utilizing tribal labor relations. Thus, instead of being contrary to tribal self-governance, unionism became a way for people to participate in the process of self-governance.

Clearly, a significant difference between the Navajo context and the California tribal gaming context (chapter 2) has much to do with the makeup of the workforce. Unlike California Native nations casino employees, Navajo Area IHS employees are predominantly tribal members and thus have a much greater investment in the local community and in their jobs and work conditions as essential parts of their community. This investment, as articulated through the Campaign for Union Recognition, constructs work and the work site as locales for commenting on and enacting tribal self-determination. It bespeaks the need for tribal unionism. Much like its counterpart, tribal capitalism—which is a commitment to improving Native communities through responsible development of economic resources—tribal unionism is a collective effort to create responsible tribal labor relations that respect both sovereignty and the unique position of tribal workers, whose work is a commitment to improving the community and the sustainability of tribal self-determination.

five
The Campaign for Union Recognition

A standard tactic of union busting is to criticize unionism as an impediment to positive and productive employer–employee relations. This criticism constructs unions as outsiders to the relationship between workers and management rather than mediators who advocate for workers in the same way corporate lawyers and consultants advise and negotiate for management. Particularly in workplaces without a history of unionism, the characterization of "outsiderness" gains traction regardless of how many workers support and participate in the union. Structurally, some elements of unionism—union representatives who work for the union and therefore are not technically employees' coworkers; union dues structures that remove money from employees' paychecks—will always act in a third-party function. Union-busting consultants seeking work in tribal communities have begun to make the third-party or outsider argument in the context of tribal labor relations, constructing unions as feared adversaries that threaten tribal sovereignty. Of course, the success of this tactic relies on the consulting firms' ability to downplay their own "foreignness."

In tribal labor relations, consultants and other anti-union forces doubly encode union outsiderness in terms of race and the politics of sovereignty—they use the racial difference of traditionally white union organizers to suggest that unions are intruding not just in labor relations but in the indigenous community as well. Anti-union arguments that construct unions as outsiders are based on conceptually severing the union from the workforce—asserting that the union and its agenda (conventionally described by anti-union consultants as only about union dues) are external to and manipulate workers' goals and needs. Union busting also tries to sever any connection between the union and the indigenous community, but it does so in a way that constructs the tribal government or tribal enterprise as tantamount to the community.

The anti-union theory of tribal labor relations is perhaps most convincing in the context of tribal gaming, in which most employees are not tribal citizens. Those who manage tribal enterprises such as casinos already perceive a disconnect between their workforce and the indigenous community. Therefore, it is easy to see a union advocating on behalf of "foreign" workers as an outsider as well. However, tribal labor relations are much more complicated when employees are also tribal citizens. Indigenous workers who participate in unionism, as well as unions that have positive interactions with tribal-member employees, are not as easily separable from a tribal community. This is not to say that unionism and its goals are isomorphic with workers' needs and agendas, but the extent to which indigenous workers support and participate in unionism can limit the outsiderness of unions. More importantly, such workers indigenize unionism by making it useful for local and specific political economic needs. One key way to closely examine how unionism resonates with indigenous workers and meets their proximate needs is to look at how they interact with union organizers, particularly on a face-to-face level. This chapter uses ethnographic methods to examine how, through the process of organizing Native workers, union organizers relate and co-articulate with them a political and economic voice. I use the term *co-articulation* to describe how political economic agendas are jointly produced and enunciated through interactions but do not necessarily have the same meaning or purpose for all parties involved.

The interactions I look at took place during the campaign to maintain LIUNA's union representation for health-care workers potentially affected by the NNC's plan to take over administration of the Navajo Area IHS. I call upon my ethnographic research on this six-month-long campaign to look at how union organizers and health-care workers collaboratively constructed the campaign at the intersection of tribal self-determination and tribal labor relations. I treat this not so much as a study of union organizers or of health-care employees but as an ethnographic observation of a union organizing campaign. I compare conversations between workers and organizers during the campaign and how both parties talked about the campaign, within the more general, community-wide debate about tribal self-determination and the delivery of health care found in public forums such as newspapers, letters to the editor, and NNC meetings (see chapter 4). This material includes workers' personal reflections about both the plan to take over health care and the union's campaign, gleaned from ethnographic interviews that I conducted during and after the campaign.

This chapter considers the multilayered alliances and discrete incongruities between the values and goals of LIUNA and those of the Navajo Area IHS workers it seeks to represent. I talk about the alliances in terms of co-articulation between health-care workers and union organizers. This terminology is the most appropriate way to describe a union campaign because it treats a campaign as a joint endeavor—something that comes from union organizers' tactics and strategic agendas and workers' concerns and needs. Thinking in terms of co-articulation underscores three important aspects of a union campaign: the role of worker agency, the actively collaborative aspects of organizing, and the conversational processes that drive the collaboration. Considering how workers co-articulate a union campaign pays attention to the various levels of workers' active participation in campaign strategy, planning, and mobilization *and* the ways in which rank-and-file workers can affect the direction of a campaign by how they interact with professional union organizers. In effect, I argue that despite the ultimate control that union leadership may have over the campaign's direction, the campaign depends on worker participation. Leaving aside the intensely honed persuasion skills of professional organizers, workers make decisions to support a campaign based on their own best assessment of their own situation—they are not duped into supporting it. Leadership might design a campaign, but it needs to be flexible and bend toward local workers' needs and interpretations of their social and political economic situation. Evidently, workers who support a campaign also bend toward the union in that they express their interests through the institutional channels of labor unionism. However, it is important not to assume that worker assent to or support for a campaign is isomorphic with the union's interests; workers may have overlapping and parallel interests with the union's. Attention to worker agency is particularly relevant when discussing workers of color, who historically have suffered the double injustice of economic structural proletarianization coupled with racism at the hands of both management and organized labor.

Additionally, the notion of co-articulation focuses on the way participants make the meaning of the campaign through their interactions. This notion privileges the meaningfulness of a campaign over its success or end results. Instead of asking why organizers succeed in persuading workers—a question that necessarily privileges organizers' skills—I ask how workers and organizers jointly set campaign goals. Moreover, attention to meaning more than results recognizes the itinerant and intermittent nature of union campaigns. They may garner significant support in certain situations but not in others; support for unionism waxes and wanes. Workers do not automatically view their participation in a union campaign as building the labor movement as a whole, but they still want the support and security benefits of union recognition. Lastly, even a campaign that ultimately does not meet its proposed economic or political goals can still be meaningful.

The third facet that co-articulation attends to is how conversational interactions make the organizing happen. In many ways, union campaigns are accomplished through talk—talk that happens in organizing conversations and participants discussing these conversations. The former happens in face-to-face interactions between union organizers; the latter occurs mainly in discussions and strategy sessions that produce a "campaign message." Face-to-face organizing interactions can be just as important as the larger institutional powers that can influence a campaign: capitalism's structural inequalities, the law-creating and law-interpreting authority of (tribal) nation-states, and the self-promoting agendas of business unionism. The importance of organizing conversations lies in the give-and-take between workers and organizers. The same conversational elasticity is found in the campaign message. It is strategically crafted by local and international union leadership and delivered by professional and volunteer organizers. It is expressed through both campaign literature and organizing conversations and is meant to distill the usefulness of unionism and contextualize it for a particular group of workers in a specific geographic locale and political milieu.

Finally, union campaigns are fundamentally based on talk. In large part, the main goal of a union campaign is to articulate the collective voice of workers to express the need and desire to achieve collective political and economic ends. Working toward the collective goals of a union campaign, such as union representation or a collective bargaining contract, does not mean that workers and organizers share the same reason for or interpretation of the campaign's ultimate goals. But through organizing conversations, the meaning of a campaign becomes co-articulated by workers and organizers. The give-and-take of union talk, the conversational aspect of organizing, makes a campaign a joint endeavor. Examined ethnographically, then, the face-to-face interaction and people's planning for and reflections on this conversational interaction can tell us a lot about how workers' collective voice is produced.

Many scholars of union organizing and the labor movement (and progressive factions within the labor movement) have called for an increase in direct organizing as a way to increase worker participation in unionism and to make union campaigns a place where workers' voices can be heard. In other words, face-to-face, direct, social movement–style organizing is key to democratizing unions and to unionism's overall success because it relies on social networking and community-based organizing (e.g., Brodkin 2007; Bronfenbrenner et al. 1998). Not enough attention has been paid to the actual talk that makes networking and organizing happen. What has not been studied in depth is the way in which conversations between workers and organizers can be the engine that drives success and democratization of unionism.

The ethnographic research on conversations between workers and organizers during the Campaign for Union Recognition presented in this chapter provides an additional model for understanding how direct organizing works. Attending to conversational interaction and the talk about these conversations (before and after they happen) helps us see how workers and organizers jointly construct a campaign in a way that meets the needs of both. In particular, conversational interaction can display how workers' voices and the union's goals can be co-articulated in ways that productively overlap without being necessarily isomorphic. This was certainly true with the Campaign for Union Recognition; LIUNA had the delicate task of articulating both a pro-union and a prosovereignty message, and Navajo Area IHS workers sought to express both their support for the concept of tribal self-determination and their frustration with how the NNC enacted self-determination in reservation health care.

Organizing conversations in this campaign illustrate how, for Navajo Area IHS workers, the Campaign for Union Recognition was about having a say in the process of self-determination and maintaining the protection of union representation. For LIUNA organizers, it was about giving voice to the workers' concerns and maintaining a foothold in representing them.

The Campaign for Union Recognition

Before the Campaign for Union Recognition officially kicked off, John Herman, the director of LIUNA's Public Employee Department and overall director of the campaign, made an organizing trip to the Navajo Nation. He came from the union's international office in Sacramento to spend a few days talking with Navajo Area IHS employees, trying to get them to sign a petition supporting the certification of union representation by the Office of Navajo Labor Relations. At this point, some union stewards and volunteer organizers had been using this same organizing tactic for a few weeks, and John wanted firsthand knowledge of how the signature gathering would work. He ended his organizing trip at LIUNA Local 1376's monthly executive committee meeting, where he had a strategy session with the stewards, who had also been trying out the new tactic. In Gallup, New Mexico, thirteen Navajo Area IHS stewards and representatives from the union international sat in the Ramada Inn's smallish, cookie-cutter conference room. None of the four international representatives was Navajo, but one had grown up on the reservation. Two-thirds of the stewards were Navajo, and the other third had been living in Navajo communities for several years. The key agenda item at this May meeting was what John had undecoratively titled the Petition Plus campaign. This title had already been used in the union's open letter to IHS management, informing IHS about the campaign; the title headed the first draft of petitions that organizers had been using. However, it would soon change.

Discussion of the campaign began when Violet Tsosie, a Navajo benefits coordinator from the Shiprock hospital, noted that she encountered some hesitancy from Navajo coworkers she had approached about the issue. She interpreted their misgivings as coming from the appellation *petition*. She stated in the meeting, "I found Navajos, my people, are very wary of the word *petition*. They automatically think of it in the negative sense, because petitions are used in chapters to oust people." On the Navajo Reservation, people can be recalled from chapter governments by local circulation of petitions that request their removal. Violet thought that her coworkers were drawing a parallel between the chapter process and the union-recognition petition and thus were worried that signing the union's petition meant they wanted to oust the tribal government for its actions surrounding 638. This local interpretation is not surprising, considering that some chapters had warned of a failure to reelect or even threatened recall elections for NNC delegates who voted in favor of 638. Indeed, one NNC delegate explained his 638 opposition to the national Native newspaper *Indian Country Today* (2002): "[Community members] pointed me out and sometimes personally threatened me, saying, 'Nelson Gorman, we will not vote for you again if you vote Yes [on the 638 contract].'" Violet further explained that, according to this interpretation, her coworkers were apprehensive about being associated with such a potentially extreme action against the tribal government, even though she felt they were supportive of continued union recognition.

John responded to Violet's appraisal of the campaign's progress by asking, "Should we call this a Positive Petition?" In response, Violet suggested using the term *Campaign for Union Recognition*.[1] While the committee mulled this idea over, John asked the group, "How do you say 'You have a voice!' in Navajo?" One person who spoke Diné blurted out a phrase; the rest of the Diné speakers laughed, and the non-Navajos looked around, trying to figure out the joke. John then asked the group, "What's so funny?" One Navajo man jovially replied, that the Diné "translation" meant "Shut up! It's my turn to talk." Everyone laughed. Finally, after more discussion among the Navajo speakers and a cell phone call to one person's Diné-fluent daughter, they came up with "Shi' zaa Iil'ee," which one speaker roughly translated as "My voice is important." This phrase became an integral part of the written document used to garner signatures in support of union representation, helping set the campaign's tone.

In the conversation about changing the title of the campaign, the committee searched for words that would express the union's goal of providing a voice for Navajo Area IHS employees. Acknowledging Violet's concerns—and her interpretation of her Navajo coworkers' anxieties, about not appearing to oppose the tribal government—the committee changed the title to one that focused more on the act of speaking up for workers rights—gaining union recognition. Heeding Violet's suggestion, John recommended that they add a phrase in Diné reminding workers of the value and power of their opinions—literally, their voice. Other Diné-speaking executive board members followed on John's lead by joking, "Shut up! It's my turn to talk." Although humorous to all, in this context the joke also indexes workers' frustration with management and the 638 process and their strong desire to have their opinions heard. Ultimately, organizers decided to display the Diné phrase and its English rendition, "My Voice Is Important," prominently on the top of the petition sheet. After this new terminology was instituted as part of the campaign, it was constantly reiterated in organizing. Organizers would say to employees, "Your voice is important," or ask, "You want your voice to be heard, don't you? Then sign the petition." Choosing the title *Campaign for Union Recognition* over *Petition Plus* and adding "My Voice Is Important" in both Navajo and English made a more emphatic statement about the petition drive's objective. Union leaders and local workplace leaders—Navajo and non-Navajo alike—co-articulated the necessity that workers' voices be heard, not necessarily as an opposition to 638, centralized tribal leadership, or Navajo health-care managers but as a public, proactive assertion of health-care workers' concerns, needs, and desires.

From IHS to Navajo Nation Control

The IHS is a fundamental social service used by nearly every member of the Navajo community; thus, the transition to tribal administration promised to affect the community as a whole. But the most vocal anxiety about 638 came from health-care employees, those who would likely be affected the most by the 638 takeover. Their dissatisfaction provided a unique opportunity for the labor union representing them. LIUNA had been a credible, well-funded organization on the reservation for nearly twenty-five years, but it had maintained a relatively low profile and garnered only moderate support from IHS workers. The uncertainty created by 638 was a chance for LIUNA to increase its support among these employees. However, LIUNA never took an official stance of opposition to 638, as the Doo' Dah 638 group had done. Instead, it preferred to remain publicly neutral on the issue. Having represented workers at the Navajo Nation and hundreds of employees on other reservations throughout Indian Country, LIUNA and its organizers recognized the importance of tribal sovereignty and the value of publicly respecting it. This stance at times required delicate political and organizing gymnastics, but LIUNA knew that taking a position that was perceived to undercut sovereignty would certainly antagonize tribal leaders and likely alienate the very tribal members whose support for unionization was necessary for its existence in Indian Country—as the discussion over the campaign title demonstrates. Initiating an organizing campaign during the political tensions surrounding 638 would require the union to walk a fine line. Taking health care 638 was directly an issue of tribal sovereignty because it was an effort to enact self-determination. But given the mixed results of the referendum on 638, the general perception of taking health care 638, let alone the local politics of tribal self-determination, was unclear. Even if many tribal members were skeptical of or frustrated with the actions of the centralized tribal government, LIUNA did not want to give the appearance that it opposed the Navajo Nation's right to decide for itself how to administer social services. At the same time, LIUNA felt certain that there was a lot of concern about the plan for 638 among the workers it represented. From LIUNA's perspective, the union's continued existence could help allay some of this concern as the administrative transition took place—to say nothing about the union's own concern about maintaining its foothold as the exclusive collective bargaining agent for Navajo Area IHS workers and receiving their dues. As the strategy session illustrates, what the Campaign for Union Recognition focused on was the extent to which union representation provided an institutionalized voice for workers' concerns.

During this time, when LIUNA presented itself as a stabilizing force in the transition from IHS to tribal control, the NHCSC was going full bore with its efforts to assuage workers' uneasiness about 638. But this corporate outreach effort to healthcare workers did not necessarily have the desired effect and in some cases further calcified people's opposition to 638. The NHCSC held several meetings at various IHS service units. Many were billed as "informal" information sessions, but others were described as mandatory meetings and their legality was so questionable that LIUNA threatened to file unfair labor practice claims against Navajo Area IHS management.[2] These meetings presented management and the tribal council's position that taking health care 638 would improve services and working conditions because it would create more local control over health-care and budget decisions and provide more money for the health-care system as a whole. Although most Navajo and non-Navajo health-care workers respected the tribal government's right and desire to enact self-determination, many were unsure what 638 would mean for their jobs and remained unconvinced.

Betty, a Navajo clerical worker from the Crownpoint hospital, told me she was afraid for her job; she felt that the tribal council and even the Navajo community as a whole were not adequately prepared to administer health care. This was a commonly held opinion—that in the abstract, 638 was a good idea because it allowed the Navajo Tribe to express its political sovereignty but that in the specific case of health care, the tribe was not prepared for the challenges and complications of running its own health services. Other employees felt that the information sessions did not answer their questions about the quality of health-care delivery and working conditions under 638. They felt that the managers running the sessions either were evasive or too frequently had to reply "I don't know" to workers' questions about their future. Laurie, a non-Navajo nurse from the Crownpoint hospital, was very disappointed with the management meeting she attended. As a volunteer organizer with the Campaign for Union Recognition, she characterized herself as aggressively seeking answers in the meeting. Not only did she feel that she received insufficient answers, but she was also agitated at one presenter's suggestion that "management felt the union would not be needed" after 638. Hank related a similar account, of a meeting at his smaller and more remote facility, Inscription House, where his coworkers asked so many questions challenging 638 that the presenter was left nearly in tears. This meeting piqued the Inscription House employees because, as Hank reported, management's presenter billed it as a meeting "to reeducate the people" and during the meeting said that "the referendum vote [on 638] didn't matter."

Some workers told me that management required them to attend these meetings. At some meetings, management even requested that workers make choices, in advance of 638, that would affect the specifics of their employment under 638. Such meetings irked LIUNA and its supporters because these potentially constituted illegal captive-audience meetings, compelling workers to make decisions about their employment without full information and in effect undercutting collective bargaining.[3] Edna, a Navajo nurse, condemned the meetings as "not right, because the corporation [NHCSC] goes and talks to less-educated Navajos…[and] tells workers to do things that they aren't educated about." Access to reliable information about 638 became a huge concern for Navajo Area IHS employees and tribal members alike. Controversy over the partiality of the referendum election was compounded by the dearth of public information about 638. Both of these factors produced the uncertain and divisive atmosphere that ultimately benefited LIUNA's claim to be a stabilizing force during 638, at least as it pertained to the workplace.

The correlation between public perceptions of 638 and the success of the Campaign for Union Recognition should not be terribly surprising, considering that whenever management proposes large-scale changes to the structure of a company or institution, it risks unnerving and alienating the workforce. Workers' responses can be particularly intense if management is not forthcoming about how such changes will affect work conditions or if it does not quell rumors of adverse consequences. A negative work environment engenders a positive environment for union organizing, because workers look to the security provided by unions (Bronfenbrenner and Hickey 2004; Bronfenbrenner and Juravich 1998). Amid the uncertainty created by the 638 transition, LIUNA organizers constructed the union as a viable option for achieving workplace security. They did so by emphasizing the fact that sustaining union recognition could provide workers with consistent labor relations in the change from federal to tribal management. The Campaign for Union Recognition was explicitly not focused on preventing a 638 transition, but instead on channeling the frustration with 638 toward a constructive political outcome that would maintain workers' voices regarding their work conditions. The idea of a workers' political voice through union representation was a key part of both the on-the-ground organizing discourse and the strategic planning for the campaign.

Union Organizers and Organizing Logistics

Planning and preparations for the campaign were conducted jointly by local and international LIUNA leadership. The international leadership consisted of five non-Navajo international representatives/organizers; local leadership came in the form of the executive committee of Local 1376, composed of stewards from several Navajo Area IHS facilities.[4] Much on-the-ground organizing was done by international representatives and organizers who came to the Navajo Reservation for three-day to two-week stints over the course of the six-month-long recognition campaign. Within the organizational hierarchy of LIUNA, there are notable differences between the job categories and responsibilities of international representatives and of international organizers. However, in the context of the Campaign for Union Recognition, these differences are only marginally relevant in that LIUNA employees with both job titles served the same function in the campaign. The most senior leader of the campaign was John Herman. John was a Euro-American with more than thirty years of experience with labor unions, organizing campaigns, and political activism. Much of his organizing experience was gained in United Farm Workers campaigns in the 1970s, and he had early experiences with Native activism in Pacific Northwest "fish-ins." He had been working with and representing Navajo Area IHS employees for more than ten years. As director of the LIUNA division that oversaw representation of public employee locals and campaigns (including campaigns on other Indian reservations), John had many responsibilities besides the Navajo Area IHS campaign. Thus, he did less on-the-ground organizing during the Campaign for Union Recognition but was a part of most planning and strategizing. Jim Kelley was another union leader from the international with a vast amount of experience organizing on the Navajo Reservation and in other Indian communities. Jim was unique in that, although Euro-American, he had grown up on the Navajo Reservation and to this day has many Diné friends still living at the Navajo Nation, some of whom hold positions in the tribal government. He would often try to index his connection to Navajos and Navajo Country by joking with the people he was organizing in a comically exaggerated "Navajo English" accent.[5] Jim was also responsible for several other locals and campaigns, and his participation in the campaign was limited to three-day to one-week visits once a month. Vanessa Redding was another international representative. She was responsible for Navajo and Albuquerque area IHS facilities. Vanessa, an American Indian but non-Navajo (Oneida/Choctaw), had a long and involved experience with the IHS. She had been an IHS employee before taking the job with LIUNA. She was also responsible for duties other than the Campaign for Union Recognition and did only a small amount of organizing during the campaign. The two international representatives/organizers who did the greatest amount of organizing were Allen Cooper and Gary Harris. Both Euro-Americans, they were stationed at a LIUNA local in Phoenix but frequently came to the Navajo Nation to spend several days organizing. Both had experience working with Native employees at IHS facilities in Phoenix, but neither had spent much time at the Navajo Nation. Allen had several years of union experience, both as a member of and as an organizer for the Teamsters before working for LIUNA. Gary's experience with labor unions came mostly from being a benefits coordinator for LIUNA and other unions. Both men brought a tremendous amount of practical organizing experience to the Campaign for Union Recognition. Although representatives from LIUNA's international did much of the organizing with their visits to specific job sites, a great deal was also done by local stewards—both with aid from the international representatives/organizers and on their own, through their daily interactions with their coworkers.

Eight key stewards consistently participated in mobilizing their coworkers to support the Campaign for Union Recognition. Those most active in the campaign were also on the union's local executive committee and thus played a large role in determining campaign strategies. The business manager (and de facto elected leader)[6] of the local was Hank Tomlinson. An African American physician's assistant, Hank worked at two of the smallest facilities in the Navajo Area IHS system, the Inscription House and Navajo Mountain clinics. Hank was very popular in the communities these units served and as a result was a highly successful organizer. Laurie Schultz and Anita John worked at the Crownpoint hospital—a moderately sized service unit in the eastern region of the reservation. Laurie, a Euro-American, worked as a nurse. Anita was a Navajo woman who did clerical work in one of the hospital's administrative departments. Both volunteered to be stewards and take active roles in the union at the beginning of the campaign because they felt strongly about maintaining the union's presence after 638. Laurie had been a member of a union at a hospital outside the reservation, and Anita had previously been a less active member of LIUNA. Organizing at the Navajo Area IHS was relatively new to both of them. Violet Tsosie, in contrast, had been active in earlier workers' rights campaigns on the reservation. Violet, a Navajo steward, represented clerical workers and worked as one at the Northern Navajo Medical Center in Shiprock, one of the largest facilities on the reservation. Calling on her past experience, Violet did a great deal of organizing in her own service unit and at others. She had help organizing from her coworker Kendra Yazzie, another Navajo clerical worker at the Northern Navajo Medical Center. Like Laurie and Anita, Kendra was relatively new to the union but was instrumental in mobilization of the Campaign for Union Recognition because of her persistence and willingness to organize. Another key figure in the organizing was Kate Hoch, a Euro-American lab technician from another large hospital, the Tuba City Indian Medical Center. Kate had been the steward at Tuba City for a few years before the campaign; she already had experience with the union and mobilizing workers. Lewis Kirkpatrick had similar experience with LIUNA. He had been the steward for some years previous and parlayed this experience into mobilizing his coworkers at the Kayenta Health Center. Lewis was also a Euro-American lab technician. His attention to detail and computer database skills were quite useful in tracking which employees had yet to sign the petition. Like Kayenta, the Winslow Health Center in Winslow, Arizona, was a moderately sized facility. The steward from Winslow was Thomas Joe. Thomas, a Navajo supplies manager, was well known and well liked at his service unit for his sense of humor and was effective at convincing his coworkers to support the campaign. Another steward who had several years experience with LIUNA was Elsie Nez, a Navajo clerical worker from the Navajo Area IHS central administration office. She was critical to the organizing because her long experience with the union, central office location, and knowledge of other service units enabled her to help organizing at several job sites, including her own. The last steward connected to the campaign was Edna Begay. Edna did not participate in on-the-ground organizing because she worked at an IHS hospital in Albuquerque—one that was part of the Albuquerque Area IHS, not the Navajo Area.[7] However, she was on the executive committee of the local, and being a Navajo woman who had worked for the IHS for several years and being a union member for almost as long, she had a tremendous wealth of knowledge about the Navajo Area IHS and LIUNA. She frequently drew upon this knowledge to contribute to and comment on strategy discussions for the Campaign for Union Recognition. Although several other workers participated in the campaign and mobilized one another in many different ways, those mentioned above did the majority of the face-to-face organizing for the campaign and participated in the planning of the campaign during executive board meetings.

On a typical day of face-to-face organizing, one to three paid organizers, local stewards, and volunteer activists would spend several hours talking to employees at IHS service units, persuading them to sign the petition calling for union recognition. For the international organizers, the day would start with an early-morning departure from one of the handful of centrally located reservation motels at which they always stayed. Given the vast size and widely dispersed population of the Navajo Nation, the organizers would usually drive one to two hours from the motel to an IHS service unit; sometimes the Phoenix-based organizers found it almost as efficient to make day trips, despite three to seven hours of driving—one way! In advance of an international organizer visit, local volunteer organizers would talk to their coworkers to drum up support for the campaign and in some cases would get a number of people to sign the petition ahead of time. When the paid organizers arrived, the volunteer organizers would show them to the room reserved for the day's organizing activities. Under LIUNA's contract, IHS management was required to provide the union with a room in which to meet with the workers it represented, although these locales were not always the most conducive for organizing. Some were out-of-the-way conference rooms or rooms in satellite buildings rarely frequented by employees, in varying states of disrepair or used as makeshift storage space. Sometimes the union was fortunate enough to get to use employee break rooms. These rooms provided prime access to workers, who would come in and out all day, retrieving food from the refrigerator or popping something into the microwave. In these rooms, the organizers set up to stay for two to six hours. They brought food, souvenirs, and petitions for the workers to sign. Under the collective bargaining agreement, organizers were not permitted to talk to employees while they were working, but they were allowed to during their breaks. In addition to word of mouth by volunteers, the announcements generally did a good job of bringing employees to the organizers. In most cases, a steady stream of employees came to talk to the organizers during the midday hours (11:00 a.m. to 3:00 p.m.), particularly when the organizers brought food (pizza, giant submarine sandwiches, or cookies) and souvenirs (pens, hats, jackets, wallets, I.D. card lanyards, and tote bags) emblazoned with LIUNA's emblem.

Bringing food and souvenirs was an effective method for getting workers to come hear the union's message—no matter the work site (in or outside Indian Country). Lunch on the union was a popular and important social event at IHS facilities—something to break up the day's monotony. Upon arrival, LIUNA organizers or a local steward would make an announcement on the hospital's PA system, letting employees know that the union was providing lunch or coffee and cookies. Gary always told local activists to make these announcements in a casual fashion. "Say, 'Come on down and have some lunch,'" he would suggest. Gary called this kind of organizing Lunch and Learn. During the Campaign for Union Recognition, employees came for the food and stayed for the union's message; nearly every worker who took food and union souvenirs signed the petition. Some organizers resented the energy and time it took to procure the food in advance of the day's organizing—especially because that time might have been better spent doing face-to-face organizing. In their weakest moments, some even complained that workers took too much food and too many souvenirs, even though these same organizers freely passed out the goods to people who did not qualify for the union and thus could not sign the petition.[8] Despite the extra time it took, offering food and souvenirs at the job site was critical to establishing face-to-face contact with workers. It brought workers to the union and helped build a social component to the campaign. When the union visited the job site, coworkers and organizers chatted amicably and interspersed social with political conversations, forging an immediate, although temporary, sense of community.

After organizers established face-to-face contact with workers, they gave a two-minute pitch about union representation in general, the Campaign for Union Recognition, and how both related to the potential 638 takeover. Despite some problems with local connotations of the word *petition*, the petition was a key vehicle for obtaining and legally proving worker support for union recognition. As organizers delivered their pitch, they handed workers a pen and a clipboard with the petition on it. Workers either signed the petition or asked organizers about the campaign and union recognition in general, yet almost all eventually signed the petition; some signed before organizers finished the pitch. What is more, a few were so motivated by the 638 controversy that they signed without even hearing the pitch. Organizers obtained from about ten to fifty signatures per day, working toward an ultimate goal of more than sixteen hundred signatures. This goal represented 55 percent of all Navajo Area IHS employees and the threshold required by the Navajo Nation Collective Bargaining Code (NNCBC) to grant automatic union recognition. Critical to achieving the goal was that professional and volunteer organizers talked to workers about the issues and gave them an opportunity to voice their feelings about tribal self-determination of health care.

Discourses of Organizing

Early in the Campaign for Union Recognition, the executive committee agreed that the union needed to maintain its respect for Navajo Nation self-governance and the NNC's desire to enact a 638 contract for health care. It decided to remain neutral on 638, both when this was first proposed and during the tribal-wide referendum. The decision was advocated most strongly by John, the LIUNA international representative leading the campaign. In an early organizing meeting, John said that the union should make explicitly clear that its only position on 638 was to support a referendum on the issue, not support or oppose the actual 638 takeover. In fact, as a demonstration of LIUNA's decision to support tribal democratic processes, LIUNA members and organizers helped obtain the signatures needed under Navajo law to put 638 to a tribal-wide referendum.[9] LIUNA organizers and stewards chose a neutral position despite the fact that a 638 takeover of health care would compel them to conduct a resource-intensive petition campaign to preserve union recognition. This was also not a simple choice, considering that a small but vocal group of Navajo health-care workers called on the union to take a wholesale stand against the 638 plan and vigorously fight its implementation.[10] Instead, the union leadership maintained its long-held position of noninterference with Navajo self-governance.

Moreover, this decision was made with a forward-looking eye to the argument LIUNA was going to make in its Campaign for Union Recognition. Actively supporting a general referendum on 638 but not interfering with the NNC's decision to go 638 allowed the union to organize from a relatively impartial position. And given that the NNC was being publicly criticized for its handling of the 638 referendum, the Campaign for Union Recognition became an alternative way for Navajo health-care workers to make their voices heard. Union organizers and workers co-articulated the notion of worker voice not as an opposition to the decision-making authority of the NNC but as a way to continue the public conversation about 638. Particularly in the wake of some tribal leaders using the referendum results to foreclose debate on the issue, the Campaign for Union Recognition presented a grassroots political venue parallel to tribal-wide representational and electoral democracy.

Fundamental to the campaign's ability to function as an alternative outlet for Navajo workers' collective voice was the very deliberate stance it took on 638 and thus Navajo tribal sovereignty in general. The union's political standpoint was set up by the first public statement LIUNA made on 638. In an open letter sent to all Navajo Area IHS employees and management, LIUNA explained its stance on 638 and the takeover's relevancy to union representation. A key part of this letter read:

> **On June 19, Navajo Nation voters will have the opportunity to vote on** the contracting out of Indian Health Service programs under the PL 93-638 process. The Union supports the referendum process because this is an important decision for the people of the Navajo Nation. However, we must be prepared to represent employees no matter what the outcome of the vote.

This statement was clearly directed at Navajo employees and the Navajo tribal government, assuring all parties concerned that LIUNA respected tribal sovereignty and the self-determination process. The public letter went on to clarify what actions the union planned on taking in regard to a potential 638 contract:

> **We will be establishing a "Petition Plus" Campaign in early June to achieve [the] 55% goal** and to solicit more membership from all employees in LIUNA Units in the Navajo Area.... Union members and Stewards will be working in "Petition Plus" teams at each Service Unit to get employees' signatures on the petition.[11]

Publicly announcing the intention of the campaign, LIUNA tried to set a tone of noninterference by stating that the campaign was being conducted to prepare for a 638 takeover, not to impede it.

This delicately phrased stance was also expressed in much of the petition itself. The text below was included on every petition sheet, above ten lines for names, addresses, and job classifications:

> The undersigned employees of Navajo Area Indian Health Service hereby designate Local Union No. 1376 of the Laborer's International Union of North America, AFL-CIO as our collective bargaining representative in all matters pertaining to labor conditions, wages and hours of employment. This authorization shall apply to the Employer for whom we are employed on this Date and all other Employers for whom we may become employed after this Date. We signed this authorization for the purpose of securing for the Union voluntary recognition and negotiation rights with our Employer and with any future Employer in accordance with applicable laws, rules and regulations including 15 N.T.C Chapter 7 Section 6. It may be revoked only by those employees of Navajo Area Indian Health Service who have signed this petition and only through written notice to the Union.

There is no direct mention of or commentary on the 638 takeover of health care. Instead, the petition consists of legal language necessary to meet tribal labor code provisions for union recognition. After all, this was the actual document the union would turn in to the Office of Navajo Labor Relations for verification of union recognition. At the same time, its bland legalese presented a neutral but strategically calculated stance of explicitly staying away from the politically charged question of whether health care *should* go 638.

However, in the interactive context of organizing conversations, LIUNA organizers and health-care workers actually did co-articulate the Campaign for Union Recognition as a commentary on the 638 takeover process. This commentary maintained much of the subtlety of the union's neutral stance on whether 638 was the right thing for tribal health care, but in conversations with workers, the union directly engaged their concerns about how the takeover was being enacted and provided them with an opportunity to voice their frustration. This was accomplished partly through how the act of signing the petition was discursively framed—both textually and orally. For example, on the top border of each petition sheet, the union's name was followed by the title of the campaign, laid out as such:

Navajo Nation Healthcare Employees
Local 1376
Laborer's International Union of North America
CAMPAIGN FOR UNION RECOGNITION

But just below the title was

**SHI' ZAA IIL'EE
(MY VOICE IS IMPORTANT)**

This was the phrase chosen by the executive committee at its first meeting about the campaign. Finally, at the bottom of the page, again in bold, was "YES, YOU HAVE A VOICE." It is with these taglines that we can see the union engaging workers about their frustrations and skepticism concerning the tribe's attempt to take health care 638.

These statements only implicitly commented on the 638 process and thus did not outwardly criticize it. But interpreted in the context of the referendum on the 638 takeover, they indexed the concern and public skepticism about how representative the referendum actually was, by implying that it was important that everyone's opinion on this issue be considered and heeded. Moreover, despite the disputed outcome of the referendum vote, the union's campaign and even union recognition might serve as political advocacy. The notion of "voice" was key to framing the campaign. The union's repeated use of the word *voice* was an attempt to connect its campaign to the public discourse about 638. Specifically, LIUNA presented the Campaign for Union Recognition as an additional opportunity for the Navajo health-care workers' perspective to enter public discussions about 638. First and foremost, the process began with talking to workers face-to-face, not only to get them to sign the petition for union recognition but also to listen to them and give them a chance to air their opinions about unionism and the 638 takeover. At their core, these may have been strategic organizing decisions motivated by a union intent on maximizing the success of its petition campaign and thereby maintaining its presence at the Navajo Nation, but Navajo Area IHS workers used the campaign for their own, local expression of political voice. This manifested face-to-face conversations between workers and union organizers.

Face-to-Face Organizing

The way in which the petition's text framed the campaign as part of Navajo public discourse was reiterated in the face-to-face conversations of the organizing drive. Gary and Allen, two of the campaign's lead organizers, did not shy away from referencing the 638 controversy when trying to persuade workers to sign the petition. Equally, the workers used the organizing conversations as an opportunity to share their aggravation about 638. Commencing the organizing only a week after the special election, the organizers used the referendum on 638 to introduce the Campaign for Union Recognition. First and foremost, they knew that because of strong feelings surrounding the referendum and the 638 takeover, mentioning it would attract attention to the union's campaign. Both men frequently began their organizing conversations by commenting on the 638 referendum. Gary, for example, often began by asking, "Have you heard about the referendum on 638?" He would follow up by commenting that although the results of the election showed voter opposition to 638, "unfortunately, they [were] still going ahead with it." He would then conclude that the tribal labor code allowed for union recognition, so if workers signed the petition, union representation for Navajo Area IHS workers would be preserved. In nearly all cases, the conversation ended with the worker signing the petition. Often, as a worker signed, he or she would comment about not wanting health care to go 638 or about concerns over how the 638 decision came out.

Although organizing conversations would vary from interaction to interaction, they consisted of three basic parts: (1) the characterization of the referendum election as an expression of voter opposition to 638; (2) speculation that 638 would proceed despite opposition; and (3) the proposition that maintaining union representation was the best response to 638. In the first part, the organizers worked to align the union with the Navajo public without necessarily criticizing the takeover itself. For example, Gary referred to the voters' opposition, not the union's opposition, yet his characterization of the results as an opposition to 638 was meant to index a sense of solidarity between the union and workers: the union understands Navajo people's interpretation of the referendum and their reaction to the result. The latter is also expressed in the second part of the organizing conversation. Stating, "Unfortunately, they are still going ahead with it," Gary referenced people's sense of the referendum's limited utility and democracy. Few workers disagreed with this assessment. Moreover, he invariably left "they" ambiguous, letting workers decide for themselves whether 638 was being predominantly pushed by hospital management or by the tribal council. Gary could thus avoid explicitly speaking against the NNC and against its sovereign decision-making authority. Presenting the petition after referring to the problems surrounding 638, Gary framed union recognition as a response to the problems, not an adversarial challenge. Not explicitly stating that the union petition could undo or counteract the tribal council's actions, Gary constructed organizing conversations to position the union's petition as a solution to workers' feelings of futility concerning the 638 referendum.

Allen followed a similar organizing pattern, typically starting out with a reference to the controversial nature of the referendum. But he would first plainly ask workers, "Have you folks signed the petition yet?" This question rhetorically normalized the campaign and the union's presence at the job site by implying that the petition was something they not only would have familiarity with but also would have likely already signed. Allen would follow this question by commenting that "638 didn't pass, but it did." This paradoxical statement acknowledged the complicated legal and political situation that allowed the 638 process to proceed even though an overwhelming majority had voted against it. The contradictory nature of this statement also indexed another common complaint about the 638 referendum: that the wording of the ballot—a vote to prohibit 638—had those against 638 voting yes and those in favor voting no. Including this comment at the beginning of organizing conversations aligned Allen and LIUNA with Navajo workers who were critical of the 638 referendum process. It indirectly connected union recognition to an anti-638 position, by echoing worker sentiment about it.

In the organizing conversations, LIUNA organizers may have been the first to bring up 638, but it took little to get health-care workers to share their frustrations about it. Many workers signed the petition sheet immediately after the organizers' pitch, often stating as they signed, "Oh, I don't want it to go 638" or "I'm not for 638," even though LIUNA organizers explained that the union was neither against nor in favor of 638. There were other, subtler reasons the Campaign for Union Recognition became articulated as an attempt to engage in the larger tribal political debate over self-determination for health care. The actual subject matter of organizers' conversations was less about unionism than about people's anxieties over 638. LIUNA organizers would take their cues from the workers, letting them guide the conversation before organizers asked them to sign in favor of unionization. In many ways, this kind of interactional assessment is common to union organizing in general (Kamper 2003). A good organizer will appraise a worker's level of support in order to figure out what he or she can say to be persuasive and how much of a commitment to actually ask of the worker. This discursive tactic requires flexibility on the part of the organizer and guards against flat-out rejection of support, which is much more damaging to a campaign than leaving a conversation with an ambivalent worker—sustaining the potential for future commitment (the proverbial "Why don't you just think about it"). In-conversation evaluation also gives a worker control over the direction of the conversation and more often than not forces the organizer to bend toward the concerns of the worker.

In the Campaign for Union Recognition, LIUNA organizers and Navajo Area IHS workers did not spend much time talking about the general benefits of unionism. The conversations were highly contextualized in tribal politics, and the need for union recognition was often more implied than asserted. Of course, situational organizing attuned to the specific, practical needs of workers is a sign of good organizing tactics. The Campaign for Union Recognition became highly intertwined with local political debates about 638 rather than pushing the merits of unionism. Organizers did construct union representation as a solution to the future uncertainty of 638, but workers seemed equally invested in the way the campaign gave them an opportunity to speak their minds on 638—it continued the public conversation forestalled by the referendum results.

Consider the following conversation, which took place at Fort Defiance Indian Hospital in Fort Defiance, Arizona, on July 13, 2001. The participants were LIUNA organizer Garry Harris (GH) and a female Navajo IHS employee (NE1). Nonparticipating observers were LIUNA organizer Allen Cooper, Navajo Area IHS steward Brad Jensen, and researcher David Kamper.

Line	Participant	Utterance
1	NE1	"What's going on?"
2	GH	"Have you been in to sign *our* petition yet?"
3	NE1	"No, I just heard it through the gossip line."
4	GH	"It's in reference to 638, not pro or con, but just so *we* keep representation after 638."
5	NE1	"What if *they* don't honor the petition, because *they* didn't honor the referendum?"
6	GH	"Well, *we* can only worry about that when it happens. Now *we* can just follow *their* laws.

Gary hardly mentions the union. His only gesture toward the idea is to refer to representation and the Navajo employee's focus on disillusionment with 638. Gary sympathizes with the woman in a way that aligns the union with her and her coworkers. Upon being asked by Gary to sign the union's petition, the Navajo worker hesitates. She then says that she doubts the tribe will respect LIUNA's petition, contending that if the tribal government did not respect the votes in the 638 referendum, why would it heed the union's petition? Utilizing in-conversation assessment, Gary responds that all that can be done is to follow the Navajo labor code and go from there. The woman concedes that he is right, and she signs the petition.

This conversation is much more about tribal politics than it is about the necessity of union recognition. As in many of Gary's organizing conversations, he makes sure not to criticize the tribal government. But he also makes no effort to distance the union from this woman's frustration with the 638 process. For example, in line 6, he asserts that the union will follow the NNCBC and trust the system. But Gary implicitly assents to her negative evaluation of the referendum as being unrepresentative, given in line 5. He does so in line 6 by acknowledging the possibility that the tribal government might not honor the union's petition ("Well, we can only worry about that when it happens") and by implying that in comparison, the union's actions were aboveboard, because all it was trying to do with the campaign was follow the tribal labor relations code. Gary also expresses the union's desire not to undercut the sovereign rights of the tribal government to make decisions about health care (line 4) and asserts that the union wants to follow the tribe's labor relations process—not to appeal to authorities outside tribal law. Gary and the Navajo worker co-articulate a positive valuation of fair and transparent tribal government actions and ultimately—with her signing of the petition—co-construct the Campaign for Union Recognition as a potential avenue for participating in responsive tribal governance.

Moreover, his use of plural first-person pronouns (italicized in lines 2, 4, and 6) is not insignificant. As in many other organizing conversations, Gary's use of these pronouns expresses solidarity with the Navajo workers. In line 2, when he speaks of *"our* petition," it is clear that he means the union's petition. However, in line 4, "so *we* keep representation" is ambiguous; he is testing whether the employee wants to be included in the idea of maintaining representation—the distinction between the union and the employees is much clearer than in line 2. Finally, after the employee uses *they* (line 5) to describe the NNC, Gary's response of *we* in line 6 is the clearest expression of solidarity with Navajo workers. Juxtaposed with her use of *they*—an explicit separation of the health-care workers from the NNC—Gary's use of *we* creates an us-versus-them opposition, with Gary clearly implying that this employee (all the employees) and Gary (the union) are on the same side. He implicates the union and the local political context by concluding, "Now *we* can just follow *their* laws." Here he suggests that it is not the union that makes the laws, nor even breaks them; it just seeks to respect them. Ultimately, she concurs by signing the petition. By using personal pronouns, the Navajo worker and Gary align the campaign with her (and her coworkers') complaints about the NNC.

By emphasizing tribal politics, some employees and organizers downplayed the campaign as a commitment to unionism. This approach was especially effective when a worker hesitated to sign the petition. Although where the hesitancy came from was not always readily apparent, Gary and Allen would often interpret it as uncertainty about the union. In some cases, uncertainty was explicitly expressed, and the organizers would often try to ease it. But more often than not, the reason behind workers' tentativeness was unclear. Gary and Allen would commonly respond to this pause by reassuring workers in a way that distanced the Campaign for Union Recognition from a more significant commitment to unionism. They did this by reminding workers that one did not have to be a union member to sign the petition—sometimes going as far as to assure workers that the campaign had "nothing to do with membership." In most cases, it was not clear at all that the commitment of membership was the problem for these employees—all of whom eventually signed the petition. What is more, even after workers had signed the petition, Gary and Allen would tell them to encourage their coworkers and friends to sign the petition and would add, "Make sure they know they don't have to be members to sign." In effect, they reified a concern about membership that was not explicitly enunciated by workers and in so doing contributed to an articulation of the campaign that was not about unionism.

It is important to remember that at the beginning of the Campaign for Union Recognition, LIUNA membership among Navajo Area IHS workers was relatively low. Over the course of the campaign, this changed. Organizers prompted the more enthusiastic supporters to join the union; many signed membership cards after signing the recognition petition. Also, since the campaign, union membership among Navajo Area IHS employees has grown significantly. Several years after the Campaign for Union Recognition, the union mobilized a membership drive that nearly doubled membership, compared with levels before the campaign. LIUNA organizers believe that much of this success was built upon the success of the Campaign for Union Recognition

In part, the distinction between support for recognition and becoming a union member is a product of the way the NNCBC is written—and is typical of how union recognition is regulated nationally. In a recognition campaign such as this one, the union needs to demonstrate only that workers want collective bargaining rights, not that they want to join a union. Irrespective of this legal low hurdle for union recognition, in the context of face-to-face organizing, union membership was downplayed in many instances. These instances represent a striking departure from the way union campaigns generally function. Membership growth is fundamental to the strength and continued existence of any union and is thus ingrained in the strategy and practice of organizing. Nearly all union campaigns have an underlying goal of increasing membership, and that is what is so significant about LIUNA organizers going out of their way to eschew the importance of membership.[12] This distinction is highly relevant to the way in which the Campaign for Union Recognition could be co-constructed as a referendum on local tribal politics and not on the union.

The organizers and IHS employees co-articulated the act of signing the petition not so much as a pledge to LIUNA but as a political response to the 638 issue. Strategically highlighting that the petition was not necessarily a commitment to the union, Allen and Gary made it more likely for the campaign to be dialogically constructed as a protest against 638 and a loss of voice. Because organizers did not ask workers to make a significant commitment to unionism, many workers began to construct the campaign as organizing against 638. Following Gary's and Allen's lead, Kate Hoch said she always made it clear to signers that the petition was distinct from union membership: "I always reassure people that this obligates them in no way to join the union. And 'You don't have to be in the union. This merely states that even though you may never use the union, you still would like to have that there as a little backup if you need it.'"

Later I asked Liz Begaye, one of Kate's Navajo lab-mates, about signing the petition. She said that Kate and other union representatives had told her that the petition was for 638: If you're against this...here sign it.' That was pretty much it.... We were against [638]. We were kind of thinking maybe [LIUNA would] do something about it for us...they're on our side. So, so that was good." She further clarified what she hoped the union would do in regard to 638: "They'll be speaking for us...that a lot of people they're not going for 638.... We still want to work underneath the government. We don't want to go under the tribe.... [The union is] on our side to, to try to hopefully make that happen." From what Kate told me about how she organized and from what I observed of Kate's organizing, it is unlikely that Kate told any employee that the union's petition was an "anti-638 petition." Nonetheless, Liz aligned the petition with a position that would stop 638. This example illustrates how organizers' coupling of comments about frustration over 638 with comments that deemphasized the significance of union membership created a context wherein workers could interpret the petition campaign as less of an overt act of support for the union and more of an act against 638. This is not to say that workers did not understand the campaign or that organizers were trying to dupe workers into supporting something different from what they were told. Rather, the campaign was dialogically articulated as a way for workers to voice their concerns, opinions, and needs in regard to 638 for Navajo Area IHS. Labor relations became a place where workers could express their feelings not just about unionism but equally about Navajo Nation politics and practices of self-determination. Workers used the campaign to protest how the tribal government was trying to enact self-determination and to assert their rights—equally as tribal members and (potential) tribal employees—to have a say in how self-determination should be enacted.

In addition to workplace organizing conversations between health-care employees and union organizers, strategy discussions in local executive committee meetings were important settings for negotiating the meaning of the Campaign for Union Recognition. In these meetings, job-site stewards and international representatives/organizers discussed health-care workers' responses to the campaign and collectively decided what to say during organizing. At one such meeting, Jim Kelley and Edna

Begay led a conversation about how the 638 takeover could potentially change healthcare delivery. The conversation began with a discussion about the process by which 638 might go forward, since the referendum had failed to stop it. Because the NNC still had to take a final vote to approve a 638 contract for health care, Edna suggested that the union needed to conduct a grassroots campaign at chapter houses and convince them to put pressure on their elected council representatives to reject 638. She said she was upset with the union and felt that the group was focusing too much on the workers' rights aspect of 638 and not enough on how patients and medical services would be affected. She also suggested that the union garner more publicity about how services would suffer cutbacks. She proceeded to list several changes that could adversely impact health care after 638, such as transportation, standards, and liability changes.

Jim Kelley and John Roberts, a non-Navajo organizer from the union's international office, vociferously agreed with her appeal to incorporate more issues beyond the workplace into the campaign. They suggested that the union formulate a public letter composed of questions to be sent to the tribal council to raise awareness of people's concerns. Months later, when the NNC was making its final decision on whether to approve 638, the union hosted a seminar, under Jim and John's direction, for council delegates. To ensure that workers' concerns about 638—both workplace and general health-care issues—were aired and factored into council members' decisions, they had three employees speak at this information session. Edna had convinced the lead organizers from LIUNA that the Campaign for Union Recognition ought to be about much more than mere union recognition, but an opportunity to meaningfully advocate for the Navajo people most affected by NNC.

Jim took Edna's guidance in his organizing conversations. For instance, at a lunchtime meeting I observed at the Crownpoint facility, Jim detailed problems with the tribal council's planned takeover of health care. He directed his criticism at the actual administration of health care. He rhetorically asked the assembled workers, "What are Grandma and Grandpa gonna do if they live near Hopi or Zuni and can no longer use those local IHS facilities and have to drive a long distance to a Navajo Nation health-care facility?" Then he asked, "Or what about your kids at school in Oklahoma? They can't go to IHS there." Both questions engaged workers' concerns about what would happen to their families' health care. As Jim suggested, under a 638 health-care contract, Navajos would potentially no longer be eligible for general IHS health care and instead would have to exclusively use Navajo Nation health care. This change could cause significant transportation hardships for some people. The nature of these concerns had more to do with problems of health care in general and less to do with workplace issues. Nonetheless, the workers at Crownpoint used the very health services facilities where they worked, and because most of them were Navajo, they were interested in the health-care issues affecting the social life of the tribe as a whole. Most agreed with Jim's comments by nodding along with him and then signing the petition. What is significant about this interaction is that Jim knew that ultimately union representation could do little to fix this circumstance. Issues of health-care delivery would clearly fall outside the purview of any collective bargaining agreement. But more importantly, Jim was following Edna's admonition, recognizing that the union needed to engage health-care workers' concerns as community members, not just employees. In this tribal context, the union's campaign meant conceiving of the union—conventionally a worker's strongest advocate in labor relations—and the campaign itself as entities through which workers could express their concerns about their political lives and their general health and well-being.

Articulating Voice

Navajo Area IHS workers held a variety of opinions about the usefulness of union recognition and how it might or might not affect a 638 takeover of health care. But workers' opinions about 638 were channeled into the Campaign for Union Recognition regardless of whether union recognition was, or even could be, the ultimate answer to people's misgivings about 638. The campaign itself conveyed a sense of optimism; it presented an alternative to the uncertainty created by the NNC's handling of 638—particularly how the referendum was perceived as foreclosing, not opening, the decision-making process. To many who were unsatisfied with the results of the referendum, the campaign allowed for continued public debate. This was important because tribal leaders supporting 638 considered the referendum to have settled the debate and IHS hospital managers even began convening meetings throughout the Navajo Area IHS system to prepare workers for the 638 takeover. The campaign's organizing conversations provided a "safer" space for worker expression than the anxiety-provoking, obligatory "information sessions." Moreover, even if most people considered 638 a foregone conclusion, from employees' and the union's perspective, what work conditions would be like after 638 was still open to discussion. Thus, the Campaign for Union Recognition stood in dramatic contrast to the referendum's passive construction of public voice over the issue. The referendum relied on people's silence, their lack of willingness to "prohibit the tribal government to take over healthcare"; union recognition was articulated as an active opportunity for Navajo people, as health-care workers, to have a say in what the delivery of tribal health care would like. Thus, the Campaign for Union Recognition mirrored some Navajo beliefs about language and how it is used, which may have added to the campaign's popularity among Navajo health-care workers.

Many key volunteer organizers reflected on how the union and the campaign were important for voicing their views. In particular, they were conscious of their roles as intermediaries between coworkers, union leadership, health-care management, and even the tribal government and of the worker's voice at the center of these forces. Laurie, the non-Navajo nurse from Crownpoint, continually referred to the need for both herself as a local leader and the people she represented to vocally demand their rights. In our conversation, she frequently told me how she tried to rally people around the concept of a public voice and sticking up for oneself. She would try to radicalize her coworkers by encouraging them: "Guys, stand up and be counted." She told me that sometimes people would ask her what they were going to get out of the union. Why should they sign it? "And I say, 'A voice. Verbalize your opinion. You need to tell them what you need.'" Other times, she used the fear of losing a voice to challenge people to not squander the opportunity the union would give them to speak up. When talking about the need to support and participate in the union's campaign, she told her coworkers, "I need you, we need you, you need you." Or she would ask them to consider what the workplace would be like without the union: "What will happen if the union isn't around after 638? Doesn't that scare you? Who's going to talk for you?" Here she implies that workers should proactively take advantage of the Campaign for Union Recognition because the alternative may be no voice at all.

Laurie recognized that as a steward, she was standing up and standing out, and she realized that this drew a lot of attention to her. However, she thought this necessary; it was critical to say to management: "We're here, we're alive, we bite." But also she saw herself as fulfilling the crucial function of getting information to rank-and-file workers. She stated, "[The] little guy needs more information…so I'm the information." Laurie regarded herself as a link between individual workers and the collective power of the union. She was there to inform workers, represent them, and fight for them, and the best way to do it was by being as vocal and proactive as possible. Her coworkers responded very positively to these actions.

Violet, the Navajo benefits coordinator, and Anita, the Navajo clerical worker, expressed similar views. Violet told me why the union was important: "We want to come to the table and have a say," and the union was the only way to do that. Violet warned against letting managers and the tribal council make decisions that affect the lives of Navajo Area IHS employees without speaking up and demanding to take part in the process. Anita also opined on the need to contest a system that might not consider workers' interests. In an interview, I asked her the best way to convince coworkers to sign the petition. She answered that it was simply to inform them that without union recognition, they would not have a public voice after 638:

> If they sign…basically they're signing because they want to have a voice. They still want to have a voice once we go under 638.… They've been signing because they know they'll still have a voice. But if they don't have a voice, the tribe [council] is gonna tell them, and [the tribal council is] gonna basically do what they want *or* [my coworkers are] gonna quit once they go 638.

If people were unsure about signing, she would tell them, "You want your opinion to matter. I know I do." To her coworkers (and equally to me), Anita asserted that IHS employees had an unquestionable right to help determine the nature of their employment. This belief is fundamental to the union ideology that it is appropriate for organizers and workers to speak with determination about issues affecting their workplaces.

However, just as important was the more localized meaning of Anita's beliefs. Her assertions contended that power and authority do not rest merely in the hands of the tribal council but rather that the workers could take control over their work conditions by being active public advocates for themselves as a collective. All three women connected speaking up to provoking political action. The connection between language and action is not alien to Navajos. Indeed, conventionally, Navajos tend to believe in a strong connection between language and causality, that words said in specific ways and specific contexts can bring things into the world and make events happens (House 2002; Reichard 1950; Witherspoon 1977). Given this view, the Campaign for Union Recognition's articulation of a particularly active role for workerss may have been appealing. However, as House (2002) notes, we must be cautious in asserting homogenous Navajo language ideologies. The volunteer organizers themselves had their own views on how notions of language use and voice related to the campaign.

Anita, like Laurie, acknowledged that articulating a strong public voice was no simple matter and did not come without political consequences. She was willing to tell her tribal council representative, in regard to the 638 referendum and takeover, "We are still going to have a voice whether you like it or not." But she knew that not everyone could be this forward. Commenting on her coworkers, she said:

> They're followers. They want somebody to speak up for them. They'd rather stay in the background...which I can understand because, you know, if you speak up and you don't really talk for yourself, then you're going to be shot down by management. And that's what a lot of people don't want. They don't want the retaliation. So for me...if I say something and I believe in what...I'm doing, and of course I'll speak up, regardless of whether I get fired or not. It's just [that] I'm gonna speak up. I'm gonna say something.

Anita illustrates an activist's conviction about standing up for what one believes in and also about the importance of workers' voices being recognized as valid and authoritative (see Brodkin 2007). This is a key part of a proactive public voice, speaking up so that workers will be heard, even if their voices contradict health-care and tribal governmental authority.

Violet's feelings about expressing a public voice resonated with Anita's conviction. However, she took this articulation one step further by suggesting that the union's notion of public voice needed to defer to local Navajo worker notions. Violet contended that public voice should be articulated cautiously and not without regard for local norms and relationships. She posited another apparent Navajo ideology of appropriate language use:

> My Navajo people aren't the most aggressive.... They always say we want to be the harmonious kind of people, but then there are some of us who...want to go in

there and ruffle somebody's feathers. But I only do it because there's stuff I know I can defend and there's documents there that allow me to defend [my rights].

Violet said that people had to be sure of their arguments when speaking up and should not speak for the sake of drawing attention to themselves and their cause. Indeed, she recognized that there is a limit to how aggressively one can campaign for workers' rights. For her, it is inappropriate to be seen as a singular, self-centered individual telling the tribal government what to do. For example, at the beginning of the campaign, John wanted to sign Violet's name to a press release quote stating that it would be a "real risk" if the tribal government went forward with 638 for IHS and that Navajos should "immediately stop" the process. Violet explained her refusal to be associated with this commentary: "It's not...anybody's place to tell the Navajo Nation Council what to do. And I'm...only one person, and I'm from Shiprock, you know. I'm not gonna...there's *no way* that I'm gonna say something like that."

Violet felt that John's suggested comments made her appear to be a self-serving individual and missed the point of the Campaign for Union Recognition. From her perspective, it was okay to speak up for people's rights, but not to appear to be one individual telling the tribal government what to do. Moreover, she suggested that a public voice, even expressed as a protest against the tribal government's actions or policies, was not a directive demanding certain actions out of leadership, but rather an appeal to public debate and an invitation to a public discussion about what is responsible and responsive leadership. Her refusal to be associated with the suggested commentary forced the union leadership to adjust its strategy and remake the campaign more in terms of Navajo workers' desires and needs to articulate their concerns and frustrations with 638, not to command their leaders to act a certain way ("immediately stop") or suffer consequences ("real risks"). The latter is the language of adversarial unionism that seeks results through credible threats backed up by job actions and withholding of labor. This was not the approach of the Campaign for Union Recognition. Indeed, it is telling that striking for recognition was never mentioned as an option by anyone involved with the campaign.

Instead, as an expression of tribal labor relations, the Campaign for Union Recognition was a way to keep the debate about 638 going. It was a way for Navajo workers to keep their voice on the issue of health-care delivery and their place within this system. Even though the standard repertoire of tribal governance—referendums and representational democracy—had been exhausted, people were not satisfied enough to conclude the debate. The standard devices had not covered all that needed to be covered. For responsive self-governance to take place, everyone needs to feel as though he or she has been heard. Public conversation needs to be kept alive, even if the way to resolution is unknowable or unreachable. In this sense, the process of articulation is as important as the results; therefore, even people who thought they ultimately could not effect change participated in the campaign. This is a hallmark of direct democracy—everyone's voice being heard—and the union campaign presented a means for this.

Conclusion

Violet's comments on the Navajo-ness of asserting public political voice reflect the notion of *hózhó*. This complex and fundamental Navajo value is commonly translated as "harmony" or "balance." Hózhó is thought to, ideally, suffuse all relations—not just between humans but also between humans and the supernatural, the natural world, and the past and future. Given the importance of this cultural value, Violet's ambivalence toward her own political activism is understandable. She, Anita, and Laurie all recognized how speaking up had the potential to draw attention to them as individuals, consequently creating the possibility of being accused of disrupting harmony. Aubrey Williams (1970), in his study of Navajo chapter house political discourse, came to a similar conclusion. He states that rather than publicly speak out against popular opinion, Navajo people will refrain from voting (taking a public position) on local issues.

It is important to attend to instances of Navajo self-censure and conformity in the name of not disrupting the harmony that is political consensus. But there is also evidence that Navajo elites have marshaled appropriate notions of language use to maintain social stratification. Connecting David Aberle's (1966) and Jerrold Levy and Stephen Kunitz's (1974) observations of Navajo socioeconomic status to Navajo ideologies of language use, Margaret Field (2009) notes that the pressure to speak Navajo appropriately in political contexts (such as in tribal council, chapter house, and school board meetings) may not be about just preserving indigeneity, but also about preserving political economic power structures (see also House 2002). Commonly, families that have lost many of their Navajo speakers are the ones forced by economic circumstances to work off the reservation and therefore learn English, use it more frequently, and place more value on it. In contrast, families that have long had traditional forms of wealth, such as livestock and good grazing land, have been able to stay on the reservation, avoid language loss, and run for and hold Navajo public office. Families that use more English and are seen as having adopted more "Anglo ways" are known to complain about the pressure to learn Navajo in schools (Field 2009; House 2002). At the same time, it is in the political interest of those in power to assert "traditional" notions of appropriate language use that map onto notions of harmony and disharmony, with accusations of disharmony being an easy way to forestall and delegitimize public criticism of political leadership.

Looked at from another perspective, employing one's political voice can be seen as an attempt to restore harmony, not to upset it. This notion is apparent in Violet's and Anita's confidence that they are doing the right thing by advocating for the collective welfare of their coworkers and their community and by trying to make change happen through the active use of their voices. Harmony does not necessarily mean silence; it is important not to oversimplify hózhó as a sort of "noble savage" stoicism, devoid of vigorous political debate. Moreover, historically, the Navajo Nation is far from devoid of vociferous political advocacy or disputes (see chapter 4). Indeed, the Navajo Nation, in large part, was able to avoid the ruin of the Dawes Act of 1887 and instead expand the size of its reservation because its leaders vigorously lobbied Congress (Bailey and

Bailey 1986). Additionally, there is a long tradition of active, translocal political debate among the Diné—much of which intensified with the development of a national council–style government. And it is not just in NNC chambers that vigorous debate takes place. It happens in many public forums, such as chapter houses and letters to the editor and opinion sections of the *Navajo Times*. It is also not uncommon to see people picketing and posting homemade political protest signs outside NNC chambers when the council is in session and making decisions on significant issues.

The political debates in these public forums are not simply based on the binary factionalism of progressives versus traditionalists. They are complicated and multifaceted and involve people actively declaring their position. Both the livestock reduction/IRA constitutional debate and the politics surrounding Peter MacDonald's presidencies demonstrate active political voice. The Campaign for Union Recognition ought to be understood within this historical political context. In all three cases, Navajo people used whatever political avenues were available to articulate a public political voice, even when there was no direct guarantee they could effect political change. In the case of livestock reduction, people actively spoke out against the policy even after the federal government began wholesale implementation. Those most displeased with the policy and its disastrous results used the referendum over the IRA constitution to express their frustration and to protest governments that would institute reduction policies. In the case of the Peter MacDonald administration, his supporters were willing to stage public protests even after he was removed; some were willing to use force to delegitimize the officials who replaced his administration. Furthermore, for many years after his removal, many people still used presidential and local ballots to speak out against MacDonald's political adversaries. Similarly, Navajo Area IHS employees used the Campaign for Union Recognition to articulate their frustration with the health care 638 decision and to continue to have a say in how tribal health care would be delivered and what their place within this system of healthcare delivery would be. They used the political avenue available to them to make sure their voices were heard.

six
Grassroots Expressions of Tribal Labor Relations

Without much warning, on the first Monday of May 2004, a picket line formed across the street from the hospital in the western Navajo Nation town of Tuba City. Among the more than one hundred protesters, a Navajo elder wielded a bullhorn. She called out one of the hospital directors by name and said, "I know your uncles! I know your dad! I know your mother! What are you doing to your people? You come from a great line of medicine men.... You are doing things you were taught not to do.... You need to root for your own people!" (Helms 2004). This woman voiced the frustration of the Tuba City hospital workers and community members who stood next to her with picket signs in hand, chanting and beating on a powwow drum. She also spoke figuratively for hundreds not at this protest, including other hospital employees and community members from Tuba City, from the hospital's western reservation regional service area and from across the Navajo Nation as a whole. She and other Diné were protesting NNC mismanagement of the process of enacting self-determination for reservation health care. She bemoaned the tribe's takeover of the Tuba City hospital and the leadership selected to manage the newly tribally run hospital. Her admonition of the board member was part of a workplace-based protest that began as outrage over the firing of a handful of Navajo employees and developed into a grassroots movement to demand both improved labor relations at the hospital and greater accountability from its managerial leaders and from tribal leadership in general.

The precursor to the protest had occurred almost two and a half years earlier, when the NNC sought to resolve the public tension surrounding its proposed 638 takeover of health care. Efforts such as the Campaign for Union Recognition (see chapter 5) and other Navajo public expressions of dissatisfaction with the NNC's takeover plan (and the process by which this plan was decided upon) succeeded in pressuring the NNC into compromising on how it would implement 638 for health care. Instead of taking the entire Navajo Area IHS system 638, the NNC approved what it called a 638 pilot program in August 2002. It established a health-care corporation to take over administration of the IHS hospital in Tuba City. About a month later, on September 30, 2002, the Tuba City Regional Health Care Corporation (TCRHCC) officially began its role as owner and operator of the Tuba City hospital. Many Tuba City community members and hospital employees had originally opposed a 638 takeover of Navajo Area IHS hospitals. When 638 became a reality at Tuba City, however, many warmed up to the idea and tried to approach the situation with a positive attitude. One short year later, hospital employees felt that their work conditions had significantly declined, to the point that many were concerned about the security of their jobs, the hostility in their work environment, the possibility of retribution from management, and the poor performance of the hospital CEO and board of directors. Concern for workplace conditions reached a boiling point in May 2004 when, three days after five employees had been terminated, more than one hundred employees and community members began a week of picket-line protests across the street from the hospital's administration building.

* * *

Tribal sovereignty and self-determination mean different things to different people in different contexts. It is clear, however, that tribal self-determination is critically linked to tribal economic development: economic growth can be instrumental in sustaining the institutions necessary for self-governance; at the same time, economic development is rarely successful without well-developed and legitimate structures of self-determination. In examining the economic development of the Seminole tribal gaming industry, Jessica Cattelino (2008:148) called this connection a form of "economic nationalism," wherein "the tribal nation increasingly is consolidated and conceived around economic life. Like other government leaders,...tribal officials appeal to discourses of nationhood that are based in economic strength, diversity, and corporate organization." Because of the consolidation of economic development and governmental functions, tribally run workplaces can be thought of as crucial front lines where people directly experience tribal self-governance. Their day-to-day experience of labor relations dramatically affects and mirrors their notion of how self-determination works.

This chapter details the conditions and events leading up to and following the firing of five employees on a day known to Tuba City hospital employees as Black Friday. Using Black Friday as a rallying point, several concerned hospital employees and community members formed an ad hoc grassroots group. Calling themselves the Hospital

Employees and Community Members Committee (HECMC),[1] they organized workplace protests, publicized what they thought to be the main problems at the hospital, and formulated a political platform to provide solutions for these problems. Here I consider how tribal employees recognize their collective interest and work together to improve their situation—both as employees and as community members—and how this interest relates to the overall ideals of economic nationalism expressed in Navajo Nation self-determination at the Tuba City hospital. The flash point in labor relations at the Tuba City hospital illustrates a layer of tribal labor relations not yet covered—that which takes place on the grassroots level. The workplace activism discussed in this chapter was not organized by a labor union but instead emerged from ad hoc protests made by workers rallying against what they saw as the unacceptable direction of tribal labor relations at the Tuba City hospital. Moreover, legal institutions did not support these workers. Under management's interpretation of its tribal government–authorized contract to run the Tuba City hospital, there was no place for collective workplace action, nor was it protected by federal or tribal law. Indeed, Tuba City hospital employees and community members took action precisely because they felt that the CEO and board of directors were acting in ways that ignored, stifled, and overrode workers' active participation in determining how the hospital would be run. This ad hoc group of workers and community members responded by publicly demanding more accountability from the hospital CEO and board of directors: they vociferously protested the firing of their coworkers, insisted on the ouster of certain members of upper management, sought greater input in how the hospital's directors were selected, and demanded union recognition. Their protestation took many forms: public rallies and picket lines, speaking up at community and workplace meetings, distributing flyers and pamphlets at the job site and in the community, placing ads in and writing letters to local newspapers, and entering a proworker float in a local, tribally sponsored parade.

This grassroots workplace activism was not necessarily a resistance to or a rejection of the idea of Navajo self-determination as expressed by taking the hospital 638. Rather, it was an assertion that tribal leadership, whether corporate or political, must be accountable to the people. Authority to lead comes from the people and from responsible leaders, not from the rank of a position. This idea could be seen at the picket line in the elder's public shaming of the hospital board member. Through the blare of the bullhorn, she voiced the community's collective reminder that this specific manager had a connection and responsibility to the community. She invoked the authority of her knowledge of the manager's relatives ("I know your uncles! I know your dad! I know your mother!") to remind the manager that she comes from these people—is a part of the community—and to remind her of the values these people taught her ("a great line of medicine men"). Lastly, the elder declared that in such a position of leadership, the manager must work at the behest of the community ("What are you doing to your people?... You need to root for your own people!"). This behavioral proscription was the main point of all the protests and grassroots activism of the

Tuba City HECMC. The committee called public attention to the need for hospital leadership to be more accountable and responsible to the community, of which hospital employees were an intrinsic part. Ultimately, this relatively spontaneous and ad hoc intervention into public discourse embodied in the picket-line protests crystallized in the formal platform of the Tuba City HECMC: that the hospital board of directors be elected by community members (not appointed by tribal bureaucracy) and that hospital employees be granted union recognition. These demands were an insistence on worker and community participation in the process of labor relations at the Tuba City hospital.

The hospital at Tuba City became a locus for employee demonstration because it represented much more than a mere job site. The hospital was crucial to the daily life of the region and was the fulcrum of local economic development and tribal self-determination. To this day, it is one of the largest employers in the region (with more than seven hundred employees) and is the most comprehensive public health-care provider for the western part of the Navajo Nation. Layered on top of these important economic and civil service roles is the fact that it was one of the largest entities to be taken 638 by the Navajo Nation. The hospital, as a tribal corporation, became an experiment in the enactment of local self-determination and thereby an opportunity to debate the processes of enactment. Hospital workers wanted their voices heard in this debate. And they wanted to be heard not just as employees but also as community members whose investment in health-care delivery and the distribution of local democracy was as important as their need for employment rights and stability.

The story of the Tuba City HECMC and its struggle to have a say in work conditions and the local process of tribal self-determination illustrates the way workplace activism at the Navajo Nation provided a crucial means for navigating the process of tribal sovereignty. This grassroots activism created a forum for debate over how self-determination should work. I examine how deliberations over labor relations fit into Navajo Nation self-determination by chronicling the implementation of 638 at the Tuba City hospital and the events surrounding Black Friday. I narrate the story, however, from the perspective of workers who participated in and played a central role in planning the grassroots activism of the Tuba City HECMC. I do so because their story tells about the process of self-determination from below—that is, from the perspective of rank-and-file tribal citizens. This vantage point is rarely discussed in depth because the processes of tribal self-determination are frequently understood to be isomorphic with tribal governmental institutions and tribal leadership (cf. Simpson 2000). Moreover, as institutional representatives of a Native nation, tribal leaders have the most access to resources that enable them to articulate their perspectives on self-determination. This certainly was the case for TCRHCC management. The employees, however, had to find inventive and alternative avenues to enunciate their feelings and beliefs about tribal self-determination. Their grassroots articulation of Navajo self-determination is what makes their example so important.

Employees and community members did an excellent job of making their voices heard in the debate over how self-determination should be enacted for Tuba City health care. To further elaborate on their frustration and their theorization of how self-determination should operate, I use ethnographic interviews to retell and reflect on their workplace activism. I specifically highlight workers' opinions about labor relations at the hospital *and* the grassroots strategies they used, such as picket-line protesting, pamphlets, and speaking up at public meetings, to implicitly and explicitly make a claim for participation in how their workplace was to be run. This chapter deliberately resists an investigative journalism that would strive toward a "balanced" account to uncover the "truth" about who was right and wrong in the incidents at Tuba City. I seek not to lay blame on managers, workers, or tribal leaders.[2] Rather, what is relevant to this discussion of tribal labor relations is worker perception of the events and what this says about workers' evaluations of the legitimacy of the NNC 638 pilot program at Tuba City.

I began to conduct the ethnographic interviews, which compose a significant part of this chapter, a month after Black Friday and continued these conversations periodically for the next five years (conducting multiple interviews with many of the same people). Interviews were conducted during the height of HECMC workplace activism and then later as tension died down, when workers had achieved some of their goals but not others. The interviews amount to reflections on ongoing events and in some cases events that were several months or even years old. Despite the passage of time, which can lead to forgetfulness about specifics, the "objective truth" of the "facts" retold in these reflections is less important to me than how the workers told their stories as expression of their feelings and beliefs (see Stephen 1994) about what happened and about the politics of tribal labor relations and self-determination.[3]

Many interviews took the form of narrative; Tuba City hospital employees narrated their perspectives on events that took place in their community and reflected on what these meant for the process of local tribal self-determination.[4] The connection is well established between the stories people tell about their participation in events and how they view themselves and the world in general (see Ochs and Capps 1996). In the context of workplace and community activism, Karen Brodkin argues, personal narratives can play a critical role in activists' asserting the right to political power and agency:

> To create a narrative is to exercise personal agency, to act upon society. Narrators create plots and social characters, not least themselves. Being the interpreter of events makes the narrator an active agent in constructing the world. In their political narratives activists construct themselves as oppositional political actors and analysts. They show historical circumstances that shaped them, and show how from this vantage point they have developed a critical analytic perspective on the state of the world. (2007:50)

Tuba City health-care workers' and community members' telling of their experiences articulates their self-asserted right to participate in the local enactment of Navajo self-determination and sovereignty.

638 Comes to Tuba City

The public protests at Tuba City were a local iteration of the tribal-wide debate over the relationship between Navajo Nation health care, Navajo Nation self-determination, and workers' rights, a debate that originated in the effort to take Navajo Area IHS 638. In Tuba City, there was as much public opposition to the NNC's original plan, to take over administration of all Navajo health care, as there was anywhere else in the Navajo Nation.[5] Tuba City hospital employees heavily participated in the Campaign for Union Recognition, and some of the most active union stewards in the campaign came from this hospital. If anything, local concern over the issue of 638 for health care only intensified after the tribal debate ebbed—mainly because, to resolve the heated deliberations over whether to go 638 on a tribal-wide level, the NNC selected the Tuba City hospital (along with two much smaller facilities) as a pilot program for tribal administration of health care.[6] This move effectively shifted the debate from a tribal-wide level to one concentrated at Tuba City and made Tuba City an experiment in the administration of self-determination. The workplace activism staged around 638 at the Tuba City hospital became an opportunity for workers to keep the discussion about labor relations and self-determination open and ongoing, as was the case with the Campaign for Union Recognition (see chapter 5). With this, however, also came a shift in the terms of the debate. Instead of discussing whether self-determination was the right move for Navajo Area IHS, employees of the hospital questioned how self-determination ought to be applied and how the hospital, as a tribal corporation, ought to be accountable to the community it served.

As a pilot program, the TCRHCC was both a prototype of a tribally run corporation and a trial run for enacting large-scale self-determination at the Navajo Nation. Management, community members, and hospital employees recognized that the stakes were high, given that Tuba City was one of only three service units to go 638 and was by far the largest of the three. Moreover, all involved at Tuba City knew that there would be much scrutiny over whether the TCRHCC would succeed or problems predicted by opponents of 638 would surface. As for the Tuba City hospital employees, nearly all consulted for this chapter had originally considered themselves in the camp against 638. Their reasoning reflected the larger debate across the Navajo Nation. Most felt that the tribal government was not ready to handle such a large, complicated administrative system, were wary of how council leaders would spend money earmarked for health care, or were anxious about job placement once tribal administrators took control of hospital budgeting and hiring. Because of these concerns, LIUNA's Campaign for Union Recognition received a great deal of attention and support from the Tuba City employees, as was the case at the other service units. A strong majority—more than 60 percent—of the Tuba City employees signed the petition for union representation. And they signed, many verbally expressed their concerns about and opposition to 638 to the LIUNA organizers who had brought the petitions (see chapters 4 and 5).

According to Stephen Cornell and Joseph Kalt (1997), concerns about equitable administration and what is called rent-seeking are not uncommon in Indian Country and are critical for tribal leaders to address in order to maintain successful economic development. *Rent-seeking* is an economist's term for manipulating governmental or managerial authority in order to benefit oneself or one's associates. In Indian Country, this usually takes the form of distribution of tribal-enterprise funds and jobs. Rent-seeking is one of the biggest threats to the legitimacy of tribal corporations and a tribal government's ability to sustain overall reservation economic development.[7] Cornell and Kalt (1997:274, box 10-1) argue that success in tribal economic development relies on formal governmental structures that provide "some mechanism of confining the government to the third-party enforcer role and [that shut] down rent-seeking." Controversy and disagreement over how leaders dispense funds and jobs call their authority into question and can hamstring the operations of a tribal corporation. The question of legitimacy was central to the tribal-wide 638 debate and was particularly crucial to the way 638 played out in Tuba City. Misgivings about the legitimacy of TCRHCC leadership were so great that they clouded any effort to dispassionately evaluate the efficacy of the hospital under 638 and TCRHCC management.

Even so, there was a brief window of time when employees did not openly question the legitimacy of 638 and gave corporate leadership at the Tuba City hospital the benefit of the doubt. They hoped that the benefits the proponents of 638 had touted—mainly the improvement of health-care delivery and technology—would come true through the increased local control of decision making. Even after significant problems with working conditions arose under 638, many employees still believed that 638 was the correct direction for the hospital. In fact, as the public outcry and protests against hospital management reached full intensity, workers never considered retrocession (returning the hospital to IHS management) a viable solution to the hospital's problems.[8] Workers grew to like the ease in acquiring new medical technology, hiring new employees, and gaining approval for hospital expansion plans that was afforded by 638's localized control but not by the previous complicated bureaucracy of the federally run IHS. Indeed, "local control" became the goal to achieve, but what was wanted was more inclusive, local control that included a grassroots voice and participation.

The idea of local control was always a key part of the 638 proponents' discourse in their lobbying of the tribal government to take over health care from the IHS. But ultimately, the way 638 was "locally" enacted at Tuba City was unsatisfactory to many employees and provoked much strong criticism. To understand how this critical response played out, it is important to consider the local implementation of a 638 contract within the larger political economy context of American Indian health-care delivery and of tribally run economic development in general. Attending to the larger political economic factors of Native health care sheds light on how the Navajo government implemented a 638 contract for the Tuba City hospital and why the NNC continued to push for some form of tribally administered health care even in the face of strong public opposition. Why several NNC representatives eventually decided to vote in favor of 638 remains opaque. Whereas chapter 5 details the public debate that surrounded the decision to go 638, in this chapter I try to elucidate the decision by focusing on how Native nations in general appear to make choices about taking over health care. The factors involved up front in decision making can heavily impact the end result of health-care self-determination, particularly the relationships among tribal health-care corporations, tribal governments, health-care employees, and local communities that use the health-care facilities.

Alyce Adams (2000) has attempted to explain this kind of tribal governmental decision making by doing a statistical analysis of factors thought to affect tribal governmental choices to take over for IHS administration. Most of her research is on the Native communities that were the first to implement 638 self-determination health-care contracts—those that went 638 within the first five years after PL 93-638 passed in 1975. She found that many complicated and contradictory determinants influenced this decision: a desire to increase tribal sovereignty, the fear that 638 was a covert attempt at terminating the federal government's responsibility to provide health care, and even the need to implement policies that could meet multiple goals all at once. According to her research, the biggest factors determining whether tribal leaders chose to go 638 had to do with how responsive IHS had been to local needs. Did the IHS employ Native managers? Did a community's health-care facilities receive adequate federal appropriations? High numbers of Native managers and high funding levels in a given IHS service unit correlated negatively to tribal governments' decisions in favor of a 638 takeover.[9]

Analysis of all these factors led Adams (2000:26) to suggest that tribal leaders ask themselves three general questions when making the decision to take over health care: "(1) Do we have a compelling reason to manage health care resources?; (2) Do we have the capacity to manage health care resources?; (3) How will other participants in the system react to our involvement?" The first two questions are closely connected. On the one hand, a lack of internal capacity may nullify the strongest reasons in favor of instituting tribal management; as inadequate as tribal leaders may assess IHS management to be, they have to have confidence that they themselves can do better utilizing their own infrastructure. On the other hand, Adams notes, the desire for independence from the federal government, manifested positively as a desire to increase sovereignty or negatively as intense dissatisfaction with IHS, can be so strong as to override a fair assessment of a tribe's internal capability for 638. The first two (interconnected) questions seemed to be particularly relevant for tribes that made their decision early in the self-determination era, when this option first became readily available to them. Stephen Kunitz (1996) suggests, however, that a fundamental shift in the 638 contracting of tribal health care has made the third question just as important. Tribal decisions on 638 for health care are now more than ever influenced by what other tribes are doing. Kunitz (1996) argues that because of budget cuts to the federal funding of Indian health care, tribes utilizing the IHS (not their 638 administrations) are competing with one another for pieces of a shrinking pie. Alternatively, 638 contracting provides some measure of economic stability in that the contracts are agreements of support and tribal governments have a significant say over internal distribution of federal money to fund 638 health-care contracts. Tribes that choose to stay with the IHS are more vulnerable to congressional budgeting. Cuts in appropriation are more likely to affect general IHS programs than those specifically stipulated in 638 contracts. Thus, at some point, a critical mass of tribes choosing 638 will adversely affect those staying with the IHS, by absorbing most of the funds. And because of economies of scale, this mass exodus from the IHS system could potentially bankrupt the IHS. As larger tribal communities such as the Navajo Nation opt out of the general IHS and go 638, it will become more and more difficult to financially sustain the IHS, because Congress will allocate more money to 638 contracts than to the IHS (Mario Garrett, personal communication, October 15, 2005).[10] Many Navajo health-care employees argued that these macroeconomic forces in Indian health care compromised Navajo 638 pilot programs.

The public outcry against 638 was enough to convince NNC representatives that the Navajo general public could not find a "compelling" enough reason to go 638 and that the general public perceived a lack of "capacity" to manage the entire Navajo service area. The NNC was also concerned about the overall funding of Navajo Area IHS. Adams notes:

> Generally, tribal members may disagree about whether the tribal government is the best institution to manage health care services. This may be particularly true when the federal government employs a large segment of the tribe's population. While the 1988 amendments guaranteed employment for federal employees should they be displaced by PL 638 contracts, tribal members employed by IHS may view the federal government as a more predictable employer than the tribe. (2000:27)

This is the same argument Navajos Area IHS employees made against 638, that the tribal government was not ready to take over health-care administration—thus a lack of capacity. Moreover, they were happy with their IHS jobs and uncertain how things might change under 638, which constituted a lack of a compelling reason. But Navajo tribal leaders knew the significant economic consequences of turning away from 638.

Indeed, on the day the NNC approved the pilot programs, it took two votes. The first vote rejected a complete 638 takeover of the entire Navajo Area IHS. After this vote, the issue appeared to be settled and the NNC went into recess. After the rejection, however, IHS administrators pointed out to key tribal leaders that the negative vote also meant a possible rejection of $20 million that would be budgeted specifically for 638 contracts (*Indian Country Today* 2002; Shebala 2002; Tohtsoni 2002). The "folk" recounting of this legislative drama, particularly by those who opposed 638, was that when the speaker of the NNC and other supporters of 638 learned of the potential loss in funds, they scrambled to reconvene the council—literally dragging legislators into the chambers from the hallways—to pass some form of legislation that would salvage the financial support. This legislation established the pilot programs at Tuba City, Winslow, and Montezuma Creek. Although we most certainly should not blame tribal leaders for looking out for the best financial interests of their tribe (that is a key part of their job, after all), this story attests to a general disagreement about why and how to take Navajo health care 638.

The NNC decided to take a few IHS service units 638. And beyond examining the decision to go 638, it is important to consider subsequent decisions: how council members and corporate managers organized and operated the emergent Navajo healthcare corporation. According to Stephen Cornell and Joseph Kalt, the relationship between tribal political governance and tribal corporate governance is critical in successfully linking economic ventures to overall tribal self-determination. Through Cornell and Kalt's vast economic policy research and applied development work in indigenous communities, they have found that the extent to which tribal corporate governance is separated or at least shielded from tribal political governance eventually determines the success or failure of the economic endeavor. It is worth noting that Cornell and Kalt consistently define success not purely in terms of finances but, more importantly, in terms of community acceptance of a venture and its ability to sustain self-determination and self-governance. To this end, they suggest that tribal economic ventures should be evaluated in terms of efficacy and legitimacy. They state that for "productive economic progress and social health, institutions of government that undergird processes of saving and investment, specialization and exchange, and rights enforcement and dispute resolution must pass tests of both *effectiveness* and *legitimacy*" (Cornell and Kalt 1997:263). Herein lay the problem with the TCRHCC; employees and community members felt it missed the mark on both counts.

Notions of effectiveness and legitimacy are not easily measured objectively. At Tuba City, there certainly was disagreement over how these valuations applied to the TCRHCC and its leadership. But it was the negative assessment on the part of hospital workers and community members, as well as their need to publicly express their discontent, that led to the workplace activism at Tuba City. Effectiveness and legitimacy are intimately intertwined. Questions about the legitimacy of TCRHCC management hampered the hospital's effectiveness. At the same time, many doubts about legitimacy were articulated in terms of questions about the efficacy of leadership. Effectiveness in this context is not about quantitatively measured health outcomes[11] but rather about a qualitative evaluation of the administrative capabilities of the managers acting as the Navajo tribal government's proxy. Community members' perceptions and acceptance of a tribally run enterprise are as important as its balance sheet, cost effectiveness, or health outcomes.

Cornell and Kalt are well aware of this issue. They and others who work with indigenous communities on planning economic development (particularly research fellows at the HPAIED, which Cornell and Kalt founded) call this "cultural fit." They encourage economic planners and tribal leaders to be attentive to the sociocultural context in which a tribal economic venture is established (see also Smith 2000). Attentiveness goes beyond just "cultural sensitivity" to ensure that an economic venture does not break local taboos or run counter to tribal values. It also means awareness of the significance of local sociopolitical relations and the intense effect they can have on emerging socioeconomic relations. This is particularly important in Native communities because Native economic ventures are quite different from private business enterprises. Despite some potentially "commercial" aspects of their business models, these ventures are enacted in behalf of the tribal community and are much more similar to nationalized or governmental enterprises. Tribal economic ventures can vary, from lumber mills to tourist attractions to public waterworks to hospitals, but the general idea remains the same. They are not created to turn a profit for investors, but rather to enrich tribal governmental coffers as a whole or to provide local services and jobs:

> For Indian governments establishing and sponsoring these tribal enterprises the pressure is on to put in place the institutional infrastructure that is needed to channel human and financial resources into productive activities so that the community is working to add to the economic "pie," rather than squiggling over how to divide the pie.... Comparative research across the spectrum of tribal contexts has found that successful economic development is most likely to occur when tribes effectively assert their sovereignty and back up such assertions with capable and culturally appropriate institutions of self-government. (HPAIED 2008:121)

Cornell and Kalt advocate minimizing the potential for sociopolitical conflict in tribal economic enterprises by isolating tribal corporate governance from tribal governance in general. They argue for corporate leaders who can run the day-to-day operations of tribal companies independently of the national and local politics of the tribe (Cornell and Kalt 1992, 1997; HPAIED 2008). This approach minimizes rent-seeking and helps establish continuity in corporate governance despite cyclical changes in the administrations of centralized tribal governing bodies; both processes are central to the effectiveness and legitimacy of a tribal enterprise.

Fears of rent-seeking and political cronyism inspired a large part of the public opposition to the original plan to put all Navajo Area IHS under tribal administration. Opponents speculated that the NNC wanted the financial and administrative control allowed for under 638 largely for two questionable reasons: (1) to siphon off health-care funds to other pet governmental projects (the most cynical version of this complaint included personal gain as a motivation) and (2) to give health-care jobs to relatives and political allies. By the time 638 was finally approved for Tuba City, the NNC and the designers of the TCRHCC were well aware of this criticism. In an effort to respond, they attempted to put in place the safeguard advocated by Cornell and Kalt. The HPAIED notes:

> Successful nation-building tribes have taken steps to isolate their enterprise managers from political opportunism by, for example, instituting independent

boards of directors. These boards encourage the use of outside business expertise and an emphasis on profitability over job creation; however, their most important contribution seems to be the isolation of enterprise from political interference. (HPAIED 2008:128)

At the Navajo Nation, the final plan for the 638 health-care contract created the TCRHCC as an independent corporate entity. The designers of the 638 contract—not the NNC—supervised its board of directors. Moreover, the board of directors—not council representatives—allocated the budget for the hospital. Lastly, the board hired corporate managers to run the day-to-day operations; the board itself met only monthly and acted in an advisory capacity to the corporate managers. The first CEO hired by the board was a nontribal member whose main experience was health-care administration and consulting in California. From the perspective of those promoting the TCRHCC's autonomy from tribal politics, this CEO's lack of experience with Navajo communities was not a weakness; it meant that he was more likely to be free from tribal political connections.

Although the CEO's lack of experience with Navajo communities could be portrayed as a political benefit, designers of the TCRHCC also knew that it was important to promote the organization's efforts to respect local cultural norms. The hospital's corporate charter commented on the importance of cultural fit, stating in a brochure that a key TCRHCC goal was to

> elevate the health status and quality of life of Navajos and other American Indians through the provision of high quality, cost effective, responsive, and culturally appropriate health care services that are prevention oriented and respect the teachings and gifts of both Western medicine and traditional Native healing.

The tribal sovereignty advanced by 638 relies on the creation of tribal corporations as entities that attempt to balance capitalist values and modes of organization with local Native philosophies and cultural norms (see also Champagne 2004). This work is particularly important for health care at places such as the Navajo Nation, where traditional healers and healing methods still hold a prominent place in society. Although projects that draw on and combine multiple values systems are common to and for the most part accepted throughout the contemporary Navajo Nation (and for that matter much of Indian Country), with the TCRHCC, this balancing act was primarily in the hands of the hospital's managerial leadership.

Ultimately, this managerial leadership was held to the standard of effectiveness and legitimacy. The initiatives set up by the TCRHCC to create a culturally appropriate, independent tribal enterprise were positive attempts at addressing the concerns of the Navajo electorate. This work was a large step forward in Navajo tribal economic development and self-governance. But, ironically, the isolation of TCRHCC corporate governance from tribal governmental institutions was so significant that, from the perspective of hospital employees and community members, there were not sufficient checks and balances on the authority of hospital management. The perception of unchecked authority ultimately led to the workplace activism that contested the legitimacy and effectiveness of the TCRHCC leadership.

Although many claimed that once 638 became a reality at the Tuba City hospital, they were willing to give it a chance to work, others maintained their skepticism. For the latter, little could change their minds about the problems they believed 638 would bring. Some were so concerned, they quit the Tuba City hospital or transferred to other IHS facilities before the 638 handover was finalized. As for the former, a large part of their willingness seemed to be based on the notion that community and worker input would be an appropriate and valued part of self-determination for the hospital. This attitude should not be surprising, considering that those pushing 638 for health care heralded "local control" as the key benefit. Indeed, Cornell and Kalt espouse a self-determination—"nation-building"—kind of economic development precisely because it can increase indigenous people's investment in their local economic success:

> Sovereignty and self-determination allow local desires, preferences, needs and ways of doing things to be more accurately perceived and acted upon so that institutions and governments can function in support of economic growth and community change. Sovereignty as an idea and self-determination and self-governance as federal policies place resources squarely in the hands of Native officials and citizens. In most cases, this translates to an increased sense of ownership over the resources, a sense which often is augmented still further when a Native Nation pools resources garnered through own-revenue generation with federal funds.... Closely linked to the idea of ownership is the idea of accountability. Here, it is important to recall that contracting and compacting are policies whereby Native nations take over the management and delivery of programs otherwise within the domain of federal government. In the "direct service" model, where BIA employees or other federal administrators manage programs, accountability runs from the program to Washington—there is little or no accountability to the Native government or its citizens about how resources are used or managed. But under a contract or compact, accountability extends to these very important parties. Tribal leaders and citizens feel ownership over the resources and hold their program managers and project leaders accountable for how federal resources—and, indeed, all tribal resources—are used. (HPAIED 2008:127)

This combination of ownership and accountability began to take hold in Tuba City once the TCRHCC became a reality. The most concrete expression of the notion was the large public protest over the way labor relations were being enacted at the hospital. The hospital, not just as a health-care facility but also as a place of work, became a focal point for communal perceptions of tribal economic enterprise.

The workplace became the central locale for the expression of ownership and accountability, in large part because hospital workers were the very same tribal members in whose interest the tribal government enacted the self-determination process for Tuba City health care. Moreover, as employees of the newly instituted tribal enterprise, they were at the front lines of the experiment in self-determination and economic development. Even nontribal hospital employees expressed a similar level of investment. Many, particularly doctors and nurses, were long-term members of the community and were recognized by Navajo tribal members for the work they had put into community health care. Their political relationship to elected tribal officials—and to the hospital leadership these officials appointed—was not the same as that of tribal members, who were fully enfranchised in tribal governance, but they still actively participated in advocating for high-quality health care and work conditions after the 638 takeover.[12] A sense of ownership and accountability was expressed by both Navajos and non-Navajos not merely in terms of the "citizenship" model proffered by Cornell and Kalt but also in terms of labor relations; employees felt invested as stakeholders in the hospital as a workplace and expected hospital administrators to be good workplace leaders. So when tribal employees became concerned about the effectiveness and legitimacy of the hospital as a health-care corporation, they felt empowered to speak out and entitled to have their voices heeded by hospital leadership.

Cornell and Kalt's analytical terms *ownership and accountability* and *effectiveness and legitimacy* are useful for understanding the disagreements and protests at the Tuba City hospital. Although these terms have their roots in public policy analysis and to some extent are limited by a structuralist notion of sociocultural and sociopolitical relations, they are useful in the context of TCRHCC employees' actions and attitudes toward hospital management. I use this terminology not so much as an objective or statistical measure of the tribal enterprise's success but rather as a measure of what workers and community members feel about their jobs and the local health care they receive. In analyzing workers' notions of ownership, accountability, effectiveness, and legitimacy, I am not trying to report on the failure of the tribal enterprise or uncover what went wrong. Indeed, the hospital exists to this day, beyond the moment of tension under examination here, and still serves a large population. Furthermore, some of the most criticized corporate leaders maintained their jobs throughout the workplace activism and went on to work in other important tribal institutions. Moreover, many of the employees who were fired or were the most critical of hospital administration still work at Tuba City. Instead, I am using tribal labor relations as a lens for understanding how community members and tribal employees evaluate, comment on, and shape tribal economic development and self-determination.

Roots of Protest

For many Tuba City employees, an early sign of problems with the new 638 administration was an exodus of hospital employees. Not everyone left for the same reason, but, overall, these departures were thought to negatively impact the effectiveness of the hospital. This opinion was particularly apparent in workers' retelling of the events at Tuba City. Most people's narratives started with these early departures of valuable assets to the hospital. Some thought that certain employees were forced to resign because of disagreements about how to manage the TCRHCC. The most extreme examples were a few upper-level managers, such as the director of human resources and the director of nursing, who disagreed with the CEO and board of directors. In other cases, nurses succumbed to pressure from upper management to resign. In still other cases, nurses, physicians, and other employees actively sought to leave the hospital for other Navajo Area IHS units or to vacate the Navajo area altogether.

For many of the workers who stayed, the departures were signs of confusion and shortcomings in the new managerial leadership. Sam Joe, a Navajo from Tuba City who works in the anesthesia department, recalled:

> I think that's where things really started...when the legislation [638 for Tuba City] actually passed the [Navajo Nation] Council.... So people started wondering, "What's going to really happen?"... And so all these people started dwindling off.... And I think [the people who left] kind of saw something, I mean, not clearly but...had this impression it's not gonna go right and so started jumping ship. I mean, they're like, "Okay, we're going here. We're going there." And...they weren't vocal about it. They didn't let anybody know about it. [They just left.] I mean, we, we're the little peons down at the bottom, you know. And [those who left saw] the administration part of the hospital and how that works. So they knew what was coming up.

Sam described the departures not as cases of employees feeling pressure to leave from management but rather as employees being concerned about and unhappy with management, so they no longer wanted to work at the hospital.

Sam made two important points about employees who resigned early on in the 638 administrations. First, many of them held positions of mid-level authority. He suggested that they might have had access to information about the hospital that other employees did not; therefore, they left because they saw the writing on the wall. Second, he noted that those who left were not very vocal about their criticism of the hospital administration or even about their decisions to leave. In fact, because they gave little explanation about why they were leaving, it is quite possible that some left for reasons other than disagreement with the hospital administration. What is important, however, is Sam's beliefs about the exodus from the hospital. The exodus was an important component of Sam's and his coworkers' narratives of how problems escalated at the hospital.

It is important to consider that many of the departing upper-level employees were in a position to leave their jobs and seek new ones. Some were not from Tuba City or even Navajo, so the decision to leave was not as difficult as it would have been for those who had longer-term commitments to Tuba City—both the town and the community. The departing employees were not necessarily representative of the average Tuba City hospital employee. Each departure could potentially be explained by individual motivations; the new hospital management might have been epiphenomenal. Nonetheless, as more people began to leave, the more concerned those who stayed behind became about the future of the hospital. Indeed, most people's narratives tell of a relative exodus of employees after the 638 transition and describe it as an early piece of the escalating problems with effectiveness and legitimacy at the hospital. In a logistical sense, employees who remained were worried about how to effectively deliver health care without the departing employees (many of whom were doctors and nurses). But there was also a growing skepticism about the legitimacy of the hospital leadership.

As their concerns and anxieties grew, TCRHCC employees and community members began to be much more vocal. They started to question more frequently and boldly the decisions made by leadership. And when they were not given answers or found the leaders' answers to be insufficient, the workers and community members became quite frustrated. Again, it is important to understand their frustration in the context of the original push for 638. In that situation, workers and community members also felt that the NNC and its appointees formulating the 638 contract did not sufficiently answer their questions about 638 and how it would affect health care; many felt that their desires not to go 638 were ignored. This was felt acutely by IHS employees because they were directed through workplace memos not to publicly talk about 638. The memos came from the IHS administrators who were pushing for 638; some became top administrators under the 638 pilot program. Employees could receive disciplinary actions for publicly questioning, criticizing, or in some cases even discussing the 638 proposal. Some Tuba City hospital employees still harbored bitterness about the management directive; they had ignored the proscription and spoken out against the 638 proposal. They felt the same stifling of their voices all over again when they tried to express their concerns about the problems at the TCRHCC.

In 2003, employees and community members responded to the perceived lack of information by trying to increase the accountability of and pressure on hospital officials. They increasingly attended monthly hospital board meetings and chapter meetings to publicly inquire about the hospital's finances. The problems became compounded when the most vocal employees began to feel threatened by management for speaking out. Thus, their concerns about legitimacy and accountability increased because they believed they were not being listened to and were attracting negative responses and consequences. Their attempts at public debate about local self-determination did not produce positive changes at the hospital but instead fueled the controversy.

Nearly all the public criticism of the hospital administration was directed at the CEO and board of directors, but the CEO caught most of the heat. This man, the non-Native from California, had been hired for his several years' experience in health-care administration, including running his own health-care consulting company. Despite these credentials, much of the criticism assailed his effectiveness and legitimacy as a leader. In the eyes of Navajos, as well as white workers who had spent a long time in Tuba City, the CEO lacked an understanding of and respect for Navajo social values and norms of civility. Workers often criticized his penchant for cursing and talking loudly and abruptly, even occasionally yelling at people. Although this behavior is certainly considered rude by most American standards, it is much more commonly tolerated in a mainstream corporate setting; it is particularly accepted and even expected in the hypermasculine world of upper corporate management. In talking about the CEO, employees and community members frequently said things like "Well, he yelled at me," "He yelled at so-and-so," "He's always cursing or yelling," and "He's just not very nice." Speaking in harsh tones and with foul language are conventionally taboos among Navajo speakers, arguably more so than within mainstream American culture. This transgression mattered most because it was happening in the context of perceived abuses of authority among TCRHCC upper management. The offensive language and behavior were seen not just as character flaws but also as evidence that the CEO did not care about hospital employees or their opinions of working conditions. His willingness to speak harshly and rudely to people was a sign of bad leadership, a steering of the hospital in the wrong direction. The verbal aggression was also interpreted as a sign that he was willing to take reprisals against people he did not like, mainly people who spoke out against the hospital. This situation made many employees anxious. They believed that it limited their ability to effectively deliver health care, and it diminished the legitimacy of hospital leadership in their eyes.

Unease and apprehension did not stop the boldest employees from speaking out at chapter meetings and other public forums, even when the CEO or board members were present. In October 2003, two Navajo employees even requested permission from the CEO to take a survey of hospital employees about their feelings regarding the workplace. After receiving permission, the two employees conducted a forum in the hospital for employees, who were encouraged to speak out about the hospital and then fill out a survey. Below are the survey questions and results as they were reported to employees throughout the hospital via e-mail:

> Staff, as promised at the employee forum, [we] agreed to communicate your concerns to the Board of Directors and the CEO. Attached as promised [are] the questions from your responses…[the questions and results will be] presented to the Board of Director and the CEO, on Wednesday afternoon.… If and when they respond, we don't know. We can either ask them to respond in writing or before an employees' forum. Your suggestions are welcome. As for the survey questionnaires, the response to the survey was overwhelming. As surveys go, a good response to a survey is usually between 30% and 40%. In this survey, 100 questionnaires were given out, with 80 answered and returned, resulting in an 80% response. This response emphasizes the seriousness with which the staff has taken this matter. Following [are] the results of the survey:
>
> > Is your concern:
> > Fear of losing your job? Yes = 69%, No = 23%, no response = 6%, and Maybe = 3%

Retribution? Yes = 74%, No = 11%, no response = 13%, Maybe = 3%
Job Security? Yes = 84%, No = 13%, no response = 4%
Hostile work environment? Yes = 71%, No = 20%, no response = 10%
Is the current work environment affecting your job performance?
Yes = 38%, No = 25%, no response = 5%, Maybe = 23%
Are you happy with the Board of Directors' Performance? Yes = 6%,
No = 83%, no response = 6%
How would you rate the Board of Directors, 1, 2, 3, 4, or 5,
with 1 = Low, and 5 = High? Survey average = 1.4

This survey shows that a significant number of employees felt a high level of workplace insecurity and distress about their work conditions. However, it would be naive to think of this survey (or any workplace survey for that matter) as fully objective or impartial. But ultimately, that is not the point. Much of the meaning of this kind of survey lies in the kinds of questions asked and who is responding to them. In this case, most of the questions are worded in the negative or imply negative views of the workplace, and the survey is explicitly about concerns, not just about work conditions. Obviously, the people who created and participated in the survey were self-selected as already having significant concerns about their workplace. This forum was a volunteer event; most likely, those with the strongest of feelings were the ones to attend the forum and participate in the survey.

The most explicit sentiment that the survey reveals is a sense of ownership and accountability. Employees who did not like where their health-care corporation was going decided to take ownership in determining its problems and starting on the road to change. Moreover, sharing the results of their survey with all hospital employees and TCRHCC leadership established an expectation of public accountability to workers and addressing their concerns. The survey was a discursive tool employed by grassroots activists to get hospital leadership to listen to them. The introductory paragraph frames it as a demonstration of workers' concerns to be delivered as a report to hospital administrators. It is important that the survey was conducted and documented in such a way as to make individual workers anonymous and to collectivize their concerns. This approach reflects both a sense of collectivity and reiterates a fear of reprisal. Moreover, the transmission of the results via e-mail to all hospital staff further created the sense of an anonymous mass of people (except, of course, the person who sent the e-mail). Thus, the survey, its results, and the presentation of the results to upper management became a grassroots, communal effort at ownership and accountability, despite the fact that the survey was organized and delivered by only two workers.

The survey was an early effort at ratcheting up pressure on hospital leadership. Criticism of TCRHCC administrative effectiveness and legitimacy soon intensified, specifically after Black Friday. After the firings, workers held large-scale picket-line protests, lobbied their local and tribal-wide representatives, and publicly advocated for change through newspaper ads and letters to the editor. Using these public venues, they called for public accountability of their leaders, demanding that some of them step down and that the fired employees be rehired. In addition, protesting employees and community members insisted on greater ownership in how the hospital was being run, by calling for union recognition and chapter approval of the hospital's board of directors.

Black Friday

In recounting the events that led up to Thomas Benally's termination, he and his wife, Josie Benally, told me about one particularly tense chapter house meeting attended by many hospital employees and the TCRHCC board of directors. The meeting had been set up to address people's concerns about 638. At the meeting, Thomas was vocally critical of the hospital administration. He was certain he had sealed his fate and would soon be fired. Josie remembered that he came home from this meeting and said, "Oh, honey…I went and talked about 638 again. The board was there, and everybody was there, and most of the employees [were] there.… I think I am going to get fired. I'm gonna lose my job. [Chuckling] Get ready, we're on for a long ride." Thomas was so sure he would be terminated that over the next week and a half, he was cleaning out his desk and boxing up his personal items. Two weeks after the meeting, Thomas's intuition proved correct. He was fired, along with four other employees, in May 2004.

Clearly, the epithet *Black Friday* for the day of the firings conveys the workers' perspective on the terminations. For protesting TCRHCC employees, the day represented a bleak moment in the short history of 638 for Tuba City health care. It was also a watershed moment in that it crystallized a collective objection to the hospital's labor relations and motivated a large-scale collective protest. The following Monday, more than one hundred people showed up at the picket line; they picketed all week. Months later, they picketed again. For nearly two years after Black Friday, workers and community members engaged in various forms of workplace protests, lobbying of elected officials, and efforts to gain public support to effect significant changes at the hospital.

In discussing Black Friday and the events surrounding it, I do not give a journalistic account or decide whether the firings were just. Instead, to examine how tribal employees think about and experience tribal labor relations, I recount the day's events through workers' narratives. Whether the terminated workers "deserved" to be fired or were fired in a "dignified" fashion are not my questions—although many workers' biases on these issues are readily apparent in their narratives. What I focus on is how workers' narratives of this day reveal their feelings about appropriate tribal labor relations and management of a tribal enterprise. On Black Friday, news of the firings spread throughout the workplace. At day's end, a large group of employees held an ad hoc meeting outside the workplace to figure out how to respond. Ultimately, employees' individual stories became a collective story that circulated among workers, creating a culture of solidarity (Fantasia 1988). These stories became collective expressions of people's disapproval of the local enactment of 638. I analyze Black Friday through these narratives as commentaries on effectiveness, legitimacy, ownership, and accountability.

For many workers, Black Friday represented a crisis in tribal labor relations and of hospital leadership. In their eyes, the CEO and board of directors were to blame for the firings. The firings were considered reprisals against outspoken employees, not the result of poor job performance. Additionally, many workers pointed to the hospital's at-will hiring policy as a sign of the illegitimacy of the firings. But it was not just the terminations that upset the workers; the way the firings were handled was seen as highly inappropriate. The terminations were handled in a way that publicly shamed the employees. To many, the situation was indicative of the hospital's ineffective leadership. Ironically, the public nature of the firings turned Black Friday into a communal event. It was a catalyst for employees and community members to take ownership of the direction of their hospital and to hold leadership accountable for how it ran the hospital.

The terminations in and of themselves became an event because the firings all happened on the same day, within a matter of hours. Even if management's decision on each termination had been independent of the others, from the employees' perspective, the firings appeared to be a planned event and each firing was connected to the others. By almost all accounts, those fired were well known, well liked, and well respected by their coworkers. They were well respected in part because they had all publicly stood up and called for improvements in hospital administration. One frequently spoke out at chapter meetings, and two others had designed the survey described above. Of course, according to most employees' interpretations of Black Friday, these actions were precisely what put their jobs in jeopardy. The employees were not fired for insubordination, though. The administration terminated the employees by using the corporation's at-will policy. They were not fired for cause, action, or offense but rather because all employees work at the will of management; therefore, management can fire them without having to provide reasons. To many, such as Naomi Johns, a Navajo public health nurse from Shiprock, the at-will policy was illegitimate. Naomi had been working for Navajo Area IHS for twenty-eight years, eighteen of them at the Tuba City hospital. In talking about her coworkers' firing, she observed:

> But there was no reason given...so he's saying "Why are you firing me? What is it for?" And [a top administrator] tells him, "Uh, I can't tell you, I can't tell you." That was all. There was no reason. No due process in terms of... counseling, verbal counseling to say, "Your performance is deficient and this and this and this." I mean, that's how you [ought to] get fired...they talk to you. It's on paper.... After that, they give you a warning. The second time, if you continue to have deficiencies or you're a poor performer, then it's written up.... If it continues, then they put you on suspension. The last alternative is, they fire. But this one didn't have...counseling, no reprimand, no suspension.... He was given the paper, "You're fired." Then, when he goes back to

ask, "What did I do? Why are you firing me?" "I don't know. We can't tell you." That was the answer.... So...to this day, it's not working.

Naomi clearly feels that terminations should follow a systematic procedure that gives employees many opportunities to correct their workplace behavior and be cognizant of where they stand in terms of job performance; that did not happen in this case. Utilizing the at-will clause, and thus not having to follow any procedure to attempt to improve an employee's poor job performance, was proof enough to hospital employees that the firings on Black Friday were not about workers' performance. Naomi was not in the room when her friend was fired, yet she tells his story as though it were her own. She was personally offended by what happened to her coworker. Like many of her coworkers, she was indignant over what she felt to be illegitimate terminations.

Others also found fault with the timing of the Black Friday firings. All the individuals terminated had been instrumental in the hospital's effort to pass its major accreditation inspection. On the day of the firings, inspectors from the Joint Commission on Accreditation of Healthcare Organizations (JCAHO), the nation's top not-for-profit health-care standards–setting and accreditation organization, were finalizing their inspection and approval. They were still in the building when the five workers were terminated. Three of those fired had met with the inspectors only hours before they were fired. One had gone to a final meeting with the inspectors, upset because her supervisor had just been fired and sensing that she would be next. She described the situation: "I went into the close-out...interview with JCAHO with my red eyes, but you [know], I sat and I wanted to make sure that it was, that [my] part [of the inspection] went well. No way, no how, was I going to jeopardize...the three-year accreditation [process] for my people." JCAHO accreditation is essential to the operation of any reputable health-care facility. So some hospital employees questioned the timing of the firings. They felt that the hospital administration had taken advantage of these employees' commitment to their jobs, their hospital, and their community and then letting them go immediately after the accreditation was approved.

A final issue suggesting that job performance was not the reason for termination was that all five got their jobs back in some form or another: and one was rehired within a few days; three were reinstated through a legal settlement; and one left the area to become a top-level administrator at another IHS facility. Although nearly all recognized the justice in these employees getting their jobs back, many employees said that this did not make up for how they had been treated in their firings. For many, the fact that these workers were terminated in a way that publicly shamed them was just as bad as the firing itself—if not worse. Much of the ill feeling had to do with lumping all the firings together on one day, drawing attention to them in a way that spreading them out over a few days might not have. Thus, Black Friday became a public event in part because news of the firings spread rapidly throughout the hospital by word of mouth. But this was not all.

Those who were terminated were removed from the building by security escorts;

they had to walk down a main corridor in the hospital. Many felt that this unnecessarily drew attention to the fired employees. Irrespective of management's intent, it had the effect of publicly shaming those fired and intimidating the rest of the hospital staff. Naomi described the scene:

> It was horrible, and, oh, everybody down the hall…saw the employees being escorted out and people looking, and you [know], I imagine the people [who had been fired] were very intimidated. They were humiliated beyond belief. They might as well put shackles on them. They were escorted out. [One employee] got escorted out all the way through the hospital. Going through the hospital, everybody was looking at her because the project security and Navajo security guards were escorting [her] out. And nobody knew, you know. "What did she get fired for? What did she do?" You know, it was just *horrible*. And [another employee] got escorted out. She's a petite little administrative officer. She lives [about 80 miles south] in Flagstaff, and they have a community bus that goes back and forth, and she's on that bus every day, but [they] escorted her out and, you know, said, "You're, you're out." And she had no ride home. She was left out, you know, out in the parking lot. Embarrassing, you know…people were crying, and it was just, it was *horrible*.

As Naomi notes, the public procession, with security guards escorting employees through the hospital, gave other employees the impression that their coworkers had not only done something very serious but also were somehow a danger and thus needed to be guarded. Combined with the fact that at first no one knew exactly why these people were being terminated, coworkers were left to speculate on what the terminated employees had done to receive such severe treatment.[13]

By almost any account, terminating an employee is well within the prerogative of management. But nearly every account of Black Friday related to me contained disappointment about the public display of the firings. A few workers confided that Black Friday and the days that followed were so traumatic that they and others relied on the hospital's psychological counseling services for several months. Some even took a few weeks of psychological leave. What is significant about the terminations is that they ran counter to Smith's (2000) recommendation that managers of tribal enterprises be attentive to local cultural norms. As in many Native communities, publicly shaming someone can be a severe transgression among the Navajo. Whether or not the hospital administration meant to intentionally shame the fired employees or intimidate their vocal coworkers, there does not seem to have been enough attention paid to how the firings would appear to the community. Coupled with the view that the non-Navajo CEO was callous toward employees, the shaming was taken as representative of how ineffective TCRHCC leadership was.

The Monday after the firings, more than one hundred people picketed, demanding that the terminated employees be rehired and that the CEO be fired, along with some key members of the board of directors. People held signs inscribed with slogans such as "C.E.O. Must GO!" The CEO was openly criticized for his ineffectiveness as a hospital administrator—certainly as an administrator who knew how to work with Navajo people. Soon rumors began to circulate about excessive spending on corporate perks, potentially inappropriate use of hospital funds, conflicts of interest, and other personal improprieties. Although these accusations relied on evidence of varying degrees of trustworthiness—some of the more salacious rumors were far from collegial or civil—they all spoke to a precipitous drop in the credibility of upper management after Black Friday. Indeed, Black Friday was the catalyst for an already growing crisis of legitimacy for the leadership enacting 638.

Much of the legitimacy issue revolved around questions of both the effectiveness of the TCRHCC administration and how these managers had been chosen to administer the 638 enterprise. Many employees and community members were disturbed that the TCRHCC's board of directors and the CEO were not elected but were appointed by the original team put in charge of designing the 638 contract and overseeing the transition from IHS to 638. This design and transition team consisted of former IHS administrators and other community members whose appointments were approved by the NNC. Workers and community members complained that not only were the TCRHCC leaders not elected but also they were not even appointed by elected officials. They were appointed by officials who themselves had been appointed, not elected. Moreover, people protested that once board members were appointed, there was no way to recall them and no institutionalized way to hold them accountable for their actions. Much of this situation resulted from NNC efforts to isolate the hospital administration from political processes. However, in the eyes of employees, this marginally democratic process severely limited the legitimacy of the leadership.

HECMC formed in response to Black Friday. The original goals of the group were to get the fired employees reinstated and get those responsible for the terminations removed from their positions. The picket line was HECMC's first action to expose what was happening at the hospital. This tactic soon expanded into questioning the legitimacy of TCRHCC leaders to make the case for their removal. HECMC members spent their personal time (and money) investigating the background of the TCRHCC leadership.[14] They began to research the CEO's previous experience in the health-care industry and even questioned whether he had falsified his job qualifications. Others looked into previous business dealings of members of the board of directors. HECMC members then used photocopied flyers and a full-page color advertisement in the tribal newspaper to broadcast the most striking inconsistencies in the leadership's record and what were felt to be egregious acts of impropriety. The flyers and newspaper ad included such titles and headings as "Lack of Accountability"; "Arrogance and Isolation"; "Abusive, Vindictive Firings, Not Based on Performance"; "Gross Incompetence"; "Lack of Credibility"; "Fiscal Irresponsibility"; "Wasted Time and Wrong Priorities"; "From the Office of Concerned Native Americans"; and "Where There Is Smoke, There Is Fire." Most messages contained laundry lists of problems and alleged offenses meant to evoke support from people in the workplace and the community in general.

Other public challenges were two May 2004 votes of no confidence in the hospital leadership by the hospital's medical staff—each result by near consensus (Thayer 2004). Although these votes were in no way binding on management, they were public calls for the CEO and board members to resign. And the calls were purposely public in that the results were sent in a letter to the NNC and the Navajo Nation president. Pressure on hospital leadership intensified further as the Tuba City chapter government overwhelmingly passed (twenty-eight to one, with eight abstentions) a resolution calling for the same resignations (*Navajo-Hopi Observer* 2004). During this time, the HECMC organized another set of picket-line protests across the street from the hospital. This demonstration drew such public attention that Joe Shirley, the president of the Navajo Nation, flew to Tuba City to see for himself what was going on and to act as a negotiator to calm the tensions. All of these actions were meant, in one way or another, to delegitimize the TCRHCC leadership. A few of the accusations bandied about relied on spurious evidence and never amounted to much action. However, others were serious enough to be picked up by and reported in an investigation conducted by the NNC's Health and Social Services Committee. The investigation was motivated by the turmoil generated after the Black Friday terminations. The committee's report and recommendation in August 2004 ultimately led to the removal of the CEO a few months later and removal of the at-will clause from corporate bylaws.

It could be argued that some public criticisms of the TCRHCC's administration were petty personal attacks, but there is little doubt that the overall purpose of the HECMC was to hold the administrators accountable for their actions. For example, one flyer stated, "There is still no Community Health Advisory Board. The Board Members only represent themselves, not the grassroots people." And a full-page ad in the *Navajo Times* (July 15, 2004) contended, "The Board is not elected, cannot be recalled and has no stockholders. It is, therefore, responsible to no one for its actions." These declarations for accountability intensified demand that had existed even before Black Friday. Indeed, as Thomas Benally asserted, using the public forum of a chapter house meeting to try to hold the board responsible for its authority was what got him fired on Black Friday.

Amber Klee, another Navajo employee fired on Black Friday, was at the same chapter house meeting that Thomas identified as leading to his demise. She, too, felt it her responsibility to use the public meeting to increase pressure on hospital management. Along with other outspoken employees, she urged chapter house officials to ask tough questions of management to get answers that might allay workers' concerns over the hospital's financial situation and its future plans to maintain acceptable community health care. Amber recalled the meeting as disquieting; she felt that it was biased in favor of the hospital administration. The CEO and board of directors attended the meeting, and although it was a community-based meeting, not a hospital board meeting, some directors sat next to the chapter officials in the front of the room. It appeared to Amber that board members where trying to cozy up to the chapter officials running the meeting and that chapter officials were doing little to contradict this appearance.

She feared that this apparent close relationship would make it hard for the chapter to publicly hold managers accountable. Nonetheless, she spoke up on behalf of the employees, asking the CEO to allow an employee-only forum and survey about the workplace environment. Under pressure of the public eye, the CEO agreed. This was a huge first step for the workers, both for holding management accountable in labor relations under 638 and for taking ownership over improving labor relations—a step that would not reach its full potential until after Black Friday.

Like Thomas, Amber traced her Black Friday firing to her outspokenness at this meeting. But the realization of the severe consequences for publicly speaking up did not deter her from boldly trying to hold management accountable for its actions on the day she was fired. In her account, midway through that day, she found out that her supervisor's superior and her supervisor had been fired in succession. Amber was so confident that she was next in line that she decided to take a proactive approach rather than let fate come to her. She went to the top of the chain of command, seeking out the head of the hospital's Human Resources Department. She wanted to ask him directly whether she would be fired. She was so convinced of her eminent firing that when he came to her office to answer this question, Amber was already boxing up her personal items. She recalled that he was perplexed by her actions and told Amber that she had nothing to worry about. He said, "I don't know...who's passing the word around. You're not going to be fired. What are you doing [packing up]?" But he could not dispel what Amber knew to be inevitable, and she kept packing.

What troubled Amber even more than getting fired for speaking up, however, was that those who fired her would not disclose that this was the reason behind her termination. As with her public criticism of hospital administrators, she wanted them to be held accountable for their actions. This attitude is clear both in her proactive querying of the human resources director and in her interactions with top hospital management throughout Black Friday. She told me a harrowing story of the tension building throughout that day. She was certain that she "would be next," but no one would give her a straight answer as to when and why she would be fired. The delaying of what she believed to be the inevitable was so stressful that twice she decided to go directly to the top get a final answer on her employment. After receiving an unconvincing answer from the director of human resources, she tried to inquire with the hospital's CEO. Both times, his secretary told Amber that he was unavailable. Eventually, toward the end of the day, she was brought into a room with the CEO, select board members, and a security guard. It was there and then that they finally informed her that she was terminated. When they would not provide her with a satisfactory explanation for her termination, she became adamant that they, not she, take accountability for her firing. She defiantly declared to them her own interpretation of why they were firing her. She recounted it this way:

> So then, um, we were in the boardroom and there was a police officer standing behind me. And, and I asked, when they showed me, gave me the letter [of

termination], I asked, "What are the charges? What are the actions?" They didn't have them, and they said, "We are firing you, firing you at will." And I said, "Okay." Then, I asked, "I, I need to know what, why you're doing this." And that's when they said, "Escort her out. Officer, escort her out." So on my way out, what I said was, "You, you're firing me because I'm a female, I'm a Native American, and I have a voice here." And so that's when I walked out.

At the very moment the CEO and board were exercising their greatest power—the power to terminate employment—Amber overtly challenged this power by evoking the greater authority of the community. She contested their corporate authority to conduct at-will firing, to make decisions about employment and the hospital without providing an explanation. She disputed the notion that employees work at the will of managers. Moreover, an at-will termination constructs Amber's firing as an isolated incident, with no connection to the other employees fired on the same day. Amber refused to accept this as an adequate justification for her termination; she instead supplied her own explanation. In this way, she attempted to make the administration accountable for its actions. She constructed her firing as not for something she did wrong—poor job performance—but for something she was—a female, a Native American, someone with a voice. She proudly proclaimed who she was, and that was apparently what got her in trouble.

In her account of the events of Black Friday, Amber highlights her agency in her termination. She attempted to take control of her situation and not passively let management define it for her. She was the one trying to make them accountable for what they were doing on Black Friday. Just as important is how her articulation of agency is also emblematic of an emergent sense of ownership of the hospital and the process of making it a successful 638 tribal enterprise. The sense of ownership comes from individuals recognizing their connection to their community and from their willingness to act upon this connection and take responsibility for the community. This is exactly what Amber did in the conclusion of her narrative of Black Friday. She declared that her connection to a community of women and Native people and speaking on their behalf had led to her firing. In asserting that it was being female, Native American, and having a voice that resulted in her termination, she took ultimate responsibility for her community. She accepted the consequences of active involvement in her community. In so doing, she declared that she, not the board or CEO, was rooted in the community and that their act of firing her was actually an act against the community.

Interestingly, in her retelling, Amber explicitly gendered her firing. She reiterated that she was targeted not only as a Native person but also as a "female" with "a voice." Her suggestion of the gendered nature of her firing flags a specifically gendered history of health-care employment at Navajo. The health-care industry has long been a space of political and economic opportunity for women in general and Navajo women in particular. Although, across the industry, women are concentrated in entry- and mid-level positions and men continue to dominate the ranks of doctors and administrators, women occupied many of the highest administrative positions within the

TCRHCC. In fact, some of the board members and CEOs most criticized by the local community were Navajo women. Gender relations within this particular hospital setting are complex; they do not map onto conventional axes of workplace gender discrimination. The complexities (and Amber's comments) are best understood by examining the larger role that health-care employment has played in gendered economic relations within twentieth-century Navajo communities and in the broader, gendered history of work on the Navajo Nation.

From the first, U.S. colonialism and capitalism have undermined the traditional political, cultural, and spiritual powers of indigenous women and the traditionally gendered balances that have sustained local indigenous communities (Barker 2008; Denetdale 2007, 2008; Smith 2005; Smith and Kauanui 2008). The livestock reduction of the 1930s caused a profound disruption in gendered economic relations among Navajos. Forced livestock reduction undermined the economic power of women because livestock were traditionally viewed as being owned by women (Shepardson 1982; Weisiger 2007). Moreover, livestock reduction intensified Navajos' interactions with market economies in general, and market economy jobs, such as mining and construction jobs, were defined by the marketplace as "men's work" (O'Neill 2005). Even though most Diné families only partially relied on wage labor and women continued to play a key role in ensuring economic subsistence, Navajo men's wage work became a key source of compensation for the economic loss of grazing (Bailey and Bailey 1986; O'Neill 2005; White 1983).

Over the long run, many jobs in construction and mining proved to be intermittent and unstable, and Navajos chose not to move too far or stay too long away from the reservation just for a job (O'Neill 2005). Consequently, unemployment rates for Navajos have remained generally high. More recently, public-sector jobs and especially health-care jobs held by women have become economic mainstays for many Navajo communities. Many women I talked to were the primary breadwinners for their families. One female TCRHCC employee joked that at shift changes, the hospital parking lot was always full of men in trucks, waiting to pick up their spouses. All these factors considered, women's jobs at the TCRHCC are critical not only for women's personal livelihood but also for the community's as a whole. Amber's firing impacted her specifically as a Navajo woman trying to provide for her family in a context of market instability.

Gender also played a significant role in the way women such as Amber viewed their activism. Clearly, at the climactic moment of her firing, Amber felt compelled to speak out on behalf of not only hospital employees in general but also women in particular. Similar public expressions of protest against TCRHCC leadership came from other women and also men, but many women discussed with me their own willingness to be outspoken. They frequently traced this trait to earlier roles for Navajo women, who traditionally and historically were outspoken and whose political opinions were respected within the community. These political opinions gave woman authority in the community, even if they did not maintain positions of leadership "sanctioned" by non-Indian military and political leaders or achieve recognition by non-Indian historians (see Denetdale 2007). By gendering her firing through her statement to the managers *and* by giving this statement a prominent role in her retelling of the day she was terminated, Amber referenced both the historical power of Diné women and the contemporary importance of female health-care workers in the Tuba City community.

Amber's actions, as well as the actions of her female coworkers and co-activists, typify what indigenous feminist scholars have called Native feminisms (Smith and Kauanui 2008:241).[15] Amber's retort to hospital management demands recognition for the role that she and other female employees played in the effort to hold local leadership accountable to the promise of self-determination. Moreover, the activism practiced by Amber and her fellow HECMC members reflects the nonhierarchical and everyday life–based organizing advocated by Andrea Smith (2008) in her call for a Native feminist politics that emphasizes collective action and replaces vanguardism with a more inclusive, creative, and emotive activism. Indeed, after Amber's and her four colleagues' firings, her coworkers and community members came together across gender and racial lines to support her and challenge the hierarchy of the hospital in very creative and quotidian ways, using flyers, T-shirts, posters, and a float in a Navajo heritage parade. In the process, workplace activism that started out as an effort to restore the jobs of those sacked became an increasing, community-wide desire to take ownership of the TCRHCC and to self-determine its administration.

Continued Workplace Activism

Eventually, those fired on Black Friday were reinstated, in large part because of a legal settlement.[16] But it was also persistent public pressure on the hospital leadership that aided these workers' cause. Employee–community solidarity gathered strength and momentum as workplace activism effected change, including the removal of the CEO and the reinstatement of the fired employees. The fact that their voices were being heeded empowered workers and community members to push for further changes in hospital leadership and for an institutionalized say in how the hospital was run. In terms of the former, the HECMC advocated for the removal of some top-ranking board members and the interim CEO (who replaced the one the committee had helped get removed). As for the latter, the committee sought collective bargaining rights for employees and chapter approval of the board of directors. A sense of ownership over the TCRHCC was initiated in the collective solidarity of workplace activism regarding issues of labor relations, but ultimately, employees and community members expressed it in the discourse of self-determination as they began to call for a grassroots articulation of self-determination.

The TCRHCC made several efforts to calm the tensions provoked by Black Friday: it fired the non-Navajo CEO, settled on rehiring the terminated employees, reconsidered aspects of its corporate bylaws (including eliminating the at-will employment policy), and engaged in public forums to open a dialogue with employees and community members. From the HECMC's perspective, however, these actions were forced on the directors more than motivated by them. For example, despite distaste for and distrust of the non-Navajo CEO, many employees ultimately felt that board members had used him as a scapegoat for problems that had deeper roots in the corporate structure of the TCRHCC. They noted how some board members tried to disavow prior knowledge of the Black Friday firings. Many employees and community members believed that the board of directors had been intimately involved in Black Friday—that it was not an act solely instigated by the non-Navajo CEO, as some board members claimed. Many employees were outraged that these board members were not removed along with the CEO. As for the rehiring of the terminated employees, as far as the HECMC was concerned, this action was established by a legal settlement, not the benevolence of management. Additionally, the change in the at-will policy was legally imposed upon the TCRHCC when the Office of Navajo Labor Relations found the policy to be a violation of Navajo Nation laws requiring formal procedures for terminated Native employees.[17] Moreover, other potential reforms to the corporate bylaws never materialized beyond the review stage.

Lastly, engagement in public dialogue about hospital policy was as much provoked by employees and community members who packed the hospital's monthly board meetings, chapter meetings, and tribal governmental committee hearings as it was by the board of directors itself. In fact, employees frequently complained about hospital leaders' using parliamentary tactics at these meetings in order to stifle workers' voices. Such tactics included agendas that rarely gave workers ample time to express their concerns and "public comment" sections that were too often relegated to last in the long meetings and were commonly tabled as a "time consideration." Further, employees decried management's attempt to limit their voices with new policies, such as a requirement that employees take leave time or be off-duty to attend board meetings. Under the new policies, a time slot at board meetings was reserved specifically for comments from "community members." However, TCRHCC employees were forbidden from speaking as community members. This effort to disassociate workers' community subjectivity from their workplace subjectivity only disappointed the employees further. It tried to undercut the bond that the HECMC had forged between employees and patients. Furthermore, it implied to employees that their opinions *as community members* were devalued or that somehow they could not be both hospital employees and community members (even though nearly all employees lived in the immediate vicinity of the hospital and used it for their health-care needs).

Most management efforts to change the TCRHCC were poorly received by the HECMC. HECMC members publicly declared that tensions still existed and more structural changes needed to come. Moreover, given that all the efforts to change the TCRHCC were imposed from the outside, a bunker mentality remained among the board mambers. The most criticized members publicly declared that they were being unjustly attacked. They tried to discount the HECMC, suggesting that it was just a handful of disgruntled employees or that its protests were culturally inappropriate and not part of the "Navajo way." To compound the stalemate, employees, emboldened by their emergent power, protested more vocally and pushed for more progressive reforms.

The next manifestation of the increased enthusiasm for workplace activism came in response to the new CEO. At the beginning of the summer of 2004, she was hired on an interim basis. She was thought to be a significant improvement over the previous CEO because she was Navajo. Early on, she said all the things the employees wanted to hear; she talked about healing and restoring harmony to the hospital from day one. This honeymoon period did not last long, though. Many hospital workers hoped that she would help buffer them from the board members they did not trust. But it was not long before the same patterns of tension between employees and hospital leadership reemerged. By this time, the ad hoc HECMC was having regular meetings. It became a means for employees and community members to maintain concerted action and an oppositional identity against what they believed to be a continuing crisis of effectiveness and legitimacy in the TCRHCC.

These meetings were mainly used for information sharing and planning.[18] Workers and community members in attendance discussed and tried to verify any workplace rumors they might have heard. They shared information about work conditions across the various departments of the hospital. They kept one another updated about upcoming public forums, such as hospital board meetings, chapter house meetings, NNC committee and general council meetings, and lobbying delegations. They discussed who would attend which public forum and who would speak, often considering who had time off from work, who had access to transportation, and how resources could be pooled to pay for gas and for the flyers they hoped to pass out at meetings. They discussed the political messages of their protest literature, including flyers posted around the hospital and community; letters to the editors of local newspapers; public letters to hospital, governmental, and union officials; and a full-page advertisement in the *Navajo Times*. Discussions over text varied, from informal group conversations about flyers to consensus-based ratification of more formal documents.

The latter was particularly the case for the full-page ad placed in the *Navajo Times* on July 15, 2004. A small group was chosen to write the ad and then present it to the HECMC for consensus approval. The small group took this undertaking quite seriously and ended up writing what became the committee's de facto position paper. The advertisement called for an elected rather than appointed hospital board of directors, union recognition, and the removal of certain board members. It was placed in the *Navajo Times* during the week of a critical NNC meeting, wherein council representatives received recommendations from two legislative committees that had investigated the turmoil in Tuba City. Additionally, the committee sent a copy of the position piece to every NNC member. This public declaration announced that hospital employees and community members wanted greater control over how their hospital was being administered.

In addition to working toward increased worker and community participation, the mere existence of the HECMC was an act of claiming ownership over tribal labor relations. HECMC meetings were safe spaces in which workers could share their feelings and discuss rumors without fear of reprisal; these created an alternative and collective-oriented source of authority. Participating in these meetings, workers and community members refused to blindly accept upper management's construction of hospital working conditions. Although the meetings remained ad hoc and never fully realized any formal structure, they were a way for workers to express an investment in and to take some responsibility for how labor relations and general administration were conducted at the TCRHCC. Through the meetings and the activism planned at them, employees and community members formed a grassroots-based, oppositional identity. The cohesion for this group was a collective sense of distrust of and frustration with official hospital leadership and a desire to change the way this leadership operated. Ultimately, the meetings threatened the authority of the official hospital leadership; the CEO warned some people that they could be fired for attending.

The sense of ownership could also be seen in the most tangible result of HECMC activism: the resignation of the new CEO. As under the hospital's previous CEO, employees were vigilant about holding top administrators responsible for their leadership. When work conditions did not improve under the new CEO, employees continued to attend hospital board meetings, question leaders about their future plans, and hold them accountable for some of their spending. Not getting the desired answers, workers began to openly criticize the new CEO and accused her of not being forthright and honest with employees. One flyer contended, "When [the new CEO] came to TCRHCC she told everyone she has an open door policy and likes transparency. There are now closed doors, secret meetings, and threats against employees. Obviously her words aren't true." Not surprisingly, this public pressure only increased tension; the CEO responded by criticizing prominent employees in the HECMC. According to another HECMC flyer, she removed an employee from an internal position on a hospital leadership council because he attended HECMC meetings, and then she threatened him by allegedly saying, "I'll make sure I find reasons to fire you."[19] It is clearly understandable that any CEO would be highly concerned about a potential conflict of interest in an employee attending high-level corporate leadership meetings and at the same time being part of a grassroots organization dedicated to critiquing this very leadership. But it was the alleged threat of termination that was most significant to employees. To them, this was the same tactic used in Black Friday and therefore illustrated a striking lack of progress in their work conditions. Indeed, one flyer on which this quote prominently appeared was titled "History Repeated" and was constructed as a two-column comparison of the previous and current CEOs. This time, however, workers responded before there could be another round of terminations.

In December 2004, workers held another week of picket-line protests outside the hospital (Dempsey 2004). This and other public pressure provoked the NNC Health and Social Services Committee to hold an on-site hearing at the Tuba City Chapter House in January 2005. At this meeting, many employees aired their grievances against the CEO and board of directors and protested board members being appointed and not elected. Under significant fire from most attending the meeting, the hospital leadership also got to present its side of the story. With great poise, the leaders defended themselves, contending that they were doing their best to be receptive to employee concerns, come up with solutions for these concerns, and maintain a positive work environment in which to treat "the most important" part of the TCRHCC, the patients. Because of the findings of this hearing, however, the CEO ultimately resigned, and a policy change was initiated to ensure chapter approval of the board of directors. As with the removal of the previous CEO, many employees saw these reforms as significant victories and a validation of workers' right to have a say in the hospital's labor relations.

Grassroots Articulation of Self-Determination

Tribal members' desire for active participation in a tribally run enterprise is predicted by Cornell and Kalt (HPAIED 2008) and is one of the main reasons they advocated for such an endeavor. Community members' interest and investment in enterprises they can genuinely claim as *theirs* lead to successful self-determination projects. As the workplace activism at Tuba City began to produce favorable results and as people's participation in the HECMC increased, workers began to adopt the discourse of self-determination. They did so in a way that attempted to formulate a grassroots tribal self-determination articulated in opposition to the more centralized and limited form of self-determination practiced by the TCRHCC board of directors. Articulating their protest in terms of self-determination emerged as employees moved beyond their initial outrage over Black Friday and sought solutions to what they believed to be the main problems with how the hospital was run. This process also marked a general acceptance that 638 was at Tuba City to stay and that it was perhaps the best model within which to work, rather than go back to IHS administration. Indeed, the workers' argument about increased community control and participation paralleled (if not co-opted) the original arguments in favor of 638. This emergent, grassroots-oppositional conceptualization of self-determination took many forms but did not necessarily rise to the level of a formalized political message. Nevertheless, among the ad hoc strategies marshaled for workplace activism at Tuba City, it became a potent articulation of a sense of community ownership of the TCRHCC.

The grassroots-oppositional form of self-determination frequently was expressed in public criticism of the TCRHCC. One common way of criticizing hospital administrators was to blame them for stifling workplace democracy and local political participation. Suppression of political voice was constructed as the antithesis to self-determination. Many HECMC flyers referred to the philosophical writings of the U.S. founders—in one case even directly quoting Thomas Jefferson—and the ACLU. Typical protest flyers contrasted the way labor relations were practiced at the TCRHCC with popular American notions of civil liberty. One flyer stated:

> [The new CEO] threatened [Dave Pearce] telling him that if he goes to one more [HECMC] meeting she will make sure she finds reasons to fire him.
>
> The framers of the Constitution regarded freedom of speech and expression and inquiry as hallmarks of political freedom and a democratic society. This is because free speech is merely the expression of free thought. Speech is merely the articulation of thought. If speech is banned, then thought is banned as well because then thought is denied expression.

Commentary such as this was clearly meant to dramatize the experiences of TCRHCC employees, but it also speaks to how many employees believed that the circumstances had become dire. Juxtaposing these two ideas invoked the larger issues employees felt were at stake: legitimate governance and the right to have a say in how self-determination is enacted. Calling on the principles of democratic governance and freedom of speech was an attempt to hold corporate leadership accountable to the reality that the TCRHCC is not merely a health-care corporation but also a tribal enterprise run under the auspices of tribal self-governance. Workers used the fact that the hospital was a 638 tribal enterprise to appeal to notions of popular democracy and to contend that employees and the community should not be shut out of the process and indeed should have an active say in determining how the TCRHCC should be run.

In addition to expressing this position in terms of a Euro-American political tradition, the HECMC and its participants focused on a more practical application of grassroots self-determination. In one instance, a flyer urged people to attend an upcoming chapter house meeting to vote on a resolution calling for the election of hospital directors. The flyer was titled "Chapter Self-Determination." It sought to notify employees and community members:

> **The Tuba City *Hospital Board* of Directors have Bylaws that say they make the final decision on who is selected as a Board Member to represent the Tuba City Chapter.**
>
> - We need to make them change their Bylaws to say that our Chapter will make the *final* decision on who represents our chapter.
>
> - Vote for the resolution that will let our Chapter *"Elect"!* a hospital Board Member to represent us. Remember, an elected representative will work for and be accountable to the chapter people and not to the Board.
>
> **Please Come and Vote on this important resolution.**

At the bottom of the flyer, in handwritten bold print, was the proclamation "This is your Hospital!! Not the Board's!!" Another flyer declared: "At TCRHCC, we do NOT have 'Self-Determination,' we have 'Board Determination.' Return the Tuba City hospital to the community; Removal of the current TCRHCC Board of Directors cannot wait!" Both examples call for a popular model of self-determination, one based on a grassroots workplace and community participation and oversight. As significant, they also defend and attempt to institutionalize active participation in the enactment of 638, the very action that got the five employees fired on Black Friday.

The grassroots-oppositional articulation of self-determination was not a call for involvement in the day-to-day operational control of the TCRHCC. But the hospital itself, through its labor relations, had become a place where community members, in their jobs as hospital employees, experienced tribal self-determination on a day-to-day basis. Given their immediate experience with the enactment of self-determination and its potentially detrimental effect on individuals' livelihoods and mental health, not to mention on delivery of the community's health care in general, employees decided to take a stand. They worked to hold tribal officials accountable for their leadership and sought to take more ownership of the tribal enterprise. Rather than rely solely on tribal officials, they sought grassroots participation in the process of tribal self-determination.

Conclusion

Conspicuously absent from the workplace activism at Tuba City was organized labor. In part, this speaks to LIUNA's principled stance of not appearing to intervene in the process of tribal sovereignty. It is also likely the reason that of the HECMC's main demands—removal of two CEOs and reinstatement of the employees fired on Black Friday; chapter-elected TCRHCC directors; and union recognition—the last is the only one that to this day is unmet. Four of the five employees got their jobs back; the fifth took a high-ranking job at another facility. The board of directors removed the two CEOs after great pressure from the HECMC and the Navajo Nation tribal government. Lastly, the chapters served by the TCRHCC all passed resolutions insisting on elected directors; the board ultimately conceded the point by changing the TCRHCC bylaws. After this change, directors with the most contentious relationship with employees were no longer on the board. The demand for union recognition has still not been met, however, despite a new petition drive that garnered majority support of TCRHCC employees.

LIUNA in no way abandoned the TCRHCC employees. In fact, because of the intricacies in TCRHCC's 638 contract, some employees technically remained IHS employees, not direct hires of TCRHCC, and therefore were still legally represented by the union.[20] Because it did have a long-term relationship with employees at the facility, the union helped the HECMC in subtle, unofficial ways, such as lending advice and even paying for a bus to transport employees to Window Rock to lobby NNC representatives for union recognition. The union found itself in a bind trying to officially represent TCRHCC employees under the 638 contract, though. Despite the union's securing the requisite number of signatures from Tuba City hospital employees for recognition under Navajo Nation collective bargaining laws during the Campaign for Union Recognition, the TCRHCC leadership declined to recognize and negotiate with the union. In response to LIUNA's inquiry about recognition, the board asserted that it was a unique institution that fell under neither the NLRA nor the tribe's labor code. From the perspective of the employees and some union representatives, hospital management was manipulating the circumstances of how the NNC had created and structured the TCRHCC in order to avoid unionization. Recall that during the debate about whether to take over administration of Navajo Area IHS, many Navajos were anxious about tribal council members having direct control over funding and hiring for a tribally run health-care system (see chapters 4 and 5). In response to these fears of impropriety, the NNC did everything it could to make the TCRHCC a tribal corporation accountable to but separate from the NNC. This left the TCRHCC in a political and administrative gray area; one hospital manager used to claim that the TCRHCC was a unique kind of Navajo tribal corporation. This legal gray area made it difficult for LIUNA to counter TCRHCC management's position if the union wanted to maintain its reputation as supporting tribal sovereignty and self-determination.

Under management's interpretation of its chartered relationship to the NNC, U.S. federal law did not apply, because the standard NLRB position at the time was to abdicate jurisdiction over tribal enterprises (this event mostly taking place before the *San Manuel* decision had been rendered). Moreover, after the *San Manuel* decision came down (which happened during the Tuba City protests), the *Yukon II* decision was released (see chapter 2). The latter case was specifically about a Native Alaskan 638 health-care facility; the NLRB ruled that it would not assert jurisdiction. Thus, the union's only recourse was tribal, not federal, labor law. For that matter, hospital management claimed that because the NNC had made an effort to isolate the TCRHCC from the NNC, the tribe's labor code did not apply. When pushed on this matter by the HECMC—and to some extent by LIUNA officials—TCRHCC management asserted that it would think about unionization but that the NNC would need to pass a special law to regulate labor relations for a 638 corporation such as the TCRHCC. Although the Office of Navajo Labor Relations did not necessarily agree with this position, it did not fight TCRHCC management on it, and LIUNA felt hamstrung over how assertive it could be on this issue. To this day, the HECMC and LIUNA have received a series of unfulfilled promises by past and current hospital leadership to consider the idea of union recognition for TCRHCC employees.[21] Given the legal complexity of this issue and the way in which it directly related to Navajo Nation sovereignty through an enactment of a 638 contract, LIUNA chose to remain neutral and out of the public eye throughout the labor relations turmoil at Tuba City.

Even so, TCRHCC employees were not deterred by their inability to gain institutional support from the union. Some privately expressed disappointment about the union's relative inaction, but there was never public criticism—most likely because employees were hopeful that LIUNA would represent them after TCRHCC leadership finally gave in to their demand for union recognition. Indeed, the hope of unionization is one indication of the multivalent nature of tribal labor relations in Tuba City and in general. Tribal labor relations at Tuba City were a complex mix of local Navajo sociocultural practices and political relations; tribal nation-state legal and economic development policies; American institutionalizations of the workplace, such as unionization and corporate capitalism; and broader Euro-American cultural notions of civil rights and political expression.

This nexus of forces was perhaps best exemplified by a small gathering of Navajo and non-Navajo hospital employees and community members during the Tuba City turmoil. The meeting consisted of a select, interracial "working group" of people from the HECMC who decided to have a strategy session in advance of a crucial hearing in Tuba City by the NNC's Health and Social Services Committee. The hearing was meant to be an update on the progress made by the TCRHCC in the eight months since the committee had conducted an investigation and called for significant reforms. The employees, feeling that things had not significantly changed, wanted to make sure that they were able to clearly communicate their concerns to the committee. This working group convened in Thomas's hogan in a remote area outside town. Members spent more than two hours sitting on the dirt floor, warmed from January's chill by a fire inside a steel drum in the center of the hogan. They covered the inside of the five earthen and wooden walls with butcher paper, on which they brainstormed and crafted a message for select Navajo employees and community members to deliver at the upcoming hearing. Despite the aggravating circumstances being discussed, participants described this meeting as comforting and uplifting because of the great ambiance and camaraderie inside the hogan. Here was an interracial group from various backgrounds discussing how best to advocate for the rights and progress of their workplace and their community. They represented different experiential and cultural backgrounds, different job titles and levels of education, and different connections to the community of Tuba City, yet they all wanted to improve TCRHCC's labor relations and delivery of health care.

In a similar fashion, the events surrounding the TCRHCC represented this nexus of forces. A coalition of community members and employees—some of whom were not Navajo—came together to oppose what they felt were unfair and unhealthy work conditions. By their reckoning, unharmonious labor relations were provoked by an abuse of corporate authority that valued the opinions of an elite leadership over those of the community. Community members and employees used multiple means to protest these abuses. Some of the protests were rooted in local articulations of community, suggesting that corporate leaders either did not understand local cultural norms of civility, responsibility, and accountability or had betrayed them. Other protestations were articulated in terms of Euro-American Enlightenment notions of citizenship and civil rights. What they shared in common was a grassroots tenor—ad hoc in nature, employing quotidian and local forms such as word of mouth, flyers, floats in local parades, and coverage in the local press. At the same time, employees and community members called on classic workplace activism such as picket-line protesting, petition drives, and lobbying public officials. Ultimately, the group proposed solutions that relied on a blend of local popular control and external oversight: community participation in the selection and accountability of leadership through local and regional forms of tribal governance and in workplace security established through collective bargaining. Much as tribal capitalism is seen as a local, communal expression of a more universal institution, the tribal labor relations enacted by Tuba City employees blended local modes and needs with conventional workplace activism.

The TCRHCC 638 pilot program proves the importance of what Cornell and Kalt find to be critical components of a tribal enterprise: effectiveness and legitimacy. In this chapter, I approach these issues from a labor relations perspective, chronicling what happens when workers believe that there has been a failure in the effectiveness and legitimacy of their tribal corporate leadership. From the same perspective, I show that what Cornell and Kalt believe to be the main benefit of tribal enterprises—a sense of local ownership and accountability—can be used and enacted by tribal employees acting as and with community members in whose interest the tribal enterprise was established. Community members as employees in a tribal enterprise are in some instances best situated to hold tribal corporate leadership accountable to the local community (and the tribe as a whole) because of their positions within the workplace. Moreover, because tribal employees' individual welfare and job security are tied to the success of the tribal enterprise, their investment in their jobs uniquely overlaps with the community's interest in having a tribal enterprise succeed. This is why tribal labor relations are so important to the health of indigenous communities.

epilogue
The Uncertain Future of Tribal Labor Relations

To provide a glimpse of what may lie ahead in tribal labor relations, I close by offering two examples of potential trends in Indian Country labor relations. The first is what I witnessed at two recent national tribal economic development conferences. The second comes from recent developments at the world's second-largest casino, Foxwoods, owned and operated by the Mashantucket Pequot Nation. In December 2007, the Council for Tribal Employee Rights (CTER) held its annual Legal Update Convention at the Imperial Palace Hotel, an aging hotel and casino on the strip in Las Vegas, Nevada. Over the course of three days, hundreds of tribal employee rights officers, labor union organizers and officials, and vendors dressed in business casual gathered in a high-ceilinged hotel ballroom to hear legal updates on labor rulings and presentations on topics such as Native-preference hiring policy compliance. The April 2008 annual meeting of the National Indian Gaming Association (NIGA), held in the gleaming, glass-walled San Diego Convention Center, located on scenic San Diego Bay, was by comparison a grander affair. It drew thousands of tribal gaming corporation officers and managers and also vendors selling everything from Native sculptures to gaming products. Both conferences offered sessions focusing on labor unions in tribal economic life. The CTER conference featured several presentations about positive collaborations between unions and the tribal leaders and institutions that manage tribal economic development, including union-sponsored job training for tribal members and tribal government–sanctioned union membership drives. But CTER and NIGA also offered seminars presenting hard-hitting union-busting tactics, illustrated in PowerPoint presentations and handouts and delivered by slick human resources consultants who had secured tribal governments as clients and were seeking more. As is now typical of union-busting consulting firms in general, the consultants made no bones about explaining how to keep tribal workplaces what they euphemistically call "union free." They talked about how to detect whether union organizers are targeting your company, how to use supervisors as information gatherers, and how to run counterorganizing campaigns in the event of a representation election. They discussed potential legal strategies to fight unionization while also making sure that tribal enterprises do not break any laws in their attempt to bust unions.[1] Their presentations included all the standard tactics of corporate America's increasing effort to keep unions out of the workplace and to decertify those that already exist (Brodkin and Strathmann 2004; Logan 2002). As a starting point, presenters assumed that their audiences agreed with them that unionization was a disease that needed to be stopped. But it is hard to tell how the audiences received the presentations. At CTER, there was certainly some murmuring of dissatisfaction from the audience; no doubt this had to do with the fact that many union organizers and Native union members were in the audience. But only a few people posed any questions challenging the presenters' presumptions about unionism's place in tribal labor relations. At the NIGA presentation, most questions from the audience were logistical inquiries about how to bolster efforts against unionization. There were no presentations by union leaders, but such a thing would be highly unexpected, given the tension between unions and the Indian gaming industry.

Perhaps most telling is that these presentations were even made at all. Whether or not tribal leaders want to employ the services of anti-union consultants, the conference organizers believed their information to be useful. What is more, the anti-union consultants certainly saw their presentations as an excellent opportunity to market their services to potential clients. The presentations alone do not necessarily signify an intensifying trend of anti-unionism in tribal labor relations. But there are some signs. A handful of tribes have passed tribal right-to-work laws. Although these laws cannot outlaw unions or union organizing, they are a clear effort to constrain on-reservation unionism. Right-to-work laws, like the tactics proffered by anti-union consultants, are another classic tactic used to create an unfriendly environment for unionism.

The *San Manuel* rulings may have paved the way for union campaigns in Indian Country, but they have not guaranteed automatic organizing success or passive acceptance of unionization by tribal political and economic leaders. Not surprisingly, the *San Manuel* rulings clearly emboldened labor unions' efforts to organize tribal casino employees. At the same time, some tribes have continued to challenge unionization of their casinos, treating the adjudication of tribal labor relations as more of an open question than one definitively settled by the NLRB and the D.C. Circuit Court. This has been the case for two tribes in particular: the Mashantucket Pequot Tribal Nation and the Saginaw Chippewa Indian Tribe of Michigan. In late 2007, the UAW won an NLRB-sanctioned election by a three-to-two margin to secure union representation for poker and game table dealers at the Foxwoods Casino. Trying to build on the momentum of this success, over the next six months both the UAW and the International Union of Operating Engineers (IUOE) filed petitions with the NLRA to hold representation elections for three other job categories of Foxwoods casino workers: the engineering, offtrack betting, and slot technician departments. But whatever momentum was gained by the UAW's victory with dealers was significantly stalled in these elections. First, the IUOE lost its bid to represent the engineers by a three-to-one margin. Then the UAW lost the representation election for offtrack betting employees by a three-to-two margin and subsequently decided to rescind its petition to request the slot technician election, effectively canceling the election.[2] During the same period, the Teamsters attempted to organize housekeepers at the Soaring Eagle Casino, owned and operated by the Saginaw Chippewa Tribe. The Teamsters lost the election by a two-to-one margin. Clearly, these campaigns illustrate that workers at these casinos were not overwhelmingly sold on the idea of union representation.

These elections also illustrate tribal leaders' unwillingness to passively accept the results of the *San Manuel* rulings. Despite the blow the rulings dealt to tribal sovereignty, Mashantucket Pequot and Saginaw Chippewa political and economic leaders still attempted to maintain significant control over labor relations at their tribal casinos. Every step of the way, they appealed the NLRB's decisions on representation elections, based on arguments of tribal sovereignty and jurisdiction. Additionally, the Mashantucket Pequots requested that the UAW and IUOE file their representation petitions under the tribe's labor code, not the NLRB. All these actions signify reluctance on the part of Native nations to accept what they believe to be the bad law created by *San Manuel*. Moreover, they also project the possibility that one of these two tribes, or another tribe in the same circumstance, will challenge the D.C. Circuit Court's ruling on *San Manuel* in the Supreme Court. The San Manuel Band of Mission Indians has been hesitant to take this ultimate step, but the Saginaw Chippewa leaders in particular have publicly refuted the NLRB's authority and have made subtle overtures that suggest a willingness to undertake such a legal endeavor in order to definitively establish their sovereignty over tribal labor relations (see Ecker 2009).

Even if these indigenous leaders do not push the issue legally, they have asserted the right to have a say in labor relations in Indian Country and at their casinos. They did not remain neutral during the representation elections—particularly the Saginaw Chippewa, who used an anti-union firm to make their case against unionization to workers. Of course, irrespective of the *San Manuel* rulings, their actions are well within the legal right of employers anywhere in the United States. What is significant to the future of tribal labor relations is the antagonistic nature of the response to the intensified unionization efforts post–*San Manuel*. Given the loss of jurisdiction over tribal labor relations, will tribal governments attempt to assert control over labor relations by fighting the unionization of their enterprises, including using anti-union consultants, or will they engage in good-faith bargaining with hopes of negotiating a contract that secures their tribal labor relations?

One possible answer to this question leads to a potentially more amicable trend in tribal labor relations. The Mashantucket Pequot example may in fact turn out to have a more cordial ending for the parties involved. At first, like the Saginaw Chippewa, Foxwoods management hired one of the country's premier union-busting firms to fight unionism and the court decisions that had limited its sovereign right to regulate labor relations. However, apparently realizing the limits of this strategy, the tribe recently fired the firm after exhausting its NLRB appeals. This act seemed to signal a new course in how the Mashantucket Pequot might handle tribal labor relations. Then, in late October 2008, the tribal government and the UAW put out a joint press release saying that both parties would pursue negotiations of a union contract primarily under tribal, not federal, labor law. This followed the historic act of the Mashantucket Pequot Tribal Nation Council, certifying the UAW to represent the dealers, who had voted overwhelmingly for union recognition.

This certification was the first of its kind under the newly amended Mashantucket Pequot Labor Relations Law (MPLRL) (Mashantucket Pequot Tribal Laws: Title 32).[3] Mashantucket Pequot labor codes represent a unique approach to balancing goals for tribal self-determination with workers' rights to unionization. The MPLRL was preceded by a tribal right-to-work law, which was recently amended (Mashantucket Pequot Tribal Laws: Title 28). Unlike many right-to-work laws, the Mashantucket Pequot code does not outlaw union security agreements per se but instead provides a guarantee that no one has to join a union to secure a job on the reservation. This law prefaces and tempers the more union-friendly MPLRL without aggressively trying to undercut unionism. Within the MPLRL itself, there is a similar strong attempt to balance various interests. The text of this labor relations code acknowledges the *San Manuel* decisions and the NLRB's claim to assertion of jurisdiction over tribal labor relations and at the same time refutes the NLRB's logic by citing the NLRA's silence on tribal enterprises and other federal laws that promote tribal sovereignty (see section 2). However, more than anything, this section provides a theoretical assertion of Mashantucket Pequot tribal sovereignty, not a practical denial of the NLRB's jurisdiction, because in this very section, the MPLRL also acknowledges the right of any union to seek representation of tribal employees under the NLRA. What the law does is to claim tribal authority to handle labor relations, and it lays out a framework for labor relations processes similar to laws governing state employees elsewhere in the United States (by calling for representation elections, limiting work stoppages, and allowing for limited waivers of sovereign immunity). Thus, while acknowledging that employees and unions have alternative legal frameworks for union recognition and regulation of labor relations, the Mashantucket Pequots also encourage unions to use tribal instead of federal law. Despite *San Manuel*'s apparent abrogation of tribal authority, the Mashantucket Pequot government is still enacting its rights of self-governance and laying claims to its legitimate ability to handle labor relations with its own laws.

Ultimately, the MPLRL posits a model of concurrent jurisdiction of tribal labor relations—a position, incidentally, not altogether prohibited by the NLRB.[4] However, as of now, the current federal legal precedent allows unions, not tribal enterprises, to choose which form of regulation of tribal labor relations to use. Apparently, the UAW is convinced enough of the legitimacy of the MPLRL to at least give this avenue a try. Of course, it does so at relatively low risk, given the option to go back under the NLRA, but this is commendable nonetheless, given its willingness to support Mashantucket Pequot self-determination and self-governance.

The UAW and Mashantucket Pequot Tribal Nation agreement to utilize tribal instead of federal law has led to huge steps in trust on either side. Elizabeth Bunn, secretary-treasurer of the UAW, noted, "It came about because both parties were willing to listen [to] and address each other's concerns. The Mashantucket Pequots have set an extraordinary example by respecting the rights of workers." And Jackson King, general counsel for the Mashantucket Pequot Tribal Nation, stated, "We are very pleased to have come to an understanding that both acknowledges employees' rights to join unions and respects the rights of Native American governments."[5] Although negotiations over actual labor relations at Foxwoods under this agreement are still in their infancy, progressive agreements like this one could become more the norm than the exception. This change would certainly signal a positive turn toward an intentionally interdependent model of self-determination in tribal labor relations and in tribal sovereignty as a whole.

Whatever the outcome, another important lesson from both the Mashantucket Pequot and Saginaw Chippewa examples is that the *San Manuel* rulings do not ensure union success in Indian Country. Indeed, success depends largely on whether the union can run an effective organizing campaign, which can be a challenge when a union does not have a historic relationship with a specific group of workers. Unions (such as LIUNA) that have been representing workers in Indian Country for a long time, before *San Manuel*, are likely to do better post–*San Manuel* than unions that have made forays into Indian Country only after the *San Manuel* rulings—in part because the established unions have more credibility with both employers and tribal leaders. Those who seek to challenge unionization can easily brand the latter unions as interlopers. Indeed, much of tribal leaders' frustration with unionization seems to come from the fact that some unions began organizing tribal casino employees only after the *San Manuel* rulings. Of course, from the perspective of union leadership, they only began organizing post–*San Manuel* because it was too risky to put resources toward an organizing campaign in the absence of standard NLRA protections for such a campaign. But tribal leaders point to this very logic—that some unions bypass tribal processes of labor relations and instead appeal to an outside jurisdiction—as a sign of disrespect for tribal sovereignty. Given the newness of their campaigns, some unions could easily be labeled dues-seeking opportunists by both management and workers. This labeling is not insignificant, given that unions organizing in Indian Country often must overcome being doubly cast as outsiders. A key anti-unionization tactic in any work context is to denounce the union as an unwanted intruder in the "positive" and "familiar" employee–employer relationship. This issue is compounded in Indian Country, where tribal leaders can declare the union to be an outside, non-Native force. Approaching a tribal workforce only after the *San Manuel* rulings might make a union look like an outsider even to non-Indian employees. New union organizing in Indian Country post–*San Manuel* might not be able to produce the kind of class solidarity among workers against management that is often key to a successful union campaign, although this situation might change in time with persistent and good-faith organizing.

Another harbinger of trouble for unions trying to organize in Indian Country may be how tribal labor relations bring out tensions between labor unions that lie just beneath the surface of the current labor movement: there have been significant fissures within the AFL-CIO, with large unions leaving the organization; union density has steadily declined in the U.S. workforce; the U.S. economy has shifted away from manufacturing jobs traditionally held by U.S.-born citizens toward service jobs that often employ recent immigrants; and U.S. companies are more aggressively attacking unionization. These factors have created greater competition among unions to stay relevant, fight to represent employees, and expand beyond their traditional industries to increase membership. Tribal labor relations amplify and reiterate these tensions within the larger labor movement. The swift growth in the tribal gaming industry that has created many new service-sector jobs reflects the larger shift away from manufacturing and toward the service industry. Some unions appear to be turning toward tribal gaming as an untapped well of potential members. New unions are vying with those that traditionally represent hotel and casino employees. Indeed, the original *San Manuel* case was about UNITE-HERE!'s complaint that the CWA was getting preferential access to employees. At the Foxwoods Casino, before the UAW rescinded its request for a representation election for slot technicians, the UAW had to appeal to the NLRB to settle a dispute between the UAW and the International Brotherhood of Electrical Workers over who would represent the slot technicians. Such competition between unions can only complicate efforts to represent casino employees and stave off challenges from tribal casino management.[6]

There is also potential conflict among unions vying to represent the different kinds of work done in Indian Country. Tension between trade unions and service unions has existed for some time in the larger labor movement, and with the growth of tribal gaming, it could potentially surface in Indian Country. For example, several trade unions have represented indigenous miners and construction workers in Indian Country for a long time, since before the *San Manuel* rulings. Although they have had their ups and downs in dealings with tribal governments, many trade unions have forged good working relationships. Perhaps CTER is the best example of how trade unions work with tribal governments in providing placement and training for high-paying jobs on construction and mining projects on and near reservations—jobs that Native applicants otherwise might not get because of lack of experience. The end results are very good working relationships between tribal governments and labor unions, based on mutual respect and symbiosis. Furthermore, positive experiences with unionization generally lead indigenous people to join unions and even become key organizers.

Still, as the antagonism between service unions (or those seeking to represent casino service employees) and tribal governments grows, some trade union leaders are nervous about unionism getting a bad reputation in Indian Country, spoiling all the hard work they have done there. I have witnessed firsthand how this anxiety brings out the worst in labor leaders in ways that can further divide the labor movement and weaken unionism in Indian Country. At the same CTER conference that featured an anti-union consultant presenting union-busting tactics, for example, a trade union organizer from Michigan went out of his way to allay tribal leaders' concerns about trade unionism by reminding them, "We aren't like the service unions, who are too aggressive and won't respect your sovereignty." This comment clearly reiterates the differences and often divisive relationship between trade unions and service unions. In many instances, this divisiveness has hampered the broader labor movement in the United States (particularly compared with other countries). Such attitudes will likely hamper unionism in Indian Country.

Historically, tensions between trade unions and service unions belie deeper racial and gender divisions.[7] In Indian Country, these tensions can also be coded in differences between tribal members and nonmember employees. Indeed, another trade union leader, in his pro-union presentation at the CTER conference, suggested that job training collaborations between unions and tribes were important because they helped preserve jobs for tribal members instead of "Mexican workers." In this double dose of xenophobia, the threat is not just against nontribal members but also against non-American (that is, undocumented) nontribal members. In their comments, both of these union organizers were trying to create solidarity based on a broader appeal to general anti-immigrant racism in America. I believe that both comments were meant to articulate solidarity with tribal leaders as much as to distinguish the speakers' own trade unions from the "radical, troublemaking" service unions. Still, they reveal the multilayered tension around tribal labor relations. It is not just unions versus tribal leaders, but unions competing with one another to organize in Indian Country and workers' being pitted against one another based on racial, gender, and tribal citizenship status.

Perhaps even more troubling is the prospect of anti-union consultants (and aggressive unions) pressuring tribal leaders down the worst roads of neoliberal global capitalism. Anti-union consultants represent some of the worst tendencies in neoliberalism: the idea that liberalizing labor policies is the best way to grow an economy. This attitude can lead to more confrontational labor relations and worsening work conditions for employees. Moreover, when tribal leaders engage in the anti-union tactics offered by these consultants, they play into the argument made by nonindigenous union leaders, U.S. judges, and the general public that tribal enterprises are like any other commercial enterprise. Engaging in union busting puts tribal enterprise in line with many other U.S. and global corporations. In the eyes of courts and the general public, it can undermine tribes' claims to the unique circumstance of sovereignty, and the importance of this politics of public perception should not be underestimated (Corntassel and Witmer 2008).

In this book, I show that union organizing in Indian Country not only reveals tensions within the labor movement and labor policy but also points toward new understandings of the workings of sovereignty. Sovereignty, of course, means that tribal leaders are empowered to make their own decisions about what is best for their communities and their communities' economic development. Tribal labor relations are an excellent framework for understanding how sovereignty is constituted in interdependency as well. This is not to suggest that unions themselves are sovereign entities with the same self-governance rights as Native nations, but by appealing to federal labor regulatory bodies, unions can access the authority of U.S. sovereignty, which is most certainly in an interdependent relationship with tribal sovereignty. Following Young (2001) and Cattelino (2008), I argue that indigenous sovereignty is best understood as a nondominant negotiation between many interested parties and that it might serve the interests of tribal self-determination for tribes to seek common ground with unions rather than aggressively fight their existence. Recognizing their mutual interdependence may lead to more productive relations between tribes and unions, with workers' protections and rights established within an indigenous context.

Common ground might be found by refocusing on how worker status is conceptualized in legal battles about labor relations. Much of the debate over tribal labor relations circulates around which laws—federal or tribal—have jurisdiction over employees of tribal enterprises. It is easy for actual workers to get lost in the shuffle when they traverse two legal regulatory systems. But more expansive notions of citizenship, particularly those offered by Jennifer Gordon (2007) and Alexander Aleinikoff (2002), who theorize citizenship in the context of transnational work and tribal sovereignty, may give us a better grasp of tribal employees' situation. Gordon argues for a transnational conception of labor citizenship that would give workers rights and protections irrespective of which side of a legal jurisdiction they work and live on. Rather than just call for universal workers' rights, Gordon posits that this formulation of rights and protections be worked out at local levels. Gordon discusses legal structures that move beyond "a single-country framework" (2007:577) and "link worker self-organization with the enforcement power of the state in a way that crosses borders just as workers do" (2007:565). This conception of the transnational citizenship of a worker acknowledges that worker rights and protections must be recognized at the intersection of multiple, interrelated entities. In tribal labor relations, the entities are unions, tribal enterprises, tribal governments, and federal regulatory institutions. Accounting for but not necessarily giving primacy to any one of these entities helps build and balance interdependent relationships. In practice, this transnationally conceived, locally negotiated and executed program of workers' rights might take shape as some form of concurrent regulation of tribal labor relations that ensures rights and protections for people who work in Indian Country and for tribal enterprises while also honoring and protecting the self-governing powers of tribal nations.

Aleinikoff (2002) makes a similar proposition in talking about tribal sovereignty's general jurisdiction over nonmembers, including nonmember employees. Arguing for what he calls "denizenship," he notes the value of recognizing the participation and contribution of nontribal members in the life of indigenous communities. He conceives of a model that "opens up a number of possible political arrangements between full voting rights and total political exclusion," in which denizens might have limited participation in tribal governance without being granted the full rights of tribal citizenship (Aleinikoff 2002:147). Rather than seek the help of an outside jurisdiction every time they have a problem, tribal governments might grant limited voting rights or even nonvoting governmental advisory positions to nontribal members. Tribes would thus reap the benefit of having nontribal members feel more invested in the community and be more respectful of tribal governance. Collective bargaining in an indigenous context and under tribal law connects the ideas of denizenship and transnational labor citizenship in a practical way. It grants nontribal workers significant participation and political voice in the political economic process of tribal economic development. Within the discrete context of labor relations, tribal governments might also consider a limited waiver of their sovereign immunity in tribal courts.[8] In fact, the MPLRL and the NNCBC go a long way toward meeting these models. Of course, the current NLRB precedent significantly limits tribal legal regulation of labor relations, but a less dominant form of interdependency could preserve sovereignty and workers' rights. Ultimately, constructing tribal labor relations in terms of interdependent sovereignty is critical because it recognizes the important contribution that all employees (tribal members or not) make to tribal enterprises, to Indian Country economies, and thereby to sustaining tribal self-determination (see Lyons 2004).

Similarly, conceiving of tribal labor relations in an interdependent way also reveals how important tribal employees in particular are to decisions about indigenous economic development. Labor unions and workplace activism provide a venue for workers to participate in such decision making. Arguably, workers who are tribal members have a much stronger reason for participating in decision making, but this does not mean that nontribal workers should be ignored. In fact, through contract negotiations, nontribal voices can be institutionalized without impeding or dominating indigenous decision-making processes or letting negative situations between unions and tribal governments dominate tribal labor relations. Additionally, examples such as that of the Navajo Nation health-care workers suggest that nontribal employees can work positively with tribal employees to improve the workplace and community.

All of this leads us back to the Navajo Nation. At Navajo, there are many signs of a positive future for tribal labor relations, particularly in terms of the legal, governmental, economic, and community structures that allow for indigenously interpreted labor relations. However, there are also signs of an ambivalent future. The workers described in this book provide the best example of this ambivalence. Through their workplace activism, they were able to claim a voice in a localized version of labor relations and in the intertwined processes of economic development and tribal self-determination. Asserting themselves on more than one occasion, they were able to force the removal of administrators they believed to be ineffective and illegitimate. Eventually, they translated their grassroots voice into an institutionalization of their power by gaining local governmental approval and oversight of the directors who managed their hospital and its labor relations. But they have yet to gain the union recognition they have sought. Unionization would further institutionalize their say in their work conditions and tribal labor relations. Equally important, it would provide additional grassroots control over how tribal self-determination is enacted at the local level. That Tuba City healthcare employees' workplace activism has yet to produce union recognition speaks to the fact that strong tribal codes are not enough. Tribal economic managers and political leaders must also actively uphold the laws of the tribe and make them useful. It is not just workplace activism but also strong and progressive leaders that will ensure successful and equitable tribal labor relations. The same can be said for the Mashantucket Pequot as they try to make their progressive labor relations code work. The practical usefulness of the MPLRL will be a much greater measure of its success than merely convincing the UAW to bargain under this code.

Although unionization has yet to be achieved at Tuba City, it is certainly not dead. The ad hoc HECMC has continued to push for union recognition, and hospital management has been considering the issue, at one point even drafting a labor relations policy. Even though the issue has stalled out, the worker-activists at Tuba City remain proud of what they have accomplished; they have created a grassroots support system that acts as an informal community union. This system may go dormant for periods of time, but workers are confident of their ability to reactivate it and call upon one another in episodes of need. These workers are on the front lines of tribal self-determination and tribal labor relations. They are the ones first and foremost affected by economic development strategies and are willing to stand up and take responsibility to make sure that this economic development and self-determination are beneficial to their lives and to the people in their community.

On the one hand, the example of Navajo Nation health-care workers reflects the broader uncertainty of the future of tribal labor relations: some significant accomplishments coupled with some unfulfilled promises; some positive instances of tribal labor relations coupled with negative ones. On the other hand, the Navajo Nation represents the great potential of how to indigenize labor relations. The tribal government asserted its sovereignty by establishing its own labor code and its Office of Navajo Labor Relations. Another Navajo Nation feature that ought to be beneficial to an indigenous form of labor relations is its well-developed legal system, which includes both Euro-American style courts and tradition-infused peacemaker courts, where disputes are resolved through open negotiations between interested parties and presided over by a respected elder. There is great potential for both kinds of courts to adjudicate tribal labor relations in a way that is fair to all parties involved and is conducted from an indigenous perspective that acknowledges tribal sovereignty and gives deference to the fact that labor relations are happening in Indian Country.

From an economic perspective, that the Navajo Nation has a broad range of industries makes it an excellent testing ground for how different workplaces within the same indigenous nation produce different modes of tribal labor relations. Tribal labor relations in Navajo Country will prove to be even more intriguing in the near future, because the Navajo Nation has finally established a tribal casino enterprise.[9] Until now, labor relations at Navajo have been insulated from the extreme context of tribal gaming. It will be interesting to see how existing Navajo labor relations trends influence labor relations in Diné casinos and whether the tension that surrounds tribal gaming impacts other labor relations in the Navajo Nation. It will also be important for the Navajos (and others throughout Indian Country) to maintain creativity and cultural integrity in formulating tribal labor relations. Relying too much on preexisting Euro-American structures of labor relations has the potential to reproduce the worst of the NLRA combined with the worst of the IRA.[10] Relying heavily on these models could create a situation in which tribal employees are stuck with a labor relations regulatory system that is too easy for management to circumvent and disregard, coupled with a political system too centralized to heed the local concerns of workers.

Lastly, the health-care workers of the Navajo Nation provide an excellent example of how workplace activism can indigenize labor relations. The Diné, as a people, have historically been willing to speak up for themselves and demand justice, whether it be from the U.S. government or from their own centralized tribal government. This determined assertiveness translated to the workplace ensures that labor relations will be shaped by the desires and needs of the indigenous people for whom tribal economic development and self-determination are enacted. The work of sovereignty is most successful when decision making is responsible to and legitimated by the people. In the words of Tuba City nurse Mary Ann Jim, tribal labor relations enacted under these conditions allow indigenous people to "walk in beauty again, with beauty all around us."

Notes

Chapter 1: Introduction

1. I use the term *Indian Country* both to connote the territorial spaces socially, culturally, and politically dominated by American Indians and to denote the legally and juridically defined areas of jurisdiction.

2. The decline of manufacturing and the rise of service-industry jobs in the United States, combined with internal drives to aggressively court new workers through direct organizing campaigns rather than just service current union members, have put service-industry organizing and service-industry unions at the forefront of the new labor movement.

3. This point is the first premise of Kate Spilde's (1998, 1999) brilliant explication of the "rich Indian" as a racist anti-Indian stereotype.

4. I do not intend to privilege the individual at the expense of the collective, something that is often frowned upon in Native communities, but rather to consider how the individual fits in with and actually contributes to creating the collective.

5. For several reasons, tribal governments generally cannot raise revenue the way most governments do, through taxes.

6. This is not to say that most workers relate to management through labor unions. Indeed, the converse is true in that union representation in the United States is currently quite low. But those who do relate collectively to management do so primarily through unionization.

7. See Hosmer 1999 and Raibmon 2005 for in-depth discussions of indigenous people's actual comprehensive and complex understanding of and participation in market economies during this time period.

8. Of course, many indigenous peoples make the decision to opt out of modern market

economies, or more commonly to partially opt out by participating in a diverse set of economic strategies (see Pickering 2000).

9. See Alfred 1999 for a critique of this method from an indigenous perspective. Alfred charts an indigenizing path that emphasizes Native philosophies more than Euro-American structures of sociopolitical organization. Interestingly, though, he does not completely eschew engagement in a capitalist market economy (see, for example, his discussion on tribal gaming), or nonindigenous society as a whole for that matter. He is not arguing for extreme separatism.

10. As a corollary to this deficit of employable tribal members, in some tribal governmental gaming communities, tribal members are making enough money not to have to work. Therefore, the importation of labor results from what we might consider an emerging leisure class. See Cattelino 2009 on the concerns of some tribal governments and efforts to deal with members who do not need or want to work.

11. What I am talking about here is more than an issue of balancing economic benefits—such as jobs and revenue—against a development plan's potential impact on cultural and natural resources. This is clearly a very important issue for indigenous community members and leaders to assess. Rather, I am suggesting that responsible economic development plans need to consider the working conditions of employees—that is, create enterprises that institutionally allow for the voice of employees to be heard.

12. It is important to note that at this point, rulings have been split between the NLRB and the various circuit courts. Attention to the differences in these rulings could provide a sense of the judicial philosophies of the judges in these circuits. Moreover, the Supreme Court has yet to rule on this issue, but as the division in the circuit courts grows, it appears more likely that the Court will hear a tribal labor relations case. This may, in some ways, be the ultimate test of whether tribal sovereignty or labor unionism is more under attack in contemporary America.

13. This provides an interesting parallel to what Jessica Cattelino (2008:148) has called "economic nationalism" among the Seminoles, in which "the tribal nation increasingly is consolidated and conceived around economic life." In her seminal (pun intended) study, Cattelino considers economic nationalism as an outcome of tribal enterprises. I look at how economic nationalism plays out in terms of indigenous labor, not indigenous management.

14. The best example of this would be the United Nations Declaration on the Rights of Indigenous Peoples, which was adopted in 2007 but had been in the works for more than twenty years.

15. See Alfred 1999, Barker 2005, Cobb 2005/2006, Simpson 2000, and Steinman 2005/2006 for problems with and the appropriateness of applying this term to indigenous nationhood and communities.

16. Regarding American Indians, the term *self-determination* does not necessarily have an unblemished past of its own. Barsh and Henderson (1980) critique the federal policy of self-determination as federally granted and supervised self-administration rather than the self-rule or full self-governance that we would associate with sovereignty. They are more critical of the application of federal Indian policy than of the meaning of the term, though. See also Steinman 2005/2006.

17. It is important to note that this sophisticated, comprehensive, and modern form of tribal governance did not just spring up overnight. It was the result of much hard work and various proactive reforms meant to address problems and inconsistencies that, as with any government, arose from political challenges and confrontations (see Denetdale 2007, 2008; Iverson and Roessel 2002; Wilkins 1999, 2002). Of course, like any government, the Navajo Nation government is a work in progress.

18. Interestingly enough, during the course of this project, the Navajo Nation government

approved and began plans to institute casino gaming at a handful of locations on the reservation. At the completion of this manuscript, only one Navajo Nation casino has opened. The Fire Rock Navajo Casino began operations in November 2008 near Church Rock, New Mexico. It will be worth noting how Navajo casinos will affect or reflect labor relations across the Navajo Nation and Indian Country as a whole.

19. The use of pseudonyms is part of the consent agreement with my consultants. I have created the pseudonyms based on common first and last Diné and non-Diné names. Moreover, to preserve the anonymity of my consultants, I have also used pseudonyms for the names of people (such as supervisors and coworkers) discussed in interviews—except for high-profile public officials. All interviews were conducted in English. Although many of my consultants spoke Diné, all were fluent in English, and English was the primary—although not the exclusive—language of the health-care facilities in which my consultants worked. A paid Navajo translator provided translations of some materials, such as notes from meetings conducted in Diné.

20. Working as a paid union organizer for the UAW as part of teaching assistants' campaigns gave me access to LIUNA's union recognition campaign at the Navajo Nation. My former organizing job produced a personal relationship with LIUNA's director of the campaign, who granted me permission to follow the campaign among Navajo health-care workers. My previous union experience also accorded me professional credibility with my union organizer consultants.

21. To maintain ethnical issues of informed consent, I have used recordings of only those public hearings whose proceedings are a matter of public record.

Chapter 2: The Legal, Political, and Social Context

1. I do not mean to suggest a strict chronology of twentieth-century noble savage tropes moving from an incompatibility with modernity to its antidote. Nor do I mean to imply that representations of the barbaric savage disappeared in the twentieth century—the Western cinematic genre attests to the staying power of imagining Indians as barbaric savages. Deloria (1998, 2006) provides far more detailed and nuanced accounts of how Indian savagery is encoded in similar and different fashions across many periods in American history. See also Berkhofer 1979; Dilworth 1996; Huhndorf 2001.

2. In proposing this conceptualization of Indians and expectations, Deloria (2006) provides a prototypic example: a 1950s photo of an indigenous woman wearing buckskin but sitting under a beauty-shop dryer. To make a similar point in my introductory American Indians studies class, I use a picture of Navajo grandmothers in traditional clothing using cell phones.

3. However, in some ways the fundaments of the rich Indian stereotype are not necessarily a recent phenomenon. Native accumulation of money certainly predates tribal gaming. Indeed, the potential for this accumulation is initiated with indigenous participation in market economies. This very participation in market economies and subsequent accumulation of wealth have posed many challenges to the conventional perceptions of Indianness. See Deloria 2006; Harmon 2003; Hosmer 1999; and Raibmon 2005.

4. The association of indigeneity with poverty is as old as the European-formed distinction between Europeans and indigenous peoples worldwide. This continued connection has both a strong empirical basis and an ideological one (and these two forces certainly work collaboratively). As for the former, worldwide material exploitation by European and American colonialism and global capitalism has resulted in indigenous communities ranking at the bottom of most economists' statistics. The latter is more bound up in the way indigeneity is linked to primitivism. Marianna Torgovnick (1990) illustrates the Western tradition of defining European (and Euro-American)

modernity in opposition to a notion of the primitive—that is, the modern can exist only with a notion of what is *un*modern or primitive. Primitivism is the process of constructing dichotomies that distinguish non-Western peoples from Western peoples based on notions of what it means to be backward, uncivilized, or premodern. One such dichotomy is that Europeans and Euro-Americans are wealthy whereas indigenous peoples are poor. See Raibmon 2005:7 for a useful chart of how these dichotomies specifically relate to notions of authentic Indianness.

5. See, for example, Cattelino's (2008) brilliant examination of how the Seminole gaming industry combines economic modernity and indigeneity through the inherent fungibility of money.

6. This reversal can also be seen as part of a trend in the jurisprudence of federal Indian law that has undercut the territorial sovereignty of tribes (see Aleinikoff 2002).

7. There are also open debates about the extent to which tribes and the federal government (and even state governments) share jurisdiction over certain issues, instead of there being a nested hierarchy. These debates are generally settled on a case-by-case level through common law.

8. Incidentally, this is not unlike the way courts often decide issues of jurisdiction in general in Indian Country.

9. Aleinikoff (2002) argues that this focus on citizenship, not race, comes from the Court's conservative move away from racially based civil rights and affirmation action policies. This move affects tribal communities in unique ways (and countermands the uniqueness of Indian Country) as the Court tries to maintain jurisprudential consistency in how it squares citizenship with race.

10. For the overall effect of these U.S. and global economic changes on the labor movement, see Clawson 2003; Fantasia and Voss 2004; Nissen 2002; Tait 2005.

11. See Bronfenbrenner et al. 1998, Clawson 2003, Fantasia and Voss 2004, Milkman 2000, Milkman and Voss 2004, and Nissen 2002 on the general upswing of social movement organizing in the U.S. labor movement. For social movement organizing by HERE, SEIU, and UNITE, see Bonacich 2000; Bronfenbrenner and Hickey 2004; Milkman 2002, 2006; Ness 1998; Nissen and Grenier 2002; Sharpe 2004; Sherman and Voss 2000; Waldinger et al. 1998.

12. California is well known for the active role that general referendums play in state politics. Several referendums appear on every ballot. The use of referendums has intensified over the past twenty-some years as initiatives have been used to take action on issues that for various reasons state politicians have not acted on. In the case of tribal gaming in California, the Wilson administration would not sign compacts acceptable to most California Native nations, mainly because the tribes were seeking a kind of slot machine that the administration argued was illegal under the state constitution. See Gede 2000 for a distillation of the Wilson administration's position. Ultimately, the Wilson administration told tribes that it would not negotiate a compact until they closed down the (in Wilson's view, illegal) slot machines that were already operating. Moreover, after negotiating a model compact with one tribe (the Pala Compact), which included what the administration deemed to be legal slot machines, Wilson threatened to shut down any tribal casino that would not sign and operate under the Pala Compact. California Native nations used the initiative process to circumvent Wilson's intransigence and the Pala Compact, calculating—ultimately correctly—that the general public would be more sympathetic than the Republican governor. See Gordon 2000 and Lombardi n.d. for the history of this referendum.

13. Although, during this campaign, California tribes had not yet signed compacts with the state to establish how to regulate tribal casinos, many existing casinos had been open for years, operating in what might be called a legal gray area. It was the employees of these operations who were used for the testimonials.

14. See Cattelino 2008 for a more refined version of this argument. She suggests that instead of necessarily being the product of a "compromise," tribal gaming illustrates the way sovereignties

are inherently interdependent. Moreover, Native nations do not simply trade political rights for economic benefits. Economic benefits of gaming lead to the expansion of tribal self-governance and political clout in ways other than that which IGRA can limit (see Cattelino 2008; Contreras 2006; Goldberg and Champagne 2002; HPAIED 2008; Lombardi n.d.; Mullis and Kamper 2000; Spilde 2004a).

15. Moreover, before Gray Davis was elected, unions even aligned with their traditional Republican political enemy Governor Wilson to gain pro-union language in the Pala Compact. Although for different reasons, both supported the Pala Compact as a way to put limits on the gaming compacts that most tribes were seeking (Gordon 2000; Lombardi n.d.).

16. Between the California gaming referendums and this court case, HERE and UNITE merged to form one union, UNITE-HERE! However, in 2009 these unions split into two again, with UNITE renaming itself Workers United.

17. A key provision of the NLRA grants different unions equal access to employees before a contract is signed. This is done to ensure against management manipulation of the collective bargaining process by limiting worker choice of representation and thereby trying to deal exclusively with just one union—potentially giving a sweetheart deal to one union in exchange for a contract favorable to management.

18. In using the word *dictum*, I am using the colloquial version of *obiter dictum*, the legal term signifing a part of a court's opinion that is unnecessary or peripheral to the ruling and facts of a case and that therefore does not carry the weight of legal precedent. However, dicta can be important insofar as they give a sense of a court's sentiment on issues related to a given case or body of law.

19. The third exception, based on "legislative histor[ical]" proof of congressional intent, is self-evident and relatively cut and dry. Still, the notion of "some other means [of proof of intent]" can lead to variation in interpretation.

20. Although, technically, Native Alaskan communities and villages are tribal corporations as a result of the Alaska Native Claims Settlement Act of 1971, the NLRB considered them to be legally analogous to tribal nations in this instance.

21. The case is called *Yukon II* because it was the second time the NLRB had heard the issue involving this health-care facility. The original case (328 NRLB 761) was decided in 1999, but upon losing, the Yukon Kuskokwim Health Corporation appealed the decision to the D.C. Circuit Court, which sent the issue back to the NLRB, requesting it specifically to consider this instance of labor relations in the context of the mandates of the American Indian Self-Determination Act—which allowed for the creation of the Yukon health-care company. *Yukon II* (341 NRLB 139) is the NLRB's decision after reviewing the issue of tribal self-governance.

22. Many states have passed their own labor relations laws to deal with this exemption and to provide collective bargaining rights for public employees, although most state laws put significant limits on job actions such as strikes. In the 1970s there was an attempt to pass federal legislation akin to the NLRA that would provide a national standard for collective bargaining rights for any (not just federal-level) public/governmental employee in the United States. However, this act, the National Public Employee Relations Act, never succeeded (see McCartin 2008). As for federal governmental employees, in 1962, Executive Order 10988 gave collective bargaining rights to many federal employees, and in 1978 the Federal Labor Relations Authority was established to govern collective bargaining for all federal employees.

23. Interestingly enough, as the dissent in *San Manuel* points out, the governmental enterprises of Puerto Rico and other U.S. territories are exempt under section 2(2), even though they are not explicitly mentioned in this provision. (See footnote 50 of 341 NRLB No. 138 for citation of the relevant cases.)

24. The sad irony of this legal discursive attempt to disconnect the commercial enterprise from the tribal governmental functions of Indian gaming is that more recently, some tribes have been denied federal recognition for fear that it will lead to tribal casinos. These denials of recognition illustrate that the link between tribal governance and casino commerce is so clear that the federal government—usually motivated by opposing state politicians—will not even grant the rights of governance, on the logic that this is a sure way to limit the tribal gaming industry. Moreover, there is an assumption that tribes want federal recognition only so that they can establish casinos. Again, this assumption is based on an accepted overlap between tribal governmental functions and commerce. However, this assumption reverses the argument, suggesting that tribal governance, in the form of gaining federal recognition, supports commerce, not the other way around—that tribal governmental functions have trouble surviving without the financial support of their gaming enterprises. See Cramer 2005 for the debates around gaming and federal recognition.

25. See, for example, *Florida Paraplegic Assn. v. Miccosukee Tribe of Indians of Florida*, 166 F.3d 1126, 1129 (11th Cir. 1999). This case is directly cited by the NLRB to uphold its commercial distinction in *San Manuel*. It also relied on the *Tuscarora–Coeur d'Alene* test's interpretation of "purely intramural" activities to argue that the Americans with Disabilities Act applied to tribal casinos. Because they engaged in interstate commerce, their operations did not qualify as self-governmental. (That is, the operation was not purely intramural.)

26. *Oliphant v. Suquamish Indian Tribe* (1978), *United States v. Wheeler* (1978), and *Montana v. United States* (1981).

27. At the time, the BIA was known as the Office of Indian Affairs. The name was officially changed in 1947.

28. The termination-era policies of the 1950s attempted to assimilate Indians into the U.S. market economy by encouraging Indians to end their relationships with the federal government, sell off reservation land, fully embrace state citizenship and jurisdiction, and move to urban centers to seek employment.

29. A similarly striking example came from television ads opposing Proposition 5 in California. Several ads criticized tribal gaming, suggesting that only a few tribal leaders get rich and the rest of the Native community and the non-Indian community do not benefit from tribal gaming. The ad that most powerfully illustrated the rich Indian backlash's obsession with personal accumulation consisted of only aerial shots of "mansions" owned by leaders of gaming tribes, accompanied by voice-overs declaring that tribal gaming benefits only a limited few.

30. In suggesting that tribal corporations are directed toward a communal goal of self-determination, I do not mean to suggest unanimity within indigenous communities about whether tribal corporatism is the best or only way to achieve self-determination—just that self-determination is a collective goal, unlike the personal accumulation often associated with capitalism.

31. In addition to Champagne's (2004) normative theorization of tribal capitalism, see, for example, Cattelino's (2008, 2009) on-the-ground investigation of the way Florida Seminoles interpret casino, per capita revenue sharing in terms of the traditional function of tribal leaders to redistribute resources among community members rather than solely in terms of personal accumulation of individual tribal members.

32. Until 1996 most tribes were able to avoid revenue-sharing agreements. Tribes had a two-pronged attack for states' attempts to negotiate revenue-sharing agreements. First, tribes argued that revenue sharing was in essence a tax that was prohibited by IGRA. Second, if states still insisted on revenue sharing, tribes cried foul—that states were engaging in bad-faith bargaining. IGRA outlawed bad-faith bargaining and allowed tribes to sue states that bargained in bad faith. However, in 1996 the Supreme Court ruled in *Seminole Tribe of Florida v. Florida* that the Seminoles

could not sue the State of Florida for bad-faith bargaining because of the state right of sovereign immunity. This ruling not only struck down the IGRA provision but also opened the floodgates for revenue sharing, since nothing stood in the way of states, demanding a hard-line stance on revenue sharing (Spilde 2003).

33. It is important to note that the economic monopoly that comes along with tribal gaming is not artificially created by sovereignty or IGRA but rather benefits the most from the fact that states severely limit what kind of gaming can be conducted within their boundaries. If a given state were to legalize gaming wholesale, sovereignty and IGRA would provide a minimal competitive advantage. For example, even though Nevada has many federally recognized tribes, only a few have opened casinos. Moreover, in *California v. Cabazon Band of Mission Indians* (1987), the Supreme Court ruled that tribal gaming was distinguishable from the legal precedent that prohibited tribes from creating economic monopolies by taking advantage of tax exemptions on consumables such as cigarettes and gas on reservations. Here, the Court decided that "tribes did not simply resell a product; they built facilities and provided services to their patrons" (Canby 1998:286). Tribes were not just marketing their tax exemption in an unfair way but were fulfilling the self-reliant and self-governing promise of sovereignty.

34. Of course, this was a negotiation. It was certainly not equal after *Seminole Tribe v. Florida* ended tribes' ability to sue to prevent bad-faith bargaining, but tribes did get something in exchange for agreeing to the revenue-sharing plan. In exchange for the hefty increase in sharing, the four tribes gained a large increase in their allotment of slot machines. The 25 percent revenue sharing, though unprecedented in California, matches what some tribal casinos share with the states of New York and Connecticut.

35. A key difference is that our Constitution grants states limited sovereignty under the structure of federalism whereas tribal sovereignty is based on pre- and extraconstitutional grounds, such as aboriginality and treaties. Nonetheless, the analogy is relevant when considering inherent nondelegated powers, because the Indian canon of construction asserts that tribes retain those self-governance rights not explicitly abridged by Congress.

36. The NCAI is the longest-operating and most prominent political group advocating on behalf of American Indians. The Employee Free Choice Act is proposed federal legislation that would make it easier for unions to organize workplaces by mandating union recognition through a majority of employees, signing membership cards rather than through representation elections.

37. What is more, most tribal casinos do provide highly competitive wages and benefits.

38. I grant that some might question the decolonizing potential of gaming, but given this argument's grounding in a Western form of capitalism, it threatens to reiterate rich Indian discourses without considering the ways in which Native peoples can indigenize economic success and institutions of modernity (see Cattelino 2008, 2009; Champagne 2004; Deloria 2006). Even the indigenous nationalist Taiaiake Alfred (1999) has argued for positive outcomes of tribal gaming.

39. Cattelino (2008) specifically addresses this question of how the uniqueness of gaming as an industry in general affects the way tribal gaming is received.

40. Undoubtedly, some of these differences in judicial opinion must also lie in the kind of federal employment laws in question. Although these laws share many common trends as employment law, they all have their own legislative and jurisprudential history and social context, which helps determine how important a given employment law is deemed to be by the courts and how respected it is by the general American public. That is, in different contexts and eras, OSHA, the ADA, Family Medical Leave, or Title VII might seem more important to a given population than the NLRA or ERISA. How these employment laws relate to Indian Country, as well as to tribal labor relations, is extremely important and relevant, but a comprehensive study of these employment

laws as applied to Indian Country is well beyond the scope of this chapter and manuscript. I have chosen to confine my analysis to labor relations, not employment law in general.

Chapter 3: Tribal Structuring of Labor Relations

1. The "American Indian Opinion Leaders" surveys are a running feature of *Indian Country Today*, covering topics important to contemporary Native communities. It is not clear how many people are questioned for each survey or how these people are chosen—other than the newspapers, soliciting opinions and editorials from people it deems to be leaders in Indian Country, such as tribal leaders, elders, activists, and people connected with national Native organizations.

2. Republican representative J. D. Hayworth of Arizona introduced the Tribal Labor Relations Act in 2004 and the Tribal Labor Relations Restoration Act in 2005. Both failed to gain any support in the House of Representatives by wide margins. Recently, the NCAI lobbied Congress to add an amendment to the Employee Free Choice Act that would expressly exempt tribal enterprises from the NLRA. The NCAI has convinced Senator Inouye to sponsor an amendment to the bill that would change the NLRA to exempt tribal enterprises. The first right-to-work ordinance was passed by the San Juan Pueblo and upheld by the Tenth Circuit Court (*National Labor Relations Board v. Pueblo of San Juan*) more than ten years before the *San Manuel* cases. However, a handful of tribes have passed right-to-work laws since—some in response to *San Manuel*. Lawyers and consulting firms that offer services to help defeat unionization advertise on the Internet, in Native trade publications, and at Native economic development conventions. The Mashantucket Pequots filed NLRB petitions to challenge the legality of the NLRB's order for two representation elections at their Foxwoods Resort Casino subsequent to *San Manuel* (*Foxwoods Resort Casino 34-RC-2230*, *Foxwoods Resort Casino 34-RC-2251*).

3. This union neutrality agreement has yet to produce union representation because the Menominee casino has not opened yet. Building an off-casino reservation takes several levels of local, state, and federal approval. Currently, the tribe is waiting for BIA approval.

4. Many tribes with IRA constitutions have legal provisions that allow tribal councils to handle judicial procedures, as well as legislative ones, but this system does not always lead to unbiased decisions, particularly when tribal leaders themselves are involved in disputes. As a result, many tribes have been looking to separate judicial procedures from legislative branches (Lemont 2006). Regional intertribal court systems are growing in popularity as tribes within geographic proximity pool economic resources to pay judges and legal clerks, who administer the laws of given tribes on a rotating basis. These courts either travel to a given reservation to hold sessions or are centrally located, with litigants traveling to the intertribal court session.

5. Of course, this kind of debate is not limited to Indian nations. There is similar debate on rights and powers of states vis-à-vis the federal government.

6. *Martin v. Indian Wildlife Commission* (D. Wis. 1992) and *Reich v. Great Lakes Indian Fish and Wildlife Commission* (7th Cir. 1993).

7. Card-check neutrality is the process by which management agrees to recognize a union if a majority of employees sign membership cards. Additionally, management agrees in advance to stay neutral during the process of attaining cards and not attempt to influence workers against unionization.

8. My subsequent description of the specific provisions of California Native nations' TLROs comes from analysis of the boilerplate or "model" TLRO included in the California tribal–state gaming compacts signed in 2000 and beyond. As soon as a tribal government signed its compact, the boilerplate TLRO became part of that tribe's general legal code, with the exception of a handful

of tribal governments that modified the boilerplate TLRO to fit local needs and desires. My description includes analysis of these locally modified TLROs as well.

9. As far back as 1834, there is a tradition of and legal precedent for preferential Indian hiring in Indian Country. This practice has even been upheld by the Supreme Court as not violating the Fifth Amendment, because Indian preference is based on political and treaty rights, not on race (see Anderson 1980; Becker and Thomas 1985).

10. It is true that not all Native communities have fully developed judiciaries or access to intertribal court systems. Frequently, this means that the tribal council acts as the judiciary. Under these circumstances, it is wise that the joint tribal-state-federal dispute resolution system ends in federal courts, given that tribal councils often oversee the decisions of their economic enterprises and therefore are less likely to be impartial.

11. I do recognize debate around the "fairness" of card checks as opposed to representation election, particularly as management (including tribal management) and unions are staking out positions on the Employee Free Choice Act that might come before Congress in the next few years.

12. More recently, some unions have attempted to get a more "union-friendly" card-check provision included in TLROs. In 2007 five California tribes began the process of renegotiating to extend the length of their compacts and to provide for more slot machines. UNITE-HERE! saw this reopening of the compacting process as an opportunity to gain card-check recognition that does not require no-striking clauses or other preconditions. It lobbied state legislatures to institutionalize card-check recognition in TLROs, but to no avail. Despite some initial support, even powerful and traditionally prolabor Democratic legislators did not demand this provision in the final version of the compacts, and the tribes involved were not inclined to include the provision. The prolabor legislators used the *San Manuel* decisions as cover, suggesting that the state may not be legally allowed to become involved in tribal labor relations. Ultimately, the new compacts, without card-check neutrality provisions, were approved by California voters and signed by tribes in 2008 (see Sweeney 2007). However, at the time of this writing, there is much discussion in the labor movement about the Employee Free Choice Act, a bill yet to be debated before Congress but one that aims to make card checks and possibly card-check neutrality the federal legal standard for labor relations across the country. There are growing discussion and debate in the labor movement in general and Indian Country in particular about this bill and its future. Important national indigenous organizations such as the NCAI and NIGA have opposed the Employee Free Choice Act, but some individual tribes, such as the Navajo Nation, have endorsed the bill.

13. Ignoring this already existing check and balance makes the NLRB's decision seem even more like a power grab.

14. The language of the law itself even references the NLRB's *San Manuel* decision and the fact that one union was trying to organize casino employees.

15. That being said, in 2008 the Navajo Nation did open a tribal governmental gaming operation. It remains to be seen whether a union will try to organize the tribal casino employees under the Navajo Nation's labor relations codes.

16. These codes were established as amendments to the Navajo Preference in Employment Act.

17. However, as many prolabor stalwarts and union organizers will likely note, language similar to "harmonious relations" is often used by anti-union managers trying to co-opt unionization with company unionism that purports to be more harmonious than adversarial labor unionism. But in this case, I think it is worth uncynically attending to the Navajo cultural meaning of "harmony" without giving in to naïveté.

18. Document in author's possession.

19. It is not uncommon for tribes to waive their sovereign immunity on a limited basis in

business contracts with outside corporations that act as service providers to tribal enterprises, particularly gaming enterprises.

20. The arguments essentially revolve around whether one believes that unionism is good for business *and* what combination of profit margins and a positive work environment makes for good business.

21. See Thompson 2001 on right-to-work codes as a tribal economic development strategy.

Chapter 4: Navajo Nation Politics and Pragmatic Unionism

1. Emigrant states support their citizens' emigration by making it easier for them to send money back home, allowing citizens to vote and in some cases even hold office while living abroad, and trying to advocate for citizens' rights within the countries to which they have emigrated (see Barry 2006; Chander 2006).

2. See Bronfenbrenner et al. 1998, Clawson 2003, Lichtenstein 2002, Mantsios 1998, Milkman 2000, Milkman and Voss 2004, and Tait 2005 for various examples of community-based organizing and a broad range of ways in which progressive unions are engaging community and social justice issues as a whole, not just workplace issues.

3. This system of hospitals and health-care facilities is called the Navajo Area by the Indian Health Services. It is one of twelve service areas, but it is the only one with a "tribal" name; the rest have city or state names. However, this name can be confusing in that the Navajo Area is not isomorphic with the boundary of the Navajo Nation; it extends beyond it to include major facilities off the reservation.

4. Much of this brief history of LIUNA in general, its Public Employee Department, and its interactions with the Navajo Nation comes from a conversation (August 31, 2009) with Robert Purcell, director of the Public Employee Department, and internal documents he shared with me.

5. This petition process does not oblige workers to join the union in order to establish collective bargaining rights; it merely requires that they demonstrate the desire to have a specific union represent them in collective bargaining. Nonetheless, signing up for membership is a more definitive indication of support for a union. Some employees who signed the petition signed union membership cards as well. Others were already members of the union, and still others have joined since the Campaign for Union Recognition.

6. Part of the reason for this lower percentage has to do with the fact that gaining union recognition under the Federal Labor Relations Authority was a two-step process. The first phase required the union only to prove that 30 percent of a bargaining unit desired representation. Completion of this step initiated a representation election, in which employees of a given collective bargaining unit were eligible to vote. But the union needed only a majority of voters to gain recognition. Consequently, in previous campaigns, the union never had to garner as much support as it needed under Navajo Nation collective bargaining codes.

7. Having worked as a union organizer for five years, I have great appreciation for this success rate. Neither I nor any organizing colleagues I have discussed this campaign with have ever witnessed anything like the success rate of this LIUNA campaign.

8. This is not surprising, considering that the bill took form under the Nixon administration. Although Nixon called for "self-determination without termination," the bill could also be interpreted in the context of Nixon's larger new federalism, decentralizing of government policy agendas (Castile 1998, 2006). Termination itself was part of a decentralization backlash against New Deal policies such as the IRA.

9. This is not to say that affiliation with national U.S. political parties is not relevant to Native peoples. But these affiliations matter much more for participation in politics beyond the local level, such as state and national politics.

10. Of course, these dichotomies themselves are oversimplifications.

11. Analysis of "factionalism" in American Indian tribal politics can be traced to Bernard Siegel and Alan Beals (1960a, 1960b, 1966), who formulated definitions of different kinds of factionalism that various scholars subsequently applied to various Native communities. For the most comprehensive review of this literature, see Fowler 2004.

12. This is also apparent in much of the recent intratribal political upheaval over enrollment and disenrollment and some intertribal tension over submissions for federal recognition (Cramer 2005).

13. This office later changed its name to its current designation, the Bureau of Indian Affairs.

14. Lawrence Kelly (1975) explains that voting in favor of IRA constitutional governments was a two-step process. Tribes had to first vote in favor of the IRA and then to approve a constitution developed by the IRA with minimal consultation with tribes. Also, if a tribe did not vote on accepting the IRA or the constitution within a given time period, neither took effect. Lastly, some small bands were consolidated with other tribes between the original referenda on the IRA and the constitution votes. Ultimately, 252 tribes had the opportunity to go with IRA constitutional governments, and only 92 did so (Kelly 1975:304).

15. This translates to Attorneys Who Contribute to the Economic Revitalization of the People (Iverson and Roessel 2002:23).

16. It is worth noting that before the council advocated this referendum, a community group had formed specifically to defeat the health-care takeover through the initiative process. At the time, the NNC was not interested in a referendum over the 638 health-care issue, but the community group attempted to force a public vote on the takeover by organizing a petition drive. The group successfully gathered ten thousand signatures, but this fell well short of the more than twenty-five thousand legally needed to force a referendum (Di Giovanni 2001a). What is significant about this failure is that initiative procedure is different from referendum procedure: referenda are called by the NNC, brought to the people for a vote, and require 50 percent of all Navajo votes plus one, whereas initiatives originate in the petition process, which brings issues to a vote of the Navajo general public, and require only a majority of those voting, a much lower threshold than passage of a referendum. Therefore, had this community group succeeded in bringing the initiative to fruition, 638 for health care likely would have been halted. Nonetheless, as the NNC's decision to hold a referendum (and the ten thousand signatures) illustrates, there was still enough public concern to compel the NNC to put the issue to the Navajo general public. The decision did not go without criticism from supporters of 638. A few complained that the referendum was a waste of money, enacted only to placate the small but very vocal group that could not garner enough support for its opposition through the referendum petition process and thus the referendum was allowing the group to pull an end run around the proper political channels (Dohi 2001).

17. The full text of the ballot measure is as follows (Shebala 2001a):

> Shall the following statute be added to Title 13 of the Navajo Nation Code: 13 N.N.C. Section 4401. The Navajo Nation shall be prohibited from contracting IHS Health Care Services for the Navajo people pursuant to the Indian Self-Determination and Education Assistance Act with the exception of Community Health Representative/Outreach, Public Health Nursing, Behavioral Health Services, Emergency Services, Health Education and Environmental Health

Programs. This provision shall be effective on May 1, 2001.

Yes ____

No ____

18. As a point of comparison, the 2000 U.S. Census recorded nearly three hundred thousand who self-identified as being Navajo or part Navajo. But this number does not reflect those the tribal government recognizes as tribal members. The other reason for the discrepancy between three hundred thousand and about eighty-six thousand registered voters is that the Navajo Nation, like many indigenous communities, has a large percentage of members under voting age.

19. Voting patterns are one potential explanation for the disparity between the public sentiment against 638 and the relatively low number of eligible voters who turned out for the election. However, a comprehensive study of Navajo referendum voting patterns has not yet been published, and such a study is beyond the scope of this book (see Russell and Henderson 1999 for an analysis of the 1994 presidential election).

20. This argument was further supported by the fact that the NNC originally did not intend even to hold a referendum on the issue; many felt that it did so under pressure.

21. In the year before the 638 referendum, a popular and controversial referendum to significantly decrease the number of elected tribal council representatives failed for the same high-threshold reasons (Shebala 2000). The outcome led to similar public complaints of tribal council members hiding behind the logistics of the referendum process (Shebala 2001b; Tohtsoni 2001).

22. Under 638 contracts, tribes can request increases in funds from the federal government and gain the authority to determine their own health-care budgets (Kunitz 1996). The team that designed the 638 contract for Navajo Nation health care projected a total increase of about $100 million in annual funding after the transition (Di Giovanni 2001a).

23. The notion that personal greed was council members' motivation was sometimes offered to me without solicitation, but frequently it was at least part of a response to my question "Why do you think the tribal council wants to take health care 638?"

24. A duallie is a pickup truck with four wheels on its rear axle to facilitate towing of heavy loads. It is very useful for the ranching and herding common on the reservation. Moreover, it is more expensive than a regular pickup truck and thus signifies status as much as utility. For interesting parallel discussions on automobiles and their function and status in Indian communities, see Cattelino 2008:101–105 and Deloria 2006:136–182.

25. As part of House Concurrent Resolution 108, studies were made to determine which Native communities were ready for termination. A study was conducted at the Navajo Nation, but there was never a recommendation to terminate the tribe. Nonetheless, the NNC was able to use the termination era's spirit of local independence, with the concomitant fear of its political and financial relationship with the federal government being terminated, to gain more control over economic, social, and governmental services (Young 1978).

26. This is not to suggest that important religious, social, and cultural reasons were not intricately bound up in the economic reasons to maintain a herding lifestyle.

27. Although currently the Navajo Nation legislative body is called the Navajo Nation Council, during the time period Strieb reports on, it was called the Navajo Nation Tribal Council.

28. A comparison between Navajo (and American Indian) unionism and the way African Americans, Chicanos, and Asian Americans have engaged unions for social movement goals would be fascinating, but it is beyond the scope of this study. See Brodkin 2007 for an excellent discussion of how young social justice activists of color in Los Angeles have drawn upon their ethnic and racial identities to shape and interpret their participation in social movement unionism and how

these activists form allegiances around shared life experiences of marginalization. O'Neill (n.d.) briefly argues by way of comparison: "While all faced discrimination in the workplace, American Indians found unions not particularly sympathetic to their concerns. Alternatively, important Latino and Black leaders emerged from the labor movement, mobilizing workers around broader social justice and civil rights issues." And in direct relationship to Navajos, she elsewhere notes that in the mining industry of New Mexico in the 1930s, "the union struggle became synonymous with the struggle for racial justice for Spanish-speaking people" whereas Navajos had a much more ambivalent and pragmatic relationship to unionism (O'Neill 2005:116).

Chapter 5: The Campaign for Union Recognition

1. Although the name of the campaign was formally changed, most organizers still used the word *petition* when referring to the document they asked people to sign. For this reason and for precision and clarity, I also use *petition* when describing the document.

2. These meetings and the entire transition fell into a legal gray area in that before a complete 638 takeover, the IHS would manage the hospitals and after 638 was complete, the NHCSC would take over as management. NHCSC leadership conducted many questionable and presumptive activities as part of the exploratory and transition process without interference from IHS management. Clouding the issue even further was the fact that many IHS managers were likely to maintain their positions as NHCSC management after the takeover was complete.

3. Federal labor law protects workers from being forced to attend meetings about work conditions where only management is present. LIUNA additionally claimed that these meetings constituted "direct dealings"—a violation of labor law because they circumvented and undercut the collective bargaining process.

4. Because of the size of some service units and some unique circumstances, not every service unit sent a steward to each executive committee meeting, but most service units were represented.

5. See William Leap 1993 on American Indian English and its regional and tribal variations.

6. Preceding the campaign, the local was in a transition phase; it was coming out of trusteeship from the international (see chapter 4) and had not elected a new local president or vice president. Thus, the business manager position became the highest elected office in the local.

7. Local 1376 represented service units in the Navajo Area and Albuquerque Area IHS and thus represented workers at clinics and hospitals that were not at the Navajo Nation. These people were not affected by the Navajo government's potential 638 takeover but were nonetheless at the Local 1376 executive committee meetings. Those who were Navajo Nation citizens were particularly interested and involved.

8. I observed some workers who had already signed the petition reply to coworkers' questions about what the petition was all about: "It's so the union stays after 638. Sign up and you get a pop." Organizers said they had some duplicate signatures because people would sign twice in order to get more food or souvenirs without arousing suspicion. But organizers on some occasions promised the most coveted union souvenirs to the volunteer organizer who collected the most signatures.

9. The signature-gathering campaign ultimately did not garner enough to put the referendum on the ballot. Rather, the referendum was put on the ballot later by the NNC's legislative action.

10. A couple of people who ultimately refused to sign the petition during the Campaign for Union Recognition did so because they were frustrated with the union for not taking a strong stance against 638. They made clear that they were unhappy with LIUNA but not against the idea of union recognition—indeed, they called for more assertive union representation than LIUNA was providing.

11. The letter was sent out before the name of the campaign was changed from Petition Plus to the Campaign for Union Recognition.

12. Even if an organizer, through in-conversation assessment, decides that a worker is not ready to commit to union membership but is willing to demonstrate support for union recognition, it is counterproductive to unionism to foreclose the issue of membership. More commonly, the organizer simply does not mention membership rather than risk a no answer to the question of membership.

Chapter 6: Grassroots Expressions of Tribal Labor Relations

1. As an attestation to the grassroots and ad hoc nature of this committee, people who participated in it variously referred to it as the Hospital Employees and Community Members Committee, the Employees Committee, or the Employee and Community Member Committee. I use HECMC for consistency and because this is the title the committee members used in one of the key publications of their demands.

2. To this end, I will not mention the hospital managers or tribal leaders by name, even though there are several journalistic accounts of these people and their participation in the events surrounding the turmoil at the Tuba City hospital. I made this decision so as not to participate in the public shaming of any individual—an act that is not culturally or politically appropriate for me to do. In this chapter, as in the others, I also use pseudonyms or impersonal designations for employees I discuss or quote. I do this to protect the identity of employees who have worked on this project with me and who still work at the hospital and are rightfully concerned about their job security, as well as per the conditions of a research consent agreement they signed with me.

3. This is not to say there are not multiple and in some cases contradictory perspectives on some aspects of the 638 takeover of the Tuba City hospital. Nevertheless, Tuba City health-care workers and community members collectively express a shared view about what happened and its meaning. I think of this collective memory not in terms of a competition for the most accurate depiction of events, but rather the way Jonathan Boyarin (1994) talks about collective memory as being an intersubjective relationship that is constantly reinforced, reshaped, and reinvented in order to connect individual identity to group membership. The collective memory and narratives of Tuba City hospital employees and community members help forge their oppositional identity to TCRHCC management.

4. Some of my questions led my consultants to respond in a narrative format, and others were much more open-ended. The latter sometimes produced explicit narratives and sometimes not. However, the ethnographic interview format itself, wherein an analyst asks questions of a consultant, can implicitly lead to a narrative of self-experience, which also may explain many of the narratives my interviews produced.

5. Moreover, there is some evidence to suggest that Tuba City and the people who live there, being on the western edge of the reservation, far away from Window Rock, are generally considered—by themselves and outsiders—to be antagonistic to the positions established in Window Rock. The maverick persona of Peter MacDonald (see chapter 4) is perhaps a paradigm example. Although there is most certainly regional social and cultural variation among the Diné people and across the Navajo Reservation as geographic space, there has been no systematic study of the tension between Tuba City and the rest of the Navajo Nation. Moreover, there is no strong evidence to distinguish this folk attitude about Tuba City from general tension between local Navajo communities and the centralized government in Window Rock.

6. The other two facilities were the service unit at the reservation border town of Winslow, Arizona, and a small clinic in the northern part of the reservation at Montezuma Creek, Utah.

7. It is important to note that when Cornell and Kalt (1997) talk about rent-seeking, they are not talking about greed—just the perception of unfair distribution of resources. See Bee 1999 for a similar argument and Cattelino 2008 for how Seminole tribal members—unlike the surrounding non-Indian press—express concerns not over how much wealth is being accumulated through tribal gaming enterprises (the focus for those outside the community), but rather how this wealth is distributed by tribal leadership.

8. In a few instances in its literature, the HECMC suggested retrocession, but most members admitted that this was not a practical option but was proposed more as a strategic and credible political threat to TCRHCC management.

9. Adams's quantitative analysis has some flaws in that the measure of managerial responsiveness is based solely on the number of Native managers already in an IHS service unit. This approach assumes that merely being Native automatically assures a manager's responsiveness—something that never proved to be unequivocally true with BIA management; tribal members who worked for this federal agency were often resented by other tribal members and deemed to be just as ineffective as non-Indian bureaucrats, if not more so. Moreover, this analysis does not take into account that within the field of reservation health care (and in federal Indian administration overall), it is not uncommon for a Native person to work for a tribe outside his or her "home" community. Cross-tribal employment greatly complicates Adams's simplified conclusion of Native managers as being inherently more responsive to local needs than non-Indian administrators. Her measurement of funding levels is based on appropriations per person. IHS appropriations vary from service unit to service unit, based on a complicated system including factors such as size of community served and proximity to other forms of health care (Kunitz 1996).

10. More recent signs show that the trend of cutting funds for Indian health care may be reversing. In early 2008, congressional debate ultimately produced a positive impact on funding for Indian health care. On February 26, 2008, the Senate reauthorized the Indian Health Care Improvement Act—a bill apportioning billions of dollars to build new facilities and improve sanitation and mental health projects (for both IHS and 638 contracts)—by an overwhelming margin. In March 2008, also by a large margin, Congress approved an additional billion dollars for the IHS's 2009 budget (Reynolds 2008). Interestingly, President George W. Bush threatened to veto the reauthorization of the Indian Health Care Improvement Act, on the grounds that an amendment to the bill extended the Davis-Bacon Act—a law ensuring that prevailing wages are paid to construction workers building governmental facilities—to the IHS. The Davis-Bacon Act will likely secure high-paying and potentially union jobs for Native construction workers building health-care facilities for their own communities.

11. *Health outcome* is the term used by public health researchers to describe and measure the endpoint of a health-care process. It is a way to quantify the success of a given health-care institution, method, or event (Brian Finch, personal communication, January 18, 2009).

12. Many of the non-Navajo hospital employees were health-care professionals who had originally come to work for Navajo Area IHS as part of fulfilling military obligations or out of a personal inclination toward social welfare and justice. Those who had been there long-term felt a real commitment to the community of Tuba City and received respect from the community. It should come as no surprise, then, that they stayed at Tuba City to try to make 638 work. In contrast, many of those who left the hospital with the implementation of the takeover were non-Navajos who either had not been working at Tuba City very long or, like many others who worked for IHS, had transient health-care careers, frequently moving around various IHS facilities.

13. Performatively criminalizing terminated employees by using security guard escorts is not an uncommon managerial strategy to stifle workplace activism—particularly unionism. It serves the function of publicly disgracing vocal activists and intimidating the rest of the workforce, thereby discouraging anyone from taking the disgraced activists' places. I am not suggesting that this was an explicit tactic of the TCRHCC's upper management, but it was certainly read by many employees as an overt public expression of management's power. The effect on employees was potentially the same as that of explicit union busting. See Penny 2004 on anti-union countermobilizations.

14. As drastic as this might seem, many employees felt that it was justified because of what they perceived to be the lack of accountability of leadership and how leadership was chosen. They argued that without looking into the background of hospital management, they would not know anything about their corporate leaders. Moreover, in conversations with me, many justified this act because later the same thing happened to some key employees and community members in HECMC. In a strange turn of events, months after the Black Friday protests, a doctor received a package containing professional background checks on himself and several other employees and community members (including a current tribal government official). The package was sent anonymously to let this doctor know that someone was looking into his background. An investigation revealed that the background checks were paid for with hospital funds (Dempsey 2004). Who specifically ordered and authorized them was never revealed—although workers have their suspicions.

15. In addition to Andrea Smith and J. Kehualani Kauanui (2008), several indigenous feminists (Audra Simpson, Joanne Barker, Dian Million, Lisa Kahaleole Hall, Jennifer Denetdale, Mishuana Goeman, and Reyna K. Ramirez) contributed to developing the idea of Native feminisms in the forum "Native Feminisms without Apology," published in *American Quarterly* in 2008. See also the important work of Speed, Aída Hernández Castillo, and Stephen (2006) on indigenous women's simultaneous and co-constitutive assertion of their political rights as indigenous peoples and women.

16. One employee was reinstated within forty-eight hours after her termination. Another decided to leave the area and took a job with another IHS facility. The other three employees won a legal arbitration that restored their jobs.

17. This was found to be a problem in the 638 contracts for all three service units (Tuba City, Winslow, and Montezuma Creek) that went under tribal administration. All three were forced to eliminate the at-will policy.

18. At the invitation of HECMC members, I attended three of these meetings. Given the confidential nature of many of the conversations and the fact that some workers were threatened with termination for attending these meetings, I chose not to record the proceedings. My discussion is from my field notes and research consultants' recounting of these meetings in our interviews and discussions.

19. This quote was thought to be so inflammatory that it was used on multiple flyers—as the title of one and the first line of complaint in another. To the employee's credit, he made light of the threat, showing up at one HECMC meeting with a paper bag over his head and joking that no one could identify him that way. This stunt got a big laugh from everyone at the meeting.

20. Even with legally recognized representation of these employees, the union found it difficult to enforce grievance procedures upon the TCRHCC.

21. The issue of union recognition for TCRHCC employees did make it as far as the NNC. A member of the Intergovernmental Relations Committee (IGRC) proposed a law to regulate unionization in this context. The proposal was tabled, however, and never received significant discussion

in the NNC as a whole. TCRHCC board members publicly claimed to have backed the legislation, but some employees suggest that they did so only because they knew in advance that the IGRC never intended to act on the legislation. These skeptical employees believed that the legislative proposal was a public relations ruse to get the board off the hook for not being willing to recognize the union (Horris 2005). More recently, the hospital leadership drafted a proposal for collective bargaining regulations for TCRHCC employees—which in many ways mirrored Navajo Nation collective bargaining codes. Nonetheless, these have never been officially approved and implemented.

Epilogue: The Uncertain Future of Tribal Labor Relations

1. Indeed, in addition to the rise in anti-union consulting firms specializing in tribal enterprises, I have noticed an increase in anti-union law firms using the Internet to promote their services to tribes.

2. Such petitions are not necessarily signs of a union defeat. There are various context-specific reasons why a union might file such a petition. Rescinding the request merely cancels a given representation election; it does not remove the right to hold such an election at a later date. Unions file these petitions when for various reasons they fear they might lose an election. Rather than lose, they postpone the election until more favorable conditions arise. As much as such a delay can stall a campaign, it is better than definitively losing a representation election.

3. The Mashantucket Pequot tribal laws are available to the public at http://www.mptnlaw.com/.

4. Although the NLRB claims ultimate jurisdiction over tribal labor relations and discretion as to when to assert this jurisdiction, there is nothing stopping a union from using a tribe's labor relations code instead of the NLRA. Indeed, John Cotter, an assistant regional director of the NLRB, suggested, "The NLRB doesn't necessarily object to [a petition to bargain] being filed with the tribes" (Toensing 2007).

5. This press release is available at http://www.uaw.org/news/newsarticle .cfm?ArtId=513.

6. Moreover, recent factionalism within UNITE-HERE! itself could have a big impact on which unions try to organize tribal workplaces. In fact, the recent history of UNITE-HERE!, the plaintiff in the *San Manuel* cases, typifies the current upheaval in organized labor. HERE first filed an unfair labor practice suit against San Manuel; as the case wound through court, HERE merged with UNITE to make each union stronger and more capable of dealing with changing labor markets. Soon thereafter, UNITE-HERE! left the AFL-CIO to join the Change to Win Federation, which attempted to push the labor movement in a more progressive direction and toward aggressive organizing campaigns. Recently, after the *San Manuel* case concluded, the union split up again as a large number of locals voted to separate from UNITE-HERE! Most of the locals that left were originally UNITE locals; they formed a new coalition called Workers United and affiliated with the SEIU, one of UNITE-HERE!'s main competitors for organizing service employees. After this split, UNITE-HERE! rejoined the AFL-CIO. It will be interesting to see which of the two unions tries to organize tribal casinos and with what success and how much of a turf war might ensue.

7. I thank Colleen O'Neill for reminding me of this during our conversation about the CTER conference.

8. Under the current NLRB precedent, to the detriment of tribal self-determination, tribal courts have limited or no jurisdiction over tribal labor relations. However, there may be ways to structure adjudication of tribal labor relations that rely almost wholly on tribal legal systems but that still defer to federal authority in a limited way. Tribal court adjudication of labor relations

could be open to a last-level, federal "abuse of discretion" appeal. In contrast to de novo review, which makes everything about a case reviewable by a higher court, "abuse of discretion" could be structured in a very limited way, allowing the federal court to review only whether tribal labor relations administrative proceedings followed their own predetermined procedures, not whether the facts of the case were judged correctly. This system might meet a minimal standard for federal jurisdiction over tribal labor relations without significant impingement on the legitimacy and sovereignty of tribal legal systems and their ability to adjudicate tribal labor relations.

9. The Navajo Nation opened its first casino—Fire Rock Casino—in Church Rock, New Mexico, on November 19, 2008.

10. I thank an anonymous reviewer for pointing this out to me.

References

Aberle, David
1996   The Peyote Religion among the Navajo. Chicago: Aldine.

Adams, Alyce
2000   The Road Not Taken: How Tribes Choose between Tribal and Indian Health Service Management of Health Care Resources. American Indian Culture and Research Journal 24(3):21–38.

Ahkeah, Sammy
2001   IHS Referendum Will Fail. Letter to the editor. Navajo Times, May 10.

Aleinikoff, T. Alexander
2002   Semblance of Sovereignty: The Constitution, the State, and American Citizenship. Cambridge, MA: Harvard University Press.

Alfred, Gerald (Taiaiake)
1995   Heeding the Voices of Our Ancestors: Kahnawake Mohawk Politics and the Rise of Native Nationalism. Don Mills, ON: Oxford University Press Canada.
1999   Peace, Power, Righteousness: An Indigenous Manifesto. Toronto: Oxford University Press.

Anaya, S. James
2004   Indigenous Peoples in International Law. New York: Oxford University Press.

Anderson, Kevin N.
1980   Indian Employment Preference: Legal Foundations and Limitations. Tulsa Law Journal 15:733–771.

Anderson, Percy Bryon
2001   Election a Given. Letter to the editor. Gallup Independent, May 12.

Apfelbaum, Sharon
1999   Cabazon Finalizes Union Regulations. Public Record, April 16.

Aprill, Ellen P.
1992   Excluding the Income of State and Local Governments: The Need for Congressional Action. Georgia Law Review 26:421–502.

Arizona Cooperative Extension
2008   The Navajo Nation Quick Facts. Electronic document, http://www.indiancountryextension.org/media/docs/az_research_pubs/navajo_nation_quick_fact.pdf, accessed September 29, 2002.

Bailey, Garrick, and Roberta Glenn Bailey
1986   A History of the Navajos: The Reservation Years. Santa Fe, NM: School of American Research Press.

Barker, Joanne, ed.
2005   Sovereignty Matters: Locations of Contestation and Possibility in Indigenous Struggles for Self-Determination. Lincoln: University of Nebraska Press.
2008   Gender, Sovereignty, Rights: Native Women's Activism against Social Inequality and Violence in Canada. American Quarterly 60(2):259–266.

Barry, Kim
2006   Home and Away: The Construction of Citizenship in an Emigration Context. New York University Law Review 81:11–59.

Barsh, Russel Lawrence, and James Youngblood Henderson
1980   The Road: Indian Tribes and Political Liberty. Berkeley: University of California Press.

Barsh, Russel Lawrence, and Ronald L. Trosper
1978   Title I of the Indian Self-Determination and Education Assistance Act of 1975. American Indian Law Review 3:361–395.

Bartelson, Jens
1995   A Genealogy of Sovereignty. Cambridge: Cambridge University Press.

Becker, Craig, and Darlene Thomas
1985   Labor Law and the Native American. Indian Law Support Center Reporter 8:1–21.

Bee, Robert L.
1999   Structure, Ideology, and Tribal Governments. Human Organization 58(3):285–295.

Begay, Jason
2009   Appeal Certain in Reform Ruling. Navajo Times, July 2.

Berkhofer, Robert F., Jr.
1979   The White Man's Indian: Images of the American Indian, from Columbus to the Present. New York: Vintage Books.

Beyal, Duane
2001   How about Another Referendum? Navajo Times, June 21.

Biolsi, Thomas
1992 Organizing the Lakota: The Political Economy of the New Deal on the Pine Ridge and Rosebud Reservations. Tucson: University of Arizona Press.
2005 Imagined Geographies: Sovereignty, Indigenous Space, and American Indian Struggle. American Ethnologist 32(2):239–259.

Bonacich, Edna
2000 Intense Challenges, Tentative Possibilities: Organizing Immigrant Garment Workers in Los Angeles. *In* Organizing Immigrants: The Challenge for Unions in Contemporary California. Ruth Milkman, ed. Pp. 130–149. Ithaca, NY: ILR Press.

Bosniak, Linda
2000 Citizenship Denationalized. Indiana Journal of Global Legal Studies (Spring):447–510.

Boyarin, Jonathan
1994 Space, Time and the Politics of Memory. *In* Remapping Memory: The Politics of Time and Space. Jonathan Boyarin, ed. Pp. 1–37. Minneapolis: University of Minnesota Press.

Brodkin, Karen
2007 Making Democracy Matter: Identity and Activism in Los Angeles. New Brunswick, NJ: Rutgers University Press.

Brodkin, Karen, and Cynthia Strathmann
2004 The Struggle for Hearts and Minds: Organization, Ideology and Emotion. Labor Studies Journal 29(3):1–24.

Bronfenbrenner, Kate, Sheldon Friedman, Richard W. Hurd, Rudolph A. Oswald, and Ronald L. Seeber, eds.
1998 Organizing to Win: New Research on Union Strategies. Ithaca, NY: ILR Press.

Bronfenbrenner, Kate, and Robert Hickey
2004 Changing to Organize: A National Assessment of Union Strategies. *In* Rebuilding Labor: Organizing and Organizers in the New Union Movement. Ruth Milkman and Kim Voss, eds. Pp. 17–61. Ithaca, NY: ILR Press.

Bronfenbrenner, Kate, and Tom Juravich
1998 It Takes More Than House Calls: Organizing to Win with a Comprehensive Union-Building Strategy. *In* Organizing to Win: New Research on Union Strategies. Kate Bronfenbrenner, Sheldon Friedman, Richard W. Hurd, Rudolph A. Oswald, and Ronald L. Seeber, eds. Pp. 19–36. Ithaca, NY: ILR Press.

Bruyneel, Kevin
2007 The Third Space of Sovereignty: The Postcolonial Politics of U.S.–Indigenous Relations. Minneapolis: University of Minnesota Press.

Buffalo, William, and Kevin J. Wadzinski
1994–95 Application of Federal and State Labor and Employment Laws to Indian Tribal Employers. University of Memphis Law Review 25:1365–1399.

Canby, William C., Jr.
1998 American Indian Law in a Nutshell. St. Paul, MN: West Group.

Castile, George Pierre
1998 To Show Heart: Native American Self-Determination and Federal Indian Policy, 1960–1975. Tucson: University of Arizona Press.
2006 Taking Charge: Native American Self-Determination and Federal Indian Policy, 1975–1993. Tucson: University of Arizona Press.

Cattelino, Jessica R.
2004 Casino Roots: The Cultural Production of Twentieth-Century Seminole Economic Development. *In* Native Pathways: American Indian Culture and Economic Development in the Twentieth Century. Brian Hosmer and Colleen O'Neill, eds. Pp. 66–90. Boulder: University of Colorado Press.
2008 High Stakes: Florida Seminole Gaming and Sovereignty. Durham, NC: Duke University Press.
2009 Fungibility: Florida Seminole Casino Dividends and the Fiscal Politics of Indigeneity. American Anthropologist 111(2):190–200.

Champagne, Duane
2004 Tribal Capitalism and Native Capitalists: Multiple Pathways of Native Economy. *In* Native Pathways: American Indian Culture and Economic Development in the Twentieth Century. Brian Hosmer and Colleen O'Neill, eds. Pp. 308–329. Boulder: University of Colorado Press.
2006 Remaking Tribal Constitutions: Meeting the Challenges of Tradition, Colonialism, and Globalization. *In* American Indian Constitutional Reform and the Rebuilding of Native Nations. Eric D. Lemont, ed. Pp. 11–34. Austin: University of Texas Press.

Chander, Anupam
2006 Homeward Bound. New York University Law Review 81:60–89.

Clawson, Dan
2003 The Next Upsurge: Labor and the New Social Movements. Ithaca, NY: ILR Press.

Cobb, Amanda J.
2005/2006 Understanding Tribal Sovereignty: Definitions, Conceptualizations, and Interpretations. Joint issue, American Studies 46:3–4 / Indigenous Studies Today 1:115–132.

Cole, Jennifer Perez, and Steven Woodruff
2008 President Bush Would Jettison Indian Health for Ideology. High Country News, February 25.

Contreras, Kate Spilde
2006 Cultivating New Opportunities: Tribal Government Gaming on the Pechanga Reservation. American Behavioral Scientist 50(3):1–38.

Cornell, Stephen, and Joseph P. Kalt
1992 Reloading the Dice: Improving the Chances for Economic Development on

American Indian Reservations. *In* What Can Tribes Do? Strategies and Institutions in American Indian Economic Development. Stephen Cornell and Joseph P. Kalt, eds. Pp. 3–59. Los Angeles: UCLA American Indian Studies Center.
1997 Successful Economic Development and Heterogeneity of Governmental Form on American Indian Reservations. *In* Getting Good Government: Capacity Building in the Public Sectors of Developing Countries. Merilee S. Grindle, ed. Pp. 257–296. Cambridge, MA: Harvard University Press.
1998 Sovereignty and Nation-Building: The Development Challenge in Indian Country Today. Cambridge, MA: Harvard Project on American Indian Economic Development.

Corntassel, Jeff, and Richard C. Witmer
2008 Force Federalism: Contemporary Challenges to Indigenous Nationhood. Norman: University of Oklahoma Press.

Cramer, Renée Ann
2005 Cash, Color, and Colonialism: The Politics of Tribal Acknowledgment. Norman: University of Oklahoma Press.

Darian-Smith, Eve
2003 New Capitalists: Law, Politics, and Identity Surrounding Casino Gaming on Native American Land. Belmont, CA: Wadsworth / Thomson Learning.

Deloria, Philip J.
1998 Playing Indian. New Haven, CT: Yale University Press.
2006 Indians in Unexpected Places. Lawrence: University Press of Kansas.

Deloria, Vine, Jr.
1979 Self-Determination and the Concept of Sovereignty. *In* Economic Development in American Indian Reservations. Roxanne Dunbar Ortiz, ed. Pp. 22–28. Albuquerque: INAD, University of New Mexico.
1988 Custer Died for Your Sins: An Indian Manifesto. Norman: University of Oklahoma Press.
1995 Red Earth, White Lies: Native Americans and the Myth of Scientific Fact. New York: Scribner.

Deloria, Vine, Jr., and Clifford M. Lytle
1983 American Indians, American Justice. Austin: University of Texas Press.
1984 The Nations Within: The Past and Future of American Indian Sovereignty. New York: Pantheon Books.

Dempsey, Pamela
2004 Protests Continue at Tuba City Hospital. Gallup Independent, December 21.

Denetdale, Jennifer Nez
2007 Reclaiming Diné History: The Legacies of Navajo Chief Manuelito and Juanita. Tucson: University of Arizona Press.
2008 Carving Navajo National Boundaries: Patriotism, Tradition, and the Diné Marriage Act of 2005. American Quarterly 60(2):289–294.

Di Giovanni, Larry
2001a Chapter Ponders Navajo Health Care Pitch. Gallup Independent, January 9.
2001b IHS Plan Proceeds—Despite Vote. Gallup Independent, June 21.

Dilworth, Leah
1996 Imagining Indians in the Southwest: Persistent Visions of a Primitive Past. Washington, DC: Smithsonian Institution Press.

Dohi, Lolita Gene
2001 Special Election Was a Needless End Run. Letter to the editor. Navajo Times, June 28.

Ecker, Patricia
2009 Tribe Denies Federal Labor Jurisdiction. Morning Sun, September 18.

Fantasia, Rick
1988 Cultures of Solidarity: Consciousness, Action, and Contemporary American Workers. Berkeley: University of California Press.

Fantasia, Rick, and Kim Voss
2004 Hard Work: Remaking the American Labor Movement. Berkeley: University of California Press.

Field, Margaret
2009 Changing Navajo Language Ideologies and Changing Language Use. *In* Native American Language Ideologies: Beliefs, Practices, and Struggles in Indian Country. Paul V. Kroskrity and Margaret Field, eds. Pp. 31–47. Tucson: University of Arizona Press.

Fink, Leon
2003 The Maya of Morganton: Work and Community in the Nuevo New South. Chapel Hill: University of North Carolina Press.

Fisk, Catherine L., Daniel J. B. Mitchell, and Christopher L. Erickson
2000 Union Representation of Immigrant Janitors in Southern California: Economic and Legal Challenges. *In* Organizing Immigrants: The Challenge for Unions in Contemporary California. Ruth Milkman, ed. Pp. 199–224. Ithaca, NY: ILR Press.

Fowler, Loretta
2004 Politics. *In* A Companion to the Anthropology of American Indians. Thomas Biolsi, ed. Pp. 69–94. Malden, MA: Blackwell Publishing.

Frickey, Philip
1999 A Common Law for Our Age of Colonialism: The Judicial Divestiture of Indian Tribal Authority over Nonmembers. Yale Law Journal 109:1–85.

Garroutte, Eva Marie
2003 Real Indians: Identity and the Survival of Native America. Berkeley: University of California Press.

Gede, Thomas
2000 Indian Gaming: The State's View. *In* Indian Gaming: Who Wins? Angela Mullis

and David Kamper, eds. Pp. 72–79. Los Angeles: UCLA American Indian Studies Center.

Goldberg, Carole, and Duane Champagne
2002   Ramona Redeemed? The Rise of Tribal Political Power in California. Wicazo Sa Review 17(1):43–63.

Goldberg, Chad Alan
2007   Citizens and Paupers: Rights, Relief, and Race from the Freedman's Bureau to Workfare. Chicago: University of Chicago Press.

Gordon, Chad M.
2000   From Hope to Realization of Dreams: Proposition 5 and California Indian Gaming. In Indian Gaming: Who Wins? Angela Mullis and David Kamper, eds. Pp. 3–13. Los Angeles: UCLA American Indian Studies Center.

Gordon, Jennifer
2007   Transnational Labor Citizenship. Southern California Law Review 80:503–587.

Grez, Kelly E. W.
2005   Stepping onto the Reservation: The National Labor Relations Board's New Approach to Asserting Jurisdiction over Indian Tribes. Administrative Law Review 57:1153–1170.

Gross, James A.
1981   The Reshaping of the National Labor Relations Board: Nation Labor Policy in Transition 1937–1947. Albany: State University of New York Press.
1995   Broken Promise: The Subversion of U.S. Labor Relations Policy, 1947–1994. Philadelphia: Temple University Press.

Harmon, Alexandra
2003   American Indians and Land Monopolies in the Gilded Age. Journal of American History 90(1):106–133.

Harvard Project on American Indian Economic Development (HPAIED)
2008   The State of Native Nations: Conditions under U.S. Policies of Self-Determination. New York: Oxford University Press.

Helms, Kathy
2004   Worker: If No One's Going to Be Fired, Why Are They Taking Our Pictures? Gallup Independent, May 5.

Herman, Joseph E.
2000   The California Tribal Labor Relations Ordinance: Overview and Analysis. Electronic document, http://library.findlaw.com/2000/Jan/1/129724.html, accessed June 20, 2008.

Hodge, W. H.
1971   Navajo Urban Migration: An Analysis from the Perspective of the Family. In The American Indian in Urban Society. Jack O. Waddell and O. Michael Watson, eds. Pp. 346–391. Boston: Little, Brown.

Holm, Tom
1985 Crisis in Tribal Government. *In* American Indian Policy in the Twentieth Century. Vine Deloria Jr., ed. Pp. 135–154. Norman: University of Oklahoma Press.

Horris, Brenda
2005 Initiating Legislation or Not? Letter to the editor. Gallup Independent, January 26.

Hosmer, Brian C.
1999 American Indians in the Marketplace: Persistence and Innovation among the Menominees and Metlakatlans, 1870–1920. Lawrence: University Press of Kansas.

Hosmer, Brian C., and Colleen O'Neill, eds.
2004 Native Pathways: American Indian Culture and Economic Development in the Twentieth Century. Boulder: University of Colorado Press.

House, Deborah
2002 Language Shift among the Navajos: Identity Politics and Cultural Continuity. Tucson: University of Arizona Press.

HPAIED. *See* **Harvard Project on American Indian Economic Development**

Huhndorf, Shari M.
2001 Going Native: Indians in the American Cultural Imagination. Ithaca, NY: Cornell University Press.

Ickes, R. Dennis
1981 Tribal Economic Independence—The Means to Achieve True Self-Determination. South Dakota Law Review 26:494–528.

Indian Country Today
2002 Navajos Reverse Vote on Health System Takeover. February 1.

Iverson, Peter, ed.
2002 "For Our Navajo People": Diné Letters, Speeches and Petitions 1900–1960. Albuquerque: University of New Mexico Press.

Iverson, Peter, and Monty Roessel
2002 Diné: A History of the Navajos. Albuquerque: University of New Mexico Press.

Ivison, Duncan, Paul Patton, and Will Sanders, eds.
2000 Political Theory and the Rights of Indigenous Peoples. Cambridge: Cambridge University Press.

Kalt, Joseph P., and Joseph William Singer
2004 Myths and Realities of Tribal Sovereignty: The Law and Economics of Indian Self-Rule. Cambridge, MA: Harvard Project on American Indian Economic Development.

Kamper, David
2000 Introduction: The Mimicry of Indian Gaming. *In* Indian Gaming: Who Wins? Angela Mullis and David Kamper, eds. Pp. vii–xiv. Los Angeles: UCLA American Indian Studies Center.

2003 When "Yes" Doesn't Mean "Yes": Determinacy of Communication in Union Organizing. SALSA Proceedings 2002 (Spring):69–75.

Kelly, Lawrence C.
1975 The Indian Reorganization Act: The Dream and Reality. Pacific Historical Review 44(3):291–312.

Kemp, Helen M.
1995 Fallen Timber: A Proposal for the National Labor Relations Board to Assert Jurisdiction over Indian-Owned and Controlled Businesses on Tribal Reservations. Western New England Law Review 17:1–28.

Kessler-Harris, Alice
2003 In Pursuit of Economic Citizenship. Social Politics 10(2):157–175.

Knack, Martha C., and Alice Littlefield
1996 Native American Labor: Retrieving History, Rethinking Theory. *In* Native Americans and Wage Labor: Ethnohistorical Perspectives. Alice Littlefield and Martha C. Knack, eds. Pp. 3–44. Norman: University of Oklahoma Press.

Krerowicz, John
1998 Casino Will Agree to Allow Unions. Kenosha News, October 22.

Kugel, Rebecca
1985 Factional Alignment among Minnesota Ojibwe, 1850–1880. American Indian Culture and Research Journal 9(4):23–47.

Kunitz, Stephen J.
1996 The History and Politics of U.S. Health Care Policy for American Indians and Native Alaskans. American Journal of Public Health 86(10):1464–1473.

Leap, William L.
1993 American Indian English. Salt Lake City: University of Utah Press.

Lee, Andrew J.
2001 Statement to the Committee on Indian Affairs. Washington, DC: United States Senate, July 18.

Lemont, Eric D.
2001–02 Developing Effective Processes of American Indian Constitutional and Governmental Reform: Lessons from the Cherokee Nation of Oklahoma, Hualapai Nation, Navajo Nation, and Northern Cheyenne Tribe. American Indian Law Review 26:147–175.

Lemont, Eric D., ed.
2006 American Indian Constitutional Reform and the Rebuilding of Native Nations. Austin: University of Texas Press.

Levy, Jerrold, and Stephen Kunitz
1974 Indian Drinking: Navajo Practices and Anglo American Theories. New York: John Wiley and Sons.

Lewis, David Rich
1991   Reservation Leadership and the Progressive–Traditional Dichotomy: William Wash and the Northern Utes, 1865–1928. Ethnohistory 38(2):124–148.

Lichtenstein, Nelson
2002   State of the Union: A Century of American Labor. Princeton, NJ: Princeton University Press.

Light, Steven Andres, and Kathryn R. L. Rand
2005   Indian Gaming and Tribal Sovereignty: The Casino Compromise. Lawrence: University Press of Kansas.

Limas, Vicki J.
1993   Employment Suits against Indian Tribes: Balancing Sovereign Rights and Civil Rights. Denver University Law Journal 70:359–392.
1994   Application of Federal Labor and Employment Statutes to Native American Tribes: Respecting Sovereignty and Achieving Consistency. Arizona State Law Journal 26:681–745.

Littlefield, Alice
1991   Native American Labor and Public Policy in the United States. *In* Marxist Approaches in Economic Anthropology. Alice Littlefield and Hill Gates, eds. Pp. 219–232. Society for Economic Anthropology, Monographs in Economic Anthropology 9. Lanham, MD: University Press of America.

Littlefield, Alice, and Martha C. Knack, eds.
1996   Native Americans and Wage Labor: Ethnohistorical Perspectives. Norman: University of Oklahoma Press.

Logan, John
2002   Consultants, Lawyers, and the "Union Free" Movement in USA since the 1970s. Industrial Relations Journal 33(3):197–214.

Lombardi, Michael
N.d.   Long Road Traveled I–III. Electronic document, http://www.cniga.com/facts/history.php, accessed July 14, 2008.

Lopez, Steven H.
2000   Overcoming Legacies of Business Unionism: Why Grassroots Organizing Tactics Succeed. *In* Rebuilding Labor: Organizing and Organizers in the New Union Movement. Ruth Milkman and Kim Voss, eds. Pp. 114–132. Ithaca, NY: ILR Press.

Louis, Hondo Baldwin
2001   NHCS Corp. Proceeding, Looking at Plans. STEP: A Publication of the Navajo Division of Health 5(3).

Lurie, Nancy Oestriech
1976   The Will-o'-the-Wisp of Indian Unity. *In* Currents in Anthropology: Essays in Honor of Sol Tax. Robert Hinshaw, ed. Pp. 325–335. New York: Mouton Publishers.

1986 Money, Semantics, and Indian Leadership. American Indian Quarterly 10(1):47–63.

Lyons, Scott Richard
2004 Unionization in Indian Country Can Be an Act of Sovereignty. Indian Country Today, July 14.

Maniaci, Jim
2001a Group Gets OK to Pursue IHS Takeover. Gallup Independent, January 17.
2001b Group Seeks Vote on IHS Takeover. Gallup Independent, April 18.
2001c Opponents of IHS Takeover Get Early Victory. Gallup Independent, December 4.
2001d Takeover of IHS by Tribe Moves Ahead. Gallup Independent, January 15.
2001e Takeover of IHS Could Go to Voters. Gallup Independent, April 13.
2001f Voters to Decide Takeover of IHS. Gallup Independent, April 21.

Mantsios, Gregory, ed.
1998 A New Labor Movement for the New Century. New York: Monthly Review Press.

Marks, Mindy, and Kate Spilde Contreras
2007 Lands of Opportunity: Social and Economic Effects of Tribal Gaming on Localities. Policy Matters 1(4):1–11.

Marshall, T. H.
1964 Class, Citizenship, and Social Development. Garden City, NY: Doubleday.

McCartin, Joseph
2008 "A Wagner Act for Public Employees": Labor's Deferred Dream and the Rise of Conservatism, 1970–1976. Journal of American History (June):123–148.

McKenzie, Taylor
2001 McKenzie: Navajo Nation Will Not Run IHS. Navajo Times, June 28.

Meeks, Eric V.
2007 Border Citizens: The Making of Indians, Mexicans, and Anglos in Arizona. Austin: University of Texas Press.

Merina, Victor
2008 Organizing against Unions. Electronic document, http://www.reznetnews.org/article/national-indian-gaming-association/organizing-against-unions, accessed August 5, 2009.

Milkman, Ruth
1997 Farewell to the Factory: Auto Workers in the Late Twentieth Century. Berkeley: University of California Press.
2002 New Workers, New Labor, and the New Los Angeles. *In* Unions in a Globalized Environment: Changing Borders, Organizational Boundaries, and Social Roles. Bruce Nissen, ed. Pp. 103–129. Armonk, NY: M. E. Sharpe.
2006 LA Story: Immigrant Workers and the Future of the U.S. Labor Movement. New York: Russell Sage Foundation Publications.

Milkman, Ruth, ed.
2000   Organizing Immigrants: The Challenge for Unions in Contemporary California. Ithaca, NY: ILR Press.

Milkman, Ruth, and Kim Voss, eds.
2004   Rebuilding Labor: Organizing and Organizers in the New Union Movement. Ithaca, NY: ILR Press.

Mohawk, John C.
1991   Indian Economic Development: An Evolving Concept of Sovereignty. Buffalo Law Review 39:495–506.

Mullis, Angela, and David Kamper, eds.
2000   Indian Gaming: Who Wins? Los Angeles: UCLA American Indian Studies Center.

Navajo-Hopi Observer
2004   Tuba City Hospital Board Sacks CEO. June 30.

Navajo Nation
2008   Navajo Election Administration. Electronic document, http://www.navajoelections.navajo.org/results.html, accessed September 29, 2009.

Navajo Nation Office of the President and Vice President
2008a Navajo President Joe Shirley, Jr., Delivers Initiative Petitions to Navajo Election Administration, Next Step Is Certification. Electronic document, http://opvp.org/cms/kunde/rts/opvporg/docs/403534392-10-31-2008-19-15-46.pdf, accessed September 29, 2009.
2008b Second Navajo Government Development Office Efficiency Report Reveals Navajo Nation Council Representation Expensive, Excessive. Electronic document, http://opvp.org/cms/kunde/rts/opvporg/docs/240295747-05-19-2008-22-45-31.pdf, accessed September 29, 2009.
2008c 2005 Efficiency Report on Navajo Nation Council Outlines Justifications for President's Government Reform Initiative. Electronic document, http://opvp.org/cms/kunde/rts/opvporg/docs/1060603117-05-05-2008-19-49-24.pdf, accessed September 29, 2009.

Ness, Immanuel
1998   Organizing Immigrant Communities: UNITE's Workers Centered Strategy. *In* Organizing to Win: New Research on Union Strategies. Kate Bronfenbrenner, Sheldon Friedman, Richard W. Hurd, Rudolph A. Oswald, and Ronald L. Seeber, eds. Pp. 87–101. Ithaca, NY: ILR Press.

Nielsen, Marianne O., and James W. Zion, eds.
2005   Navajo Nation Peacemaking: Living Traditional Justice. Tucson: University of Arizona Press.

Nissen, Bruce
2002   The Labor Movement in a New Globalized Environment: An Introduction. *In* Unions in a Globalized Environment: Changing Borders, Organizational Boundaries, and Social Roles. Bruce Nissen, ed. Pp. 3–13. Armonk, NY: M. E. Sharpe.

Nissen, Bruce, ed.
2002   Unions in a Globalized Environment: Changing Borders, Organizational Boundaries, and Social Roles. Armonk, NY: M. E. Sharpe.

Nissen, Bruce, and Guillermo Grenier
2002   Unions and Immigrants in South Florida: A Comparison. *In* Unions in a Globalized Environment: Changing Borders, Organizational Boundaries, and Social Roles. Bruce Nissen, ed. Pp. 130–160. Armonk, NY: M. E. Sharpe.

Norrgard, Chantal
2009   From Berries to Orchards: Tracing the History of Berrying and Economic Transformation among Lake Superior Ojibwe. American Indian Quarterly 33(1):33–61.

O'Brien, Sharon
1989   American Indian Tribal Governments. Norman: University of Oklahoma Press.

Ochs, Elinor, and Lisa Capps
1996   Narrating the Self. Annual Review of Anthropology 25:19–43.

O'Neill, Colleen
2005   Working the Navajo Way: Labor and Culture in the Twentieth Century. Lawrence: University of Kansas Press.
N.d.   Jobs and Sovereignty: Tribal Employment Rights and Energy Development in the Twentieth Century. *In* Indians & Energy: Exploitation and Opportunity in the American Southwest. Sherry L. Smith and Brian Frehner, eds. Santa Fe, NM: School for Advanced Research Press.

Ong, Aihwa
2006   Neoliberalism as Exception: Mutations in Citizenship and Sovereignty. Durham, NC: Duke University Press.

Pacheco, Michael
1994   Toward a Truer Sense of Sovereignty: Fiduciary Duty in Indian Corporations. South Dakota Law Review 39:49–92.

Parman, Donald L.
1976   The Navajos and the New Deal. New Haven, CT: Yale University Press.

Pasquaretta, Paul
1994   On the "Indianness" of Bingo: Gambling and the Native American Community. Critical Inquiry 20(4):694–714.

Penny, Robert A.
2004   Workers against Unions: Union Organizing and Anti-Union Countermobilizations. *In* Rebuilding Labor: Organizing and Organizers in the New Union Movement. Ruth Milkman and Kim Voss, eds. Pp. 88–113. Ithaca, NY: ILR Press.

Pfister, Joel
2004   Individuality Incorporated: Indians and the Multicultural Modern. Durham, NC: Duke University Press.

Philp, Kenneth, ed.
1995 Indian Self-Rule: First-Hand Accounts of Indian–White Relations from Roosevelt to Reagan. Logan: Utah State University Press.

Pickering, Kathleen Ann
2000 Lakota Culture, World Economy. Lincoln: University of Nebraska Press.

Porter, Robert B.
1997a Strengthening Tribal Sovereignty through Governmental Reform: What Are the Issues? Kansas Journal of Law and Public Policy (Winter):72–99.
1997b Strengthening Tribal Sovereignty through Peacemaking: How Anglo-American Legal Tradition Destroys Indigenous Societies. Columbia Human Rights Law Review 28:235–304.

Povinelli, Elizabeth A.
2002 The Cunning of Recognition: Indigenous Alterities and the Making of Australian Multiculturalism. Durham, NC: Duke University Press.

Raibmon, Page Sylvia
2005 Authentic Indians: Episodes of Encounter from the Late-Nineteenth-Century Northwest Coast. Durham, NC: Duke University Press.

Reichard, Gladys
1950 Navaho Religion: A Study of Symbolism. New York: Bollingen Foundation / Pantheon Books.

Reynolds, Jerry
2008 Budget Blueprint Includes $1 Billion More for IHS. Indian Country Today, March 21.

Rice, G. William
1996 Employment in Indian Country: Considerations Respecting Tribal Regulation of the Employer–Employee Relationship. North Dakota Law Review 72:267–297.

Robbins, Lynn A.
1975 Navajo Participation in Labor Unions. Lake Powell Research Project Bulletin 15.

Roessel, Ruth, and Broderick H. Johnson, eds.
1974 Navajo Livestock Reduction: A National Disgrace. Chinle, AZ: Navajo Community College Press.

Rosenthal, Nicolas G.
2004 The Dawning of a New Day? Notes on Indian Gaming in Southern California. *In* Native Pathways: American Indian Culture and Economic Development in the Twentieth Century. Brian Hosmer and Colleen O'Neill, eds. Pp. 91–111. Boulder: University of Colorado Press.

Rudy, Preston
2004 "Justice for Janitors," Not "Compensation for Custodians": The Political Context

and Organizing in San Jose and Sacramento. *In* Rebuilding Labor: Organizing and Organizers in the New Union Movement. Ruth Milkman and Kim Voss, eds. Pp. 133–149. Ithaca, NY: ILR Press.

Russell, Scott C., and Eric Henderson
1999 The 1994 Navajo Presidential Election: Analysis of the Election and Results of Exit Poll. American Indian Quarterly 23(2):23–37.

Scott, Craig
1996 Indigenous Self-Determination and Decolonization of the International Imagination: A Plea. Human Rights Quarterly 18(4):814–820.

Sharpe, Teresa
2004 Union Democracy and Successful Campaigns: The Dynamic of Staff Authority and Worker Participation in an Organizing Union. *In* Rebuilding Labor: Organizing and Organizers in the New Union Movement. Ruth Milkman and Kim Voss, eds. Pp. 62–87. Ithaca, NY: ILR Press.

Shebala, Marley
2000 Back to the Drawing Board: Referendum to Reduce the Council Fails. Navajo Times, September 7.
2001a "Attorney Language" or Layman's Terms. Navajo Times, May 3.
2001b Support for Referendum Change Is Rising. Navajo Times, May 3.
2002 IHS Actions Raise Distrust. Navajo Times, February 14.

Shepardson, Mary
1982 The Status of Navajo Women. American Indian Quarterly 6(1–2):149–169.

Sherman, Rachel, and Kim Voss
2000 "Organize or Die": Labor's New Tactics and Immigrant Workers. *In* Organizing Immigrants: The Challenge for Unions in Contemporary California. Ruth Milkman, ed. Pp. 81–108. Ithaca, NY: ILR Press.

Shirley, Joe, Jr.
2001 People Are Disenchanted with Government. Letter to the editor. Navajo Times, March 22.

Shklar, Judith N.
1991 American Citizenship: The Question for Inclusion. Cambridge, MA: Harvard University Press.

Siegel, Bernard J., and Alan R. Beals
1960a Conflict and Factional Dispute. Journal of the Royal Anthropological Institute of Great Britain and Ireland 90:107–117.
1960b Pervasive Factionalism. American Anthropologist 62:394–417.
1966 Divisiveness and Social Conflict. Palo Alto, CA: Stanford University Press.

Simpson, Audra
2000 Paths toward a Mohawk Nation: Narratives of Citizenship and Nationhood in Kahnawake. *In* Political Theory and the Rights of Indigenous Peoples. Duncan Ivison, Paul Patton, and Will Sanders, eds. Pp. 113–136. Cambridge: Cambridge University Press.

Singel, Wenona T.
2004 Labor Relations and Tribal Self-Governance. North Dakota Law Review 80:691–730.

Smith, Andrea
2005 Conquest: Sexual Violence and American Indian Genocide. Cambridge, MA: South End Press.
2008 American Studies without America: Native Feminisms and the Nation-State. American Quarterly 60(2):309–315.

Smith, Andrea, and J. Kehualani Kauanui
2008 Introduction: Native Feminisms Engage American Studies. American Quarterly 60(2):241–250.

Smith, Dean Howard
2000 Modern Tribal Governments: Paths to Self-Sufficiency and Cultural Integrity in Indian Country. Walnut Creek, CA: AltaMira Press.

Smith, Linda Tuhiwai
1999 Decolonizing Methodologies: Research and Indigenous Peoples. London: Zed Books.

Smith, Paul Chaat, and Robert Allen Warrior
1996 Like a Hurricane: The Indian Movement from Alcatraz to Wounded Knee. New York: New Press.

Smith, Victoria
2001 Ethnographies of Work and the Work of Ethnographers. *In* Handbook on Ethnography. Paul Atkinson, Amanda Coffey, Sara Delamont, Lyn Lofland, and John Lofland, eds. Pp. 220–233. London: Sage Publications.

Speed, Shannon, Shannon R. Aída Hernández Castillo, and Lynn Stephen, eds.
2006 Dissident Women: Gender and Cultural Politics in Chiapas. Austin: University of Texas Press.

Spilde, Katherine A.
1998 Acts of Sovereignty, Acts of Identity: Negotiating Independence through Tribal Government Gaming on the White Earth Reservation. PhD dissertation, University of California, Santa Cruz.
1999 Indian Gaming Study. Anthropology Newsletter (April):11, 16.
2003 The Unfair Argument: How Indian Gaming Has Provided Benefits for California. Global Gaming Business (December):16–19.
2004a Creating a Space for American Indian Economic Development: Indian Gaming and American Indian Activism. *In* Local Actions: Cultural Activism, Power and Public

Life in America. Melissa Checker and Maggie Fishman, eds. Pp. 71–88. New York: Columbia University Press.
2004b Why Indian Gaming Works. Tribal Government Gaming Annual Report:14–20.

Stacey, Helen
2003 Relational Sovereignty. Stanford Law Review 55:2029–2059.

Steenrod, Susan S.
1979 The Navajo and Peabody Coal Company: A Case Study of Communication in Intercultural Labor Relationships. Master's thesis, University of Denver.

Steinman, Erich
2005/2006 The Contemporary Revival and Diffusion of Indigenous Sovereignty Discourse. Joint issue, American Studies 46:3–4 / Indigenous Studies Today 1:89–114.

Stephen, Lynn
1994 The Politics and Practice of Testimonial Literature. In Hear My Testimony. Maria Teresa Tula and Lynn Stephan, eds. Pp. 223–234. Boston: South End Press.

Strieb, Gordon F.
1952 An Attempt to Unionize a Semi-Literate Navaho Group. Human Organization 11(1):23–31.

Sturm, Circe Dawn
2002 Blood Politics: Race, Culture, and Identity in the Cherokee Nation of Oklahoma. Berkeley: University of California Press.

Sweeney, James P.
2007 Gaming Impasse Beginning to Thaw. San Diego Union Tribune, June 8.

Tait, Vanessa
2005 Poor Workers' Unions: Rebuilding Labor from Below. Cambridge, MA: South End Press.

Thayer, Rosanda Suetopka
2004 Tuba City Doctors Vote "No Confidence." Arizona Daily Sun, June 5.

Thompson, Julie
2001 Application of the National Labor Relations Act to Indian Tribes: Preserving Indian Self-Government and Economic Security. Dayton Law Review 27:189–215.

Toensing, Gale Courtney
2007 Federal Labor Board OKs Union Vote at Mashantucket. Indian Country Today, November 7.

Tohtsoni, Nathan J.
2000 Turf Battle: "State of Distress" Causes International Union to Intervene in Local IHS Union. Navajo Times, December 7.
2001 IHS Vote "Not Clear." Navajo Times, June 7.
2002 Special Session Set for IHS Contract: Council Votes to Disapprove, Recall, Then Table Proposal. Navajo Times, February 7.

Tomlins, Christopher L.
1985 The State and the Unions: Labor Relations, Law, and the Organized Labor Movement in America, 1880–1960. Cambridge: Cambridge University Press.

Torgovnick, Marianna
1990 Gone Primitive: Savage Intellects, Modern Lives. Chicago: University of Chicago Press.

Tsuk, Dalia
2001 The New Deal Origins of American Legal Pluralism. Florida State University Law Review 29:189–268.

UCLA Office of Instructional Development
1998 Townhall Meeting Proposition 5: The Tribal Gaming Initiative. Electronic document, http://www.oid.ucla.edu/Webcast/Misc/TG_Live.html, accessed August 25, 2000.

Waldinger, Roger, Chris Erickson, Ruth Milkman, Daniel J. B. Mitchell, Able Valenzuela, Kent Wong, and Maurice Zeitlin
1998 Helots No More: A Case Study of the Justice for Janitors Campaign in Los Angeles. In Organizing to Win: New Research on Union Strategies. Kate Bronfenbrenner, Sheldon Friedman, Richard W. Hurd, Rudolph A. Oswald, and Ronald L. Seeber, eds. Pp. 102–119. Ithaca, NY: ILR Press.

Warrior, Robert Allen
1994 Tribal Secrets: Recovering American Indian Intellectual Traditions. Minneapolis: University of Minnesota Press.

Weisiger, Marsha
2007 Gendered Injustice: Navajo Livestock Reduction in the New Deal Era. Western Historical Quarterly 38(4):437–455.

Wells, Miriam J.
2000 Immigration and Unionization in the San Francisco Hotel Industry. In Organizing Immigrants: The Challenge for Unions in Contemporary California. Ruth Milkman, ed. Pp. 109–129. Ithaca, NY: ILR Press.

Weppner, Robert S.
1971 Urban Economic Opportunities: The Example of Denver. In The American Indian in Urban Society. Jack O. Waddell and O. Michael Watson, eds. Pp. 245–273. Boston: Little, Brown.

White, Brendan
2002 American Indian Opinion Survey. Indian Country Today, February 28.

White, Richard
1983 Roots of Dependency: Subsistence, Environment and Social Change among the Choctaws, Pawnees and Navajos. Lincoln: University of Nebraska Press.
1991 The Middle Ground: Indians, Empires, and Republics in the Great Lakes Region, 1650–1815. New York: Cambridge University Press.

Wilkins, David E.
1999   The Navajo Political Experience. Lanham, MD: Rowman and Littlefield.
2002   Governance with the Navajo Nation: Have Democratic Traditions Taken Hold? Wicazo Sa Review 17(1):91–129.

Wilkins, David E., and K. Tsianina Lomawaima
2001   Uneven Ground: American Indian Sovereignty and Federal Law. Norman: University of Oklahoma Press.

Wilkinson, Charles F.
1987   American Indians, Time, and the Law: Native Societies in a Modern Constitutional Democracy. New Haven, CT: Yale University Press.
2005   Blood Struggle: The Rise of Modern Indian Nations. New York: Norton.

Williams, Aubrey W., Jr.
1970   Navajo Political Process. Washington, DC: Smithsonian Institution Press.

Williams, Robert A., Jr.
2005   Like a Loaded Weapon: The Rehnquist Court, Indian Rights, and the Legal History of Racism in America. Minneapolis: University of Minnesota Press.

Witherspoon, Gary
1977   Language and Art in the Navajo Universe. Ann Arbor: University of Michigan Press.

Wolf, Eric R.
1982   Europe and the People without History. Berkeley: University of California Press.

Wolfe, Patrick
1998   Settler Colonialism and the Transformation of Anthropology: The Politics and Poetics of an Ethnographic Event. London: Cassell.
2001   Land, Labor, and Difference: Elementary Structures of Race. American Historical Review 106(3):866–905.

Yazzie, Duane "Chili"
2001   Window Rock Style Legal Mumbo Jumbo. Letter to the editor. Navajo Times, May 10.

Young, Iris Marion
2000   Hybrid Democracy: Iroquois Federalism and the Postcolonial Project. *In* Political Theory and the Rights of Indigenous People. Duncan Ivison, Paul Patton, and Will Sanders, eds. Pp. 237–258 Cambridge: Cambridge University Press.
2001   Two Concepts of Self-Determination. *In* Human Rights: Concepts, Contests, Contingencies. Austin Sarat and Thomas R. Kearns, eds. Pp. 25–44. Ann Arbor: University of Michigan Press.

Young, Robert W.
1978   A Political History of the Navajo Tribe. Tsaile, AZ: Navajo Community College Press.

Zatz, Noah D.
2008 Working at the Boundaries of Markets: Prison Labor and the Economic Dimension of Employment Relationships. Vanderbilt Law Review 61:857–958.
2009 Prison Labor and the Paradox of Paid Nonmarket Work. *In* Economic Sociology of Work. Nina Bandelj, ed. Pp. 369–398. Bingley, UK: Emerald Press.

Index

Aberle, David, 161
abrogation, and *Tuscarora–Coeur d'Alene* test, 40
accountability, and workplace activism in Tuba City hospital case study, 175–76, 178, 180, 182, 187, 199, 228n14
accreditation, of Tuba City health-care facility, 182
ACLU (American Civil Liberties Union), 194
Adams, Alyce, 170, 171, 227n9
AFL-CIO, 206, 229n6
agency, and termination of employees at Tuba City hospital, 188
Aída Hernández Castillo, Shannon R., 228n15
Alaska Native Claims Settlement Act of 1971, 217n20
Aleinikoff, Alexander T., 32, 102, 208, 209, 216n9
Alfred, Gerald (Taiaiake), 214n9, 219n38
American Indian studies, and methodology, 16–17
Americans with Disabilities Act, 218n25, 219n40
Aprill, Ellen P., 46
Arizona, and right-to-work law, 132
attentiveness, in context of tribal economic ventures, 173
at-will policy, and employment at Tuba City hospital, 182–83, 186, 188, 191, 228n17
authority, and worker activism in Tuba City hospital case study, 165, 175, 188
autonomy, and tribal sovereignty, 12, 13

Barry, Kim
Barsh, Russel Lawrence, 214n16
Beals, Alan R., 223n11
Bee, Robert L., 116, 117–18, 227n7
Begaye, Kelsey, 118–19
Berkhofer, Robert F., Jr., 113
Biolsi, Thomas, 75
Black Friday (Tuba City hospital), 164, 166, 181–90
Bosniak, Linda, 9
Bosque Redondo (Navajo), 98, 127
Boyarin, Jonathan, 226n3
Brodkin, Karen, 64, 167, 224–25n28
Brose, Thomas, 131–32
Brunswick Corporation, 30
Bunn, Elizabeth, 205
Bureau of Indian Affairs (BIA), 15, 52, 89, 227n9
Bush, George W., 227n10
Bustemante, Cruz, 61

Cabazon Band of Mission Indians, 72, 219n33
Cahuilla Nation, 81
California: casino gaming and revenue sharing in, 61; labor unions and casino gaming in, 33–37; and referendums on casino gaming, 1–2, 35–36, 216n12–13, 218n29; and trial labor relations ordinances, 79–86, 220–21n8, 221n12
California v. Cabazon Band of Mission Indians (1987), 219n33
Campaign for Union Recognition, 104,

105–108, 132, 133, 135–62, 168, 225n10
Campisi, Jack, 25
capitalism: as model of tribal economic development, 8–9; and Navajo Nation collective bargaining codes, 88; and traditional political, cultural, and spiritual powers of indigenous women, 189; tribal capitalism as unique form of, 48
card check procedures, and union organizing, 81, 82, 87, 220n7, 221n11
casino gaming: and anti-union theory of tribal labor relations, 136; California referendums on, 1–2, 35–36, 216n12–13, 218n29; economic success of and centrality in debates about tribal labor relations, 3–4, 65–66; and federal recognition of tribes, 218n24; IGRA and economic impact of, 49–50; and labor unions in California, 33–37; and Navajo Nation, 215n18, 221n15, 230n9; and revenue sharing with states, 60–61, 218n32, 219n34; and rich Indian stereotype, 57, 219n38; states and regulation of, 219n33; and tribal gaming as commercial enterprise, 48–49; and tribal labor relations ordinances (TLROs), 79–86
Castile, George Pierre, 108, 109–10
Cattelino, Jessica R., 12, 13, 24, 56, 164, 208, 214n10, 214n13, 216n5, 216–17n14, 218n31, 219n39, 227n7
Champagne, Duane, 48, 74, 96, 218n31
chapters, and tribal government of Navajo Nation, 113
Cherokee National of Oklahoma, 110
Christie, Thomas, 87
citizenship: and concept of "emigrant states," 102; in context of research on tribal labor relations, 8, 9–10; and democratic deficit for nontribal employees, 32–33; and race in civil rights litigation, 216n9; and transnational concept of labor, 208–209
civility, and Navajo cultural values, 178–79
civil liberty, and grassroots articulation of self-determination, 194–95

co-articulation, and conversational interactions between health-care workers and union organizers, 136–38, 157–60
Cohen, Felix, 54, 113
collective bargaining: and Navajo tribal labor relations codes, 86–87, 147, 154; and state labor relations laws, 217n22
Collier, John, 114
colonialism: and centralization of power in indigenous communities, 111–12; and concept of settler colonialism, 6, 65, 112; and livestock reduction on Navajo reservation, 113; and traditional political, cultural, and spiritual powers of indigenous women, 189
Communication Workers of America (CWA), 36, 72, 206
community members, and worker activism at Tuba City hospital, 191, 196, 198–99
Coeur d'Alene decision (1985), 39, 50, 51. *See also Tuscarora–Coeur d'Alene* decisions
conflict: livestock reduction and Navajo politics, 114–15; potential for among unions in Indian Country, 206–207; tribal labor relations and indigenous methods of resolution, 96. *See also* harmony
conversations: and concept of co-articulation, 137–38; LIUNA and face-to-face organizing, 150–57
Cornell, Stephen, 169, 172–73, 175, 176, 194, 199, 227n7
Cotter, John, 229n4
Council for Tribal Employment Rights (CTER), 89–90, 201–202, 206, 207
Coyotes Indian Reservation, 81, 82
Crownpoint Health Care Facility (New Mexico), 101

Davis, Gray, 37, 78
Davis-Bacon Act, 227n10
Dawes Act (1887), 6, 53, 128, 161
Deloria, Philip J., 23–24, 25, 215n1–2
Deloria, Vine, Jr., 14, 53
democratic deficit, and tribal jurisdiction over nontribal employees, 32–33

"denizenship," and tribal sovereignty, 209
Department of the Interior, 112
Devil's Lake Sioux Mfg. Corp. (1979), 30
Devil's Lake Sioux Reservation, 30
Diné Be'iiná Náhiilna' Bee Agha'diit'aahii (DNA) Legal Services, 115
Dodge, Chee, 114
Dodge, Tom, 114, 115
Donovan v. Coeur d'Alene Tribal Farm (1985), 38
Doo' Dah 638, 124, 141

economic development: and exceptionalism of tribal gaming, 4, 37; IGRA and impact of tribal gaming on, 49–50; and Indian Reorganization Act of 1934, 52–53, 54–55; and rent-seeking, 169, 173, 227n7; review of literature on, 7–8; rich Indian imagery and public discourse on tribal sovereignty and, 61; and tribal self-determination, 164. *See also* capitalism; poverty; tribal enterprises
effectiveness, and worker activism at Tuba City hospital, 172–73, 174–75, 178, 182, 199
emigrant states, 102, 222n1
Employee Free Choice Act, 63, 67, 219n36, 220n2, 221n11–12
employees: balancing of rights of with sovereignty rights, 13; democratic deficit and nontribal, 32–33; grassroots activism by at Tuba City hospital as case study of tribal labor relations, 19, 69, 163–99, 210, 226n2–3, 227n12, 228n21; "relational markers" and legal definition of, 31; role of in tribal economic development, 8; *San Manuel* decision and non-Indian, 51; and trial employee rights ordinances (TEROs), 89–90. *See also* at-will policy; labor relations; labor unions
ethnography: methodology of in workplace, 17–18, 226n4; and observation of union organizing campaign, 136

factionalism: in tribal politics, 110–11, 223n11; in UNITE-HERE!, 229n6

federal government: and funding of Indian health care, 227n10; tribal sovereignty and application of NLRA to Indian Country, 28. *See also* law; National Labor Relations Board; policy
Federal Labor Relations Authority, 217n22, 222n6
Federal Power Commission v. Tuscarora Indian Nation (1960), 38
feminist politics, and indigenous peoples, 190, 228n15
Field, Margaret, 161
Florida Paraplegic Assn. v. Miccosukee Tribe of Indians of Florida (1999), 218n25
Fort Apache Timber Co. (1976), 29–30, 41
Fort Defiance Indian Hospital (Arizona), 152–53
Fowler, Loretta, 110
Foxwoods Resort Casino (Connecticut), 201, 203, 204, 205, 206, 220n2
freedom of speech, and grassroots articulation of self-determination, 195
free market ideology, and rich Indian stereotype, 60
free-rider problem, and right-to-work laws, 94
Frickey, Philip, 66

Garcia v. San Antonio Metro Transit Authority (1985), 47, 62
Gede, Thomas, 216n12
gender relations, and worker activism at Tuba City hospital, 189–90
General Allotment Act of 1887, 52
"general applicability," and legal theory in labor relations cases, 31–32, 39, 40
globalization, and labor relations, 9
Gordon, Jennifer, 208
government. *See* federal government; law; policy; self-governance; states; tribal government
Great Lakes Fish and Wildlife Commission (Wisconsin), 77
Grez, Kelly E. W., 41
Gross, James A., 44
guardianship, and federal government's view of tribal sovereignty, 28

harmony, and Navajo culture values, 87, 161, 221n17
Harvard Project on American Indian Economic Development (HPAIED), 73, 88
Hayworth, J. D., 67, 220n2
health care: and concept of *health outcome*, 227n11; federal funding of, 227n10; Native nations and administration of, 16; and politics of Navajo self-governance and self-determination, 108–18; and public debate over self-determination in Navajo, 118–25, 223–24nn16–20; traditional healing and healing methods in Navajo society, 174. *See also* Indian Health Service; Laborer's International Union of North America (LIUNA); Public Law 638; Tuba City Regional Health Care Corporation
Henderson, James Youngblood, 116, 120, 214n16
Herman, John, 139, 140, 143–44
Herman, Joseph E., 81–82
Hosmer, Brian C., 213n7
Hospital Employees and Community Members Committee (HECMC), 164–99, 210, 226n1, 227n8, 228n14, 228n18–19
Hotel Employees and Restaurant Employees International Union (HERE), 33–37. *See also* UNITE-HERE!
House, Deborah, 159
hózhó, and Navajo cultural values, 87, 161
Hubbard-Pourier, Lydia, 123–24

immigrants: and concept of "emigrant citizenship," 102; and organizing strategies in service industry, 34
Indian Country, use of term, 213n1
Indian Country Today (newspaper), 71, 72, 139–40, 220n1
Indian Gaming Regulatory Act of 1988 (IGRA), 35, 49–50, 219n32
Indian Health Care Improvement Act (2008), 227n10
Indian Health Service (IHS), 17, 18–19, 101, 106, 141–43, 171, 222n3, 227n10

Indianness: modernity and concept of, 23–24, 215n1–2; rich Indian trope and mainstream racial and legal classifications of, 57–58; and stereotypes of barbaric and noble savage, 23, 215n1. *See also* indigeneity
Indian New Deal, 53–54
Indian Reorganization Act (IRA) of 1934, 49, 52–55, 220n4, 223n14
Indian Self-Determination Act of 1975, 16, 49, 108, 217n21
indigeneity and indigenous peoples: and feminist politics, 190, 228n15; and notion of poverty, 24, 215–16n4. *See also* Indianness
information sharing, and worker activism at Tuba City hospital, 192
Inouye, Daniel, 67, 220n2
Internal Revenue Service (IRS), 46–47
International Brotherhood of Electrical Workers, 206
International Brotherhood of Teamsters, 29–30, 42
International Union of Operating Engineers (IUOE), 85, 203
Iverson, Peter, 115, 116

Jefferson, Thomas, 194
job performance, and terminations of employees at Tuba City hospital, 182–83
Joint Commission on Accreditation of Healthcase Organizations (JCAHO), 183
Johnson, Lyndon, 109
jurisdiction, types of legal, 28, 31, 32

Kalt, Joseph P., 73, 169, 172–73, 175, 176, 194, 199, 227n7
Kauanui, J. Kehualani, 228n15
Kayenta Health Center, 145
Kelly, Lawrence C., 223n14
Kemp, Helen M., 41
King, Jackson, 205
Kunitz, Stephen J., 161, 170

Laborer's International Union of North

America (LIUNA), 14, 18, 72, 101–33, 135–62, 168, 196–97, 205, 215n20, 222n4, 225n3, 225n10
labor relations. *See* National Labor Relations Board; tribal labor relations
labor unions: and casino gaming in California, 33–37; and organization of nontribal vs. tribal employees, 32; and outsiderness in tribal labor relations, 135–36; place of in discussion of labor relations, 6; and pro-union actions by tribes, 71–73; and rich Indian discourse, 63–64, 76; and right-to-work laws, 91; *San Manuel* ruling and organizing efforts of in Indian Country, 71; and tribal labor relations ordinances (TLROs), 80–81; and tribal sovereignty in cases involving tribal gaming, 3, 4; and union-busting consultants at CTER and NIGA conferences, 202, 207–208. *See also* card check procedures; collective bargaining; Laborer's International Union of North America (LIUNA); representation process; United Auto Workers; UNITE-HERE!
language: Navajo ideology of appropriate, 159–60, 161; and translation of Navajo material, 215n19. *See also* conversations; narrative; voice
law: ambivalence toward Native economic success and tribal sovereignty in employment, 66–67; and concept of worker status in legal relations cases, 208; legal context for discussion of tribal labor relations and federal, 26–29, 37–44, 219–20n40; and tribal labor relations ordinances and codes, 80, 86–88; and tribal right-to-work laws, 90–95. *See also* National Labor Relations Act
Leap, William L., 225n5
legitimacy, and worker activism at Tuba City hospital, 172–73, 174–75, 178, 182, 199
Levy, Jerrold, 161
Limas, Vicki J., 87
livestock reduction, and political conflict in Navajo Nation, 113–15, 125, 128, 162, 189

local control, and debate on Public Law 638 and management of health care, 169
Local Governance Act (1998), 113
Long Walk (Navajo), 98, 127
Lyons, Scott Richard, 72–73, 82
Lytle, Clifford M., 53

Macarro, Mark, 36
MacDonald, Peter, 110, 113, 115–17, 162, 226n5
Marquez, Deron, 36
Marshall, John, 38
Martin v. Indian Wildlife Commission (1992), 220n6
Mashantucket Pequot Labor Relations Law (MPLRL), 85, 204–205, 209, 210
Mashantucket Pequot Nation, 85, 201, 202, 204–205, 210, 220n2, 229n3
McKenzie, Dr. Taylor, 123
"means test," and *Tuscarora–Coeur d'Alene* decisions, 56
Menominee Indian Nation, 72, 220n3
Merrion v. Jicarilla Apache Tribe, 92
methodology, of study on tribal labor relations, 16–19. *See also* ethnography
mining industry, and employment of Navajo workers, 125, 129
modernity, and conceptualization of Indians and Indianness, 23–24, 215n1–2
Mohawk, John C., 48
Montana v. United States (1981), 218n26
Morgan, Jacob, 114, 115

Naalnishí (Navajo Central Labor Council), 131
narrative, and interviews with Tuba City hospital employees, 167, 181–82, 226n3–4
National Congress of American Indians (NCAI), 63, 67, 71, 219n36, 220n2
National Indian Gaming Association (NIGA), 67, 71, 72, 201, 202
National Labor Relations Act (NLRA), 11, 13, 27, 217n17
National Labor Relations Board (NLRB): analysis of opinions of, 10–11; and commercial versus traditional tribal/

INDEX 255

governmental enterprises, 45–55, 58, 59–60; and interpretive shift in recent decisions on tribal labor relations, 37–44; and jurisdiction over tribal labor relations, 29–33, 229n4; and labor relations in context of tribal health-care facilities, 16; and Navajo Nation, 15; and *San Juan Pueblo* case, 92; and *San Manuel* ruling, 65, 69–75; and tribal right-to-work laws, 93; *Tuscarora–Coeur d'Alene* test and tribal labor relations, 56; and *Yukon II* decision, 197

National Labor Relations Board v. Pueblo of San Juan (2002), 91–92, 93, 220n2

National Public Employee Relations Act, 217n22

Native American Rights Fund, 71

Navajo Construction Workers Association, 130

Navajo Health Care System Corporation (NHCSC), 106, 118–25, 141–42, 225n2

Navajo Nation: and ambivalent future of tribal labor relations, 209–11; basic characteristics of as indigenous community, 98–99; and casino gaming, 215n18, 221n15, 230n9; and NLRB, 29; LIUNA and organization of health-care workers as case study of tribal labor relations, 14–16, 101–33, 135–62; and Navajo Area of Indian Health Service, 222n3; and tribal labor relations codes, 86–88; worker activism at Tuba City hospital as case study of tribal labor relations, 19, 69, 163–99

Navajo Nation Collective Bargaining Code (NNCBC), 147, 154, 209

Navajo Nation Council (NNC), 102, 103, 106, 110, 112, 113, 115, 118, 132, 172, 223n16, 228–29n21

Navajo Nation Historic Preservation Department, 18

Navajo Times (newspaper), 121, 122, 162, 186, 192

Navajo Tribe v. NLRB (1961), 15, 29, 86, 131

Nelson, Fred, 113–14

neoliberalism: and anti-union consultants, 207–208; and tribal economic development, 9; tribal and U.S. citizenship rights and, 10

New Deal, 53–54, 222n8

Nixon, Richard, 222n8

O'Brien, Sharon, 28

Occupational Safety and Health Act (OHSA), 39, 219n40

Office of Economic Opportunity, 109, 115

Office of Indian Affairs (OIA), 113, 114, 115

Office of Navajo Labor Relations (ONLR), 86, 130, 131–32, 139, 149, 191, 197, 210

Oliphant v. Squamish Indian Tribe (1978), 66, 218n26

O'Neill, Colleen, 89, 104, 125, 132, 225n28, 229n7

Ong, Aihwa, 9–10

outersiderness, of unions in tribal labor relations, 135–36

ownership, and workplace activism in Tuba City hospital case study, 175–76, 180, 182, 188, 190, 193, 199

Pala Tribe, 79, 216n12, 217n15

Pauma Band of Mission Indians, 81, 82

Peabody Coal Co., 129

peacemaker court system, and Navajo Nation judiciary, 88

peacemaking process, and uniqueness of labor relations in Native communities, 96. *See also* harmony

personnel jurisdiction, 28, 31

petition, implications of term in Navajo context, 139, 147, 225n1

Peyotism, 115

Pine Ridge Reservation, 110

policy: and Indian Self-Determination Act, 108; and power of NLRB in decisions affecting Native communities, 42–43; role of "rich Indian" imagery in, 58; and termination, 218n28, 222n8, 224n25; and use of term *self-determination*, 214n16

politics: and historical context of Campaign for Union Recognition, 162; of Navajo self-governance and self-determination, 108–18: and referendums in California, 216n12; tradition of active debate in Navajo, 162. *See also* citizenship; factionalism; feminist politics; neoliberalism; referendums
poverty, association of indigeneity with, 24–25, 215–16n4
power: colonialism and demand for centralization of in indigenous communities, 111–12; and management of Tuba City hospital, 228n13; tribal sovereignty and expansion of NLRB's discretionary, 41
pragmatism, in Navajo tribal labor relations, 125–31, 132
primitivism, and indigeneity, 215–16n4
protests, and worker activism at Tuba City hospital, 163–64, 176–81, 186, 193–94. *See also* resistance
pseudonyms, use of in study, 18, 215n19, 226n2
public debate: on management of Tuba City hospital, 191; in Navajo politics over power and role of centralized government, 116; over self-determination in Navajo health care, 118–25; tradition of in Navajo politics, 162; in tribal communities about supervision of tribal resources, 117–18
Public Law 93-638, 106, 108–10, 118, 133, 141–43, 147–50, 157, 168–76, 223–24nn16–20
public shaming, and termination of employees at Tuba City hospital, 183–84, 226n2
Purcell, Robert, 222n4

Raibmon, Page Sylvia, 213n7, 216n4
Ramirez, Ken, 36
referendums: on casino gaming in California, 1–2, 35–36, 216nn12–13, 218n29; Public Law 638 and health care system in Navajo Nation, 119–23, 124
Reich v. Great Lakes Indian Fish and Wildlife Commission (1993), 220n6
rent-seeking, and economic development, 169, 173, 227n7
representation process, of LIUNA and Campaign for Union Recognition, 106–107
resistance, of Navajos to livestock reduction, 114, 128. *See also* protests
revenue sharing, and casino gaming, 60–61, 218n32, 219n34
"rich Indian": and backlash against tribal sovereignty, 24–25, 55–64, 76, 78; and debates on casino gaming, 218n29, 219n38; replacement of barbaric or noble savage image by new trope of, 24, 215n3; and right-to-work codes, 94; *San Manuel* and trope of, 44
right-to-work laws: and anti-union consultants, 202; and Mashantucket Pequot Labor Relations Law, 204; and Navajo Nation Council, 132; and tribal self-governance, 90–95
Robbins, Lynn, 130
Roessel, Monty, 115, 116
Russell, Scott C., 116, 120

Sac and Fox Nation, 30, 41
Sac & Fox Industries (1991), 30, 41
Saginaw Chippewa Indian Tribe, 203
San Juan Pueblo, 91–92, 93, 220n2
San Manuel Band of Mission Indians, 36, 37–38, 67, 203
San Manuel rulings, 37–39, 41–45, 47–52, 58–60, 64–67, 69–75, 82–84, 91–92, 202, 205, 217n23
savage, stereotypes of barbaric and noble, 23, 215n1
Scott, Craig, 76, 77
Schwarzenegger, Arnold, 61, 80
self-determination: debate on in case of Tuba City hospital, 167, 190; and federal Indian policy, 214n16; grassroots-oppositional conceptualization of, 194–96; and politics of Navajo self-governance, 108–18; and public debate over role of in Navajo health care, 118–25; and rich Indian imagery in discussions of public policy, 61–62; and

tribal court adjudication of labor relations, 229–30n8; and tribal economic development, 164, 218n30; and tribal right-to-work laws, 91; and use of term *sovereignty*, 14; Young's model of interdependent, 74–75. *See also* tribal sovereignty

self-governance: and communal identity of indigenous communities, 12; and politics of Navajo self-determination, 108–18; and protection of tribal sovereignty rights, 78; and tribal right-to-work laws, 90–95. *See also* tribal government

Seminole Tribe, 56, 164, 214n13, 216n5, 218–19nn31–32, 227n7

Seminole Tribe of Florida v. Florida (1996), 218–19n32, 219n34

Service Employees International Union (SEIU), 2, 33–34, 229n6

Shi' zaa Iil'ee (my voice is important), 140, 149

Shirley, Joe, Jr., 112

Siegel, Bernard J., 223n11

Singel, Wenona T., 38–39, 42–43, 49, 50–52, 83, 93, 94

Singer, Joseph, 73

Sioux Nation, 30

Smith, Andrea, 190, 228n15

Smith, Dean Howard, 184

Smith, Victoria, 18

Soaring Eagle Casino (Michigan), 203

solidarity, workplace activism at Tuba City hospital and employee-community, 190

sovereignty. *See* tribal sovereignty

Speed, Shannon, 228n15

Spilde, Katherine A., 55–56, 57, 63, 213n3

states: casino gaming and revenue sharing with, 60–61, 218n32; and collective bargaining rights, 217n22; and regulation of tribal gaming, 219n33; and right-to-work laws, 132; and tribal labor relations ordinances (TLROs), 80. *See also* California

Steenrod, Susan S., 129

Stephen, Lynn, 228n15

Stevens, Ernie, Jr., 72

Strieb, Gordon F., 126–27, 128

strikes, and California gaming TLROs, 81

subject matter jurisdiction, 28, 31, 32

Teamsters. *See* International Brotherhood of Teamsters

territorial jurisdiction, 28, 31

Texas-Zinc Minerals Corp. (1960), 29

Torgovnick, Marianna, 215–16n4

tradition: and commercial versus governmental forms of tribal enterprise, 45–55, 58, 59–60; healing and healing methods in Navajo health care, 174; and political, cultural, and spiritual powers of indigenous women, 48; and public debate in Navajo politics, 162; and use of term *traditional governmental functions*, 47

travel, and concept of tribal citizenship, 10

treaty rights, and *Tuscarora–Coeur d'Alene* test, 40

tribal corporations: and hospital at Tuba City, 166; IRA's statutory provision for, 53–55; marketplace competition and commercial nature of, 60; and NLRA definition of government employer, 93; and self-determination, 218n30. *See also* tribal enterprises

tribal employee rights ordinances (TEROs), 89–90

tribal enterprises: commercial versus traditional/governmental forms of, 45–55, 58, 59–60; definition of, 5–6; NLRB and concept of surplus in definition of, 56. *See also* tribal corporations

tribal government: and commercial versus traditional tribal/governmental enterprises, 45–55, 58, 59–60; and IRA constitutions, 220n4, 223n14; Navajo Nation system of, 15, 99, 111–12; public debate in Navajo Nation over power and role of centralized, 116; tribal corporations and NLRA definition of government employer, 93

Tribal Labor Panel (California), 81–82

tribal labor relations: characteristics of in tribal communities, 69–96; development of author's interest in, 1–2; economic success of Indian gaming in debates about, 3–4; and globalization, 9; interrelation of variables in, 5; legal, political, and social contexts for discussion of, 23–67; methodology of study on, 16–19; Navajo health-care workers and organization efforts of LIUNA as case study of, 14–16, 101–33, 135–62; place of labor unions in discussion of, 6; relationship of to tribal sovereignty, 10–13; review of literature on, 6–7; self-determination and tribal court adjudication of, 229–30n8; uncertain future of, 201–11; use of term, 5; value of studies on, 3; workplace activism at Tuba City hospital as case study of, 19, 69, 163–99, 226n2–3, 227n12, 228n21

tribal labor relations ordinances (TLROs), 79–88, 220–21n8, 221n12. *See also* Mashantucket Pequot Labor Relations Law; tribal employee rights ordinances

tribal sovereignty: activism in academic literature on, 12; definition of, 3; and economic benefits of Indian gaming, 37; and expansion of NLRB's discretionary power, 41; and future of tribal labor relations, 208; legal basis of, 219n35; and limitations on applicability of NLRA in Indian Country, 27–28; relationship of labor relations to, 10–13; rich Indian trope and backlash against, 24–25, 55–64, 76, 78; self-governance and protection of rights, 78; *Tuscarora–Coeur d'Alene* exceptions and limitations of, 42; use of term *self-determination* and, 14. *See also* self-determination

tribe: casino gaming and federal recognition of, 218n24; perception of in popular imagination and by IRA, 55

Tuba City Regional Health Care Corporation (TCRHCC): author's meeting with employees of, 69; as case study of tribal labor relations, 163–99, 210, 226n2–3, 227n12, 228n21; and methodology of study, 19

Tuscarora–Coeur d'Alene decisions (1985), 39–41, 42, 44, 46, 56, 66, 83, 218n25

unfair labor practices (ULPs), and National Labor Relations Act, 37–38, 63, 80–81
Union of Needletrades, Industrial, and Textile Employees (UNITE), 33–34. *See also* UNITE-HERE!
United Auto Workers (UAW), 2, 85, 203, 204, 205, 206, 210, 215n20
United Farm Workers, 34, 143
United Garment Workers of America, 41
United Mine Workers of America (UMWA), 129
United Nations Declaration on the Rights of Indigenous Peoples, 12, 214n14
U.S. Commission on Civil Rights, 131–32
United States v. Wheeler (1978), 218n26
UNITE-HERE!, 37–38, 63, 64, 77, 78, 81, 88, 206, 217n16, 221n12, 229n6. *See also* Hotel Employees and Restaurant Employees International Union (HERE); Union of Needletrades, Industrial, and Textile Employees (UNITE)
University of California at Los Angeles (UCLA), 2

Viejas Band of Kumeyaay Indians, 72
voice: and Campaign for Union Recognition, 140, 149, 150, 157–60; and concept of *hózhó*, 161; and worker activism at Tuba City hospital, 191

War on Poverty, 109
Warrior, Robert, 14
White Mountain Apache Tribe, 29–30
Wilkins, David E., 116, 117
Williams, Aubrey W., Jr., 120, 161
Wilson, Pete, 35, 79, 216n12, 217n15
Winslow Health Center, 145
Wisconsin, and Great Lakes Indian Fish and Wildlife Commission, 77
Wolfe, Patrick, 6, 65
women, and work activism at Tuba City hospital, 189–90
workers. *See* employees

workplace activism, and tribal labor relations at Tuba City hospital, 163–99, 228n13

Young, Iris Marion, 13, 74–75, 80, 208
Young, Robert W., 127, 208
Yukon I decision (1999), 49
Yukon II decision, 41–42, 45, 48–49, 60, 65, 69, 83, 197, 217n21
Yukon Kuskokwin Health Corporation, 41–42, 49, 217n21

Zah, Peterson, 115–16
Zatz, Noah D., 31, 43

David Kamper, PhD, Associate Professor, Department of American Indian Studies, San Diego State University

David Kamper worked as a union organizer for the United Auto Workers while earning his MA in American Indian studies and PhD in anthropology from the University of California, Los Angeles. He is the co-editor of *Indian Gaming: Who Wins?* (1999), a collection of essays on American Indian tribal governmental gaming.

E 99 .N3 K27 2010
Kamper, David.
The work of sovereignty

JUN 15 2011